NEW HISTORIES OF GUN RIGHTS AND REGULATION

New Histories of Gun Rights and Regulation

Essays on the Place of Guns in American Law and Society

Edited by
JOSEPH BLOCHER
JACOB D. CHARLES
DARRELL A.H. MILLER

OXFORD
UNIVERSITY PRESS

Oxford University Press is a department of the University of Oxford.
It furthers the University's objective of excellence in research, scholarship,
and education by publishing worldwide. Oxford is a registered trade mark of
Oxford University Press in the UK and certain other countries.

Published in the United States of America by Oxford University Press
198 Madison Avenue, New York, NY 10016, United States of America.

© Oxford University Press 2023

All rights reserved. No part of this publication may be reproduced, stored in
a retrieval system, or transmitted, in any form or by any means, without the
prior permission in writing of Oxford University Press, or as expressly permitted
by law, by license, or under terms agreed with the appropriate reproduction
rights organization. Inquiries concerning reproduction outside the scope of the
above should be sent to the Rights Department, Oxford University Press, at the address above.

You must not circulate this work in any other form
and you must impose this same condition on any acquirer.

Library of Congress Cataloging-in-Publication Data
Names: Blocher, Joseph, editor. | Charles, Jacob D., editor. |
Miller, Darrell A. H., 1972– editor.
Title: New histories of gun rights and regulation : essays on the place of
guns in American law and society / edited by Joseph Blocher,
Jacob D. Charles, Darrell A. H. Miller.
Description: New York : Oxford University Press, 2023. |
Includes bibliographical references and index.
Identifiers: LCCN 2023033258 | ISBN 9780197748473 (hardback) |
ISBN 9780197748480 (epub) | ISBN 9780197748497 | ISBN 9780197748503
Subjects: LCSH: Fire arms—Law and legislation—United States—History. |
United States. Constitution. 2nd Amendment—History. |
Gun control—United States—History. | Fire arms—Law and
legislation—United States—Cases. | Heller, Dick Anthony—Trials,
litigation, etc. | Washington (D.C.).—Trials, litigation, etc.
Classification: LCC KF3941.N39 2023 | DDC 344.7305/33—dc23/eng/20230802
LC record available at https://lccn.loc.gov/2023033258

DOI: 10.1093/oso/9780197748473.001.0001

Printed by Integrated Books International, United States of America

Note to Readers
This publication is designed to provide accurate and authoritative information in regard to the subject
matter covered. It is based upon sources believed to be accurate and reliable and is intended to be
current as of the time it was written. It is sold with the understanding that the publisher is not engaged
in rendering legal, accounting, or other professional services. If legal advice or other expert assistance is
required, the services of a competent professional person should be sought. Also, to confirm that the
information has not been affected or changed by recent developments, traditional legal research
techniques should be used, including checking primary sources where appropriate.

*(Based on the Declaration of Principles jointly adopted by a Committee of the
American Bar Association and a Committee of Publishers and Associations.)*

You may order this or any other Oxford University Press publication
by visiting the Oxford University Press website at www.oup.com.

FSC
MIX
Paper
FSC® C183721

Contents

1. Firearms Law and History in a New Doctrinal Era   1
   Joseph Blocher, Jacob D. Charles, and Darrell A.H. Miller

2. U.S. Expansion and the Development of a National Firearms Industry   9
   Lindsay Schakenbach Regele

3. Scottish History, Presbyterian Culture, and the Right to Bear Arms   25
   Neil McIntyre

4. "A Well-Regulated Militia": Constitutional Politics, the Second Amendment, and the Militia in the Jacksonian Era and the American Civil War   47
   Nicholas Mosvick

5. Gun Laws in Early America: The Sometimes Contradictory Regulations of Gun Use in the Colonial South   77
   Sally E. Hadden

6. To Brandish or Not to Brandish: The Consequences of Gun Display   97
   Robert J. Spitzer

7. The Life She Saves May Be Her Own: The Radical Feminist Argument for Women's Gun-Armed Self-Defense   115
   Mary Zeiss Stange

8. Historical Gun Laws Targeting "Dangerous" Groups and Outsiders   131
   Joseph Blocher and Caitlan Carberry

9. Strange Bedfellows: Racism and Gun Rights in American History and Current Scholarship   149
   Brennan Gardner Rivas

10. A Brief Overview of Gun Registration in U.S. History   167
    Genesa C. Cefali and Jacob D. Charles

11. Historical Militia Law, Fire Prevention Law, and the Modern
    Second Amendment 195
    Mark Anthony Frassetto

12. Abolition, Armed Self-Defense, and Firearms Regulation in
    Antebellum America: The Enforcement of Surety Laws in Boston 213
    Saul Cornell

13. Constitutional Liquidation, Surety Laws, and the Right to
    Bear Arms 233
    Robert Leider

14. Prohibitions on Private Armies in Seven State Constitutions 263
    Darrell A.H. Miller

Index 279

1
Firearms Law and History in a New Doctrinal Era

Joseph Blocher, Jacob D. Charles, and Darrell A.H. Miller

In 2008, the U.S. Supreme Court issued a groundbreaking opinion in *District of Columbia v. Heller*.[1] Relying heavily on historical sources, the Court concluded that the Second Amendment to the U.S. Constitution guarantees a personal right to keep and bear arms for purposes unrelated to a government-run militia. *Heller* not only marked the judicial culmination of a decades-long historical dispute but also ushered in a new wave of legal challenges that in turn raised the need for further scholarship on the historical scope of gun rights and regulation in Anglo-American history. In hundreds of cases over the next fifteen years, judges relied on both historical research and contemporary evidence in evaluating the constitutionality of gun laws designed to address contemporary problems of the most visceral kind.

Then, in 2022, the Court decided *New York State Rifle & Pistol Association v. Bruen*.[2] In *Bruen*, the Court announced a new approach to Second Amendment doctrine where history appears to be not only probative but conclusive:

> In keeping with *Heller*, we hold that when the Second Amendment's plain text covers an individual's conduct, the Constitution presumptively protects that conduct. To justify its regulation, the government may not simply posit that the regulation promotes an important interest. Rather, the government must demonstrate that the regulation is consistent with this Nation's historical tradition of firearm regulation. Only if a firearm regulation is consistent with this Nation's historical tradition may a court conclude that the individual's conduct falls outside the Second Amendment's unqualified command.[3]

---

[1] 554 U.S. 570 (2008).
[2] 142 S. Ct. 2111 (2022). The opinion came down as this manuscript was going to press and cited a draft of Robert Leider's chapter. *Id.* at 2149.
[3] *Id.* at 2126 (internal quotation marks and citations omitted).

As with *Heller* before it, *Bruen* raises a host of challenging questions for constitutional law. What does it mean to have a "historical tradition"? What kinds of evidence satisfy that test? How will courts and scholars conduct the kind of historical-analogical reasoning that the majority's test appears to require?

Whatever the answers to those questions, it is entirely clear that historical sources are even more important now and that the future of Second Amendment law and scholarship will be determined in large part by history. In this area of constitutional law perhaps more than in any other, our understanding of the past continues to shape the present—the scope of the constitutional right and, accordingly, the government's power to regulate in the interest of public safety hang in the balance.

And yet gaps remain in our knowledge about the relevant history. Research has been sparse on local firearms regulation, the enforcement of early laws aiming to prevent gun violence, the motivations of legislators enacting gun regulations, and much more. The nascency of the Court's modern Second Amendment doctrine, the new research agenda it helped inspire, the availability of novel research databases and methods, and the time it takes to do careful historical work all have meant that the supply of historical research is still catching up to the demand.

One resource not available to scholars, researchers, or judges at the time of the *Heller* decision in 2008 is the Repository of Historical Gun Laws, maintained by the Duke Center for Firearms Law at firearmslaw.duke.edu/repository. The Repository is a freely searchable database that, as of this writing, contains records of more than eighteen hundred state and local laws regulating firearms throughout Anglo-American history. These laws range in time from the medieval ages in the United Kingdom up through 1934 in the United States, when the federal government first began passing national gun laws. The laws are organized by jurisdiction, category of law, and year. Although the repository contains a large collection of laws, it is not comprehensive, and careful historical research about the historical setting of these laws often provides useful context.

This volume aims to further broaden the growing scholarly conversations over firearms law history. The contributors, which include distinguished historians and legal scholars, add valuable new context and content to the place of guns in American law and society. Drawing on the Repository as well as original research, the essays are rich and varied. Several approach topics in gun history with a theoretical lens, while others are data heavy. Some are primarily descriptive, laying out the state of gun history at a point in time, while others carry normative or prescriptive arguments through the analysis.

Lindsay Schakenbach Regele unearths the story of early American firearms development and innovation that relied heavily on government intervention and support. In her chapter, "U.S. Expansion and the Development of a National Firearms Industry," she recounts how even the development of private firearm manufacturing facilities in the Connective River Valley—where notable firearm makers still manufacture guns to this day—was aided by the federal government's investment in sites that would be close to the federal armory in Springfield, Massachusetts. As the new nation expanded westward into lands owned by Indigenous tribes, firearms became an indispensable tool of state power; government contracts kept up production levels and advanced improvements in firearms technology that were at times expressly designed to assist in combat environments against Native peoples. Schakenbach Regele argues that "under the pretense of minimal military power, the early U.S. government simultaneously bolstered a gun industry and westward expansion." The heavy government investment in arms manufacturing helped to produce, sustain, and stabilize the American gun manufacturing industry that has made the United States today one of the biggest gunmakers in the world.

Neil McIntyre's chapter, "Scottish History, Presbyterian Culture, and the Right to Bear Arms," describes Scottish Presbyterian and covenanting traditions in British North America. His chapter illuminates how Scottish Presbyterian and covenanting history and culture shaped views of legitimate arms-bearing in parts of America in the decades leading up to the Second Amendment's ratification. McIntyre shows the diversity of non-English legal, political, and theological influences on self-defense and arms-bearing in the early United States. This history grounded both rights and duties to resist tyrannical government initially in religious understanding and obligations, before it shifted to a more individualized level as the American Revolution approached.

In his chapter, Nicholas Mosvick argues that, contrary to Justice Scalia's reading of the Second Amendment in *District of Columbia v. Heller*, it was understood throughout the nineteenth century "as a federalism provision." In the chapter, "'A Well-Regulated Militia': Constitutional Politics, the Second Amendment, and the Militia in the Jacksonian Era and the American Civil War," Mosvick argues that the Second Amendment was understood to protect state sovereignty and the institution of the militia in light of historic concerns associated with a standing army. He traces Jacksonian- and Civil War–era arguments in support of state militias and against a national draft on the grounds that the Second Amendment guaranteed federal support and protection for state militias. From the drafting up to the Civil War, Mosvick contends that "the militia clause of the amendment was consistently read not under Justice Scalia's *Heller* interpretation as merely prefatory language announcing the purpose of the amendment, but instead as text which imposed duties both upon the states and their citizens to maintain their militia units to properly defend their communities."

Sally E. Hadden describes in detail the precarious position facing colonists in the seventeenth and early eighteenth centuries and the concomitant need for both regulation of firearms and laws mandating arms-bearing and service for community defense. Her chapter, "Gun Laws in Early America: The Sometimes Contradictory Regulations of Gun Use in the Colonial South," chronicles the way legislators tried to keep up with—and effectively prohibit—arms-supplying to Native Americans in Virginia, as locals continually evaded enacted laws and the legislature kept coming back again to expand the provisions. "Why" she asks "would European settlers sell guns to Indians, or hire, arm, and register them in the seventeenth century, given that Native attacks upon White settlements happened with regularity? Answer: Hunting for profit." The fear settlers had was not enough to overcome their desire to turn a profit.

She also highlights how supplying arms to friendly Native tribes could help in eventual battles with the colonies' foes. A similar theme was true for enslaved African Americans. "Throughout the colonial period," Hadden writes, "slaves with guns provided protection and yet constituted a danger, too." She concludes that the "the sometimes contradictory interplay of these laws" regulating especially Native gun use complicate easy narratives about motives. "A mixture of many motives, these laws reveal the complexity of challenges faced by early American settlers attempting to tame the forest, its animals, and the people living there—including themselves."

Robert J. Spitzer, in "To Brandish or Not to Brandish: The Consequences of Gun Display," sheds light on an underexplored aspect of the gun debate: brandishing a gun. He describes the recent uptick in public, and especially open, gun carrying at protests and gatherings during the heightened period of unrest in summer 2020, amidst racial justice rallies and anti-lockdown fervor. Spitzer details a deep and long history of Anglo-American regulation of arms-displays, often through laws punishing brandishing as the exhibition of a weapon in a threatening or intimidating way. From this history, he argues that, in a contemporary setting, gun displays—particularly at public gatherings like protests—are threatening and intimidating, regardless of the gun carrier's subjective intentions. "The fact of gun carrying outweighs the stated intentions of the carrier, no matter how benign or well intentioned."

Mary Zeiss Stange brings a critical lens to analyzing feminist arguments for arming women to deal with aggressive violence. In her chapter, "The Life She Saves May Be Her Own: The Radical Feminist Argument for Women's Gun-Armed Self-Defense," Stange foregrounds a 1977 self-defense case involving Yvonne Wanrow that reached the Washington State Supreme Court. Stange argues that the legal saga "turned out to be a textbook case of all that was wrong—when issues of gender, race, and class were factored in—with conventional jury instructions regarding self-defense." In its decision, the state supreme court reversed Wanrow's murder conviction because (among other deficiencies) the jury instruction regarding self-defense was improper. The instruction inappropriately precluded the jury from considering the context and Wanrow's perceptions of threat.

Through the prism of the case, Stange traces the contemporary history of feminist thought on armed resistance, writing that "Second Wave feminist theory and practice was universally opposed to the notion of women arming themselves—in self-defense or for pretty much any other reason." On the other hand, she argues, some radical feminists embraced the idea that women were to defend the attacks on their bodies "by any means necessary." The *Wanrow* case played out against the backdrop in debates about feminist assertions of a woman's ability "to exercise her human right to self-defense, in whatever form that takes, and to count on support from her feminist sisters."

Joseph Blocher and Caitlan Carberry explore the historical scope of the government's power to disarm those perceived to be dangerous. In "Gun Laws Targeting 'Dangerous' Groups and Outsiders," they show that the scope of this power was quite broad, notwithstanding the fact that the Founding generations applied that power to very different groups than law does today—both more narrowly (for example, by not disarming domestic abusers) and more broadly.

As to the latter, they analyze two sets of historical gun laws that seem historically distant, but which the "dangerousness" approach makes relevant: laws regulating Native Americans and laws regulating those "disaffected to the cause of America." These groups—much more so than felons, drug users, domestic abusers, and other groups targeted by contemporary restrictions—were subject to gun regulation by the Founding generations, apparently based on the perceived threat they posed. Relying largely on the Repository of Historical Gun Laws, the first part of the chapter provides a historical overview of these laws, which have not received the same level of scholarly attention as some other historical prohibitions, such as those involving public carry or certain classes of arms. The second part of the chapter grapples with a question such regulations raise: What is to be done with the many historical gun laws that lack modern equivalents?

Brennan Gardner Rivas also explores the history—and historiography—of gun regulations targeting minority groups in her chapter, "Strange Bedfellows: Racism and Gun Rights in American History and Current Scholarship." Charting both the history of race and gun regulation and the development of historical claims about that history, Rivas takes issue with those who suggest that gun regulation is an inherently racist undertaking. She notes that such claims have made "strange bedfellows" of gun rights and ethnic studies scholars, who correctly see that race and gun regulation are connected, but go too far in their assessment of that relationship.

Rivas argues that racism in the passage and administration of gun laws became a primary theme only in the Jim Crow era. The enforcement of Texas's deadly weapon law provides an illustrative example, as discriminatory enforcement of that law developed only over time as the Republican Party collapsed. Prior to that, and even "[d]uring the period of most strident pro-slavery virulence, when some four million Black persons were enslaved in this country, the overwhelming majority of arms regulations *were* intended to be applied to the general population—which in most of the settled sections of America, was White." In various ways, then, the story of race and guns is more complicated than some accounts make it seem.

Genesa C. Cefali and Jacob D. Charles trace laws requiring firearms registration. Their chapter, "A Brief Overview of Gun Registration in U.S. History," identifies the different mechanisms government has historically used to track weapons ownership through varied registration schemes. They highlight early laws requiring firearms registration in the late nineteenth century and many more that followed in the early twentieth. Cefali and Charles observe differences in whether laws required registration of both long guns and handguns or only the latter, as well as the entity responsible for registration—the individual owners themselves or retailers who sold the weapons. They show that, despite some laws requiring intrusive reporting by gun owners themselves, the response to the mandates in these early laws appears to be rather muted.

Mark Anthony Frassetto focuses on another set of historical gun regulations that have not received as much attention in the broader legal and scholarly debate: historical militia laws and laws intended to prevent fires and explosions. In "Historical Militia Law, Fire Prevention Law, and the Modern Second Amendment," Frassetto begins by explaining the Supreme Court's decision in *Bruen* and the primacy that it accords to historical analysis—above and beyond the attention to history that was already part of the preexisting two-part framework in the federal courts of appeal. As Frassetto shows, and many other chapters demonstrate, historical analysis of gun laws before and in the immediate aftermath of *Bruen* has tended to focus on laws designed to reduce the risk of violent crime.

But some laws regarding militia service and fire prevention imposed burdens on gun owners that were even more stringent than those crime-focused laws. How, then, do they fit into *Bruen*'s analysis of the burdens and justifications of historical gun laws? Drawing on existing case law, Frassetto argues that these laws, too, are an essential part of the history of gun regulation and should factor into the calculus of governments' modern regulatory authority.

Saul Cornell's "Abolition, Armed Self-Defense, and Firearms Regulation in Antebellum America: The Enforcement of Surety Laws in Boston" offers a nuanced historical account of Boston's abolitionists who advocated both armed resistance to the slave power and aggressive principles of self-defense. It counterposes this view with mainstream legal thought that sought a well-regulated society. The maintenance of the public peace required prohibitions on carrying concealed firearms in public without adequate cause. The chapter questions the contemporary gun debate's focus on southern gun culture as representative of the national tradition, and instead argues how surety laws were adopted in many states. This "Free States Model" became the dominant approach to firearms regulation in antebellum America. The chapter examines changes in the law of self-defense, the enforcement of surety bonds to keep the peace and good behavior, and the abolitionist movement's sometimes fraught relationship with armed violence in service of their cause.

In "Constitutional Liquidation, Surety Laws, and the Right to Bear Arms," Robert Leider challenges the claims by some scholars that the nineteenth century was an age of heavy regulation of public carriage of weapons through surety laws—the "Massachusetts Model" (or "Free States Model" in this volume)—and that this model is relevant to constitutional interpretation. Leider's chapter argues that the relevance of nineteenth-century laws and judicial decisions is tied to the notion that postenactment practice can settle the meaning of legal text, commonly known as "constitutional liquidation." He argues that right to bear arms did not liquidate in support of a general prohibition of individuals publicly carrying arms. Instead, the surety laws in this "Massachusetts Model" merely required a person to post a bond on complaint of a plaintiff who had "reasonable cause to fear an injury, or breach of the peace." Moreover, according to Leider, there's no evidence that, in passing these surety laws, legislatures considered whether broad restrictions on public carry were consistent with the right to bear arms. Finally, Leider argues, as applied to the carriage of weapons for lawful purposes, the surety laws went largely unenforced.

Darrell A.H. Miller, in his "Prohibitions on Private Armies in Seven State Constitutions," tracks the rise and fall of corporate employment of private militias to protect property and suppress labor unrest during the Gilded Age, as marked by the fortunes of the most prominent of these private forces—the Pinkerton Detective Agency. He then shows how anti-Pinkerton sentiment manifested itself in express prohibitions in seven state constitutions on a corporation's ability to either employ, or import, armed agents and explains what that prohibition means for notions of public and private power with respect to the right to keep and bear arms.

* * *

The Great American Gun Debate will not be settled by historical analysis, no matter how well done. But the ongoing dialogue over the tensions between gun rights and gun regulation, and the trade-offs between protecting individual rights to armed self-defense and protecting the safety of citizens to leave without fear of gun violence, can be aided by understanding how past generations navigated these conflicts. And the past can demonstrate not just successful balances our ancestors struck but problematic ones to avoid as well. For scholars, policymakers, public officials, and engaged laypeople, this history promises to provide important context for contemporary discussions. From a deeper understanding of the confluence of gun laws and race, gender, and other identities to a richer appreciation for the intellectual heritage and theoretical baggage that accompanies notions of gun rights, the volume offers something to all those interested in the present conversations around firearms law in the United States.

As these chapters recount, guns have been tools of oppression, repression, liberation, and self-defense since their invention. They have been symbols connected to broader themes of conquest, colonization, racial subordination, religious freedom, individual liberty, and personal autonomy. To guard against social ills—and, at times, to further them—gun regulation has existed as long as the weaponry has. This history continues to shape the present.

2
U.S. EXPANSION AND THE DEVELOPMENT OF A NATIONAL FIREARMS INDUSTRY

Lindsay Schakenbach Regele

I. INTRODUCTION

This chapter focuses not on citizens' rights to have guns but on the federal government's historical role providing and regulating them. This historical role had much to do with improving and growing the arms industry in the service of westward expansion and frontier warfare. In the early national United States, firearms innovations and the forced removal of Native peoples at gunpoint were codependent components of territorial expansion and the American imperial project.[1]

In the decades following independence, the United States was always at war, as soldiers and settlers worked to minimize Native presence within and beyond U.S. political borders. Generations of historians, however, tended to minimize the military realities of westward expansion. The dominant narrative emphasized relatively seamless expansion with limited military intervention.[2] More recently, less sanguine historians rightfully refer to the early national era as a period of conquest and state-sanctioned violence.[3] Although these historians

---

[1] John O'Sullivan, *Annexation*, 17 U.S. MAG. DEMOCRATIC REV. (July/Aug. 1845). THEDA PERDUE & MICHAEL D. GREEN, THE CHEROKEE NATION AND THE TRAIL OF TEARS (2007). Forced removal at gunpoint characterized Cherokee experience more than that of Creek Indians. CHRISTOPHER D. HAVEMAN, RIVERS OF SAND: CREEK INDIAN EMIGRATION, RELOCATION, AND ETHNIC CLEANSING IN THE AMERICAN SOUTH (2016). STEPHEN WARREN, THE WORLDS THE SHAWNEES MADE: MIGRATION AND VIOLENCE IN EARLY AMERICA (2014); James P. Ronda, *"We Have a Country": Race, Geography, and the Invention of Indian Territory*, 19 J. EARLY AM. REPUBLIC 739 (1999). Patrick Minges, *Beneath the Underdog: Race, Religion, and the Trail of Tears*, 25 AM. INDIAN Q. 453 (2001); Brian Delay, *The Wider World of the Handsome Man: Southern Plains Indians Invade Mexico, 1830-1848*, 27 J. EARLY AM. REPUBLIC 83 (Spring 2007). BRAD AGNEW, FORT GIBSON: TERMINAL ON THE TRAIL OF TEARS (1980); ROBERT V. REMINI, ANDREW JACKSON AND HIS INDIAN WARS (2002).

[2] Historian C. Vann Woodward described the one hundred thirty years between the end of the War of 1812 and the Second World War as an era of "free security," in which the majority of White Americans enjoyed safety with minimal military spending. C. Vann Woodward, *The Age of Reinterpretation*, 66 AM. HIST. REV. 3, 3–4 (1960). Fareed Zakaria, *The Myth of America's "Free Security,"* 14 WORLD POL'Y J. 35 (1997).

[3] John Craig Hammond, *Midcontinent Borderlands: Illinois and the Early American Republic, 1774–1854*, 111 J. ILL. STATE HIST. SOC'Y 31 (2018). Michael Witgen, *Seeing Red: Race Citizenship, and Indigeneity in the Old Northwest*, 38 J. EARLY AM. REPUBLIC 581 (2018).

Lindsay Schakenbach Regele, *U.S. Expansion and the Development of a National Firearms Industry* In: *New Histories of Gun Rights and Regulation*. Edited by: Joseph Blocher, Jacob D. Charles, and Darrell A.H. Miller, Oxford University Press. © Oxford University Press 2023. DOI: 10.1093/oso/9780197748473.003.0002

have done much to explore military state-building and frontier warfare, they have paid less attention to the specific relationship between continental geopolitics and the firearms industry throughout the first half of the nineteenth century.[4] This chapter shows how, under the pretense of minimal military power, the early U.S. government simultaneously bolstered a gun industry and westward expansion.[5]

---

[4] Max M. Edling, A Revolution in Favor of Government: Origins of the U.S. Constitution and the Making of the American State (2003), and A Hercules in the Cradle: War, Money, and the American State, 1783–1867 (2014); William D. Adler, *State Capacity and Bureaucratic Autonomy in the Early United States: The Case of the Army Corps of Topographical Engineers*, 26 Stud. Am. Pol. Dev. 110 (2012); William D. Adler & Andrew J. Polsky, *Building the New American Nation: Economic Development, Public Goods, and the Early U.S. Army*, 125 Pol. Sci. Q. 87 (2010); Christopher Klyza, *The United States Army, Natural Resources, and Political Development in the Nineteenth Century*, 35 J. Ne. Pol. Sci. Ass'n 1 (2002); Stephen J. Rockwell, Indian Affairs and the Administrative State in the Nineteenth Century (2010). Military bureaucrats, more than individual pioneers, were responsible for frontier development. As they acted on behalf of a federal state that sought new commercial opportunities, a consolidation of power, and accurate knowledge of its territory, they helped build an expanding and prosperous republic. William H. Bergmann, The American National State and the Early West (2012); William H. Goetzmann, Army Exploration in the American West 1803–1868 (1959); Robert Wooster, The American Military Frontiers: The United States Army in the West, 1783–1900 (2009); Samuel J. Watson, Jackson's Sword: The Army Officer Corps on the American Frontier, 1810–1821 (2012). Rachel St. John cautions that "active" on the frontier did not necessarily mean "strong." Rachel St. John, *State Power in the West in the Early American Republic*, 38 J. Early Am. Republic 88, 88 (2018). For the importance of war-making for national science, *see* Cameron B. Strang, *Perpetual War and Natural Knowledge in the United States, 1775–1860*, 38 J. Early Am. Republic 387 (2018); William Goetzmann, Exploration Empire: The Explorer and the Scientist in the Winning of the American West (1966). Paul Frymer, however, argues state weakness prevented traditional state-building but that it engineered racialized settlement to achieve imperial ends. Paul Frymer, Building an American Empire: The Era of Territorial and Political Expansion (2017).

[5] There is a wealth of scholarship on the arms industry, but this tends to focus on its influence on manufacturing. Merritt Roe Smith, Harper's Ferry Armory and the New Technology: The Challenge of Change (1977); Merritt Roe Smith, *Army Ordnance and the "American System" of Manufacturing, 1815–1861*, in Military Enterprise and Technological Change: Perspectives on the American Experience 39 (Merritt Roe Smith ed., 1985). While Merritt Roe Smith and David Hounshell argue that armory practices led to the achievement of interchangeability by the 1840s, historian Donald Hoke asserts that interchangeability was far from an absolute concept for manufacturers and was not solely a product of federal arms-making. Hoke maintains that interchangeability varied not only across industries but also from factory and factory and developed slowly throughout the nineteenth century, largely in the private sector. Smith, Military Enterprise and Technological Change; David Hounshell, From the American System to Mass Production (1984); Donald R. Hoke, Ingenious Yankees: The Rise of the American System of Manufactures in the Private Sector 3 (1989). The first conventional musket made entirely of interchangeable parts was manufactured in 1844, but historians disagree about exactly when and by whom interchangeability was achieved. Merritt Roe Smith, *John H. Hall, Simeon North, and the Milling Machine—The Nature of Innovation Among Antebellum Arms Makers*, 14 Tech. & Culture 589 (1973). Not all historians of technology agree. Robert B. Gordon emphasized the importance of improvements in artificers' handwork over the influence of ordnance officers and superintendents. Robert B. Gordon, *Simeon North, John Hall, and Mechanized Manufacturing*, 30 Tech. & Culture 179 (1989); and *Who Turned the Mechanical Ideal into Mechanical Reality*, 29 Tech. & Culture 744 (1988). James Farley, on the other hand, argues for the persistent importance of the Ordnance Department in driving innovation: James Farley, Making Arms in the Machine Age: Philadelphia's Frankford Arsenal, 1816–1870 XV, at 64 (1994). Decius Wadsworth to Roswell Lee, 15 December 1818, Box 1, Target #2, Letters Received from Officials and Officers of

II. Government Support for Gun Manufacturing

Following independence, the early American state confronted the geopolitical demands of the Napoleonic Wars, as well as countless named and unnamed Indian wars.[6] Its response was little different from the imperial governments of Europe.[7] Historian Ken Alder has shown how in Revolutionary France the gun became an "artifact essential to the authority of the state."[8] It became this for the United States as well. Geopolitical ambitions superseded liberal republican ideals, and even as the United States sought to distinguish itself from the Old World, it emulated European arms production until American weapon-making surpassed that of any other empire in the world.[9]

To make this happen, the new U.S. government embraced firearms mandates and government-subsidized arms manufacturing.[10] Americans' use of arms for both warfare and private defense owed more to Article 1, Section 8 of the Constitution—which gave Congress the power to support armies and provide arms for the militia—than it did to the Second Amendment. The amendment, which states, "A well regulated Militia, being necessary to the security of a free State, the right of the people to keep and bear Arms, shall not be infringed,"

---

the War and Treasury Departments, Records of the Springfield Armory, RG 156 (National Archives, Waltham, MA). Lawrence D. Cress argues that fears of centralized power led to the celebration of the militia. LAWRENCE D. CRESS, CITIZENS IN ARMS: THE ARMY AND THE MILITIA IN AMERICAN SOCIETY TO THE WAR OF 1812 (1982).

[6] Anthony Gregory, *"Formed for Empire": The Continental Congress Responds to the Carlisle Peace Commission*, 38 J. EARLY AM. REPUBLIC 643 (2018); Mark R. Wilson, *Law and the American State, from the Revolution to the Civil War: Institutional Growth and Structural Change*, in 2 CAMBRIDGE HISTORY OF LAW IN AMERICA 35 (Michael Grossberg & Christopher Tomlins eds., 2008).

[7] The United States' trajectory toward sovereignty in some ways fit the European model that Charles Tilly laid out, in which states' four responsibilities are war-making, state-making, protection, and extraction. Charles Tilly, *War Making and State Making as Organized Crime*, in BRINGING THE STATE BACK IN 181 (Theda Skocpol, Peter Evans, & Dietrich Rueschemeyer eds., 1985). For the relationship between economic interest and liberal internationalism, *see* Glenda Sluga, *"Who Hold the Balance of the World?" Bankers at the Congress of Vienna, and in International History*, 122 AM. HIST. REV. 1403 (2017). For the contingency of the relationship between capitalism and the sovereign state, *see* Jonathan Levy, *Appreciating Assets: New Directions in the History of Political Economy*, 122 AM. HIST. REV. 1490 (2017).

[8] KEN ALDER, ENGINEERING THE REVOLUTION: ARMS AND ENLIGHTENMENT IN FRANCE, 1763–1815, at 131, 223, 249 (2010).

[9] H. DOC. NO. 2, at 9, 22ND CONG., REPORT OF THE SECRETARY OF WAR, NOVEMBER 21, 1831 (1st Sess., Nov. 21, 1831).

[10] Historians have debated the extent to which Americans subscribed to economic liberalism or mercantilism. John E. Crowley argues that before, during, and after the war, Americans preferred to maintain their privileged relationship with British or European metropole, rather than achieve manufacturing self-sufficiency or free trade. JOHN E. CROWLEY, THE PRIVILEGES OF INDEPENDENCE: NEOMERCANTILISM AND THE AMERICAN REVOLUTION (1993). Margaret Newell, on the other hand, characterizes New Englanders as economic liberals whose self-interested commercialism helped the colonists achieve independence. MARGARET NEWELL, FROM DEPENDENCY TO INDEPENDENCE: ECONOMIC REVOLUTION IN COLONIAL NEW ENGLAND (1998).

was rarely invoked in the century after its passage. The first reported appellate court case to address the "right to bear arms" was the 1822 case of *Bliss v. Commonwealth of Kentucky*, and not until 1857 did the amendment undergo debate in the Supreme Court, when the Court observed that if Black men were citizens, they would have the constitutional right to bear arms.[11] It received little legal attention until the 1960s, when an increase in gun violence, compounded by the assassinations of President John F. Kennedy, Martin Luther King Jr., and Robert Kennedy, provided impetus for the passage of the Gun Control Act of 1968 and sparked jurisprudential and scholarly contentiousness around the Second Amendment. Throughout early U.S. history, the federal government, in accordance with its constitutional obligation, subsidized and improved arms manufacturing and expanded the market for guns.

The Militia Act of 1792 required militia members to provide themselves with a musket, but many struggled to arm themselves in the face of postwar shortages. As a short-term solution, Congress prohibited the export of arms and kept import duties low in the early 1790s. Its long-term strategy involved the construction of two federal armories, in Springfield, Massachusetts, and Harpers Ferry, Virginia. In 1795, the Springfield Armory manufactured the nation's first public musket. It was modeled after the French Charleville, which many American soldiers had fought with during the Revolution and considered superior to other European guns.[12] Because production was slow at first—fewer than one thousand muskets annually—the second part of the long-term strategy was to subsidize production in private armories.[13]

First, the government had to actually develop private armories. During the American Revolution, the Continental Army had relied on imported arms, and following the war, private producers had little incentive to increase output for a limited civilian market. What gun manufacturing did exist was mostly small-scale craftwork. Throughout the eighteenth and early nineteenth centuries, the most established of these gunsmiths worked in Pennsylvania. Government intervention, however, shifted the loci to the Connecticut River Valley in New England for its proximity to the federal armory at Springfield, Massachusetts. One of the region's draws was its skilled craftsmen, who were not specialized gunsmiths. Government officials in fact complained about established gunsmiths' unwillingness to conform to government standards.[14] It was difficult

---

[11] Bliss v. Commonwealth of Kentucky, 12 Littell 90 Ky. (1822); Dred Scott v. Sandford, 60 U.S. (19 How.) 393 (1857).

[12] S. REP. NO. 25, at 104, 4TH CONG., MILITARY FORCE, ARSENAL, AND STORES COMMUNICATED TO THE SENATE, DECEMBER 15, 1795 (1st Sess., Dec. 15, 1795); JAMES B. WHISKER, THE UNITED STATES ARMORY AT SPRINGFIELD, 1795–1865, at 19 (1997).

[13] Compared with ten thousand muskets in 1810. S. REP. NO. 37 at 130, 6TH CONG., ARMORY AT SPRINGFIELD, COMMUNICATED TO THE SENATE, JANUARY 7, 1800 (1st Sess., Jan. 7, 1800).

[14] Oliver Wolcott, *Oliver Wolcott to Daniel Gilbert, September 8, 1798*, in Record Group 45, POST-REVOLUTIONARY WAR PAPERS (National Archives and Record Administration).

to rely on manufacturers who "did not consider themselves bound to the pattern," and felt "entirely free to act on their own judgment."[15] This issue would gain considerable salience when the War Department had to adjust to the demands of particular kinds of frontier warfare in the 1820s and 1830s.

By the second decade of the nineteenth century, the U.S. government established a cohort of regular contractors in New England. One of these was Eli Whitney, who had no prior experience making guns. Whitney, however, convinced federal officials that "it is in the interest of national security to train men to make arms."[16] Whitney received one of the government's first contracts for ten thousand muskets in 1798. This included a cash advance and funding for several storehouses at his armory-in-progress in New Haven, Connecticut.[17] His willingness to conform to military standards made him a suitable contractor. Officials also appreciated his knowledge of the manufacturing techniques France used to mass produce weapons for major warfare throughout the Napoleonic period, especially as the United States prepared for a potential war against France.[18]

Whitney signed his second contract for fifteen thousand muskets at the start of the War of 1812.[19] In that span of almost fifteen years, the national arms industry changed dramatically. The Militia Act of 1808 required Congress's "making provision for arming and equipping the whole body of the militia of the United States," giving $200,000 annually for states to arm their militias. It stipulated that these funds go to private manufacturers (the choice of private armories reflected many congressmen's apprehensions about centralizing all national arms production at the federal armories). These appropriations would shape the development of the arms industry and its capacity to supply weapons for frontier violence. For the next three decades, the War Department issued five-year renewable contracts that came with 10-20 percent cash advances, which enabled Whitney and other New England contractors to expand their operations.[20] By the War of 1812, the United States could supply all its own firearms.

---

[15] *Memorial to John Armstrong, April 3, 1813*, and *Sketch Memorial of William and J.J. Henry to Secretary of War, April 20, 1813*, Folder 7, Box 8, HENRY FAMILY PAPERS (The Hagley Library and Museum).

[16] Eli Whitney, *Eli Whitney to Oliver Wolcott, June 15, 1798*, Box 1, Folder 12, ELI WHITNEY PAPERS (Yale University Manuscripts and Archives).

[17] Henry Dearborn, *Henry Dearborn to Eli Whitney, February 25, 1803*, in Record Group 107, Entry 10, ORDER BOOK, LETTERS SENT REGARDING PROCUREMENTS, RECORDS OF THE OFFICE OF THE SECRETARY OF WAR (National Archives, Washington, D.C.); Wolcott, *supra* note 14.

[18] DAVID HOUNSHELL, 4 FROM THE AMERICAN SYSTEM TO MASS PRODUCTION, 1800-1932: THE DEVELOPMENT OF MANUFACTURING TECHNOLOGY IN THE UNITED STATES 32 (1985); KEN ALDER, ENGINEERING THE REVOLUTION: ARMS AND ENLIGHTENMENT IN FRANCE, 1763-1815 (2010).

[19] Dearborn, *supra* note 17.

[20] During the first rounds of contracts, contract forms varied—some were handwritten and they came with different terms. Robert S. Woodbury, *The Legend of Eli Whitney and Interchangeable Parts*, 1 TECH. & CULTURE 235, 238 (1960).

This meant that America's second war against Britain was truly a war of independence, at least in terms of weapons. This independence had particular salience as government officials increasingly recognized that American liberties had been won through armed force and that they could be threatened at any time by despotic Europeans and Native Americans.[21] The United States was involved in almost never-ending warfare as the Jeffersonian ideal of an agrarian republic collided with the broader national phenomenon that would become known as Manifest Destiny. Once the War of 1812 settled border issues with Britain, the Shawnee, and other British allies, the United States turned its attention to the Indian and Spanish presence in Florida.[22]

Financial expenditure in the service of armed force is usually associated with eighteenth- and nineteenth-century European nation-states, but the early American republic was no stranger to it. Public expenditures for territorial acquisition and defense became commonplace as the United States required ever more land to overcome constraints on its economic growth.[23] In the years between the Louisiana Purchase and the Mexican-American War, the United States consolidated land on which to establish a sound political economy. Private citizens and government agents participated in the violence, settlement, and state-building that accompanied the process of westward expansion.[24] Although to many Americans the United States seemed to be at peace between the War of 1812 and the Mexican-American War, fighting on the frontier never ceased. The United States fought a series of undeclared wars against the Seminoles, Arikara, Winnebago, Sauk, Fox, and Creek Indians, among others.

Firearms had played an important role in imperial contests on the continent for centuries. Natives traded and raided for European guns and used them, for example, to interrupt the French fur trade, compete with other Native groups, and combat White encroachment.[25] Native groups also successfully negotiated

---

[21] H. REP. NO. 152, at 663, 14TH CONG., RE-ORGANIZATION OF THE MILITIA, COMMUNICATED TO THE HOUSE OF REPRESENTATIVES, JANUARY 7, 1817 (2d Sess., Jan. 7, 1817).

[22] GREGORY EVANS DOWD, A SPIRITED RESISTANCE: THE NORTH AMERICAN INDIAN STRUGGLE FOR UNITY, 1745–1815 (1992). For "manifest destiny" as an American ideology from settlement to the twentieth century, see ANDERS STEPHANSON, MANIFEST DESTINY: AMERICAN EXPANSIONISM AND THE EMPIRE OF RIGHT (1995).

[23] DREW MCCOY, THE ELUSIVE REPUBLIC: POLITICAL ECONOMY IN JEFFERSONIAN AMERICA 198–99 (1980). Martin Öhman argues that early republican policymakers understood that territorial expansion was linked with economic security and an improved status in the international trading system. The Louisiana Purchase, in fact, was executed with the understanding that the manufacturing sector would subsequently expand. Martin Öhman, *Perfecting Independence: Tench Coxe and the Political Economy of Western Development*, 31 J. EARLY AM. REPUBLIC 397 (2011).

[24] For example, the Monroe administration was always willing to forgo acquisition of Texas, which other scholars have pegged as the site of American imperial and racial ambitions during the 1830s and 40s, in its negotiations with Spain for Florida. WILLIAM WEEKS, JOHN QUINCY ADAMS AND AMERICAN GLOBAL EMPIRE 167 (1992).

[25] DAVID SILVERMAN, THUNDERSTICKS: FIREARMS AND THE VIOLENT TRANSFORMATION OF NATIVE AMERICA (2016).

for firearms in treaty terms with Europeans and Americans. The United States' power was always contested, but the challenges became easier to overcome because of developments in the arms industry.[26] This did not, of course, mean that the ability to manufacture increasingly efficient firearms immediately led to geopolitical dominance. Centuries of North American history disprove notions of technological determinism. Rather, in response to political desires to remove Native challenges to U.S. territorial consolidation, the federal government prompted arms manufacturers to innovate. Over time, these innovations had major consequences for the fate of U.S. empire.

The Seminole Wars in particular vexed U.S. military strategy; they consumed an incredible amount of resources from the 1810s through the 1850s.[27] The first major conflict started on November 21, 1817, when General Edmund P. Gaines attacked an Indian settlement after a small band of Seminoles refused to vacate lands just north of the Florida border. Over the next two years, American troops led by General Andrew Jackson waged war against the Seminoles in Spanish territory.[28] Following the War of 1812, many Americans wanted a reduction in military size and spending. Regardless, both Secretary of War John C. Calhoun and President James Monroe advocated violence against the Seminoles for the sake of punishment and national interest, only later appealing to Congress that the military action was necessary for the "safety of our fellow-citizens."[29] Legislators continued to push for a reduction in the military's budget. The House of Representatives requested that the War Department present a report on the feasibility of reducing the army and called for "the attention and effort of the government to be roused to confine its excesses within the most moderate limits which may be practicable."[30]

---

[26] Michael Witgen, *Seeing Red: Race Citizenship, and Indigeneity in the Old Northwest*, 38 J. EARLY AM. REPUBLIC 581, 610 (2018). For Natives' border crossing, see LAWRENCE B.A. HATTER, CITIZENS OF CONVENIENCE: THE IMPERIAL ORIGINS OF AMERICAN NATIONHOOD ON THE U.S.-CANADIAN BORDER (2017).

[27] Beginning in 1835, the second round of Florida Seminole Wars absorbed a tremendous amount of resources (between $30 million and $40 million—50 percent of annual expenditures—and forty thousand troops). H. REP. NO. 739, at 466, 25TH CONG., ESTIMATES AND APPROPRIATIONS FOR SUPPRESSING HOSTILITIES OF THE SEMINOLE INDIANS IN FLORIDA, SEPTEMBER 15, 1837 (1st Sess., Sept. 15, 1837). H. DOC. NO. 26-8, at 10, 26TH CONG., EXPENDITURES IN SUPPRESSING INDIAN HOSTILITIES IN FLORIDA, DECEMBER 15, 1840 (2d Sess., Dec. 15, 1840). Annual federal expenditures, exclusive of public debt, were $17.5 million in 1835, $30.9 million in 1836, $39.2 million in 1837. AM. STATE PAPERS NO. 497, at 16–20, 25TH CONG., STATEMENT SHOWING THE AMOUNT OF ANNUAL ESTIMATES SUBMITTED BY THE SECRETARY OF TREASURY, AND ANNUAL EXPENDITURES, JUNE 29, 1838 (2d Sess., June 29, 1838).

[28] Weeks, *supra* note 24, at 107.

[29] *Id.* at 109–10; H. REP. NO. 163, at 680, 15TH CONG., WAR WITH THE SEMINOLE INDIANS, MARCH 25, 1818 (1st Sess., Mar. 25, 1818).

[30] H. REP. NO. 168, at 779, 15TH CONG., REDUCTION OF THE ARMY CONSIDERED, DECEMBER 4, 1818 (2d Sess., Dec. 4, 1818); ANNALS OF CONG., at 391, 15TH CONG., REDUCTION OF THE ARMY, DECEMBER 11, 1818 (2d Sess., Dec. 11, 1818).

In spite of petitions to reduce the military budget, the Ordnance Department—the branch of the War Department tasked with overseeing weapon production—assertively pushed for increased efficiency and output. War Department officials made routine presentations to the president and to members of Congress about increasing appropriations for arms production.[31] Sometimes they waited "until the temper of Congress has cooled" to ask for more money.[32] As skirmishes between Seminole Indians and Americans increased along the Florida border, Secretary of War John C. Calhoun hoped to "increase the product of the national armory." He told Chief of Ordnance Decius Wadsworth to authorize contracts for five thousand barrels and rods prior to receiving approval from Congress. Wadsworth, accustomed to circumventing the legislative hurdles, "expected [the plan for new contracts] to be fully understood at the next session of Congress and measures taken to make it effectual."[33] At another point, Wadsworth instructed the Springfield Armory to produce at least twelve thousand stands of arms, even if it meant exceeding congressional appropriations.[34] As Wadsworth and other officials pushed arms supply, manufacturers at both federal and private armories responded by increasing output, but Americans had not yet figured out how to fight warfare in Florida or make weapons that could withstand the conditions. The First Seminole War petered out as a stalemate at the end of the 1810s.

Throughout the 1820s and 1830s, federal officials began to speak about the relationship between guns and Indian defense.[35] As the national political message out of Washington increasingly conflated Indian relations and firearms productions, the War Department began to strategize about how to manufacture weapons for the particularities of warfare against Natives in different regions across the continent.[36] Small military victories, such as the Arikara War in the mid-Missouri River plains in the early 1820s did little to secure White Americans' dominance of borderlands. In 1829, the department requested a report from General W.H. Ashley, who had overseen both defeat and victory against the Arikara, about the "military force best calculated for the protection of our Western frontier." In his letter to Washington, Ashley distinguished between the "bands of Indians from whom we may expect the greatest immediate danger" and "the bands with whom we have friendly intercourse," but also recognized

---

[31] John Morton, *John Morton to Roswell Lee, December 16, 1817, in* Box 3, Folder 3, SA-LRM.
[32] Decius Wadsworth, *Decius Wadsworth to Roswell Lee, November 10, 1818,* Box 1, Target #2, SA-LRO.
[33] Decius Wadsworth, *Decius Wadsworth to Roswell Lee, July 25, 1818,* Box 1, Target #2, SA-LRO.
[34] Decius Wadsworth, *Decius Wadsworth to Roswell Lee Springfield Armory, August 30, 1817,* Box 3, Folder 9, SA-LRM.
[35] AM. STATE PAPERS NO. 39, at 2, 21ST CONG., MESSAGE FROM THE PRESIDENT OF THE UNITED STATES, JANUARY 25, 1831 (2d Sess., Jan. 25, 1831).
[36] ANNALS OF CONG., at 1953, 18TH CONG., INDIAN FUR TRADE, MARCH 29, 1824 (1st Sess., Mar. 29, 1824); AM. STATE PAPERS, *supra* note 35; AM. STATE PAPERS, at 18, 21ST CONG., REPORT FROM THE INDIAN BUREAU, NOVEMBER 19, 1831 (1st Sess., Nov. 19, 1831).

that all Natives posed some threat to U.S. ambitions. In making his case that all should be met with a display of U.S. military force, Ashley assessed the weapons best suited for different situations. He noted first that "the patent rifle which I examined . . . appears, in one particular, to be well calculated for this service, in as much as it can be conveniently and quickly charged on horseback . . ." He was worried, though, that these rifles could not be repaired quickly. Ashley ultimately recommended rifles, which were "admirably well constructed for general use, but more particularly for the prairies, where severe winds and rains prevail at certain seasons of the year."[37] Additionally, he distinguished among fighting against Native peoples in different contexts: "The sabre will be found useful, and almost indispensable in operations against Indians mounted on horseback . . ." and "[T]he Indians in the vicinity of the Rocky mountains are very much in the habit of fortifying some strong point convenient to where they intend attacking their enemy, . . . they fight desperately before they can be ousted. It is in cases of this kind, as well as in many others, that artillery would be found convenient."[38]

This knowledge about specific Native combat context would eventually pay off, as the connection between Indian relations and firearms became particularly acute under Jackson's administration (1829–1837). The Indian Removal Act of 1830's pretensions to good will and mutual benefit are easy to dismiss on the grounds of unequal power dynamics and imperial ambitions, but these power dynamics were by no means secure.[39] The administration's ability to carry out this policy depended on violence—both real and perceived—and, often, guns.[40] Secretary of War John H. Eaton reiterated Ashley's advice to Congress following the passage of the Removal Act: "No half way measures should be adopted; show a sufficient force in the country to put down all opposition, and all opposition will cease without shedding of blood."[41] U.S. military leaders were right about the need for force, but wrong about bloodshed. The Seminoles in particular would pose a major threat to removal policy.

In the meantime, the United States had a victory in the Old Northwest that nonetheless revealed military inadequacies.[42] Fighting began in the spring of

[37] William Ashley, *Letter from General Ashley to the Secretary of War, March 1829*, in CONGRESSIONAL RECORD BOUND, at 92–93, 21ST CONG., APPENDIX TO THE REGISTER OF DEBATES (2d Sess., Mar. 3, 1831).
[38] *Id.*
[39] They were threatened not only by Natives but also White Americans, many of whom did not share or actively opposed imperial policies. *See, e.g.*, AM. STATE PAPER NO. 310, 21ST CONG., MEMORIAL OF INHABITANTS OF NORTHAMPTON, EASTHAMPTON, SOUTHAMPTON, AND WESTHAMPTON, MASSACHUSETTS, ON REMOVAL OF INDIANS, MARCH 17, 1830 (1st Sess., Mar. 17, 1830).
[40] Ethan Davis, *An Administrative Trail of Tears: Indian Removal*, 50(1) AM. J. LEGAL HIST. 49 (2008); Michael Morris, *Georgia and the Conversation over Indian Removal*, 91(4) GA. HIST. Q. 403 (2007).
[41] AM. STATE PAPERS, *supra* note 35.
[42] PATRICK J. JUNG, THE BLACK HAWK WAR OF 1832 (2007).

1832 over land disputes. Sauk Indians had ceded land to the U.S. government that traders purchased from federal land officials. Sauk Indians remained divided about the terms of the cession, and some refused to vacate their land. When Black Hawk led a band of Sacs and Foxes across the Mississippi, General Atkinson was forced to retreat. The governor of Illinois called out three thousand mounted volunteers to reinforce the regular troops, which enabled them to pursue Black Hawk, killing close to two hundred (while fewer than a dozen U.S. troops died). This experience bolstered Ashley's claims about the efficacy of mounted rifleman, and following this war, mounted rangers were sent south to police Indian removal.[43] In August, the fighting effectively ended, but the U.S. military held Black Hawk and other tribal leaders in prison for another year out of fear.[44] Although the conflict had revealed the power of U.S. army numbers against Native resistance, the conflict had also highlighted shortcomings. Just as Ashley had pointed to the problems of faulty firearms in the 1820s, during the Black Hawk War, wet conditions caused widespread firearms malfunctioning, which delayed at least one major pursuit of Black Hawk's troops.[45] And in general, commanders commented on soldiers' struggles using guns.[46]

These experiences were met with a federal initiative to improve firearms production throughout the 1830s and shore up imperial power, especially as the second war against the Seminoles, a more formidable foe than the U.S. faced during the Black Hawk War, geared up.[47] In 1832, the United States signed a vastly unequal treaty that required Seminoles to move west of the Mississippi over the ensuing three years.[48] As cotton production pushed further south, Florida was of great strategic imperial importance.[49] The formal acquisition of Florida from Spain in 1821 promised aspiring planters new opportunities for profitable landholding and guaranteed coveted commercial access to Caribbean and Atlantic markets. As a haven for runaway slaves from nearby states, however, the territory also threatened national security.[50] The territory passed a

---

[43] AM. STATE PAPERS No. 532, at 30–31, 22ND CONG., ANNUAL REPORT OF THE SECRETARY OF WAR, NOVEMBER 25, 1832 (2d Sess., Nov. 25, 1832).
[44] ROGER L. NICHOLS, BLACK HAWK AND THE WARRIOR'S PATH 155–56 (2d ed. 2017).
[45] AM. STATE PAPERS, *supra* note 43, at 30.
[46] Jung, *supra* note 42, at 34; AM. STATE PAPERS, *supra* note 43.
[47] For the most recent scholarship on the Second Seminole War, see C.S. MONACO, THE SECOND SEMINOLE WAR AND THE LIMITS OF AMERICAN AGGRESSION (2018). See also ANDREW K. FRANK, BEFORE THE PIONEERS: INDIANS, SETTLERS, SLAVES AND THE FOUNDING OF MIAMI (2017). For an account of Seminoles' persistent resistance to removal, made possible by their effective system of arms supply, see DAVID SILVERMAN, THUNDERSTICKS: FIREARMS AND THE VIOLENT TRANSFORMATION OF NATIVE AMERICA 190–220 (2016).
[48] COLIN G. CALLOWAY, PEN AND INK WITCHCRAFT: TREATIES AND TREATY MAKING IN AMERICAN INDIAN HISTORY (2013).
[49] ANDREW K. FRANK, BEFORE THE PIONEERS: INDIANS, SETTLERS, SLAVES AND THE FOUNDING OF MIAMI (2017).
[50] Weeks, *supra* note 24, at 26–27, 30–33.

series of laws in the 1820s and 1830s meant to curtail the movement and gun ownership of nonwhites. In 1827, the territory proclaimed that any slave who shot a White person would be executed. Several years later, in 1833, the territory prohibited "any slave, free negro, or mulatto" from owning a gun.[51] Several laws also focused on "Indian" gun ownership and movement. In 1827, the territory passed a law that stipulated that "any male Indian, of the years of discretion, venture to roam or ramble beyond the boundary lines of the reservations which have been assigned to the tribe or nation to which said Indian belongs, it shall and may be lawful for any person or persons to apprehend, seize, and take said Indian, and carry him before some justice of the peace, who is hereby authorized, impowered, and required, to direct . . . not exceeding thirty-nine stripes . . . to be laid on the bare back of said Indian; moreover, to cause the gun of said Indian (if he has one) to be taken from him."[52] A law passed in 1847 contained almost exactly the same wording, indicating that Native movement and gun ownership were still a problem.

In the interim, the government's solution was to use weapons more effectively against Native Americans in an attempt to eradicate the Seminole population. In 1837, former president Andrew Jackson wrote to the War Department: "A well-chosen brigade with such officers as I could select, numbering 1000 bayonets and rifles, in addition to the regulars now in Florida would destroy the Seminole Indians in 30 days from the time of their reaching Tampa Bay."[53] He was wrong. Indians knew the land in a way that intruders did not. Former Adjutant General and Florida politician James Gadsden complained about their hiding places. Based on the logic of American superiority, he assumed that "when the tomahawk was raised the seminal [sic] should have been crushed in six weeks."[54] Instead, the war was "shamefully prolonged," and U.S. failure was a constant source of humiliation for army officers.[55] Gadsden was "embarrassed, as an American, at how ineffective we have been against them . . . a small band of savages has alluded us."[56] The Second Seminole War would prove more difficult for the United States to win than the Black Hawk War.[57]

---

[51] An Act concerning patrols, in Compilation of the Public Acts of the Legislative Council of the Territory of Florida, Passed Prior to 1840, at 65 (1833), in THE MAKING OF MODERN LAW: PRIMARY SOURCES (John P. Duval ed., 1839).

[52] An Act to prevent Indians from roaming at large throughout the Territory, in Compilation of the Public Acts of the Legislative Council of the Territory of Florida, Passed Prior to 1840, at 46 (1827), in THE MAKING OF MODERN LAW: PRIMARY SOURCES (John P. Duval ed., 1839).

[53] Andrew Jackson, *Andrew Jackson to Joel Roberts Poinsett, August 27, 1837*, in Folder 3, Box 9, JOEL ROBERTS POINSETT PAPERS (Historical Society of Pennsylvania) [hereinafter JRPP].

[54] James Gadsen, *James Gadsden to Joel Roberts Poinsett, September 17, 1837*, in Folder 6, Box 9, JRPP.

[55] Jackson, *supra* note 53.

[56] James Gadsen, *James Gadsden to Joel Roberts Poinsett, August 24, 1837*, in Folder 3, Box 9, JRPP.

[57] Jung, *supra* note 42, at 34.

There were two outcomes to these challenges. The first was that the War Department placed increased importance on the improvement and experimentation of arms during the late 1830s. In 1837, a board of officers conducted a series of experiments on guns produced at private and public armories. Their comments on the trials reveal a preoccupation with combat in Florida. The board noted that one particular rifle was superior because it could transition between infantry and cavalry use seamlessly, which was important in Florida, where many operations relied on dragoons (soldiers who fought as cavalry when mounted, as infantry when dismounted). The board was particularly sensitive to on-the-ground conditions; one note specifically mentioned the heat and damp of Florida.[58] It also learned to supply weapons for guerrilla warfare.[59] Buck and ball cartridges were used, for example, because they dispersed more widely than traditional ones and facilitated fighting against opponents camouflaged among swampy forests.[60]

There was no real victory in Florida, but neither was there a defeat. Instead of negotiating a peace, the commander of U.S. troops offered remaining Seminoles money and a rifle to move to a reservation in southwest Florida, while Congress passed a law on August 4, 1842, for the "armed occupation" of Florida by settlers who would receive federal money to defend their land. Most settlers wanted statehood because the national government guaranteed weapon security and military protection against the diminished but effective Seminoles.[61] They got their wish when Florida became a state in 1845. Persistent violence erupted into the Third Seminole War a decade later, but by the eve of the Civil War, the American military had forcibly removed four thousand Seminoles to Oklahoma.[62]

III. Continued Expansion and Continuing Armament Needs

Empire, however, was far from secure. Insecurities about Britain persisted. Once Texas became an independent republic in 1836, Americans debated admitting it to the union, along with other Mexican territory to which they had dubious

---

[58] S. Rep. No. 743, at 525, 25th Cong., Report of the President of a Board of Officers on Improvements in Fire-Arms by Hall, Colt, Cochran, Leavitt, and Baron Hackett, as Compared with the United States Musket, October 3, 1837 (1st Sess., Oct. 3, 1837).

[59] For a description of the nature of warfare in Florida, see John T. Sprague, The Origin, Progress, and Conclusions of the Florida War (1848).

[60] Andrew Jackson, *Andrew Jackson to Joel Roberts Poinsett, October 14, 1837*, in Folder 8, Box 9, JRPP. M.L. Brown, *Notes on U.S. Arsenals, Depots, and Martial Firearms*, 61 Fla. Hist. Q. 449, 450 (1983).

[61] The Floridian 1 (Tallahassee, Jan. 13, 1838).

[62] Theda Perdue, *The Legacy of Indian Removal*, 78 J. S. Hist. 3 (2012).

claims.[63] Many Americans argued that if the United States did not annex Texas, Britain, which urged Texas to maintain its sovereignty, would foment Indian and slave rebellions. President John Tyler had long identified Great Britain as America's chief rival in its quest for global commercial supremacy.[64] He and pro-slavery expansionists argued that England would prohibit the spread of slavery, but even northern opponents of Tyler's administration argued for annexation because they feared that British presence would stymie trade.[65] France was also a problem. Although the United States had supported France in a minor war against the British-backed Mexican government in the 1830s, France, like Britain, opposed annexation. The French government wanted unfettered access to Texan markets and hoped to check U.S. geopolitical power in the region.[66]

U.S. geopolitical power was in fact increasing: the late 1840s marked the first time the country was prepared for war, at least from a supply standpoint. Gone were the insecurities over weapon supply. As one Philadelphia area newspaper noted, the government had plenty of "muskets ready for shipment at a moment's notice. There need not, therefore, be much fear of a scarcity of guns."[67] During the 1837 tests, the examiners determined that, "the arms now in use in service of the United States . . . combine all the requisites of convenience, durability, simplicity, and efficiency."[68] Ten years later, the War Department was also impressed by quantity. Two months after fighting commenced, it reported that the number of arms produced at Springfield greatly exceeded that of the previous year.[69] By June the following year, the United States had over $8.4 million worth of small arms in its inventory.[70] Many of these guns represented the latest in firearm technology, including the first conventional musket made entirely of interchangeable parts.[71]

Even as American officers repeatedly wrote about the superiority of the enemy's numbers (in 1846, Mexico had a standing army of about 36,000, compared to just over 7,000 men in the U.S. armed forces, fewer than before

---

[63] Adams as president attempted to purchase Texas from Mexico for $1 million (1827), and Jackson imitated the action by offering $5 million in 1829. Both efforts were rebuffed by Mexico.

[64] Edward P. Crapol, *John Tyler and the Pursuit of National Destiny*, 17 J. EARLY REP. 467, 469 (1997).

[65] Paul E. Sturdevant, *Robert John Walker and Texas Annexation: A Lost Champion*, 109 Sw. HIST. Q. 188, 196 (2005). Britain had long been developing an informal empire in Mexico that threatened U.S. interests there. ROBERT D. AGUIRRE, INFORMAL EMPIRE: MEXICO AND CENTRAL AMERICA IN VICTORIAN CULTURE (2004).

[66] R.A. McLemore, *The Influence of French Diplomatic Policy on the Annexation of Texas*, 43(3) Sw. HIST. Q. 342 (1940).

[67] EVENING NORTH AMERICAN 1 (Philadelphia, May 23, 1846).

[68] S. REP., *supra* note 58, at 529.

[69] AM. STATE PAPERS NO. 1, at 165, 29TH CONG., LIST OF PAPERS ACCOMPANYING THE REPORT OF THE SECRETARY OF WAR, DECEMBER 5, 1846 (1st Sess., Dec. 5, 1846).

[70] AM. STATE PAPERS NO. 8, at 686, 30TH CONG., LIST OF PAPERS ACCOMPANYING THE REPORT OF THE SECRETARY OF WAR, NOVEMBER 30, 1847 (1st Sess., Nov. 30, 1847).

[71] Brown, *supra* note 60; H. Doc., *supra* note 27, at 9.

the War of 1812), they also wrote about the efficacy of American weaponry.[72] New Yorker Gouverneur Kemble wrote that the February 1847 "[Battle of] Buena vista was gloriously won" and that "the quality of the metal of our guns is now superior to my home country in Europe."[73] This U.S. victory has largely been attributed to the superiority of American artillery over Mexican troop numbers, and Kemble had founded the West Point Foundry, one of the nation's major producers of artillery.[74] That winter, however, it was not just howitzers that enabled American soldiers to kill more Mexican soldiers than killed them, but also rifles, pistols, and muskets. Colonel Humphrey Marshall of the Kentucky cavalry reported that his regiment of four hundred, "armed with rifles, or with carbine, pistol and sabre," was successful against almost fifteen hundred men. Another commander noted that, "notwithstanding the great superiority of their numbers, [our] riflemen kept up a deliberate and well-directed fire upon them," and General Zachary Taylor boasted that Americans "maintained their ground handsomely against a greatly superior force, holding themselves under cover and using their weapons with deadly effect."[75]

Many of these guns represented the latest in firearm technology, including the first conventional musket made entirely of interchangeable parts.[76] Some featured Samuel Colt's new revolving technology, which the government had first tested during the Second Seminole War. The Texas Rangers used Colt's revolvers successfully against Mexican troops in the early 1840s, and Captain Samuel Walker heartily endorsed them to the Ordnance Department. The Department purchased two thousand for use during the Mexican-American War.[77] The revolvers received glowing reports from the battlefront.[78] Colt specifically asked the secretary of war for government reports on his firearms for marketing purposes.[79] These positive endorsements would be regular features in gun advertisements in the 1850s, as gun companies transitioned from big government orders to smaller, widespread civilian orders—a trend that would continue

---

[72] JAMES B. WHISKER, THE RISE AND DECLINE OF THE AMERICAN MILITIA SYSTEM 333 (1999).

[73] Gouverneur Kemble, *Gouverneur Kemble to Joel Roberts Poinsett, April 15, 1847*, in Box 16, Folder 17, JRPP.

[74] Gouverneur Kemble, *The West Point Foundry*, 15 PROC. N.Y. STATE HIST. ASS'N 190 (1916).

[75] AM. STATE PAPERS No. 8, at 133–34, 166–67, 190, 29TH CONG., LIST OF PAPERS ACCOMPANYING THE REPORT OF THE SECRETARY OF WAR, NOVEMBER 30, 1847 (2d Sess., Nov. 30 1847).

[76] Brown, *supra* note 60, at 449–51; H. DOC., *supra* note 27, at 9.

[77] AM. STATE PAPERS No. 3, at 1–3, 30TH CONG., PETITION OF SAMUEL COLT, DECEMBER 12, 1848 (2d Sess., Dec. 12, 1848).

[78] For example, D.E. Twiggs, Florida war veteran and commander under both General Zachary Taylor and General Winfield Scott, endorsed them to Congress. David E. Twiggs, *David E. Twiggs to Thomas Jefferson Rusk, 21 April 1848*, in SAMUEL COLT'S OWN RECORD OF TRANSACTIONS WITH CAPTAIN WALKER AND ELI WHITNEY, JR. IN 1847, at 84–85 (Connecticut Historical Society, 1949).

[79] Samuel Colt, *Samuel Colt to Joel Roberts Poinsett, August 3, 1840*, in GABRIEL J. RAINS PAPERS, 1840–1865 (South Carolina Historical Society).

after the Civil War. By then, firearms became a ubiquitous feature of frontier settlement, warfare, and empire.[80]

IV. CONCLUSION

Warfare in the 1830s and 1840s changed the gun market. Although civilian gun ownership remained fairly consistent throughout early America (around 50 percent), the middle of the 1800s saw shifts in America's gun culture.[81] Advertisements changed as guns were marketed for want rather than need. Military violence across the North American continent led to the gun's transition from ordinary everyday item to symbol of conquest and the American frontier. Mass-produced handguns became available in the 1840s and 1850s because of the federal government, and advertisements boasted as such.[82] Remington ads from the 1860s, for example, proclaimed that their revolvers were "Approved by the Government."[83]

This close link between gun production and the federal government suggests that as today's courts decide what kinds of gun regulation the Second Amendment permits, they ought to consider the federal government's historic role in structuring the firearms industry and its market, and in testing and regulating individual firearms. In the long history of American gun production and ownership, the federal government has always had a constitutional responsibility, and thus a right, to be involved. Indeed, its own administering of violence is responsible for the very industry that today seeks freedom from gun regulation.

---

[80] PAMELA HAAG, THE GUNNING OF AMERICA: BUSINESS AND THE MAKING OF AMERICAN GUN CULTURE (2016).

[81] Probate inventories reveal greater percentages of guns than Michael Bellesiles's discredited study of gun ownership in early America showed, but few arms manufacturers had an easy time profiting from the civilian market. Michael A. Bellesiles, *The Origins of Gun Culture in the United States, 1760–1865*, 83 J. AM. HIST. 425 (1996); MICHAEL A. BELLESILES, ARMING AMERICA: THE ORIGINS OF A NATIONAL GUN CULTURE (2000). James Lindgren & Justin L. Heather, *Counting Guns in Early America*, 43(5) WM. & MARY L. REV. 1777, 1838 (2001).

[82] Randolph Roth, *Counting Guns: What Social Science Historians Know and Could Learn about Gun Ownership, Gun Culture, and Gun Violence in the United States*, 26 SOC. SCI. HIST. 699, 705 (2002).

[83] Army and Navy Revolver Advertisement, HARPER'S WKLY., Dec. 31, 1864.

3

SCOTTISH HISTORY, PRESBYTERIAN CULTURE, AND THE RIGHT TO BEAR ARMS

Neil McIntyre

I. INTRODUCTION

On Thursday, December 10, 1743, "a poor unskilful and small Handful of People" gathered outdoors at Middle Octorara in Lancaster County, Pennsylvania, to "renew" the National Covenant of 1638 and the Solemn League and Covenant of 1643.[1] The service opened with prayer and a public reading of the Covenants as well as the "Acknowledgment of Sins and Engagement to Duties" issued by the General Assembly of the Church of Scotland in 1648. The reading was "not only for the clearer understanding of these Things" but also to make a "deep and abiding Impression of the Holiness and Sublimity of that great Transaction that [they] were to be employed in."[2] The only minister present—unnamed in the printed account, but almost certainly Alexander Craighead, minister of Middle Octorara from 1735 until his controversial departure in 1741—followed the reading with a sermon on John 11:56: *What think ye, that he will not come to the feast?*—a text that, as the minister explained, revealed the necessity of "the solemn Renewal of our Holy Covenants" as the community prepared to celebrate the Lord's Supper.[3] Indeed, both covenanting and communion were held to be "a very solemn and near Approach unto God," and "if Jesus be not with us therein, no Good can be had to our Souls, but dreadful Guilt contracted."[4]

The participants returned the following day and, after prayer, reading, and singing, the minister preached on Jeremiah 50:5: *Come and let us join ourselves to the Lord in a perpetual covenant that shall not be forgotten.* While he emphasized "the Lawfulness of Covenanting personally, family and national" as well as the

---

[1] ALEXANDER CRAIGHEAD, RENEWAL OF THE COVENANTS, NATIONAL AND SOLEMN LEAGUE; A CONFESSION OF SINS; AND ENGAGEMENT TO DUTIES; AND A TESTIMONY; AS THEY WERE CARRIED ON AT MIDDLE OCTARARA IN PENSYLVANIA [SIC], NOVEMBER 11, 1743, at viii (1748) [hereinafter RENEWAL OF THE COVENANTS].
[2] *Id.* at ix.
[3] *Id.*
[4] *Id.* at ix–xi.

importance of memory in the fulfillment of their obligations, he conceded that it had been much neglected in recent years, where "almost every one in his Station, according to his Capacity, appears evidently to use their utmost Endeavours to mar and hinder one another in this great Duty of National Covenanting."[5] "[I]n this perjured, blood guilty, apostate and backslidden Age," then, a renewal of the Covenants was never more required.[6] The service continued with more prayer and psalm-singing before another public reading of their acknowledgment of sins, the Covenants, and their testimony.

That author of the printed account of the renewal recognized that their issuing of a testimony required further explanation. In accordance with Revelation 12:11, *And they overcame him by the blood of the lamb, and by the word of their testimony; and they loved not their lives unto the death*, committed Christians were to issue a joint testimony if the constitution or membership of church or state institutions became corrupted by error or immorality. In such cases, testimonies were understood to be divinely warranted, publicly issued statements by the faithful that demanded "the right Regulation of Judicatures."[7] They evidently had as much to say about law and politics, then, as they did matters of ecclesiology. The lengthy title of their testimony also revealed much about their identity and ideological orientation. This was *The Declaration, Protestation and Testimony of a suffering Remnant of the Anti-Popish, Anti-Lutheran, Anti-Prelatick, Anti-Erastian, Anti-Latitudinarian, Anti-Sectarian, true Presbyterian Church of Christ, in America.*[8]

After another reading of the key documents, they were sworn with uplifted hands. While the author asserted that there had been "no material Alteration made" to the texts, "the Names of several Ranks of People" were removed and comments regarding the "Supreme Magistrate" included in the margins.[9] The Covenants may have been understood to have contained truths that were unchanging, but they were also clearly subject to editing and adaptation, as they had been previously when renewed by their forbears, the Presbyterian secessionists the United Societies, at Lesmahagow, Lanarkshire, in the midst of the "Glorious Revolution" of 1688–1690.[10] As we will see later, these were not insignificant alterations.

Swords had been drawn throughout the ceremony in a gesture that was clearly loaded with symbolism. This had led to much local gossiping regarding their

---

[5] *Id.* at xi–xvi.
[6] *Id.* at xv.
[7] *Id.* at xvii–xviii.
[8] *Id.* at 43.
[9] *Id.* at xviii–xix.
[10] *E.g.*, THE NATIONAL COVENANT AND SOLEMN LEAGUE & COVENANT, WITH THE ACKNOWLEDGMENT OF SINS, AND ENGAGEMENT TO DUTIES, AS THEY WERE RENEWED AT LESMAHEGO, MARCH 3. 1688 [SIC] WITH ACCOMMODATION TO THE PRESENT TIMES (1689).

intentions—Had they feared for their lives? Were they in rebellion?—but the author specified three reasons that reveal much about the ideological framework in which this covenanted community operated. First, "[b]ecause no War is proclaimed without a drawn Sword."[11] Second, "[b]ecause our renowned Ancestors were constrained to draw the Sword in the Defence of their own Lives, and for their maintaining of a true covenanted Presbyterian Reformation."[12] They drew the sword, therefore, "to testify to the World, that we are one in Judgment with them, and that we are to this Day willing to maintain the same defensive War in defending our Religion and ourselves against all Opposers thereof."[13] This was not, however, a call for offensive action; "not for falling upon Persons to take away their Lives, but a defending our Religion and ourselves from all unjust Assaults."[14] Finally, they drew their swords because it had been "the Practice of the faithful witnessing Remnant, to renew the Covenants with a drawn sword," and, as per the Song of Solomon 1:8, they were commanded to *follow the footsteps of the flock*.[15]

Lasting several days, this deeply spiritual and emotional but also heavily political performance was a conspicuous expression of the community's recent withdrawal from the Presbyterian church in Pennsylvania. The church was deemed to have been ideologically compromised due to its Erastian (that is, state-controlled) foundation in the Glorious Revolution, its recognition of the House of Hanover as the British monarchy, its relatively relaxed terms of communion, and the general denial of the all-binding nature of the Covenants by Presbyterian ministers and parishioners in North America. In the renewal we can see four elements of the Scottish Presbyterian and covenanting traditions that had been exported to North America in the later seventeenth and eighteenth centuries: (1) a religious conviction that often led to secession; (2) a deeply held suspicion of governments in general and the British state in particular; (3) words, gestures, and symbols that connected American Presbyterians to the histories of Old Testament Israel and Reformed Scotland; and (4) an enduring martial ethos that legitimized arms-bearing.

What can this renewal of Scotland's seventeenth-century covenants tell us about the framing of the right to bear arms in the eighteenth century? By focusing on the Presbyterian and covenanting traditions in British North America, this chapter seeks to address two lacunae in Second Amendment scholarship: the theory that underpins the right to bear arms, and the way that religion has shaped attitudes to arms-bearing. In order to address these lacunae, the

---

[11] RENEWAL OF THE COVENANTS, *supra* note 1, at xix.
[12] *Id.*
[13] *Id.*
[14] *Id.* at xx.
[15] *Id.* at xix–xx.

chapter uses the development and transmission of Scottish covenanting ideology as a case study that allows us to explore how religious and constitutional ideas became integrated in debates on the right of self-defense, resistance, and even first-strike action against tyrannical state officials—what the preacher and polemicist Alexander Shields (c. 1660–1700) termed the right of "vindictive & punitive force."[16]

The choice of a Scottish study is intentional and serves as a counterpoint to the Anglocentrism of historical scholarship in the field. English common law was, of course, the inherited legal code in which debates on arms took place, but, as this chapter reveals, there were diverse and highly influential non-English legal, political, and theological sources that informed ideas on self-defense and arms-bearing.

II. THE EXISTING HISTORICAL ACCOUNT IN AMERICA

In a recent illuminating blog post for the *Northwestern University Law Review*, Jacob Charles issued a call for more scholarship on the theory that underpins the Second Amendment.[17] Echoing his colleagues Joseph Blocher and Darrell Miller's observation that "few theorists [had] engaged with the Second Amendment on its own terms after *Heller* codified the private purposes reading of the right,"[18] Charles argued that the COVID-19 pandemic had served only to underscore "the degree to which the debate over what values motivate the Second Amendment right remain undertheorized."[19] He has, at the same time, cautioned us against "focusing too narrowly on those twenty-seven words of constitutional text," and particularly in light of "the vast and expansive sub-constitutional protection for gun rights" that exist currently in the United States.[20]

The urgent need to properly consider the right to bear arms in its historical and legal context has, indeed, been driven by the landmark 2008 Supreme Court case *District of Columbia v. Heller*, where, as Patrick Charles has noted, the historical and philosophical origins of the Second Amendment were litigated heavily. As

---

[16] ALEXANDER SHIELDS, A HIND LET LOOSE, OR, AN HISTORICAL REPRESENTATION OF THE TESTIMONIES OF THE CHURCH OF SCOTLAND, FOR THE INTEREST OF CHRIST 88, 639 (1687).

[17] Jacob D. Charles, *Covid Lays Bare the Need for Attending to Second Amendment Theory*, NW. UNIV. L. REV. (May 28, 2020), https://blog.northwesternlaw.review/?p = 1441 [hereinafter "Second Amendment Theory"].

[18] JOSEPH BLOCHER & DARRELL A.H. MILLER, THE POSITIVE SECOND AMENDMENT: RIGHTS, REGULATION, AND THE FUTURE OF HELLER 151 (2018). The notable exception is Michael Green. *See* Michael Green, *Why Protective Private Arms Possession? Nine Theories of the Second Amendment*, 84 NOTRE DAME L. REV. 131 (2008).

[19] "Second Amendment Theory," *supra* note 17.

[20] Jacob D. Charles, *Securing Gun Rights by Statutes: The Right to Keep and Bear Arms Outside the Constitution*, 120 MICH. L. REV. 581 (2022).

is well known, the Court embraced an interpretation that was supported by individual right scholars: that armed individual self-defense was the "central component" of the Second Amendment and thus the District of Columbia had acted unconstitutionally when it sought "prohibition against rendering any lawful firearm in the home."[21] Charles has observed similarly of *McDonald v. City of Chicago* that petitioners had to show how "armed individual self-defence in the home is 'fundamental to the American scheme of justice.'" An apparent "Anglo-American tradition" of the right was traced from classical Greece and Rome to Magna Carta and the English Declaration of Rights, becoming the constitutional standard for the Court.[22] For Charles, however, *Heller* grossly misinterpreted the Declaration's "have arms" provision, while history did not support the claim that armed individual self-defense was a fundamental American right. In fact, the historical and legal evidence revealed instead that the *Heller* decision did not "comport with the true meaning and understanding of an ancient Anglo-American right to 'keep and bear arms.'"[23]

In challenging *Heller*, Charles has recognized that the right to bear arms must be placed in a much broader historical context. His own work has paid particular attention to the development of doctrines of resistance during the "English Civil War" and "Glorious Revolution."[24] This necessary and entirely understandable focus on English history has, however, failed to appreciate that the mid-century civil wars and 1688–1690 revolution were Britannic and indeed global events: the civil wars began first in Scotland with the rioting that greeted the introduction of the Book of Common Prayer in 1637, while the Revolution was triggered by the stadtholder William of Orange's invasion from the Dutch republic in 1688. Both events were of international significance.[25] Beyond these specific moments in time, the right to resist had been hotly debated for centuries in the British Isles and continental Europe, evolving rapidly during the reformations and revolutions of the sixteenth and seventeenth centuries.[26] We cannot, therefore,

---

[21] Patrick J. Charles, *The Right of Self-Preservation and Resistance: A True Legal and Historical Understanding of the Anglo-American Right to Arms*, 18 CARDOZO L. REV. DE NOVO 18, 18 (2010).

[22] *Id.* at 19.

[23] *Id.* at 20–22.

[24] *See id.* generally. *See also* Patrick J. Charles, *The Faces of the Second Amendment Outside the Home, Take Two: How We Got Here and Why It Matters*, 64 CLEV. ST. L. REV. 373 (2016); *see also* PATRICK J. CHARLES, ARMED IN AMERICA: A HISTORY OF GUN RIGHTS FROM COLONIAL MILITIAS TO CONCEALED CARRY (2018).

[25] Recent scholarship has preferred "British Civil Wars" or "Wars of the Three Kingdoms" to reflect the multinational nature of the mid-century upheavals. For this conceptual turn, *see generally* J.G.A. Pocock, *British History: A Plea for a New Subject*, 47 J. MOD. HIST. 601 (1975); THE NEW BRITISH HISTORY: FOUNDING A MODERN STATE, 1603–1715 (Glenn Burgess ed., 1999). For the international significance of the Revolution, *see, e.g.*, Steven Pincus, *The European Catholic Context of the Revolution of 1688–89: Gallicanism, Innocent XI, and Catholic Opposition*, *in* SHAPING THE STUART WORLD, 1603–1707: THE ATLANTIC CONNECTION (A.I. Macinnes & A.H. Williamson eds., 2006).

[26] The Scots were active and notable contributors. *See, e.g.*, ROGER A. MASON, KINGSHIP AND THE COMMONWEAL: POLITICAL THOUGHT IN RENAISSANCE AND REFORMATION SCOTLAND (1998).

fully comprehend American "tradition" by sole recourse to the English past.[27] What, then, of diverse non-English yet Anglophone contributions to doctrines of resistance and early American political thought?

David Konig has, certainly, grounded the right to bear arms in an earlier eighteenth-century struggle by the Scots for a militia after it had been denied them by the British Parliament at the same time as it had remodeled the militia in England.[28] But although Konig is cognizant of the contribution of Scottish thinking on the subject, his emphasis on the influence of the Scottish Enlightenment misses the longer-term roles played by Presbyterian politics and religious culture. As we shall see, a right of resistance was developed to such an extent that it could be counted an integral feature of Scottish, certainly Scottish Presbyterian, identity.

Scottish trade, migration, and settlement in the American colonies has, to be sure, generated a wealth of scholarship, with the intellectual and cultural influence of Scottish Presbyterians receiving noteworthy attention.[29] Ulster Scots—seventeenth-century Scottish colonists and settlers in the plantations of Ulster in the north of Ireland—have likewise been subject to significant scholarship,[30]

For elsewhere in Europe, *see, e.g.,* QUENTIN SKINNER, THE FOUNDATIONS OF MODERN POLITICAL THOUGHT, VOLUME TWO: THE AGE OF REFORMATION (1978); J.H.M. SALMON, RENAISSANCE AND REVOLT: ESSAYS IN THE INTELLECTUAL AND SOCIAL HISTORY OF EARLY MODERN FRANCE (1987); MARTIN VAN GELDEREN, THE POLITICAL THOUGHT OF THE DUTCH REVOLT 1555–1590 (1992); R.M. Kingdon, *Calvinist Resistance Theory, 1550–1580*, and J.H.M. Salmon, *Catholic Resistance Theory, Ultramontanism, and the Royalist Response, 1580–1620*, in THE CAMBRIDGE HISTORY OF POLITICAL THOUGHT, 1450–1750, at 193–208, 219–53 (J.H. Burns & Mark Goldie eds., 4th ed. 2008); DAVID P. HENRECKSON, THE IMMORTAL COMMONWEALTH: COVENANT, COMMUNITY, AND POLITICAL RESISTANCE IN EARLY REFORMED THOUGHT (2019).

[27] The wider historiography has, indeed, emphasized the importance of situating the early republic in continental and global contexts. *See* MICHAEL D. HATTEM, PAST AND PROLOGUE: POLITICS AND MEMORY IN THE AMERICAN REVOLUTION 11–15 (2020).

[28] David Thomas Konig, *The Second Amendment: A Missing Transatlantic Context for the Historical Meaning of "The Right of the People to Keep and Bear Arms,"* 22 L. & HIST. REV. 11 (2004). *See also* JOHN ROBERTSON, THE SCOTTISH ENLIGHTENMENT AND THE MILITIA ISSUE (1985).

[29] For Scots in the Americas, *see* NED C. LANDSMAN, SCOTLAND AND ITS FIRST AMERICAN COLONY, 1683–1765 (2016); David Armitage, *Making the Empire British: Scotland in the Atlantic World, 1542–1707*, 155 PAST & PRESENT 34 (1997); ALLAN I. MACINNES ET AL., SCOTLAND AND THE AMERICAS, C. 1680–C. 1939: A DOCUMENTARY SOURCE BOOK (2002); Alexander Murdoch, *Scotland and America, c. 1600–c. 1800*, 4 N. SCOT. 90 (2010); David Dobson, *Scottish Emigration to Colonial America, 1607–1785*, 16 SCOT. ECON & SOC. HIST. (2011). For Presbyterians in particular, *see* Gideon Mailer, *The Influence of the Scottish Covenant on the "Election" of Representatives in The New American Republic*, 27 PARLIAMENTS, EST. & REPRESENTATION 57 (2007); Gideon Mailer, *Anglo-Scottish Union and John Witherspoon's American Revolution*, 67 WM. & MARY Q. 709 (2010); Joseph S. Moore & Jane G.V. McGaughey, *Holy Heritage: Covenanters in the Atlantic World*, 11 J. TRANSATLANTIC STUD. 125 (2013); J.S. MOORE, FOUNDING SINS: HOW A GROUP OF ANTISLAVERY RADICALS FOUGHT TO PUT CHRIST INTO THE CONSTITUTION (2016); Craig Gallagher, *"Them That Are Dispersed Abroad": The Covenanters and Their Legacy in North America, 1650–1776*, 99 SCOT. HIST. REV. 454 (2020). For a wider colonial lens, *see* VALERIE WALLACE, SCOTTISH PRESBYTERIANISM AND SETTLER COLONIAL POLITICS: EMPIRE OF DISSENT (2018).

[30] H. TYLER BLETHEN ET AL., ULSTER AND NORTH AMERICA: TRANSATLANTIC PERSPECTIVES ON THE SCOTCH-IRISH (2001); PATRICK GRIFFIN, THE PEOPLE WITH NO NAME: IRELAND'S ULSTER

with transnational and transatlantic Presbyterianism considered most recently by Andrew Holmes.[31] Presbyterians are also well-attested prior to 1776 in Robert Middlekauf's authoritative account of the Revolution: Middlekauf has observed, for example, that the Presbyterian Church had more members than any other in the middle colonies by the middle of the eighteenth century and highlighted the emergence of a powerful Presbyterian political alignment in Pennsylvania that was animated by the fear of Anglican episcopacy being imposed by the metropole.[32] Middlekauf's account, above all, emphasizes the critical role played by religion in the shaping of American culture, and in the years leading up to the Revolution, we can see traces of a Scots Presbyterian influence in anti-episcopal sentiment, certainly, but also in federal political thought, the formation of committees of correspondence, and the language of local declarations.[33] Remarkably, the Boston committee even drafted a "Solemn League and Covenant" in 1774 that bound signatories to cease commercial activity with Britain, refuse purchase of English goods, and disrupt trade with those who refused to sign.[34]

There is, all told, clear evidence for the settlement and influence of Scottish and Irish Presbyterians in the American colonies and later the United States, who brought with them a complex and dynamic religious culture. As we will see, Presbyterian ideologies had much to say about self-defense, rights of resistance, and the bearing of arms. There was, in fact, an extensive crossover of intellectual concerns between Presbyterians of the later seventeenth century and American patriots in the eighteenth—most notably on tyrannical government, the fiscal-military state, church-state relations, political representation, and the right to secede from political and religious associations. In an assessment of the development of these ideas in context, this chapter highlights how religious and

SCOTS, AMERICA'S SCOTS IRISH AND THE CREATION OF A BRITISH ATLANTIC WORLD, 1689–1764 (2001); K.A. Miller, *The New England and Federalist Origins of "Scotch-Irish" Ethnicity*, in ULSTER AND SCOTLAND, 1600–2000: HISTORY, LANGUAGE AND IDENTITY 105–18 (William Kelly & John R. Young eds., 2004); D.N. Doyle, *Scots Irish or Scotch-Irish*, and K.A. Miller, *Ulster Presbyterians and the "Two Traditions" in Ireland and America*, in MAKING THE IRISH AMERICAN: HISTORY AND HERITAGE OF THE IRISH IN THE UNITED STATES 151–70, 255–70 (J.J. Lee & Marion R. Casey eds., 2006); ULSTER TO AMERICA: THE SCOTS-IRISH MIGRATION EXPERIENCE, 1680–1830 (Warren R. Hofstra ed., 2011); BENJAMIN BANKHURT, ULSTER PRESBYTERIANS AND THE SCOTS IRISH DIASPORA, 1750–1764 (2013).

[31] A.R. Holmes, *Irish Presbyterian Commemorations of Their Scottish Past, c. 1830 to 1914*, in IRELAND AND SCOTLAND IN THE NINETEENTH CENTURY 48–61 (Frank Ferguson & James McConnel eds., 2008); A.R. Holmes, *Presbyterian Religion, Historiography, and Ulster Scots Identity, c. 1800 to 1914*, 52 HIST. J. 615(2009); A.R. Holmes, *Religion, Anti-Slavery, and Identity: Irish Presbyterians, the United States, and Transatlantic Evangelicalism, c. 1820–1914*, 39 IRISH HIST. STUD. 378 (2015).
[32] ROBERT MIDDLEKAUF, THE GLORIOUS CAUSE: THE AMERICAN REVOLUTION, 1763–1789, at 47–48, 148 (rev. ed. 2005).
[33] *Id.* at 221–22, 223, 251, 334. It should be noted, however, that "a few Presbyterians in the southern colonies" were loyalists. *Id.* at 564.
[34] *Id.* at 238.

constitutional imperatives could be woven together in the justification of arms-bearing. This observation may give us pause for reflection when considering debates not only on the Second Amendment or subconstitutional law but also on extraconstitutional doctrine.

III. The Role of Reformation

Middle Octorara was a frontier outpost when settlers first petitioned the presbytery of New Castle in 1727 for a settled ministry, with the county of Lancaster formed two years later from territory lying to the west of the Octorano Creek. Situated between Dutch and German migrants in the north and Quakers in the valleys of the east and south, Scottish and Scots-Irish communities occupied the lands south of the Mine Ridge and westward beyond the Susquehanna River.[35] Other Presbyterians had settled in New York and the Carolina backcountry, with contingents of covenanters existing within wider colonial Presbyterian congregations.[36] In Pennsylvania, then printer Benjamin Franklin—no friend of Presbyterians—published stories in his *Pennsylvania Gazette* as well as pamphlets that contributed to the intra-Presbyterian paper war that was sparked by the Middle Octorara testimony.[37] It was Franklin, indeed, who published the only contemporary account we have of the renewal of the Covenants.[38] These events courted the ire of the Crown, with English officials well aware of an historic Presbyterian capacity to challenge authority and foment resistance. It is to their past—"the Precedents of our renowned Ancestors"—that we now turn.[39]

We begin with the Protestant Reformation in sixteenth-century Scotland. Unlike the Crown-led "magisterial" reformations in England and Lutheran Germany, the Scottish Reformation was a rebellion—a rebellion in defiance of the Scottish Crown but also French control of Scottish government. From 1554 until 1560, Scotland had been governed by the queen mother, Mary of Guise, whose regency government had ruled in the name of her daughter, Mary, who had become queen upon the death of her father, James V, in 1542, and had married the French dauphin, Francis II, in 1558. At the same time as the clamor for religious reform had grown in the 1550s, Frenchmen had come to dominate political offices held traditionally by the Scottish nobility. It was this combination

---

[35] M.E. McElwain, Faith and Works at Middle Octorara Since 1727, at 2–3 (1956). With thanks to Mr. J. Barry Girvin, session elder of Middle Octorara Presbyterian Church, for providing me with this text.
[36] Moore, *supra* note 29, at 37–39.
[37] *Id.* at 40–42.
[38] Local church records for the critical 1740–1753 period have not survived.
[39] Renewal of the Covenants, *supra* note 1, at vii.

of demands for religious reform and a sense of Scottish patriotism which had contributed to the eventual success of the Reformation.

The Reformation had been led by a group of noblemen known as the Lords of the Congregation. This group adapted the medieval practice of "banding"—a mechanism used primarily to form alliances and settle feuds—toward the goal of achieving religious reform. Their bond duly became a "covenant" to advance the Protestant cause.[40] The leading clerical reformer, John Knox (c. 1514-1572), had also spoken of covenanting in polemical tracts addressed to the nation, which, crucially, included a letter addressed directly to the "commonalty."[41] There was, indeed, significant popular participation that found expression in rioting, iconoclasm, and the "Beggars' Summons" of 1559. Although not—or not immediately—a social revolution, the dynamics of the Scottish Reformation spoke to the popular nature of the Protestant movement and had radical sociopolitical implications that were spelled out in the next century.[42]

The Reformation also constituted a diplomatic revolution. The Franco-Scottish "auld alliance" had been forged in the Middle Ages and was a product of the fraught triangulated relationship between England, Scotland, and France. It was, however, the crucial intervention of England at the behest of Elizabeth I that had tipped the scales decisively in favor of the Lords of the Congregation and the Reformation movement. The Anglo-Scottish border had become a confessional boundary when Henry VIII had broken from Rome, but English assistance in the Scottish Reformation held out the possibility of a closer Anglo-Scottish relationship grounded in a shared Protestantism.[43] Some contemporaries even imagined the withering away of national identities and the creation of a Protestant Britain.[44]

The Protestant cause was secured by the "Reformation Parliament" of August 1560, where a sizeable contingent of lairds and burgesses had sat for the first time in several generations.[45] Returning from France to begin her personal rule of

---

[40] J.E.A. Dawson, *Bonding, Religious Allegiance, and Covenanting*, in KINGS, LORDS AND MEN IN SCOTLAND AND BRITAIN, 1300-1625: ESSAYS IN HONOUR OF JENNY WORMALD 155-72 (Steve Boardman & Julian Goodare eds., 2013); J.E.A. Dawson, *Covenanting in sixteenth-century Scotland*, 99 SCOT. HIST. REV. 336-48 (2020).

[41] JOHN KNOX, ON REBELLION 72-127 (Roger A. Mason ed., 1994).

[42] For the Reformation as a long-term social revolution, *see* WALTER MAKEY, Chapter 1 *in* CHURCH OF THE COVENANT, 1637-1651 (1979).

[43] CLARE KELLAR, SCOTLAND, ENGLAND, AND THE REFORMATION, 1534-1561 (2003); JOHN KNOX AND THE BRITISH REFORMATIONS (Roger A. Mason ed., 1st ed. 1998).

[44] Marcus Merriman, *James Henrysoun and "Great Britain": British Union and the Scottish Commonweal*, *in* SCOTLAND AND ENGLAND, 1286-1815, at 85-112 (Roger A. Mason ed., 1987); ROGER A. MASON, Chapter 9 *in* KINGSHIP AND THE COMMONWEAL: POLITICAL THOUGHT IN RENAISSANCE AND REFORMATION SCOTLAND (1998); DAVID ARMITAGE, *The Empire of Great Britain: England, Scotland and Ireland c. 1542-1612*, *in* THE IDEOLOGICAL ORIGINS OF THE BRITISH EMPIRE (2000).

[45] K.M. Brown, *The Reformation Parliament*, *in* THE HISTORY OF THE SCOTTISH PARLIAMENT, VOLUME I: PARLIAMENT AND POLITICS IN SCOTLAND, 1235-1560, at 203-31(K.M. Brown & R.J. Tanner eds., 2004).

Protestant Scotland, the avowedly Catholic Queen Mary was deposed violently in 1567. During and after the Marian civil wars, which ran until 1573, a series of regents ruled in the stead of Mary's Protestant son, James VI—later James I of England and Ireland—until he came to power in the mid-1580s. In the midst of these oscillations in political affairs, serious questions remained about the governance of the reformed church and the Scottish commonwealth.

Calls for further reform of the Scottish church were first sounded in the 1570s and are associated most famously with the reformer Andrew Melville, who was well connected to Calvinist Geneva.[46] On account of their overwhelmingly ecclesiological concerns, they have become known to us by their preferred form of church government—Presbyterians. Unlike in England, where the monarch was the supreme head of the established church, Scottish Presbyterians believed the king to be a member of the church only, albeit with an important role to play in the promotion of "true religion" and punishment of sin. At the same time—and, again, contrary to England—Scottish Presbyterians advocated a system of hierarchical church courts—from parochial kirk sessions, presbyteries, and synods to the General Assembly—in place of the singular authority of diocesan bishops. By the early seventeenth century, however, King James had implemented a hybrid system, with bishops imposed upon the lower church courts and the General Assembly called upon only sporadically.[47] Although they should not be conflated, Scottish Presbyterians were in some ways analogous to the puritans of England.[48]

The alignment of Protestantism and patriotism, the popular nature of the Scottish Reformation, and the emergence of a distinct Scottish Presbyterian subculture in the late sixteenth and early seventeenth centuries converged in both the framing and signing of the National Covenant. The Covenant was a response to the unconstitutional imposition of the English Book of Common Prayer in Scotland but also wider political and economic grievances arising from the authoritarian kingship of Charles I. The orchestrating of riots and petitioning in 1637 culminated in the formation of a revolutionary provisional government of nobles, gentry, burgesses, and clergy known as "the Tables." Two of its members, the Presbyterian lawyer Archibald Johnson of Wariston and the minister Alexander Henderson, drafted the Covenant in February 1638. It has been

---

[46] For Melville, *see, e.g.*, ANDREW MELVILLE (1542–1622): WRITINGS, RECEPTION, AND REPUTATION (S.J. Reid & Roger A. Mason eds., 2014).

[47] For the Church of Scotland at this time, *see* ALAN R. MACDONALD, THE JACOBEAN KIRK: SOVEREIGNTY, POLITY, AND LITURGY (1998) (describing the Church of Scotland at this time).

[48] D.G. MULLAN, SCOTTISH PURITANISM, 1590–1638 (2000). *Cf.* John Coffey, *The Problem of "Scottish Puritanism", 1590–1638*, *in* ENFORCING REFORMATION: SCOTLAND AND IRELAND, 1560–1690, at 66–90 (Elizabethanne Boran & Crawford Gribben eds., 2006); Margo Todd, *The Problem of Scotland's Puritans*, *in* THE CAMBRIDGE COMPANION TO PURITANISM, 174–88 (John Coffey & P.C.H. Lim eds., 2008).

described by Allan Macinnes as "revolutionary" and by the present author as "a vehicle to confront royal authority whilst galvanising Scottish society against the prerogative rule of absentee Britannic monarchy."[49]

We shall return to the ideas contained within the National Covenant in the following section. For the moment, we should consider that its central thrust—its ambiguities and tensions notwithstanding—was to limit permanently the exercise of magisterial power and abolish episcopacy. Despite undeniably novel elements in the Covenant, however, Presbyterians could tap into a tradition of covenanting that allowed them to frame it as a "renewal" and the revolution as a "second reformation" that would return the church to an imagined golden age in the later sixteenth century. Thus, the Covenant also represented the staking of a claim by Presbyterians for ownership of the Reformation, which was crucial not only in legitimating their ecclesiology but also their armed resistance.[50] The mass swearing and subscribing of the Covenant in parish communities, moreover, alongside innovations in publicity and print, led to unprecedented levels of popular political engagement, mobilization, and participation in this period.[51]

The covenanting revolution was exported to England via the Solemn League and Covenant of 1643. The covenanting movement recognized that the permanence of their revolution was dependent on a settlement being reached across the British Isles. The Scots covenanters—now in control of the machinery of government and transforming the fiscal-military capacity of the state to wage war against Charles—offered military assistance to English parliamentarians in exchange for the imposition of their revolutionary model in England and Ireland. As a confederal union the Solemn League came close to realizing the vision of a uniform Protestant Britain that had been mooted in the previous century, but Scotland and England were soon at odds despite their common faith.[52] The Solemn League also had profound long-term implications for Scottish colonists and migrants in Ireland.[53] By 1648, however, the Solemn League had collapsed; at the same time, the unity of the covenanting movement was compromised when two factions claimed to be acting in the best interests of the Covenants. The intensification of factionalism between 1649 and 1651 contributed to the eventual downfall of the covenanting regime. The war-torn and fiscally exhausted nation

---

[49] ALLAN I. MACINNES, CHARLES I AND THE MAKING OF THE COVENANTING MOVEMENT, 1625–1641, at 173 (1st ed. 1991); Neil McIntyre, Saints and Subverters: The Later Covenanters in Scotland, c. 1648–1682, at 2 (2016) (Ph.D. thesis, University of Strathclyde) [hereinafter Saints and Subverters].

[50] *See* LAURA A.M. STEWART, RETHINKING THE SCOTTISH REVOLUTION: COVENANTED SCOTLAND, 1637–1651, at 128–47 (2016).

[51] *Id.* at 116–21, 153–68.

[52] ROGER A. MASON, *Divided by a Common Faith? Protestantism and Union in Post-Reformation Britain*, *in* SCOTLAND'S LONG REFORMATION: NEW PERSPECTIVE ON SCOTTISH RELIGION, C. 1500–C. 1660, at 202–25 (John McCallum ed., 2016).

[53] R. Scott Spurlock, *The Solemn League and Covenant and the Making of a People in Ulster*, 99 SCOT. HIST. REV. 368–91 (2020).

was then occupied by the new English republic until the restoration of monarchy in the three kingdoms in 1660.

Despite having taken the Covenants several times—including at his stage-managed coronation on January 1, 1651—Charles's son, Charles II, was not restored on a covenanted basis.[54] The revolution was overturned in 1661.[55] At the same time, the royal prerogative was reasserted, episcopacy restored—albeit in Erastian form—and oaths of allegiance framed to abrogate covenanting principles, such as "that it wes lawfull to subjects, for reformation, to enter into covenants and leagues or to take up armes against the king or those commissionated by him."[56] The final settlement led to the ejection of over two hundred Presbyterian ministers from their parishes as well as extensive fining of laypeople exempted from the king's indemnity.[57]

It was in this period that the covenanting tradition of martyrdom and fighting for liberty began to properly germinate; it was also in this period that Scots and Scots-Irish Presbyterians first began emigrating to North America. Although resistance to Restoration governance was nationwide, in the covenanting heartlands of the south and west it culminated in an armed insurrection in 1666 and an even larger uprising in 1679. The repressive policies of state—resorting variously to bonds, fines, imprisonment, banishment, and military intimidation to enforce the Restoration—fanned the flames of protest and dissent in the 1660s and 1670s. Dissenting Presbyterians, meanwhile, held illegal meetings in houses and fields known as "conventicles," which soon became a potent expression of defiance in the face of the new regime.[58] They were organized and supported by networks of dissenting laypeople and defended by armed followers who operated essentially as vigilantes or guerrillas—for the Professor Divinity at the University of Glasgow, Gilbert Burnet (1643-1715), "a sort of banditti"[59]—complete with command structure, tactical awareness, military drilling, and improvised weaponry. But while Presbyterians were initially united in their nonconformity, it was not long before ideological divisions led to the splintering of dissenting Presbyterianism. At the Revolution of 1688-1690, where Presbyterian church government was restored but the Covenants met with silence, a vocal minority

---

[54] For the covenanted coronation, see THE FORME AND ORDER OF THE CORONATION OF CHARLES THE SECOND (1651).

[55] See GILLIAN I. MACINTOSH, THE SCOTTISH PARLIAMENT UNDER CHARLES II, at 1-36 (2007).

[56] CHARLES II, Act for preservation of his majesties' person, authoritie and government, Recs. of the Parliaments of Scot. to 1707 1662/5/20 (Keith Mark Brown et al. eds. 2007) [hereinafter RPS]. See also id. at 1661/1/16.

[57] THE REGISTER OF THE PRIVY COUNCIL OF SCOTLAND 269-70 (P. Hume Brown ed., 3d series, 1908); RPS, supra note 56, at 1662/5/96.

[58] Neil McIntyre, Conventicles in the Restoration Era, 45 SCOT. CHURCH HIST. 66-81 (2016); Neil McIntyre, Conventicles: Organising Dissent in Restoration Scotland, 99 SCOT. HIST. REV. 429-53 (2020).

[59] GILBERT BURNET, THE HISTORY OF MY OWN TIME ii, at 104 (M.J. Routh ed., 2d ed. 1833).

of dissenters refused to return to the uncovenanted church. The covenanting past did, nevertheless, inspire elements of the Revolution settlement, with clear echoes of covenanting constitutional thought in the Claim of Right of 1689.[60] It was in this period—between Restoration and Revolution—that the key elements of the Presbyterian and covenanting traditions so clearly displayed at the Middle Octorara renewal took shape. With this historical context in view, we can now consider the ideological development of rights of resistance and arms-bearing by Scottish Presbyterians.

IV. CALVIN, COVENANTS, AND SELF-DEFENSE

While Calvin himself was famously circumspect on the topic of resistance, sixteenth-century Calvinists were less hesitant to argue in this direction.[61] In brief, resistance was held to be lawful if led by an "inferior magistracy"—a term that could refer to a wide range of officeholders depending on geography or political context. In Scotland, certainly, John Knox had asserted the duty of just such an inferior magistracy to resist—meaning, in effect, the Scottish nobility. There was, indeed, a long history of Scottish magnates acting as "guardians of the realm" during royal minorities and crises in the fourteenth and fifteenth centuries. The humanist scholar George Buchanan (1506–1582)—who had justified the deposition of Queen Mary in his infamous *De Jure Regni apud Scotos* (1579) and *Rerum Scoticarum Historia* (1582)—meanwhile went further and advocated for popular resistance in the form of single-handed tyrannicide; that is, for Buchanan, every citizen had a duty to resist a tyrant—although precisely who constituted Buchanan's citizenry was unclear.[62] It was Knox and Buchanan, above all, who provided the foundations for a distinctively Scottish theory of resistance that could be expanded and pushed in new directions by Presbyterians in the next century.[63]

In the same century that Knox and Buchanan were writing, the first firearms laws in Scotland were passed by the Scottish Parliament. In 1535, statute required landholders to provide quantities of arms, ammunition, and trained men scaled to the size of their estates.[64] By mid-century, however, firearms were beginning to

---

[60] John R. Young, *The Scottish Parliament and the Covenanting Heritage of Constitutional Reform*, in THE STUART KINGDOMS IN THE SEVENTEENTH CENTURY: AWKWARD NEIGHBOURS, 226–50 (A.I. Macinnes & J.H. Ohlmeyer eds., 2000); Karin Bowie, *"A Legal Limited Monarchy": Scottish Constitutionalism in the Union of Crowns, 1603–1707*, J. SCOT. HIST. STUD. 131–154 (2015).

[61] "Second Amendment Theory," *supra* note 17.

[62] GEORGE BUCHANAN, LAWS OF KINGSHIP 12–15, 15–18, 98–109, 141–45 (Roger. A. Mason trans. & ed., Martin S. Smith ed., 2006).

[63] Saints and Subverters, *supra* note 49, at 69–72; John Coffey, *George Buchanan and the Scottish Covenanters*, in GEORGE BUCHANAN: POLITICAL THOUGHT IN EARLY MODERN BRITAIN AND EUROPE 189–203 (Caroline Erskine & Roger A. Mason eds., 2012).

[64] RPS, *supra* note 56 at, 1535/29.

be regulated. Such regulation emerged at a time when the Scottish Crown sought to curb violent feuding among the landed classes.[65] In 1567, and again in 1575, statute declared that "na maner of person nor personis of quhatsumever estate, conditioun or degree" were to carry or use firearms publicly or privately outside of licensed homes. There was, however, a list of exceptions, including soldiers in royal service and officers charged to assemble subjects at "wappenschawing" (that is, local musters).[66] By the turn of the seventeenth century, nevertheless, it was clear that regulation was the guiding principle in royal policy: the "act regarding bearers and shooters of hackbuts and pistols," for example, noted that even in cases where there was no evidence of slaughter, mutilation, or "uther odious violence," the bearers of firearms were to be pursued at law because they had bred "sic truble to pairteis and assyssouris [i.e., jurymen] and sic difficultie in the tryell that oftymes innocent persones ar thairby vexit."[67] The private carrying of firearms had evidently had a negative impact on the effective administration of justice in early modern Scotland.

Regulation, then, was the watchword. But although feuding certainly declined and litigation grew,[68] few historians would consider seventeenth-century Scotland to have been especially peaceful. The confrontation between Charles I and the covenanting movement sparked, as we saw earlier, revolution and civil war throughout Britain and Ireland, with violence used to both enforce and resist the Restoration counterrevolution.[69] Covenanting ideology was, indeed, inherently a call to arms. While a broader analysis is not possible here, the critical conceptual mechanism was that of "mutual association": in the National Covenant, subscribers were bound "to the mutual defence and assistance every one of us of another in the same cause of maintaining the true Religion, and his Majesties Authoritie, with our best counsell, our bodies, meanes, and whole power against all sorts of persons whatsoever," while the Solemn League required subscribers to "assist and defend all those that enter into this League and Covenant [. . .] all the dayes of our lives zealously and constantly [. . .] against all opposition."[70]

---

[65] *See* KEITH M. BROWN, BLOODFEUD IN SCOTLAND, 1573–1625: VIOLENCE, JUSTICE AND POLITICS IN EARLY MODERN SOCIETY (1986).

[66] RPS, *supra* note 56, at A1567/12/22, A1575/3/2.

[67] *Id.* at 1600/11/25 ("Such trouble to parties and assizers and such difficulty in the trial that oftentimes innocent persons are thereby vexed.").

[68] *See* A. Mark Godfrey, *Rethinking the Justice of the Feud in Sixteenth-Century Scotland*, *in* KINGS, LORDS AND MEN IN SCOTLAND AND BRITAIN, 1300–1625, at 136–54 (Steve Boardman & Julian Goodare eds. 2014).

[69] Apparent "lawlessness" in the Scottish Highlands was also used as a pretext for military intervention. *See* A.I. Macinnes, *Repression and Conciliation: The Highland Dimension, 1660–1688*, 65 SCOT. HIST. REV. 167 (1986); A.D. KENNEDY, GOVERNING GAELDOM: THE SCOTTISH HIGHLANDS AND THE RESTORATION STATE, 1660–1688 (2014).

[70] THE CONFESSION OF FAITH OF THE KIRK OF SCOTLAND, SUBSCRIBED BY THE KINGS MAJESTIE AND HIS HOUSEHOLDE, IN THE YEARE OF GOD, 1580, at 14 (1638); A SOLEMN LEAGUE AND COVENANT FOR REFORMATION, AND DEFENCE OF RELIGION, THE HONOUR AND HAPPINESSE OF

Although ambiguous, class-based limitations were inserted in both texts—"according to our vocation and power," "according to our places & callings"—widespread subscription to the Covenants had quietly but significantly expanded the right to resist. When the covenanting revolutionaries were united and in power, the implications of this shift were not fully in view, but the Mauchline rising of 1648 and Western Association of 1650—when grassroots protests broke out against perceived backsliding by the covenanting regime—both hinted at the ways in which covenanting had unleashed militant and socially subversive political impulses that were not easily contained.

If there was already plenty of scope in the Covenants for dispute—not least on the definition of such slippery terms as the "true Christian religion"—there was far less in the way of a philosophical justification for covenanting opposition to the king. This ideological gap was plugged in large part, however, by the Presbyterian minister Samuel Rutherford (1600–1661)—a leading figure in the mid-century British revolutions as a church commissioner and theorist—whose *Lex Rex* (1644) responded to Bishop John Maxwell's *Sacro-sancta Regum Majestus* of that same year.[71] Rutherford made three key claims: that "Wars raised by the Estates and Subjects for their owne just defence against the Kings bloody Emissaries" were lawful; that "in the case of defensive War," a distinction had to be drawn between opposition to the monarch's person and their office; and that "selfe-defence by opposing violence to unjust violence" accorded with both divine and natural law.[72] These views were also expressed in answer to the royalist argument that only kings could wage war: "[T]he King cannot take from one particular man the power of the sword for naturall self-preservation, because it is the birth-right of life; neither can the King take from a community and Kingdome a power of rising in Armes for their own defence."[73] Like Knox, however, Rutherford restricted the right of resistance to the inferior magistracy—a magistracy now assumed to comprise the three Estates of nobles, gentry, and burgesses[74]—but he also created a conceptual space in which popular rights could be asserted. If it was lawful for the political community to defend religion and liberty by force of arms, did ordinary subjects not have the same rights and duties when their leaders and political representatives subverted "the

THE KING, AND THE PEACE AND SAFETY OF THE THREE KINGDOMES OF SCOTLAND, ENGLAND, AND IRELAND 6 (1643).

[71] For Rutherford, *see* JOHN COFFEY, POLITICS, RELIGION AND THE BRITISH REVOLUTION: THE MIND OF SAMUEL RUTHERFORD (1997).
[72] REV. SAMUEL RUTHERFORD, LEX, REX: THE LAW AND THE PRINCE 257–65, 265–80, 326–39 (1644).
[73] *Id.* at 373
[74] *Id.* at 38.

fundamental constitution of our Christian and reformed Kingdome?"[75] It was this line of thinking that was pursued by dissenting Presbyterians after 1660.

Five years after the Restoration, John Brown (1610–1679), an ejected minister exiled in Rotterdam, published the first defense of the covenanting revolution as part of a wider vindication of Presbyterian dissent.[76] Although guided by Rutherford's *Lex Rex* and puritan lawyer William Prynne's *Soveraigne Power of Parliaments and Kingdomes* (1643), and drawing liberally from Cicero, Calvin, Knox, and Buchanan, Brown's consideration of additional "particulars" hinted at the way in which the "just war" doctrine of the covenanting regime could be reshaped to meet the needs of what was effectively a Presbyterian protest movement. There was, Brown explained, a difference between rising in arms without any "lawfull ground," or for "trifles," and rising in arms "in extreme necessity, when religion, lawes, lives, & liberties" were at risk.[77] There was, similarly, a difference between a war carried out by "privat persons when grievously oppressed" and a war carried out by "the body of a land in their representatives in Parliament, against a king."[78] The parenthesis in his qualifying statement is significant: "Suppose, the first could not be well defended (which yet is not absolutely denied) yet this last is clear."[79] This lukewarm denial of resistance by private persons was suggestive of a critical conceptual and ideological shift that took place shortly afterward, when resistance began to be defined explicitly in covenanting discourse as an individual right.

It is in the anonymous publications of the lawyer James Stewart of Goodtrees (1635–1713)—son of financier and former provost of Edinburgh, James Stewart of Kirkfield and Coltness (1608–1681), a donor to the covenanting regime—that the shift can be detected. It was Stewart who supplied the bulk of *Naphtali* (1667), a tract published in large part to vindicate the Pentland rising of 1666, when around one thousand dissenters had risen in arms and marched on Edinburgh to petition the Scottish Privy Council.[80] In his "True and short Deduction," Stewart outlined the extent of what he termed the "right & Priviledge of Self-defence"—a right he believed to have been activated justly by the Pentland rebels.

Stewart began with the Reformation. Rather than deny the popular nature of the rising, Stewart claimed instead that criticism of it on the basis of a lack of aristocratic leadership amounted to a denial of the principles and practices of the early reformers. Reimagining the Reformation in the image of later Presbyterian

---

[75] JAMES STEWART, JUS POPULI VINDICATUM, OR THE PEOPLES RIGHT TO DEFEND THEMSELVES AND THEIR COVENANTED RELIGION, VINDICATED 5 (1669).

[76] JOHN BROWN, AN APOLOGETICALL RELATION, OF THE PARTICULAR SUFFERINGS OF THE FAITHFULL MINISTERS & PROFESSORS OF THE CHURCH OF SCOTLAND SINCE AUGUST 1660 (1665).

[77] *Id.* at 154–55.

[78] *Id.* at 156–57.

[79] *Id.* at 157.

[80] For the rising, *see* Saints and Subverters, *supra* note 49, at 61–66.

dissent was, indeed, a successful rhetorical strategy undertaken by Presbyterians. Unlike the "illimited submission" advocated by their Episcopalian adversaries, Stewart believed it clear that the early reformers had not resigned "that First, and most just Priviledge of *Self-defence*" for self-preservation and evangelism. In fact, "the whole course of our Reformation" provided "unquestionable evidence" of "the Necessity of Convocations and Combinations (though not only without but even against Authority)" as well as justifying "the breach of any Law or Act then standing against the same."[81] This "right & Priviledge" was expansive: not only was it founded upon the law of nature, it was "the very first instinct of pure Nature"; it was, therefore, "competent to, and exercised by every individual, before that either Society or Government were known." But where other thinkers would transfer it to the sovereign,[82] Stewart maintained that self-defense was not alienated upon the formation of government—especially as it was "the great End & motive, for which all voluntary Societies and Policies were introduced and continued."[83]

This right of self-defense was then married to a Reformed political theology that, although uncontroversial on the surface, held the capacity to incite radical action. Stewart emphasized that religion was "the most important, dear and precious of all interests," its violation "the most wicked and insupportable of all injuries," and the "propelling by force of such injuries [. . .] the justest case and quarrell, that men in their Primaeve Liberty could be engaged in."[84] A breathless logic then moved quickly to rationalize popular resistance: as "the glory of God" was "the end of all things," the security of religion was thus the primary motivation for "the erecting of Rule and Government"; but if "Powers appointed for Preservation [. . .] endeavour Subversion," and "every man is bound to obey God rather then [sic] man" as stated in Acts 5:29, then such unjust violence "maketh both the End, the Means of Government, and Authority, and the injured persons Obligation thereunto, to cease."[85] In such a situation, "being called, whither to their own Defence, or the Assisting of their Brethren in so just a cause"—surely recalling the mutual association clauses in the Covenants—"they ought therein valiantly to acquit themselves, for the Glory of God, the maintenance of his Truth, and the mutuall preservation of one of another."[86]

---

[81] JAMES STIRLING & JAMES STEWART, NAPHTALI, OR THE WRESTLINGS OF THE CHURCH OF SCOTLAND FOR THE KINGDOM OF CHRIST 7–8 (1667).

[82] Stewart's theory of government anticipates that of John Locke, *see* JOHN LOCKE, TWO TREATISES OF GOVERNMENT (Peter Laslett ed., 1988) (1689). But where Locke saw a transfer of individual rights to the sovereign, Stewart emphasized that such rights were inalienable.

[83] STIRLING & STEWART, *supra* 81, at 14.

[84] *Id.* at 15.

[85] *Id.* at 16. Such logic also allowed Presbyterians to circumvent the Pauline injunction in Romans 13 to submit to higher powers.

[86] *Id.* at 16.

Similar views were given expression in the rebels' own declaration, where it was held "that nature and religion doth sufficiently teach all men to acknowledge the lawfulnesse of sinlesse self-defence," with specific obligations "to assist & defend all those that entered into the League & Covenant with us."[87] Neither the rebels nor Stewart, however, denied that magistrates held a "Reforming Power"—the power of the sword invested in them to maintain true religion. But Stewart asked his readers what Christians in general, and Presbyterians in particular, were to do "if not only the Supreame Magistrat, but with him all the Nobles and *Primores* of the Realme shall turn the principal perverters, and chief Patrons of these abominations?"[88]

The answer to this question, as well as the radical sociopolitical thrust of Stewart's theory, were laid out in his later *Jus Populi Vindicatum, or The Peoples Right to defend themselves and their Covenanted Religion, vindicated* (1669)—a title indicative of his insistence that resistance was a popular right rooted in divine, natural, and positive law. With other theorists conceding that resistance was lawful in certain cases, Stewart aimed to show that if the *grounds* of resistance justified subjects' virtual resistance through nobles or parliament, those grounds remained unchanged if the nobility or parliament no longer represented the people. Echoing the language used by Brown in this section, private persons could resist in such moments of "extreme necessity."[89] They could also, furthermore, resist a tyrannical parliament, because the law of nature gave all men a right of self-defense that "municipal laws" could not infringe; the "good of the commonwealth," that is, had to accord with natural law.[90] Leaving aside subtle shifts in thinking on Scottish parliamentary representation,[91] the examples Stewart used to evidence popular rights of resistance in the covenanting revolution—those moments "most recent in our memories"—reveal how that period could be used to justify popular political agency and participation in its widest sense, including "violent resistance."[92] In doing so, Stewart broke radically from early modern Scottish and mainstream Reformed political thought by asserting that neither the revolution in 1638–1639 nor the grassroots protests of 1648–1650 were predicated on aristocratic leadership or the authority of inferior magistrates. While recognizing that the covenanting movement had benefited from the support of "Noble Patriots: and renowned Nobles," they had not, he claimed, wielded "publick authority and Parliamentary power" or their

---

[87] "The declaration of the western party why they lifted arms," National Library of Scotland, Wodrow Quarto XXXII, fol. 123.
[88] STIRLING & STEWART, *supra* note 81, at 18.
[89] STEWART, *supra* note 75, at 22–38.
[90] *Id.* at 38–40, 44–45.
[91] Neil McIntyre, *Representation and Resistance in Restoration Scotland: The Political Thought of James Stewart of Goodtrees (1635–1713)*, 38 PARLIAMENTS, EST. & REPRESENTATION 161 (2018).
[92] STEWART, *supra* note 75, at 63.

own "inferiour, subordinat civil power" (that is, their heritable jurisdictions) in order to resist. The covenanting nobility, as others, had operated as "private persons," and it was this suggestion that allowed Stewart to innovate. For him, they acted "by vertue of that fundamental power belonging to all the members of the Commonwealth, according to their several places and relations."[93] Not only did this allow him to sidestep any accusation of an illegitimate assumption of magisterial power in the name of covenanting resistance, their walking "upon the ground of that fundamental right" theoretically expanded the right of resistance to encompass all subjects irrespective of rank or class.[94] Such covenanting radicalism extended also to "the Peoples power, in erecting Governours" and their relapsing into a state of "primaeve liberty and privilege" when government was "perverted," thus empowering them to "associate into new societies for their defence and preservation"[95]—an ideological framework used to justify secession from and war against the Restoration regime and its network of civil and military agents.

It was in this fraught political context that a militant wing emerged within the Presbyterian dissenting community that proved instrumental in the murder of the primate of Scotland, James Sharp, in May 1679, and another armed uprising that followed in June. In a series of declarations they renounced their allegiance to Charles II, declared war on his government, and separated from their erstwhile Presbyterian allies. They demanded a covenanted king, godly magistrates, and a Presbyterian church free of episcopal or state intrusion. They became known as the United Societies or "society people" on account of the confederal organizing structure of their society meetings. It was this group that the Middle Octorara communicants had in mind when they stated that "our active Testimony commences from the Year 1680."[96]

Vindicating the violence carried out by the Societies—for some, thuggish religious fanaticism, for others, a measured response to oppression—required a conceptual move so startling that it had few parallels until the emergence of revolutionist and anarchist political thought in the nineteenth century.[97] It was carried out by Alexander Shields, whom we met earlier, in *A Hind Let Loose*

---

[93] *Id.* at 64–65.
[94] *Id.* at 68.
[95] *Id.* at 80–94, 374–75.
[96] RENEWAL OF THE COVENANTS, *supra* note 1, at 46–47, 50.
[97] Shields was certainly at odds with contemporary European theorists, with the "age of assassinations" held to have ended by about 1630. *See* Colin Kidd, *Assassination Principles in Scottish Political Culture*, in GEORGE BUCHANAN: POLITICAL THOUGHT IN EARLY MODERN BRITAIN AND EUROPE 269–88 (Caroline Erskine & Roger A. Mason eds., 2012). For political thought in the wake of the French Revolution, *see* Gregory Claeys & Christine Lattek, *Radicalism, Republicanism and Revolutionism: From the Principles of '89 to the Origins of Modern Terrorism*, in THE CAMBRIDGE HISTORY OF NINETEENTH-CENTURY POLITICAL THOUGHT 200–53 (G.S. Jones & Gregory Claeys eds., 2013).

(1687). Shields's innovation was to divide the question of resistance in two: he sought to vindicate not only "The Principle of, and Testimony, for Defensive Arms" but also the "murdering [of] publick Enemies by private Persons in the Circumstances wherein they were stated"—what he also termed "vindictive & punitive force [. . .] executed upon men that are bloody *beasts of prey*."[98] Not only was defensive resistance vindicated, in other words, but an active, *offensive* form of resistance that moved far beyond the injunctions of previous theorists. A summary of his argument and apocalyptic worldview is worth quoting in full:

> That when the ruine of the Countrie, suppression of Religion, destruction of the Remnant professing & suffering for it, and the Wrath of God is threatened in & for the impunity of Idolaters & Murderers, that by the Law of God & Man should die the death, and supposing always such as are in publick Office not only decline their duty, but encourage those destroyers, yea Authorize them themselves; we may not only maintain defensive Resistance according to our Capacity, but endeavour also vindictive & Punitive force in executing Judgment upon them in cases of necessity.[99]

In the mode of Presbyterian writers before him, Shields maintained that such views were supported by the Reformation: that "practising this principle" had been "the Judgement & pleading of our Reformers."[100] But by the close of the 1680s, and on the eve of the Revolution of 1688–1690, covenanting ideology had been pushed in directions the likes of Knox and Rutherford would not have recognized. In the hands of Shields, covenanting implied an individual right to defend and advance the religious and constitutional imperatives of the Covenants by force of arms. The issue was, of course, how and by whom those imperatives were to be interpreted, understood, and adapted with the passage of time; and indeed, it was precisely this question that was wrestled with by the Middle Octorara communicants as they sought to understand their duties in eighteenth-century Pennsylvania.

V. Conclusion

After the Glorious Revolution, establishment and dissenting Presbyterians alike moved to secure the memory of the Restoration period as one of Presbyterian

---

[98] SHIELDS, *supra* note 16, at 88 (quote), 575–633, 633–93. For more on this conceptual turn, *see* Neil McIntyre, *Alexander Shields (c. 1600–1700) on the Right of Punitive Arms*, *in* SCOTLAND AND THE WIDER WORLD (Alison Cathcart & Neil McIntyre eds., 2022).

[99] *Id.* at 639.

[100] *Id.* at 638.

courage in the face of a tyrannical and licentious regime. The Societies, for example, began erecting gravestones "for our Late Martyrs" and collating "Martyrs Testimonies" which culminated in the publication of *A Cloud of Witnesses for the Royal Prerogatives of Jesus Christ* (1714)—a collection of scaffold testimonies emitted since 1680.[101] The Church of Scotland minister Robert Wodrow, meanwhile, researched the period assiduously if not impartially for his famous *History of the Sufferings of the Church of Scotland from the Restauration to the Revolution* (1721-1722). *Naphtali* and *A Hind Let Loose* were also republished several times, thereby cementing their status as important texts in the covenanting canon.[102] Presbyterian dissenters continued to engage in subversive political activity—refusing to pay taxes or customs and declining the authority of local magistrates, for example—and the martial ethos of the covenanting tradition was maintained by their sourcing and meeting in arms.[103] Eighteenth-century critics drew on the seventeenth-century upheavals to lambast Scottish Presbyterianism as violent, uncouth, seditious, and rebellious, but Presbyterians of all stripes emphasized instead their credentials as defenders of Protestantism and political liberty—a position made easier by the prevailing political climate and rise of Jacobitism. English colonists, indeed, tended to see Scottish Presbyterians as reliably Protestant stalwarts well equipped for frontier life despite lingering suspicion of their political principles.[104] No other religious culture in North America had a comparable canon of texts that covered rights of resistance so extensively or demonstrated their application so widely.

The right to resist and its corollary, the right to bear arms, had thus been grounded for centuries in religion and forms of constitutionalism that were also bound up in cultures and identities. But the radicalism of covenanting did not extend these rights as unfettered: the legitimacy of resistance depended on context and arms-bearing did not preclude regulation. The problem was, of course: Who decided when such rights became active, especially if the state was not trusted to monopolize legitimate violence? And how might arms-bearing be debated when its foundations were located in divine and natural law, to which positive law must give way? If we follow Charles, Blocher, Miller, and others in seeking to theorize the values that underpin the Second Amendment, what happens if we discover those values are embedded in a fundamentally religious ideology held to embody timeless and unchanging truths?

---

[101] "Conclusions of the General Meeting of the United Societies," National Records of Scotland, CH3/269/2, fols. 43, 54, 105, 129; A Cloud of Witnesses, for the Royal Prerogatives of Jesus Christ (1714).
[102] *Naphtali* was republished in 1680, 1693, 1721, and 1761; *A Hind Let Loose* in 1744, 1770, and 1797.
[103] McIntyre, *supra* note 98.
[104] Gallagher, *supra* note 29, at 457–58, 469.

In terms of Second Amendment theory, this chapter has suggested that attending to the intellectual origins of rights of arms-bearing in the United States requires more than sole consideration of a narrowly defined and ahistorical "Anglo-American tradition." As the renewal of the Covenants at Middle Octorara has revealed to us, the idea that all people, irrespective of social status, could bear arms in defense of themselves, their religion, and their co-religionists reflected a culture of righteous protest and resistance that was exported by Presbyterian Scots and Scots-Irish in the seventeenth and eighteenth centuries. Religious culture, in other words, was surely no less important than English common law or Whig political thought in shaping ideas on rights of arms-bearing in the American colonies in the eighteenth century.

4

"A WELL-REGULATED MILITIA"

CONSTITUTIONAL POLITICS, THE SECOND AMENDMENT, AND THE MILITIA IN THE JACKSONIAN ERA AND THE AMERICAN CIVIL WAR

Nicholas Mosvick

I. INTRODUCTION

This chapter aims to make a simple but significant point about the current predominant constitutional interpretation of the Second Amendment from the Early Republic period to the Civil War. The militia clause of the amendment was consistently read not under Justice Scalia's *Heller* interpretation as merely prefatory language announcing the purpose of the amendment,[1] but instead as text which imposed duties both upon the states and their citizens to maintain their militia units to properly defend their communities and the federal government to properly support these state institutions. Leaders from Federalists to Jeffersonian Republicans to Jacksonians, Whigs, and Republicans interpreted the "militia" clause as the stalwart principle by which states and the federal government should take a more active and purposeful role in organizing, arming, and disciplining the militia in order to avoid the expansion of a peacetime standing army that would be made necessary by the failure of the militia to provide security to the states. Combined with the observations made by Saul Cornell about the "civic" interpretation of the Second Amendment in the early republic and antebellum periods,[2] it is not surprising that political leaders and leading legal figures of the time saw the Second Amendment as a federalism provision which could be destroyed neither by the federal government's creation of a standing army nor by its inaction to secure the necessary support for the militia.

---

[1] District of Columbia v. Heller, 506 U.S. 570, 592–99 (2008); *see also* Reva Siegel, *Dead or Alive: Originalism as Popular Constitutionalism in District of Columbia v. Heller*, 122 HARV. L. REV. 191, 193 (2008) (arguing that the "majority presents this account as the original public meaning of the Second Amendment, yet draws upon evidence that may incorporate understandings that emerged long after the founding" and that an "*originalist* interpretation of the Second Amendment would treat civic republican understandings of the amendment as antiquated.").

[2] *See generally* SAUL CORNELL, A WELL-REGULATED MILITIA: THE FOUNDING FATHERS AND THE ORIGINS OF GUN CONTROL IN AMERICA 137–66 (2006).

The purpose of this chapter is not to persuade readers of the veracity of Justice Stevens's analysis in his *Heller* dissent and the numerous scholars who employ the "collective rights" understanding of the Second Amendment. Nor is it to suggest that there is not, under a proper interpretation of the Constitution, an individual right to a handgun in the home. Rather, my intent is to show that through the nineteenth century, courts and legal actors predominantly understood the Second Amendment as a federalism provision—its twin goals being the maintenance of state sovereignty over its internal objects, namely, the militia, and the protection of a core state republican institution made up of armed *state* citizens, the militia as part of the greater object of attending to the self-defense of *the people*. This "federalism" interpretation did not, notably, deny an individual right to own arms both because natural law and common law tradition maintained the right to armed self-defense and because the Second Amendment was commonly understood as a limitation upon the *federal* government's power to regulate arms-bearing rather than the states.[3] Thus, the historic evidence indicates

---

[3] *See* Joyce Lee Malcolm, To Keep and Bear Arms: The Origins of an Anglo-American Right 141 (2000) ("If the development of an armed citizenry in the American colonies was influenced by English law, liberty, and custom and enhanced by the perils of the wilderness and racial tensions, it was undergirded by the antigovernment and antiarmy legacy from seventeenth and eighteenth-century England."); Michael Steven Green, *Why Protect Private Arms Possession? Nine Theories of the Second Amendment*, 84 Notre Dame L. Rev. 131, 155–58 (2008) (suggesting that a Lockean justification for the Second Amendment would "argue that individuals have a right to bear arms in the state of nature and that they reserved this right when entering into the social contract," but noting that because many arguments in favor of the right are tied to a natural executive right to enforce our own vision of natural rights suggests the natural right of self-defense "include only justified self-defense."); Hon. Diarmuid F. O'Scannlain, *The Natural Law in the American Tradition*, 79 Fordham L. Rev. 1513, 1523–26 (2011) (noting that the *Heller* majority argued that the Second Amendment codified a preexisting natural right to self-defense); Jud Campbell, *Natural Rights, Positive Rights, and the Right to Keep and Bear Arms*, 83 Law & Contemp. Probs. 31, 36–39 (2020) (arguing that the natural right to "possess and carry weapons" required the legislature to act impartially, but did not "correspond to determinate, legalistic restrictions on legislative power" because the "constitutional lodestar" was the "police power" authority to promote the common good. But Campbell is also clear that the right to maintain weapons in self-defense was not a "collective" right held by state governments but instead the right and duty of self-defense was maintained by the *body politic* over "disaggregated individuals."); *but see* Steven J. Heyman, *Natural Rights and the Second Amendment*, 76 Chi.-Kent L. Rev. 237, 279 (2000) (arguing the Second Amendment secured the right of collective self-preservation found in Locke and Blackstone but did not secure an individual right to bear arms because the natural rights tradition did not provide for such a protection). For more on the potential drawbacks of the use of the English common law in the *Heller* decision and other notable originalist decisions, *see* Nicholas M. Mosvick & Mitchell A. Mosvick, *The Heller-ization of Originalism:* Ramos v. Louisiana *and the Problem of Frozen Context*, 19 Cato Sup. Ct. Rev. 309–38 (2020) (arguing that pinning too much interpretative value upon the state of English common law in 1791 as determinative of American constitutional provisions is a "flawed enterprise" which tends to open the door the "subjective scorekeeping of which historical conditions of 1791 'stick' from a constitutional perspective and which may be discarded as relics of a bygone era"). In the 2022 *Bruen* decision, Justice Thomas recognized this potential methodological concern with the historic method and use of English common law and stated that courts should look for unbroken lines of common law practice in determining its application to American constitutional rights. *See* New York State Rifle & Pistol Association v. Bruen, 142 S. Ct. 2111, 2136 (2022) ("As with historical evidence generally, courts must be careful when assessing evidence concerning English common-law rights. The common law, of course, develops over time. And English common law practices and

that in the period before the Civil War, there was evidence in support of both the "collective" rights or federalism interpretation and the individual rights view.[4] While most of the early state constitutional interpretations of the Second Amendment have focused on its meaning for the *individual* right in the modern period, less has been said about how they reflect a common nineteenth-century understanding of the amendment based on federalism and popular sovereignty principles, which continued to embrace the framing generation's concerns about the threat "standing armies" posed to liberty.[5]

This chapter examines several sources which reflect this continued affirmation of the "states power" interpretation of the Second Amendment in constitutional politics. State militia committees, petitions to Congress, and reports of military commissions and officers offer some of the clearest examples of this widely shared antebellum constitutional belief. This chapter will then consider how the "states power" interpretation reached its zenith during the American Civil War, through the public debates and legal challenges to the Conscription Act that often involved use of the Second Amendment as a limitation upon the federal government's power over the militia, which protected against the rise of peacetime permanent standing armies and maintained the "citizen soldier" tradition thought to be fundamental to the American system. Thus, in the early republic and antebellum period, the "militia clause" was understood to have

understandings at any given time in history cannot be indiscriminately attributed to the Framers of our own Constitution... A long, unbroken line of common law precedent stretching from Bracton to Blackstone is far more likely to be part of our law than a short-lived, 14th-century English practice.").

[4] David Thomas Konig noted that historians Saul Cornell and Nathan DeDino had recognized the "civic right" of bearing arms as not being a "purely 'individual' right in the sense of a personal right removed from civic obligation," but were the "rights and obligations associated with a citizen's duty to society," such as jury duty and militia duty. See *The Persistence of Resistance: Civic Rights, Natural Rights, and Property Rights in the Historical Debate over "The Right of the People to Keep and Bear Arms,"* 73 FORDHAM L. REV. 539, 541 (2004) (quoting Saul Cornell & Nathan DeDino, *A Well Regulated Right: The Early American Origins of Gun Control*, 73 FORDHAM L. REV. 487, 508 (2004)); see also David Thomas Konig, *The Second Amendment: A Missing Transatlantic Context for Historical Meaning of "the Right of the People to Keep and Bear Arms,"* 22 LAW & HIST. REV. 119, 120–21 (2004) (arguing that the Second Amendment protected an individual right exercised collectively and adding that the "civic right" was a "peculiarly eighteenth-century" concept unlike the "individual" or "collective" models argued for today).

[5] Note that historians like Lindsay Schakenbach Regele in a recent important study on the creation of the federal arms industry argued that while early Americans feared the large standing armies of Europe and believed state militias provided the best protection for republican citizens, the early federal government better resembled the "resource-gathering, surplus avoiding, and military-wielding behaviors" of seventeenth- and eighteenth-century European states. See LINDSAY SCHAKENBACH REGELE, MANUFACTURING ADVANTAGE: WAR, THE STATE, AND THE ORIGINS OF THE AMERICAN INDUSTRY, 1776–1848 (2019). Thus, she says, American fears of militarism lost out "to violent conflicts with Indian nations over land and threats of warfare with Europe, which necessitated greater armed forces than local militias could provide." *Id.*

independent and significant purpose apart from the protection of the existing common law right to armed self-defense.[6]

II. The Militia Before Congress: Secretary of War Poinsett's Militia Plan, 1839–1840

The constitutional politics of the early American republic were contentious and vibrant, the product of an immediate need to settle the meaning of the Constitution postratification. With regard to the Second Amendment, there was continuous debate over the meaning of the "militia clause" and what it *protected* and *required*.[7] The regulation of the militia and debates over the role of the volunteer army against a professional standing army started during the Revolution and under the Articles of Confederation with the struggles of Congress to get states to meet their requests for militia quotas. The earliest examples of such constitutional engagements were over Secretary of War Henry Knox's 1790 proposal for a military draft and the first militia acts passed in 1792 and 1795.[8] In the wake of the Whiskey Rebellion, President George Washington himself wrote to the Senate in late 1794 of his desire for "decisive measures" to support his "fellow-citizens of the militia who were the patriotic instruments of that necessity" by providing adequate organization and reflecting that "desiring and establishing of a well-regulated militia, would be a genuine source of legislative honor, and a perfect title to public gratitude" by providing for the institution under the powers of Article I.[9] Washington elaborated further upon the militia as a republican institution in this letter, offering that the service of the militia was proof that citizens understood the "true principles of government and liberty" and the marching of the "most and least wealthy of our citizens standing in the same ranks as private soldiers" was a "spectacle, displaying to the highest advantage,

---

[6] *See, e.g.*, Malcolm, *supra* note 3, at 129–30 ("It is interesting to note that these defences of the legitimate need for firearms did not rest upon, or even mention, the need to keep weapons for the militia . . . the Whig view that armed citizens were a necessary check on tyranny became orthodox opinion.").

[7] *Id.* at 136 ("Two hundred years after its passage there is no agree why [the militia clause] is there or what it means. Was it meant to restrict the right to have arms to militia members; to indicate the most pressing reason for an armed citizenry, or simply to proclaim the need for a free people to have a conscript, rather than a professional, army?").

[8] Neither the Militia Act of 1792 nor the Militia Act of 1795 attempted to create a national standing army by military draft, despite the early efforts of President Washington's secretary of war, Henry Knox, to put conscription into place. The 1790 bill of Knox was to include all free male inhabitants between eighteen and sixty divided into three classes by age with drafted persons to serve three years as regulars. *Conscription*, The Independent, Aug. 20, 1863, at 4; *Washington the Father of Conscription*, Chicago Tribune, Aug. 1, 1863, at 2.

[9] George Washington to Congress (Nov. 19, 1794), *in* 2 George Washington Papers, 346, 336–49 (transcript available in the Library of Congress).

the value of Republican Government."[10] Those early congressional debates saw references to the importance of the militia as a body of citizen soldiers against the baleful specter of a standing army, but the Second Amendment was ignored in these exchanges.[11] Similarly, the New England opposition to the War of 1812 and the requisitioning of state militias alongside the prospect of a military draft failed to produce any notable discussion of the Second Amendment.[12] However, as concerns over the state of the nation's military and state militias grew, congressional debates in the Jacksonian period saw an emphasis upon the "militia clause" of the Second Amendment.

Joel Roberts Poinsett, President Martin Van Buren's secretary of war and an experienced diplomat and South Carolina Unionist, provoked one of the more intensive periods of debate over the meaning of the phrase "well-regulated militia." Poinsett proposed to Congress a plan to reorganize the militia, which critics claimed would effectively create and maintain a large standing army.[13] Poinsett

---

[10] Id. at 345.

[11] During the debates over the Militia Bill of 1792, Virginia's John Page argued that proponents of the bill, which required the use of martial law should the people and militas refuse to submit to the law, were in fact embracing the "very doctrine which dismembered the British Empire" and that "soldiers, not militia, must be the proper tools for the Government that wishes to enforce its laws by arms" because "the virtuous, patient, submissive and truly patriotic citizens of the United States" did not deserve the suspicion which was being "excited against them." See, e.g., 2 ANNALS OF CONG. 575–76 (1792). Most of the objections were to the granting to the president the power to call forth the militia. See also 3 ANNALS OF CONG. 738 (1794). James Madison rejected the bill to expand the regular army, saying he did not see any prospect of immediate war "as could induce the House to violate the Constitution," because he thought it a wise constitutional principle to make one branch raise an army and another conduct it in order to guard against danger from either side in favor of public safety. See also 4 ANNALS OF CONG. 1215 (1795) (Massachusetts Federalist Theodore Sedgwick noted in the debate over the Militia Act of 1795 that there were two military systems available to the country—one based on "compelling every citizen, capable of performing the duties of a soldier, to arm himself, or to receive arms, to be in readiness to be called forth in defence of his country" or a system that selected part of those "capable of performing military duties" which would prepare such citizens should to be called forth to act as soldiers. Sedgwick had previously argued that which Republicans bore standing armies with jealousy, the efficacy of the militia before the Revolution "perhaps in a degree injured us" and the militia as a "means of retaliation" he thought should be abandoned in favor of a standing army. Id. at 1214–15. Maryland Jeffersonian Samuel Smith chastised the militias of the Southern states as being undeserving of "that name," but noted that the government must "either have a good militia or a standing army" and the militia was "more agreeable to Republican principles." Id.)

During the 1790s, numerous protracted debates occurred concerning the expansion of the army as well due to fear of invasion by European powers, and Federalists worried reliance on the militia was insufficient. Id. at 736. Massachusetts Senator and Federalist leader Fisher Ames argued that weak parts of the country might be attacked before a body of militia could be ready for effective service, and he found the concerns about granting the president power to raise ten thousand men a "Utopian dread" of standing armies when it was "infinitely cheaper to raise and embody an Army at leisure, when the storm is seen to be approaching than all at once." Id.

[12] See generally THEODORE LYMAN, A SHORT ACCOUNT OF THE HARTFORD CONVENTION, TAKEN FROM OFFICIAL DOCUMENTS (Boston, O. Everett 1833).

[13] JOEL ROBERTS POINSETT, MILITIA OF THE UNITED STATES: LETTER FROM THE SECRETARY OF WAR TRANSMITTING A SYSTEM OF REORGANIZATION OF THE MILITIA OF THE UNITED STATES (Washington, D.C., J. & G.S. Gideon 1840). This was not the first time that a secretary of war had proposed a reforming of the state militias in light of the importance of a "well organized militia" to the defense of a free people. Secretary of War James Barbour had made such a proposal in July 1826. See James Barbour, Official Circular, War Department, Washington, MARTINSDALE GAZETTE, Aug.

was responding and complying with a resolution of the House of Representatives which had asked him as secretary of war to communicate a detailed plain for the reorganization of the militia of the United States.[14] Problems of the moral condition, training, knowledge, and organization of the militia were foremost on Poinsett's mind.[15] In his proposal, he cited the right of a "well-regulated militia" in connection with the plan, one to be "taken from the people, and making part of the people, equally interested when their fellow-citizens in the preservation of free institutions, and ready at all times to defend the territory and the liberty of their country."[16] Poinsett added that his plan did *not* interfere with the constitutional rights of the states to train their own militia according to the discipline prescribed by Congress, because the active militia would be employed by the president during any military service in the field once called out.[17]

In a letter exchange with Poinsett, George Keim, the chairman of the House Committee on the Militia, pointed to several points of disagreement between Poinsett and the committee on reorganizing the militia—"the great bulwark of the country."[18] The first concern was that the plan, in dividing the United States into ten territories, gave the president power to call out the whole force of any one of the districts at the same time, and at any point he might designate. In particular, Keim and the committee were concerned about the interpretation of the words "territory of the United States," since it was understood by some to mean the public lands and the District of Columbia and could not therefore "embrace the limits of the several States unless there be a misconstruction of the letter and spirit of the Constitution, which declares 'a well-regulated militia as being necessary to the security of a free state.'"[19]

10, 1826, at 2 (Barbour, in a July 11, 1826, memo, stated that one of the universal political maxims of the United States was that a well organized and disciplined militia was the "natural defense of a Free People," and he recommended the establishment of a uniform system for militia training).

[14] *Id.* at 2.
[15] *Id.* at 1.
[16] *Id.* at 3.
[17] *Id.*
[18] George Keim, Reorganization of the Militia, Letter from the Secretary of War, to the Chairman of the Committee of the Militia, explanatory of the plan for Reorganizing the Militia of the United States, heretofore submitted to the House, H.R. Doc. 171, at 2 (1840) [hereinafter Reorganization]. Keim was a Pennsylvania representative, a Jacksonian Democrat, and a major general of the militia.
[19] *Id.* at 1. In Keim's majority report in 1840, the House Committee on the Militia gave a similar statement in their conclusion critical of Poinsett's plan, stating:

> In conformity with the rights reserved to the States, it is important that they should direct their attention to carry into effect the militia system under the existing laws, or instruct their representatives to modify them in a manner best calculated to ensure such a degree of military discipline and knowledge of tactics, as will render the militia in fact a sure and *permanent bulwark of the national defense*. Your committee, believing that the powers necessary to produce an efficient militia are divided between the general government and the States, that the Constitution gives to Congress only a qualified agency on the subject, and that no

Poinsett responded to Keim's letter by arguing that the Article I language referring to "disciplining" the militia was

> susceptible of a different interpretation from that given to it here, yet the subsequent reservation to the States of the power to train the militia according to the system of discipline adopted by Congress would seem to define its meaning; and as we cannot be too scrupulous in our interpretation of the Constitution, I propose that, in the event of its becoming necessary to resort to draughts in order to fill the ranks of the active class of militia, to apply to the States to place by law their contingents at the disposition of the General Government, for a period not more than thirty days of every year, for the purpose of their being trained in conjunction with regular troops, and by veteran officers.[20]

Keim responded in the House Committee on the Militia's majority report, which argued that the Constitution, "strictly construed," opposed concentrations of military power and preserved to the states "of the confederacy a sovereignty that alone claims the right of training troops until called into service under the contingencies (defined by Article I)." Congress, they asserted, only had authority through an enrollment to organize, distribute arms, and reserve training to the states given that the Constitution both guaranteed a republican form of government to each state and could not "impair the right of the people to keep and bear arms, nor exercise any power to call forth the militia, unless to execute the laws of the Union, suppress insurrection, and repel invasions."[21]

By the following year, the Senate Committee on the Militia responded to Poinsett's plan with a formal report. The report was submitted by Senator Clement Comer Clay of Alabama, a Jacksonian Democrat who was formerly a state judge and the governor during the Creek War of 1836. Clay's report immediately looked to the Second Amendment; the first two lines reference specifically

---

suggestions can be made more beneficial that those which years have sanctioned, conclude that nothing can be done effectually upon the subject by Congress, unless the foundation for it shall be laid by the previous action of the States.... MILITIA, H. R. REP NO. 584, at 13 (1839) [hereinafter MILITIA] (emphasis added).

Keim's report also found that history suggested that the militia was an "aggregation of citizens who have assembled *without coercion*, to effect whatever may be required at their hands in defending their constitutional and individual rights." This suggested an "aversion to any kind of conscription for military purposes, unless an exigency require[d] it," among the people and a sense that members of the state militia, even when under the rules of discipline of the regular army of the United States, remained citizens "of the states from whence they came." *Id.* at 11 (emphasis added).

[20] REORGANIZATION, *supra* note 18, at 2. Under the plan, the president was also given power to call forth and assemble such numbers of the active force of the militia as he might deem necessary and subject them to such regulations as he might think proper, which the committee thought was inconsistent with the language of Article I, Section VIII.

[21] *Id.* at 10.

to the Second Amendment for its protection of not only state power but its grant of a duty to Congress: "That, duly appreciating the importance of the subject, and fully concurring in the opinion that 'a well-regulated militia' is 'necessary to the security of a free state,' they have thought proper to examine it, in reference to the powers of Congress, the various plans which have been proposed, and such measures as have the adoption of the Constitution."[22] The report continued along the same lines, noting since the earliest history of the American republic, there was consensus "that a well-organized militia is not only the most economical, but the most safe and reliable means of national defen[s]e."[23]

The committee then employed the popular sovereignty interpretation of the Second Amendment, saying, "When we take into view that our Government originated in the spontaneous will of the people; that it was organized, and its fundamental law constructed by them; that, recognizing man's capacity for self-government, and the leading principle that a majority shall govern, all are alike interested in its preservation, the conclusion follows necessarily, that the national defen[s]e must be most secure in the hands of a citizen-soldiery." They followed with a paean to the rejection of standing armies of the founding period, reminding the reader about the danger of standing armies to liberty known since antiquity and the experience of the Revolutionary War, in which it was "proven that freemen, almost without organization, and without discipline, were invincible, when battling in defen[s]e of their own rights, and for the safety of their own families and firesides." The powers expressly granted to Congress in Article I, Section VIII, they believed, reflected the confidence and assurance the founding generation placed in the militia.

Clay's report looked to the history of the early republic and every president since Washington to suggest a consistent reading of both the constitutional powers and duties granted to Congress and the president as well as the meaning of the Second Amendment. In particular, it found President James Madison's frequent invocation of the words "well-regulated militia" in conjunction with the Article I powers to be a powerful example—it was the subject of "almost constant solicitude with Mr. Madison throughout his administration."[24] As an example, Clay provided Madison's 1810 December annual message: "'These preparations for arming the militia having thus far provided for one of the objects contemplated by the power vested in Congress with respect to that *great bulwark of the public safety*, it is for their consideration whether further provisions are not requisite

---

[22] CLEMENT COMER CLAY, REPORT: THE COMMITTEE ON THE MILITIA, TO WHOM WAS REFERRED SO MUCH OF THE REPORT OF THE SECRETARY OF WAR, AS RELATES TO THE REORGANIZATION AND DISCIPLINE OF THE MILITIA, SUBMIT THE FOLLOWING REPORT, S. DOC. 509 (1840), at 1.
[23] *Id.*
[24] *Id.* at 7.

for the other contemplated objections of organization and discipline."[25] And, in his last annual message in December 1816, Madison once more pleaded for action on a subject of the "highest importance to the national welfare," the need for serious congressional action to reorganize the militia because in its present organization it was "universally regarded as less efficient than it ought to be made." According to Clay, Madison, in invoking the spirit of the "militia clause," stated that "[a]n efficient militia is authorized and contemplated by the Constitution, and required by the spirit and *safety of a free Government*."[26] That sensibility was shared by members of Congress in the wake of the War of 1812 as well. In Keim's majority report for the House Committee on the Militia concerning Poinsett's plan, Keim cites the statement of the committee during the Fourteenth Congress (1815–1816) that "an energetic national militia is to be guarded as the capital security of a free republic, and that it is desirable it should be so organized and trained to the use of arms as to supersede, under any circumstances, the necessity of a standing army."[27]

During the same period with which Keim submitted his report, Secretary of War Joel Poinsett proposed to Congress a plan for reforming the militia in response to persistent pressure from the states and militia organizations to better support the militia. As an example of this state pressure, one notable petition to Congress, in the form of a memorial, came through the House Committee on the Militia in 1839. The memorial was the product of a military convention the previous July assembled at Norwich, Vermont on the Fourth of July and composed of about three hundred citizens of New Hampshire and Vermont who were "friendly to the improvement of the militia."[28] Captain Alden Partridge,[29] the former superintendent of West Point who presented the memorial to Congress, called the convention to order and was among those chosen to present resolutions of the convention. In August 1838, before issuing the resolutions to

---

[25] *Id.* (emphasis added). And in his 1815 annual message after the end of the War of 1815, President Madison spoke to the urgent need for Congress to create "such a classification and organization of the militia as would most effectually render it the *safeguard of a free State.*" *Id.* (emphasis added).

[26] *Id.* at 7–8.

[27] REORGANIZATION, *supra* note 18. Keim's report concluded that in its "essential particulars," Poinsett's plan followed those recommended to Congress by Presidents Washington, Jefferson, Madison, and Jackson, as well as former Secretaries of War Knox, James Barbour, and Lewis Cass by adapting a classification of the militia and more frequent instruction and training at public expense. The major differences, they stated, were the introduction of "rotation," by which portions of the militia were liable to duty and training, and the rejection of classification by age. It thus mostly followed from the 1792 Militia Act, but reduced training requirements significantly.

[28] ALDEN PARTRIDGE & EDMUND BURKE, IN HALF OF THE STATE MILITARY CONVENTION OF VERMONT, PRAYING THE ADOPTION OF A PLAN PROPOSED BY THEM FOR THE REORGANIZATION OF THE MILITIA OF THE UNITED STATES, S. DOC. 197, at 8 (1839).

[29] Partridge founded Norwich University and, through his experience as an army engineer during the War of 1812, led a movement to establish military schools (most of which were short-lived), which aimed to promote a citizen soldiery and against the evils of a standing army by fixing the problem of training and organization among the militia.

Congress, the leaders of the convention released a report to the public which argued that the "second article of the amendments is an unequivocal and decided expression of the importance which the wise and patriotic founders of our republic attributed to a well regulated militia."[30] The first resolution followed directly from the language of the Second Amendment:

> That an efficient and well-regulated militia is absolutely necessary for the preservation of our national independence, and of our political, civil, and religious liberty; and that, consequently, all attempts to discourage the militia from the prompt and efficient discharge of the high and important duties devolving upon them as *citizen-soldiers* and to depress their martial energies, dampen their patriotic efforts to discharge their duties, are anti American, anti-constitutional, hostile to civil and religious liberty, and well calculated to prostrate our national independence at the footstool of tyrannical and lawless aggressions, or to build up a mercenary standing army, to eat out the people's substance and trample down their rights.[31]

The memorial also powerfully linked the preamble and Second Amendment, suggesting that Congress not only had sufficient power to organize, arm, and discipline the militia, but a *duty* to properly support and strengthen the militia: "Whereas the public revenue of the United States was evidently intended by the framers of the Constitution to enable Congress to carry out into practical effect the provisions of that sacred instrument: and whereas none of these provisions are of greater importance than that which empowers Congress to provide for 'the common defen[s]e:' and whereas, by the second article of the amendments to the constitution, it is expressly declared 'that a well-regulated militia is necessary to the security of a free state:' therefore ... all the expenses necessary to provide such an organization for the militia, and to furnish such instruction for the officers and non-commissioned officers as will ensure a correct and efficient discipline, ought to be paid from the public Treasury of the United States."[32]

---

[30] PARTRIDGE, *supra* note 28, at 8.

[31] *Id.* at 4–5.

[32] Referring to the Article I power to organize, arm, and discipline and the Second Amendment, the Memorial stated:

> By the first of these provisions, Congress is invested with full power to adopt all the necessary measures to render the militia, in every respect, effective for military service; while, by the second, the absolute necessity of this great constitutional power for the security of a free State, is unequivocally asserted. *Id.* at 1.

The resolutions of the convention made clear that they believed the preamble and Second Amendment informed each other's meaning, stating that "such 'common defence' is, by the aforesaid constitution, vested in the great body of the *people*, capable of bearing arms" as referred to in the Second Amendment. *Id.* at 4.

In a separate "Address to the People of the United States," the Vermont state military convention repeated their insistence that Congress's powers over the militia and the Second Amendment reflected the commitment of the framers to an independent state militia as the proper republican means of national defense. After setting up the typical contrast between the professional permanent standing armies of European despots and the "great body of the people," they stated that the framers "were well aware of the absolute necessity of a well regulated and efficient national militia, for the preservation of our national independence and of public liberty. They, therefore, wisely invested Congress with full power to adopt all the necessary and proper measures for establishing and rendering efficient, for the military defence of the country such national force."[33] The convention leaders argued not only that "[t]he necessity of a well regulated militia to the security of our free institutions is established by the high authority of the framers of the Government" but also that it was sustained by the people themselves upon ratification of the Constitution.[34]

Ultimately, Poinsett's plan was not adopted, much to the disappointment of state committees pleading for militia reform, with New York's militia calling for a national convention in 1841.[35] While officers and militia organizations continued to call for reform, as they had in the Jacksonian period,[36] governors more vocally took on the public push for Congress to act, given their Article I and

---

[33] *Id.* at 11. That Congress was given ample powers to organize, arm, and improve the militia, and that the militia was protected by the Second Amendment, was "proof of the importance which was attached to the militia" by the framers.

[34] *Id.*

[35] *See* Wm. H. Bayne, *The Militia System*, N. CAROLINIAN, Dec. 11, 1841, at 2. In a petition to Congress in 1841, the *New York Military Magazine* spoke on behalf of the officers of the New York state militia. The officers complained to Congress that the condition of the state militia, and likely that of other states, was "not such as was contemplated by the framers of the Constitution when they declared, 'A well-regulated militia to be necessary to the security of a free government.'" Their assessment was, despite the pleas of presidents from Washington on down and the militia plan of Secretary of War Joel Poinsett in 1839, Congress had shown no interest in passing a law to create an efficient system, despite its constitutional duty to "provide for organizing, arming, and disciplining the militia." *Id.* Pennsylvania's state military convention, in March 1846, petitioned the House Committee on the Militia and similarly stated that "our republican fathers," through the preamble's requirement of providing for "the common defence," the Second Amendment's militia clause and Congress's Article I powers were "instituted in view of the principle that the people, being the source of power in a republic, should be prepared to defend their liberties and the rights of the nation at large." Thus, a standing army was "contrary to the spirit of our institutions" and history. JAMES ROSS SNOWDEN & OTHERS, COMM. ON BEHALF OF MIL. CONVENTION OF PA., ASKING MORE PERFECT ORGANIZATION OF THE MILITIA OF THE UNITED STATES, S. DOC. NO. 226, at 1 (1846).

[36] *See* REPORT OF A BOARD OF OFFICERS IN RELATION TO THE ORGANIZATION OF THE MILITIA, H. DOC. NO. 62, at 1–16 (1834). (This was a January petition to the House responding to Secretary of War James Barbour's 1826 militia reorganization plan demanding a "well regulated, armed, and instructed militia, of 400,000 men." The petition stated that the Second Amendment's militia clause is what allowed Congress in the past to provide, under the Militia Acts of 1792, 1798, and 1808, that every citizen enrolled for militia service have "a good rifle" or "good musket." Both the acts and the Second Amendment were "conceived in the same spirit" that "the whole body of the militia held to service might be effectively armed and instructed.").

Second Amendment duties to organize, arm, and discipline the militia in a time in which the country's sectional divisions were raising the prospect of bloodshed and civil war.

III. Governor's Messages

Throughout the nineteenth century until the end of the Civil War, state governors regularly invoked the "militia clause" of the Second Amendment and the language of a "well-regulated militia" in their calls for a better regulated and supported militia capable of protecting their states. These messages consistently reflect the same understanding of the "militia clause" found in the debates surrounding Poinsett's plan and the various reports of militia officers and organizations to Congress in the antebellum period and reminded audiences of the republican tradition of opposing peacetime standing armies.[37]

Such public declarations began in the early republic period, in the buildup to the War of 1812 and as New England fretted over the involvement of the state militias in a war which served the Southern interest. Federalist Massachusetts Governor Caleb Strong, in an 1807 address to the state senate following a controversial bill to reverse a court martial, noted that while he felt he could not censure the officers in question, he argued if the resolution would pass, it would cause "great disorder and disorganization in the Militia" on whom the state "principally rel[ied] for public security and defense" against the guarantee of an "well regulated militia."[38]

A common theme was the fear of standing armies in connection with the Second Amendment. South Carolina Governor Patrick Noble, in his 1839 annual address, argued that all free governments had a jealousy of standing armies because the historic record was filled with instances of their danger to liberty. He believed that the founders structured the Constitution to rely upon the militia system by giving Congress power to provide for "organizing, arming, and disciplining [the militia]" precisely because they had "practical knowledge on the subject."[39] And it was for this reason, Noble asserted, that the framers recognized the "great political truth" embedded in the Second Amendment of

---

[37] President James Polk agreed in his 1845 State of the Union, before he called for an increase to the national standing army to fight the Mexican-American War, saying that it had "never been our policy to maintain large standing armies in time of peace," which were "contrary to the genius of our free institutions," imposed "heavy burdens on the people," and were "dangerous to public liberty." Thus, he concluded we must rely upon "our citizen soldiers." James Knox Polk, President, State of the Union (Dec. 8, 1845).

[38] *Legislature of Massachusetts*, Portland Gazette and Me. Advertiser, Mar. 9, 1807, at 2.

[39] Patrick Noble, *Governor's Message*, Farmer's Gazette and Cheraw Advertiser, Nov. 29, 1839, at 4.

a well-regulated militia being necessary to a free state. He did so in the context of South Carolina politics in the wake of the Nullification Crisis and the rise of abolitionism. In his inaugural address the prior year, Noble talked about the one question remaining which in its "direst consequences menaces the safety of the Union"—abolitionism and the potential war for which "admonishes us to be prepared for the crisis."[40]

The "standing army" maxim was equally employed by opponents of slavery. Following the Mexican-American War, which was fought and won by a largely volunteer army, and in the atmosphere of growing threats of disunion, state governors in the 1850s reminded their constituents of the significance of state militias. In his 1850 inaugural, the anti-slavery Whig governor and former chief justice of the state supreme court, Charles Kilbourne Williams, treated the principle of rejecting standing armies in favor of a "well-regulated militia" composed of citizen soldiers as axiomatic and, as such, secured by both the federal and state constitutions.[41] To leave the militia in such a state of disrepair as it was after years of neglect flouted the requirements of federal law.

Similarly, when famed anti-slavery lawyer Salmon Chase, a former Democrat turned Republican, became Ohio's governor in 1856, his inaugural address, like many of the period, dealt with the derelict state of the militias.[42] In Ohio, the report of the attorney general stated there were no general or field officers in the state militia, and the public arms of the state were scattered throughout the state.[43] Chase's address stands out for its explicit endorsement of the popular sovereignty interpretation of the Second Amendment and rejection of standing armies. In prosaic language, Chase stated that a "well-regulated militia system is almost essential to the preservation of an efficient military spirit among the people," because peacetime standing armies were always viewed with distrust by republican governments.[44] Thus, the state's defense must rest upon an "intelligent and well organized militia . . . to a great extent, even in war." Chase continued, noting that in other governments, the military force was organized in support of tyranny and the mass of people were disarmed. In the United States, the military force was organized for the support of popular government and the right of the people to bear arms was explicitly protected by the Constitution. He concluded that the liberties of the people and the "maintenance of public order" were "confided to the hands of the free and independent citizens of the State."

---

[40] Patrick Noble, *Gov. Noble's Inaugural Address*, EDGEFIELD ADVERTISER, Dec. 20, 1838, at 2. (Noble added that a "well regulated militia" was up to "us to cherish and invigorate this right arm of our security and protection, by keeping up the military spirit of the country and preparing our citizens to defend their firesides").
[41] Ch. K. Williams, VT. WATCHMAN & STATE J., Oct. 17, 1850, at 4.
[42] *Governor's Message*, EATON DEMOCRAT, Jan. 24, 1856, at 1.
[43] *Id.*
[44] *Id.*

The following year, in 1857, Massachusetts Governor and future Vice President Hannibal Hamlin sounded similar notes, bemoaning that the state legislature in the past had tended to act to lessen the efficiency and bring into disrepute the militia—an institution he emphasized was created by the federal constitution and of which the past had "conclusively demonstrated" its importance.[45] He believed that the disregard of the public for an efficient military system inevitably led to an increase of the standing army of the United States, a result feared by the founding fathers and "all true friends of Constitutional liberty."[46] The pattern continued in 1858 with a well-publicized speech of Ryland Fletcher,[47] Vermont's Republican governor and a former brigadier general of the state militia. His military experience likely informed both his respect for the significance of the militia as a republican institution and his despair at its state of ruin. Thus, Fletcher pushed for the first drills of the Vermont militia since the Mexican-American War, reasoning that a "well regulated and disciplined militia force has long been regarded by our wisest statesmen and firmest patriots as the right arm of defense, and one of the most important pillars in our national edifice."[48] Fletcher concluded by preaching the virtues of citizen soldiers against standing armies to preserve peace and civil order, with the knowledge that his audience did not need to be reminded of the necessity and propriety of a well-regulated militia.[49]

Northern governors were not alone in such appeals in the years before the Civil War. North Carolina Governor Thomas Bragg, a graduate of Alden Partridge's military academy in Vermont who would join the Confederate government as Jefferson Davis's attorney general, called attention to the regrettable state of the militia in his 1858 annual address. Bragg deemed the condition so desperate that the state would be "almost powerless" should an emergency military situation arise and that outside a few volunteer companies, there was "hardly any military organization in the [s]tate."[50] He appealed to the assembly that if a "well regulated militia be of the first importance in our system of government" as the "wisest . . . civil and military" men agreed to, then something had to be done to "infuse vitality into that of our [s]tate to reach," if not "positive

---

[45] *The Inaugural Address of Gov. Hamlin*, ELLSWORTH AM., Jan. 16, 1857, at 1.

[46] Like other political leaders of the era, Hamlin fused the Second Amendment with Congress's Article I power to organize, arm, and discipline the militia—along the state constitutional requirement of militia duty for able-bodied males—as creating constitutional requirements for maintaining an efficient militia system.

[47] A political veteran who had been a member of the Whig Party, the Liberty Party, the Free Soil Party, and the Know Nothings before the Republicans, Fletcher was more known for his leadership of the Vermont State Temperance Society and the Vermont Anti-Slavery Society.

[48] *Military at Brandon*, GREEN MOUNTAIN FREEMAN, Sept. 9, 1858, at 2.

[49] *Id.* Fletcher thought the real danger before the state and the nation was not merely the destruction of the militia but Fletcher's sense that citizens had stopped exhibiting the true characteristics of the citizen soldier—a growing "selfish and sordid spirit" of individualism which ran against the commitment to duty, to the public welfare, and to institutions of volunteer citizen soldiers.

[50] *Governor's Message*, HILLSBOROUGH RECORDER, Nov. 24, 1858, at 2.

efficiency as a military body," then at least to meet an emergency. Bragg's expectations were low—he did not expect that, even if amendments to the current law were enacted, a high degree of military readiness and drilling would be attained. The failure to do so, he warned, would result in the abolition of the entire militia system. In both the North and the South, the fracture of growing sectionalism unsurprisingly led governors to invoke the "state powers" tradition of the Second Amendment to call for appeals to support the militia to meet future emergencies—Civil War.

IV. Usage in Congress during the Secession Crisis

Unsurprisingly, the period between the Mexican-American War and the American Civil War not only saw the frequent use of the "federalism" or "civic" interpretation of the Second Amendment, including among prominent members of Congress. In the months before the beginning of the Mexican-American War in 1846, James Augustus Black, the South Carolina Democrat and chairman of the House Committee on the Militia, issued a report on the state of the militia. As part of the report, the committee submitted to the House a bill to respond to the ill state of the militia, aimed to more effectively provide for national security by organizing and classifying the militia and providing for calling them into service of the United States. The report claimed to reflect the "grave consideration" given by the committee to the issue, but noted that they felt no "labored argument[s]" were necessary to "vindicate the importance, not to say the necessity, of a well regulated militia."[51] The committee felt the language of a "well regulated militia" meant that in order to preserve our institutions and liberties, "our main defense must essentially remain in the hands of a well-armed and organized citizen soldiery."[52] Large peacetime standing armies, the report stated, were still understood to be "contrary to the nature of our institutions," but also uncalled for under American conditions and inefficient as a means of national defense—a fact the committee thought shown by three decades of peace since the War of 1812, which was due not to a standing army "ill calculated for the active duties of the field," but rather the fact that the United States was at a distance from European powers such that the committee expected there would be few wars in the nation's future.[53] The committee's bill proposed a peacetime system of universal militia enrollment of those male citizens between twenty-one and thirty, with a wartime enrollment of all eighteen to forty-five-year-olds, looked

---

[51] *The Reorganization of the Militia*, Wilmington J., Feb. 13, 1846, at 2.
[52] *Id.*
[53] *See id.*

much like earlier proposals going back to the Washington administration that had likewise failed to pass through Congress.

Black's report was hardly the only moment during the Mexican-American War, which saw Congress examine the constitutional power of the federal government over the militia. Months later, in the context of the military trial of General Edward Gaines for having issued an order to raise voluntary militia regiments independently, Congress debated the propriety of Gaines's actions. Senator Daniel Webster, the most rhetorically powerful opponent of military conscription during the War of 1812, dissented from defenses of General Gaines, arguing that in the "history of free government," the military authority was only ever given for the defense and security of the general weal and the Constitution, "which so sedulously guarded against military power, which everywhere exhibited such dread of it," gave Congress power to raise armies but gave it "nothing to do with the militia, except in cases of invasion or insurrection, or to aid in the execution of the law." To defend Gaines's usurpation, to Webster, was to assert that the Constitution and laws were but general rules below another paramount law of necessity.[54] Before the Court of Inquiry in August 1846, General Gaines justified his actions both on account of the executive power to "suppress insurrections and repel invasions" as well as the Second Amendment, stating that the provision mean that the "sovereign people of this Union had an unquestionable right to offer their services to any Commander of the United States Army, or to any of the State authorities threatened with invasion, or at once to repair to the threatened frontier, and voluntarily repel any attack."[55] Gaines thought that the right of the *people* to "bear arms" included to use those arms freely in the national defense and maintenance of their rights.

The Mexican-American War was fought primarily by volunteers recruited into the regular army next to the existing army forces, with the militia failing to provide citizen soldiers to fight the first major war in over three decades. President James Polk, upon the closing of the war, proclaimed that the war had demonstrated that a volunteer army of citizen soldiers, who are armed and "accustomed from their youth up to handle and use firearms" and who patriotically served was evidence that no drafts or conscriptions standard for other warring nations were necessary.[56] Polk thus reminded his audience of that which

---

[54] *Twenty-Ninth Congress, First Session, in Senate, June 5, 1846*, NAT'L INTELLIGENCER, June 13, 1846, at 1. Gaines had given an order to raise volunteer regiments in May 1846 at the outset of the war, trying to raise troops in order to support General Zachary Taylor, whose army faced a superior Mexican force. *See Acquittal of Gen. Gaines*, AMERICAN REPUBLICAN AND BALTIMORE DAILY CLIPPER, Aug. 26, 1846, at 1.

[55] Edmund P. Gaines, *Defence of Major General Edmund P. Gaines read before the Court of Inquiry convened at Old Point Comfort, on Monday the 10th day of August 1846*, THE NEW ERA, Aug. 11, 1846, at 2.

[56] President James K. Polk, Fourth Annual Message to Congress (Dec. 5, 1848).

was axiomatic at the time—that a republican army of citizen soldiers was precisely what made American democracy unique in a war of capricious, autocratic powers.

In March 1850, just two years after the end of the Mexican-American War, Captain John McClernand issued a report to the House Committee on the Militia through Illinois Democrat William Richardson, giving a stern indictment on the state of the military while again striking the connection between Congress's powers and the Second Amendment's protection of the state militia. Congress's Article I powers over the militia, he said, were "one of the strongest inducements to the adoption of our federal institutions; and should they fail in fulfilling it, they would be responsible for any harm that might befall our citizens or the republic through so gross a neglect."[57] Congress was not only vested with the power to provide means necessary and proper for the public security, but "the provident exercise of that power fairly deducible from the power itself" and "such an exercise of it is unmistakably enjoined by the spirit, if not by the very terms, of the amendment to the constitution, which declares that 'a well-regulated militia being necessary to the *security* of a free State, the right of the people to *keep* and *bear* arms shall not be infringed.'"[58]

In a final prominent use of the "states power" interpretation of the Second Amendment in constitutional politics on the precipice of civil war, Ohio Democratic Congressman Clement Vallandigham[59] gave a speech concerning a bill to amend the Militia Act of 1808 in March 1860. Vallandigham began by asserting if there was a sentiment more fixed in the minds of "those who founded this Republic than any other, it was jealousy of standing armies," and it was a maxim among the founders that large military establishments in peacetime were dangerous to liberty.[60] This maxim, he argued, remained "to this day in the bill of rights in many of our State constitutions" and held sway over the policy of the national government since the founding.[61]

---

[57] JOHN A. MCCLERNAND, ARMORY AND FOUNDRY AT FORT MASSAC, H. REP. NO. 214, at 5 (1850). McClernand was a powerful Illinois Jacksonian Democrat before the Civil War who went onto become a Union general and a thorn in the Lincoln administration's side.

[58] The Michigan legislature, spurred by a report from another future Civil War General, George McLellan, issued instructions to its representatives to push for the passage of an act of Congress which would authorize the secretary of war to detail annually an officer of each corps of the U.S. Army for the proper military instruction and training of the militia. The Michigan legislature cited both the Second Amendment and the Article I power to prescribe and provide for the discipline of the militia, along with McClellan's 1857 report to the Senate after his time in Europe during the Crimean War. JOINT RESOLUTION OF THE LEGISLATURE OF THE STATE OF MICHIGAN RELATIVE TO THE MILITARY INSTRUCTION OF UNIFORMED VOLUNTEER MILITIA OF THAT STATE, S. MISC. DOC. 50, at 1–2 (1859).

[59] Vallandingham soon become such a thorn in the side of the Lincoln administration that he was prosecuted for an antiwar speech in May 1863 and banished from the North.

[60] CONG. GLOBE, 36th Cong., 1st Sess. 1129 (1860) (statement of Sen. Vallandigham).

[61] *Id.*

This, Vallandigham believed, was the central role of the militia since the founding—hostility to standing armies combined with a zealous desire to provide for the public safety by looking to the militia of the several states to protect against both foreign and domestic enemies. Thus, he thought the Second Amendment stood "a part, though a forgotten part, of the Constitution," the language of a "well regulated militia," was implicitly "acknowledged, in all its force, in the several clauses relating to the subject" in Article I.[62] In a familiar understanding, Vallandigham thus read the Second Amendment in relation to Congress's Article I powers concerning the militia—its power to provide for calling forth the militia to suppress insurrection and repel invasion, to organize, arm, and discipline the militia and to govern them when in the service of the United States.

Yet Vallandigham bemoaned that "no subject has been more utterly neglected by Congress" even if the Constitution granted the exclusive power when Congress used it to organize, arm, and discipline the militia. The 1792 Militia Act, he complained, had long been imperfect in its details and provisions for discipline but remained in force, even if largely disregarded. He thought Congress had "abdicated our power over the subject" even though Article I not only empowered Congress but *required* them to organize and discipline the militia. Thus, the states were compelled by Congress's "negligence" to provide for the militia separately, as Congress had so "totally abandoned all attention" to it that the word "militia," he claimed, had "disappeared for years" from congressional lawmaking. Vallandigham, again invoking the long tradition of "states power" constitutionalism, cited Justice Story as a figure "deeply imbued with the spirit of the revolutionary period" who warned Americans "solemnly of the danger to be apprehended from the growing indifference to this great bulwark of our public liberties."[63] Vallandigham closed by quoting from Washington's 1794 annual message while reminding his colleagues again of their "high constitutional duty of organizing and disciplining the citizen soldiery of the States."[64]

---

[62] *Id.* at 1130. Like the Clay Report in 1840, Vallandigham noted that all presidents in the early republic, starting with Washington, paid close attention to the issue. Washington, in particular, drew attention to the militia in every formal communication to Congress. John Adams and Thomas Jefferson followed the push for additional and more effective legislation. And like the Clay Report, Vallandigham noted that James Madison spoke often of the militia as the "great bulwark of public safety." Subsequent presidents followed and continually pressed the subject to Congress. And beyond the president, for fifty years, secretaries of war and the executive officials followed suit in begging for reform.

[63] *Id.* He quoted Story for asking whether there was "any escape ... from a large standing army, but in a well-regulated militia?"

[64] *Id.* Washington remarked that "devising and establishing a well regulated militia would be a genuine source of legislative honor, and a perfect title to public gratitude." *See* George Washington to Congress (Nov. 19, 1794) (transcript available in the Library of Congress).

Ultimately, a new militia bill would pass, but not for the reasons Vallandigham asserted. The coming of the Civil War, starting April 1861, forced Congress to twice revisit and amend the Militia Act of 1795 before finally in March 1863 passing the first legislation creating a national military draft. The decades-old rhetoric used to support militia reform and organization now was employed to fight against an act of Congress detractors believed would destroy the militia. Opponents of conscription, including Vallandigham, believed that Congress was now using those very Article I powers he thought gave a duty to Congress to support, arm, train, and organize the militia to render it nugatory in favor of a national standing army.

V. THE AMERICAN CIVIL WAR AND THE LAST STAND FOR THE "STATE POWER" THEORY

For the most steadfast proponents of the "state power" or federalism theory of the Second Amendment and the militia clauses, the American Civil War presented the hardest challenge yet. Toward the final months of the War of 1812, when the American situation appeared most precarious, Secretary of War James Monroe proposed national conscription,[65] but the bill was tabled and never revisited once the Treaty of Ghent was signed. As this chapter has shown, there were multiple pushes to build a peacetime military presence and support for greater militia discipline and organization at times of crisis in the antebellum period. But the American Civil War brought manpower demands unmatched in American history and thus, very quickly, the enduring militia system and its volunteer citizen soldier ideal were shattered by the realities of a bloody, internecine struggle. By the time Congress passed the Militia Bill of 1862, the military situation was already feeling desperate in many corners of the North, and the push for national conscription began well before it was passed early the next year. Adoption of national conscription in March 1863 under unified Republican government generated a furious challenge to its constitutionality from Democrats constitutional conservatives who relied on Jacksonian understandings of federalism, including the Second Amendment, to mount their assault.[66]

---

[65] Monroe's plan was described in a letter to Congressmen G.M. Troup, Chairman of the House Committee on Military Affairs. *See* THEODORE DWIGHT, HISTORY OF THE HARTFORD CONVENTION: WITH A REVIEW OF THE POLICY OF THE UNITED STATES GOVERNMENT WHICH LED TO THE WAR OF 1812, at 318 (New York, N. & J. White; Boston, Russel, Odiorne, & Co.1833).

[66] Constitutional conservative was a term consistently used throughout the Jacksonian period by both Democrats, who saw it as a way to describe old, national Whigs whose democratic principles were Jacksonian, and Whigs, who saw candidates like Zachary Taylor as a constitutional conservative alternative to the libertarian anarchist principles of Lewis Cass, the New York Locofocos, and the Dorr Rebellion in Rhode Island. *See The Speakership*, N.Y. HERALD, Jan. 28, 1860, at 10 (Pennsylvania Representative Thomas Florence arguing in support of a new Speaker of the House who was a "conservative, national old line whig" who would resist sectionalism under the principles of the "old

During the congressional debates over Senator Henry Wilson's Enrollment Act in February 1863, several constitutional conservative representatives and senators used the Second Amendment to support their opposition. To be certain, the Second Amendment was not the first nor the primary basis for objecting to the constitutionality of the Conscription Act.[67] Almost all the dissent, unsurprisingly, came from Democrats (conservative Republicans like Edgar Cowan and Lyman Trumbull were the exception) who considered themselves to be constitutional conservatives and strict constructionists. Kentucky Unionist Senator Lazarus Powell was one of the leading senators trying to filibuster the bill as the session of Congress came toward its closing days even though Democrats did not have the votes to block the bill. On February 28, in a long speech later reprinted in Democratic newspapers and pamphlets, Powell summed up his constitutional case:

> I regard the bill, Mr. President, as dangerous to the liberties of the people. It is calculated to strike down the rights of the States of this Union. It is calculated, if passed and carried out, to make this Union of confederate, independent States, a grand, consolidated despotism. The bill, if carried out, will sweep from existence the militia of the States and consolidate them into one grand national army under the control of the President alone. It will take away the control of the executives of the States over their own militia. That is a principle that never

---

man of the Hermitage"); *The Whig Nominations*, CARROLL FREE PRESS, June 16, 1848, at 2 (arguing that General Taylor was a constitutional conservative in favor of "beneficial policy at home" and "peaceful, just, non-intervention policy" abroad against Lewis Cass, the "representative of Dorrism and Locofoism," meaning liberal legislation at home and "intervention, war, conquest, and annexation" abroad); The Nominations, Litchfield Enquirer, June 29, 1848, at 1 (arguing that the general term Whig meant the "great Constitutional Conservative party" and the nomination of Taylor was evidence of this commitment). The *New York Herald* also applied the term to the first Republican candidate for president, John C. Fremont, in 1856, bolstering that while James Buchanan and Franklin Pierce supported the "Southern session platform of forcing slavery into Kansas," Colonel Fremont occupied alone the "conservative ground of the constitution in this contest, in his foreign and domestic policy" and the "only reliable Union candidate." *Our Political Statistics from 1789 to 1856 Issues and Prospects of the Approaching Presidential Election*, N.Y. HERALD, Sept. 24, 1856, at 6. Notably, during the war, the term could be applied critically by Republicans against so-called "peace Democrats" like Fernando Wood, and during Reconstruction, Southern Democrats co-opted the term to oppose and prevent the "success of the ultra-Republican or radical rule." See *Conservatism in North Carolina*, COLUMBIA DAILY PHOENIX, Sept. 24, 1867, at 3; *The Meeting at Morgantown Last Saturday*, WHEELING DAILY INTELLIGENCER, Oct. 8, 1863, at 2 (reporting about the meeting of "certain men who call themselves constitutional conservative, union, peace men, generally looked upon as Butternut, Copperhead Democrats.").

[67] These constitutional objections also included opposition to the arbitrary power given to the provost marshal and executive branch, claims that Congress had improperly delegated legislative power to the executive branch, and the argument that the act was fundamentally unfair in that it discriminated against poorer citizens.

should be incorporated into the law of *any free people*. Such a policy, to say the least of it, will endanger the public liberties.[68]

Powell was not alone in this invocation of the "states power" theory. Another key opponent, and constant obstructionist to the administration, was Delaware Senator Willard Saulsbury Sr., a former state attorney general who had long been a resolute opponent of the Lincoln administration and the president's suspension of *habeas corpus*.[69] Saulsbury first restated the maxim regarding standing armies: "The whole theory, therefore, of those who framed the Constitution, as evidenced by the debates both in the Federal Convention and in the conventions of the several States which ratified it, was this, that large standing armies were dangerous to public liberty."[70] Saulsbury explicitly referenced the Second Amendment at several points to agree with Powell about the threat to the militia as a state institution traditionally protected by the structure of federalism because the national draft would reach the whole body of the people. As Saulsbury argued:

> The power to raise and support armies is conferred by the Constitution upon Congress, and the right to have and maintain a well organized militia is reserved to the States. The instrument conferring this power and recognizing the reservation of this right was designed for the government of a free people. The power may be exercised in the modes employed by a free people, and as such a people had theretofore exercised it as evidenced in their history and policy. . . . The right to raise armies by conscription, if it exists, is unlimited, and may extend to the *whole body of the people*. Such a right exercised would destroy not only the recognized right of the States to officer their militia, but the existence

---

[68] CONG. GLOBE, 37th Cong., 3d Sess. 1382 (1863) (statement of Sen. Powell) ("This bill prevents the States from controlling the militia in the manner in which I have indicated, and subjects them to martial law before they are mustered into the service of the United States, and in both these particulars, I hold it to be unconstitutional").

[69] At the end of January 1863, just before the Senate began its debate over the Enrollment Act, Saulsbury, apparently inebriated, called Lincoln "an imbecile" who was the "weakest man ever placed in a high office" and when asked by president of the Senate, Vice President Hannibal Hamlin, to take his seat, Saulsbury refused. When the Senate's sergeant-at-arms tried to remove Saulsbury from the Senate floor, Saulsbury showed his revolver and said, "Damn you, if you touch me I'll shoot you dead!" Saulsbury would not return to the Senate for weeks, just in time for the debate over conscription, while some Republicans call for his permanent removal from the Senate. *Exciting Scene in the Senate—The President Denounced as an Imbecile—Senator Saulsbury Arrested*, HUNTINGDON GLOBE, Feb. 4, 1863, at 1; *see also* JONATHAN W. WHITE, ABRAHAM LINCOLN AND TREASON IN THE CIVIL WAR: THE TRIALS OF JOHN MERRYMAN 72 (2011) (noting that Saulsbury denounced secession but believed slavery should be preserved as a slaveholder and boomed that if he could paint the portrait of a despot, he would "paint the hideous form of Abraham Lincoln.").

[70] CONG. GLOBE, 37th Cong., 3d Sess. 1387-88 (1863) (statement of Sen. Saulsbury). ("It is true a small regular Army might be necessary even in times of peace, to repress sudden outbreaks of popular violence, but the mode of raising such an Army, compatible with republican liberty, was only by voluntary enlistment, which experience had always proved to be amply sufficient.").

of a State militia itself. If Congress can directly of itself call into the regular Army the entire body of the people, and are not compelled to call upon the States for their people, as militia of the States, then the right of the States to have a well organized militia, a constitutional right, may be entirely destroyed by an act of Congress.[71]

Saulsbury clearly indicates here that the right is held by the *states* under the Second Amendment, but for the benefit of their people. Fellow Democrat and Delaware Senator James Bayard likewise saw the act as dangerous to the security of the states and civil liberties. He agreed with Saulsbury that the bill did not comport with the demands of the Second Amendment, which was meant to restrict federal power. It was, Bayard pleaded, rendered "nugatory" by the Conscription Act. Bayard felt that without the Second Amendment's restrictions on federal power, the Constitution would not have been ratified.[72]

During the House debates, the sole Democrat to invoke the Second Amendment explicitly was Ohio's Samuel Smith Cox. In line with his Senate brethren, he interpreted the Second Amendment to be an additional bulwark against federal usurpation of the right of states to control their own militias. No emergency could alter this constitutional structural protection unless the militia was called into federal service.[73] Like Saulsbury and others within the "states power" tradition, Cox cited Justice Story for the proposition that the only way to conscript citizens as militia of the country was the intervention of the states themselves, as the "vital purpose" of the Second Amendment was to reserve to the states control of their militias.

Following the March 3 passage of the bill, a public constitutional debate immediately began in the Northern press between constitutional conservative and constitutional nationalist editors. Democratic newspapers made the Second Amendment's militia clause part of their core objections to the constitutionality of the Conscription Act. In a widely reprinted article demonstrating the clear unconstitutionality of the act, the *New York Copperhead* focused on the threat to state control of militias. For them, the danger was nothing less than the republic itself and the liberties guaranteed by a republican constitutional government after too many unconstitutional actions of the Lincoln administration left unchallenged. The first complaint was that the Constitution gave the federal government no power to interfere with the right of states to organize, arm, and regulate their own militias or to say which of their citizens would or would not be liable to military duty. This, the *Copperhead* claimed, was guaranteed by the

---

[71] *Id.* at 1388 (emphasis added).
[72] *Id.* at 1363.
[73] *Id.* at 1269.

Tenth Amendment. The right of a state to raise its own militia, not interfered with by any powers granted to Congress in Article I, included the power to say which citizens would be exempt and which would be liable to duty. And because the Conscription Act put the whole military power of the country in the hands of the federal government, it defeated the right of the states to have any militia at all contrary to the Second Amendment's guarantee of a "well-regulated militia" being necessary to the security of a free state.

In a widely distributed New York pamphlet, New York City attorney Dennis A. Mahoney joined congressional constitutional conservatives in arguing that the Second Amendment protected state militia power. Mahoney echoed the arguments of Democratic senators, proclaiming that the Conscription Act violated the Second Amendment by putting the state militias "out of existence" and turning American citizens into conscripts instead of subjects of the militia. He posited the federal government only had the right to call out the state militias in accordance with state laws but had no right to call people out "against their will" to perform military service in any manner outside of what conformed to the Constitution.[74] Similarly, Democratic lawyer and constitutional historian George Ticknor Curtis, the constitutional historian and co-counsel for Dred Scott before the Supreme Court, suggested in an early February letter to his brother Benjamin, the former Supreme Court justice and *Dred Scott* dissenter, that national conscription conflicted with both the Second Amendment and Article I, Section VIII.[75] Kentucky Court of Appeals Judge Samuel Smith Nicholas saw the Second Amendment as a protection against both "domestic usurpation as well as against foreign enemies" and thought the right of Congress to "call forth the militia" still expressly reserved to the states the power to appoint officers.[76]

---

[74] D.A. MAHONY, THE FOUR ACTS OF DESPOTISM: COMPRISING I. THE TAX BILL, WITH ALL THE AMENDMENTS. II. THE FINANCE BILL. III. THE CONSCRIPTION ACT. IV. THE INDEMNITY BILL 19–20 (1863). In another New York City pamphlet, fellow attorney John Joseph Freedmen expanded on Mahony's arguments. Freedman believed that conscription was not an acceptable practiced during ratification, as the broad understanding was that the regular army would always be raised by voluntary enlistment. He saw "[t]he power granted to Congress to raise and support armies" as a distinct, independent power that did not apply to the militia. If it did, the Constitution would have a general authority making the "subsequent provisions relating to the militia . . . worse than useless" and "would only tend to perplex and bewilder." The framers intended for the sovereign states to maintain power over their militias, and Freedmen argued the Second Amendment only confirmed this understanding by further restricting Congress's powers over the militia. JOHN JOSEPH FREEDMAN, IS THE ACT, ENTITLED "AN ACT FOR ENROLLING AND CALLING OUT THE NATIONAL FORCES, AND FOR OTHER PURPOSES," COMMONLY CALLED THE CONSCRIPTION ACT, PASSED MARCH 3, 1863, CONSTITUTIONAL OR NOT? 22 (1863).

[75] Letter from George T. Curtis to Benjamin Curtis (Feb. 26, 1863) (on file with the University of Virginia Special Collections).

[76] SAMUEL SMITH NICHOLAS, CONSERVATIVE ESSAYS, LEGAL AND POLITICAL 44 (Philadelphia, J.B. Lippincott & Co. 1863).

Leading Republican newspapers such as the *New York Tribune*, in denying the persistent cries of unconstitutionality from "Copperheads and Rebel sympathizers," could agree that the Second Amendment meant to "enlarge the powers of the States" because the Constitution otherwise in Article I and II had put all military power in the hands of the general government.[77] Yet the *Tribune* also believed that the Second Amendment did not deny the power of Congress to raise and maintain an army by any chosen means it saw fit, but only secured to states the right to have a "well-regulated militia."[78] It did, therefore, require the general government to call on the states for their quota of men, as the Constitution granted Congress the power to raise armies without providing the method by which to do so and was a "bold and naked" unqualified power which allowed the government to create a standing army by legislative act.

It is not, however, the case that *all* Democratic newspapers, or even the majority of them, or Democratic politicians, explicitly referred to the Second Amendment to publicly assail the constitutionality of conscription. Broadly, Democratic newspapers tended to focus their arguments on the limited grants of power in Article I and II and the maintenance of state power over their internal militia. In particular, they homed in on the ways the policy of national conscription would erase state governments, thus applying the federalism-based "states power" limits on Congress without specifically citing the Second Amendment.[79] Similarly, when several state legislatures reacted to the Conscription Act with resolutions condemning its unconstitutionality, they did not cite the Second Amendment when addressing the perceived threat to state sovereignty.[80] Yet

---

[77] *Constitutionality of the Draft*, HILLSDALE STANDARD, Aug. 11, 1863, at 1 (quoting N.Y. TRIB.).
[78] *Id.*
[79] *See* Note, *in* THE OLD GUARD: A MONTHLY JOURNAL DEDICATED TO THE PRINCIPLES OF 1776 AND 1787, at 67 (C.C. Burr ed., 1863–1870) (The Conscription Bill threatened to "sweep[] out of existence the State militia" and "clothe[d] the President with unlimited and unchecked military powers" which made him as "absolute a monarch as the Autocrat of all of the Russians."); *State Rights*, DETROIT FREE PRESS, Mar. 7, 1863, at 2 (the danger of the act was in creating a "central despotic government," and the whole scope of the bill was to take away from states the "only safeguard they have"); Pamphlet 34, *The Draft, or Conscription, Reviewed by the People*, *in* FREIDEL, UNION PAMPHLETS OF THE CIVIL WAR 787–89 (Frank Freidel ed., 1863) (It would be a "ridiculous nullity" if the federal government could freely control the militia for any purpose the president or Congress choose and would nullify all reserved rights of the states to merge the "whole in one central despotism"); *The Revolutionists*, GOSHEN DEMOCRAT, Mar. 4, 1863, at 2 (the Conscription Act overturned the foundational principle that states controlled their own militia until called into actual service under Article I by placing every man between twenty and forty-five under the "arbitrary disposition of the President" and accusing Congress for the first time in history of "surrendering their rights" and "evading their duty").
[80] *The New Hartford Convention: Thomas H. Seymour Nominated for Governor*, N.Y. TIMES, Feb. 20, 1863, at 1 (Connecticut's Democratic Convention used language "precisely similar" to the Hartford Convention of 1814 to attack Senator Wilson's Conscription Act as "subversive of the sovereignty and the rights of the states and designed to make them mere dependencies upon the central government."). One Honorable Alvan P. Hyde, after the resolution passed unanimously, of Teiland and running for Congress, spoke after accepting the nomination about the need to sustain the Constitution. Hyde attacked the Militia Conscription Bill of Senator Wilson, which transferred from the states "all authority over their own militia to the authorities of the United States or the central government" and suggested that Congress had lost confidence in the public by "forcibly" taking

not only did these arguments align with antebellum constitutional politics concerning the Second Amendment and its relation to the structure of federalism which protected state sovereignty, but other major constitutional conservatives did explicitly and powerfully invoke the Second Amendment to condemn conscription. Additionally, these arguments did appear both in the rhetoric and reasoning of perhaps the most powerful opponent of conscription, New York Governor Horatio Seymour, and into the reasoning of the only state supreme court to strike down the Conscription Act as unconstitutional, the Pennsylvania Supreme Court.

The most consequential conscription case came before the Pennsylvania Supreme Court in the fall of 1863 and saw the sole major judicial victory for constitutional conservatives who opposed the draft.[81] On July 31, three plaintiffs who had been drafted in the Philadelphia area filed for injunctions against the local draft board and provost marshal on the basis that the Conscription Act was unconstitutional. The initial complaint did not cite the Second Amendment. However, during the September oral argument, Philadelphia Democratic

---

possession of the militia of the states. *Connecticut Politics—The Conscription Bill*, CINCINNATI DAILY ENQUIRER, Mar. 1, 1863, at 3. In Rhode Island on March 14, State Senator Elisha Reynolds Potter used similar language, "The power of compelling the militia and other citizens of the United States, by a *forcible draft or conscription* to serve in the regular armies, . . . is not delegated to Congress by the Constitution; and the exercise of it would be not less dangerous to their liberties, than hostile to the *sovereignty of the States*. The effort to deduce this power from the right of raising armies, is a flagrant attempt to pervert the sense of the clause in the Constitution which confers that right, and is incompatible with other provisions in that instrument."

ELISHA REYNOLDS POTTER, SPEECH OF HON. ELISHA R. POTTER, OF SOUTH KINGSTON, MARCH 14, 1863, UPON THE PRESENT NATIONAL DIFFICULTIES 7–8 (1863). The Rhode Island Democratic State Convention adopted similar resolutions in March, stating, "[W]e adhere to the wise division of power established by the framers of the Constitution" and look "with alarm upon any encroachment of one branch of the government upon the prerogatives of another, or upon the reserved rights of the States, as tending to a most dangerous centralization of power." *Id.* at 52. A set of resolutions adopted by the Maine Democratic Convention in August 1863 simply called the Conscription Act an "unnecessary, unwise, unequal and oppressive law" which was "destructive" to the "rights of the States" and the "liberties of the people." *Refuge of Oppression: MAINE COPPERHEAD DEMOCRACY*, LIBERATOR, Aug. 21, 1863, at 134. A month later, the Massachusetts Democratic Convention passed a resolution with nearly identical language, stating that the Conscription Act was "unwise and needless" and "oppressive and unequal" as well as unconstitutional. *Resolutions of the Massachusetts State Convention*, THE DAILY OHIO STATESMAN, Sept. 11, 1863, at 1.

[81] There was one other notable judicial victory for constitutional conservatives. In New York City, Judge John McCunn, a Democratic judge on the city court, while the New York City Draft Riots roiled the city ruled that the entire law was "clearly unconstitutional" and violated the rights of the people. McCunn found that the Conscription Act contravened both New York law and the Article I powers to "raise and support armies" and to "provide for calling forth the militia." Additionally, both the Second Amendment and the "Commander-in-Chief" clause of the Article II did not authorize the Conscription Act because the act did not create a force which was militia force of the states nor part of the standing army of the United States. But because he was merely a city judge, McCunn found his decision quickly challenged, and by the end of the month, the New York Supreme Court had reversed on jurisdictional grounds. *Judge McCunn on Conscription: THE VALIDITY OF THE LAW DENIED*, N.Y. TIMES, July 15, 1863, at 8.

attorney George Wharton used the Second Amendment to buttress his argument that Article I denied the federal government power to conscript male citizens. If Congress could conscript every male citizen, he warned, the reserved powers of the states could not be preserved and state forces would be absorbed by the federal army and cease to be a separate state militia force. Wharton argued that the Second Amendment's protection of a "well-regulated militia" guaranteed to states a militia system composed of able-bodied citizens who rendered military service in emergencies for defensive warfare. All of the Article I provisions granting Congress power over the militia recognized and affirmed the existence of the militia as a body distinct from the U.S. army.[82]

The Pennsylvania Supreme Court, by a 3–2 majority, struck down the Conscription Act as unconstitutional on November 9, 1863.[83] They did so principally on the basis that the act exceeded Congress's Article I power to "raise and support" armies and a national military draft was not a "necessary and proper" mode of raising armies because Article I already provided for the express purposes as to why Congress could "call forth" the militia.[84] Of the three Pennsylvania judges in the November majority, only Judge James Thompson's concurring opinion referred explicitly to the Second Amendment as an additional protection for antebellum federalism. He felt the Second Amendment was evidence the framing generation were apprehensive about such a "dubious power" as the power of the federal government to coercively conscript.[85] Thompson agreed with Wharton and the loudest Democratic voices throughout 1863 that the threat to state militias was dire, writing that the militia could not be destroyed by an act of Congress.[86] The Constitution forbade this by granting Congress power to provide for organizing, arming, and disciplining as a means of supplying states' security against the federal government. The Court's injunction against the Conscription Act was short-lived. The bench shifted in December when Republican Daniel Agnew replaced Chief Justice Walter Lowrie, a member

---

[82] *Legal Intelligence*, PHILADELPHIA PRESS, Sept. 23, 1863, at 4; *News*, PHILADELPHIA PRESS, Sept. 24, 1863, at 2

[83] Kneedler v. Lane, 45 Pa. 238 (Pa. 1863).

[84] *Id.* at 240–42.

[85] J. Norman Heath, *Exposing the Second Amendment: Federal Preemption of State Militia Legislation*, 79 U. DET. MERCY L. REV. 39, 55 (2001) (referring to Thompson's "contention about the Second Amendment," which was based on a "states' right" interpretation of the text that understood it as a protection for the state militia, as "short-lived." The Supreme Court in 1918 would make no mention of the Second Amendment in its unanimous opinions upholding national conscription in the Selective Draft Law Cases, 245 U.S. 366, 383 (1918); Cox v. Wood, 247 U.S. 3, 6 (1918)).

[86] Kneedler, 45 Pa. at 269–70 (Thompson, J., concurring). For Thompson, the act "plainly and directly destroys the militia system of the states" through the text of the act mandating that "[e]very able-bodied man in the United States, between twenty and forty-five" be enrolled to "constitute the national forces."

of the majority who lost his seat in the October elections, and the Court reversed itself and dissolved the injunctions in January.[87]

It is apparent that had the case, or another like it, ever reached the Supreme Court as constitutional conservatives so desperately wanted, at least one justice not only would have struck down the Conscription Act but done so on the basis of the Second Amendment. That is because in the spring of 1863, Chief Justice Roger Taney drafted a private, unofficial opinion finding the Conscription Act unconstitutional.[88] In his unofficial opinion, Taney wrote that the Constitution recognized two distinct and separate military forces with their own obligations and duties. The power to "raise and support" armies was a general grant of power exclusively federal which necessarily carried with it the power to select personnel and officers and make rules and regulations necessary to control federal military forces completely independent of control by any state.[89] Following the "state powers" tradition, Taney combined Article I and II with the Second Amendment as embodying the "sharp distinction" between the two bodies, noting that the militia was composed of state citizens who "retain all their rights and privileges as citizens who when called into service by the United States are not to be fused into one body—nor confounded with the Army of the United States, but are to be called out as the militia."[90] And Taney agreed with other constitutional conservatives that the Conscription Act, by making every able-bodied male citizen belong to the national forces, effectively eliminated the militia.[91]

The defeat in the courts continued over the course of 1863 and into early 1864, during which state and federal courts in Michigan and Pennsylvania ultimately upheld the Conscription Act and defanged, but did not destroy, the "states power" interpretation of the Second Amendment.[92] Democratic clubs and

---

[87] On December 12, 1863, special counsel John C. Knox, who refused to appear before the Court in September because the federal government did not recognize the jurisdiction of the state court under orders from the Lincoln administration, appeared for the government to ask the Court to dissolve the preliminary injunction granted in the case. Just over two months after the November decision, Justice Strong, joined by Justices Read and Agnew, issued his majority opinion in *Kneedler II* dissolving the injunction issued in November and upholding the constitutionality of the Conscription Act. *See* Kneedler, 45 Pa. at 295; *Legal Intelligence*, PHILADELPHIA INQUIRER, Dec. 14, 1863, at 3.

[88] CHARLES GROVE HAINES & FOSTER H. SHERWOOD, THE ROLE OF THE SUPREME COURT IN AMERICAN GOVERNMENT AND POLITICS, 1835–1864, at 488–95 (1957).

[89] *Id.* at 490. The militia was the other separate and distinct military force established by the Constitution, which "expressly forbade federal control of the militia in peacetime" and only allowed control under "limited and defined" circumstances.

[90] *Id.*

[91] *Id.* at 491–92. To Taney, despite the general grant of power given to Congress to "raise and support armies," "few general words" could not void "plain and specific provisions related to the militia." Further, the general grant itself did not justify "such an extreme construction." He wrote that such a construction "created a paradox" of a document, with "provisions so repugnant to each other." Finding Congress had the power to pass the Conscription Act would in turn declare "all constitutional clauses relating to state militia[s] meaningless" and able to be "set aside at the pleasure of Congress."

[92] *See, e.g., Governor's Address*, PORTLAND DAILY PRESS, Jan. 8, 1864, at 2. (In his inaugural address as Governor of Maine in January 1864, Samuel Cony, a Jacksonian Democrat turned Republican

newspapers consistently referenced the Second Amendment in denouncing conscription until the end of the war.[93] Most notably, New York Governor Horatio Seymour, likely the most consistent and popular opponent of conscription throughout 1863, continued to publicly profess the veracity of the "states power" theory. In the wake of Jubal Early's June 1864 invasion of Maryland to threaten Washington, D.C., Governor Seymour pleaded with New York male citizens to join the National Guard in order to meet President Lincoln's call to the states for more volunteers. First, on July 8, Seymour issued a proclamation as governor and commander in chief of the militia. In it, he quickly noted that events of the three years of the Civil War had "shown the necessity of a well-organized militia to uphold the laws; to put down disorders; to suppress insurrections, and to repel invasions," as the state militia had been called three times to protect Washington, D.C., from Confederate invasion and now the president had called them once more. Seymour pleaded that only the militia units of New York and Brooklyn were able to meet the call, which was not only "unequal and unjust, but in violation of the theory of our Government" because the calls made by the national government must be met by all states.[94]

Four days later, Seymour issued a call to the people of the state to join the National Guard or otherwise support measures to meet the call. In language mirroring his January annual address, he reminded the people that the

during the war, argued that "[t]he doctrine of the founding fathers was, that every able-bodied citizen, during the period of full, manly strength, owed military service to his country," and with the experience of the Civil War, Cony urged the passage of state legislation to supply this "deficiency and omission," as it was a duty of the state and its representatives to ensure that a "well-regulated militia" no longer be neglected.).

[93] *See Coal Valley Democratic Club*, ILLINOIS DAILY ARGUS, Feb. 9, 1865, at 2 (noting the resolutions adopted by the January 28 meeting of the Coal Valley Democratic Club, including that the Pennsylvania Supreme Court had declared the Conscription Act "unconstitutional and void" and that the act "annihilates the 'reserved right' of Illinois to maintain 'A Well regulated Militia,'" protected against the despotism of conscription against voluntary citizen soldiers); *see also The Right to Bear Arms*, NEW OREGON PLAIN DEALER, Apr. 1, 1864, at 1 (claiming that Republicans would accuse them of "sedition" should they take notice of the Second Amendment and quoting Story's *Commentaries* for the notion that the militia was the "national defense of a free country" against standing armies and that the "right of citizens to keep and bear arms has justly been considered as the palladium of the liberties of a republic" as a "strong moral check against the usurpation and arbitrary power of rulers").
[94] *The Response of Governor Seymour*, NAT'L INTELLIGENCER, July 21, 1864, at 4. A decade before, in his first gubernatorial term, Seymour had likewise admonished the legislature as to the need for "efficient organization of the militia" to maintain and preserve good order as reflected by the language of the Second Amendment. *See Message from the Governor*, N.Y. DAILY TIMES, Jan. 3, 1854, at 1. And in his January 1864 annual address, like Governor Cony, Seymour argued that the events of 1863 showed that the "neglect of this truth has exposed us to dangers of invasion, to the disgrace of riots, and to the hazards of still greater calamities" and proved that the militia of the states should be "armed and equipped in the manner set forth" in the Constitution. *See Governor's Address*, ALBANY MORNING EXPRESS, Jan. 6, 1864, at 2.

Constitution declares that a well-regulated militia is necessary to the security of a free state and "if we had acceded to this truth we should have not been exposed to invasion, to the disgrace of (New York City Draft Riots) and to the hazards of still greater calamities."[95] Seymour not only read the Second Amendment as a federalism provision which left undisturbed the state institutional control of the militia, but agreed with past constitutional thought regarding the *duty* given to Congress to organize, arm, and discipline the militia. Seymour implored the New York legislature and the people of the state to learn from past mistakes, as the costs of arming and equipping the National Guard would have been far lower than meeting the Lincoln administration's quota following the threat to the capital. For over a year, Seymour consistently argued against the constitutionality of conscription, called often for the Lincoln administration to allow for a judicial resolution of the question, and upheld himself as the Northern leader of constitutional conservative tradition. Ultimately, the war itself was won by an army of regular army volunteers, substitutes, and conscripts and as a result, only further eroded the "states power" understanding of the Second Amendment.[96] Yet that tradition, despite prior challenges, remained in constant use throughout the early republic and antebellum period and even in the midst of the greatest national emergency yet known, constitutional conservative Democrats held steadfast to it during the war.

---

[95] *General Order by Gov. Seymour: The State Militia to be Held in Readiness*, TROY DAILY WHIG, July 13, 1864, at 2; *The Situation*, N.Y. HERALD, July 12, 1864, at 4. In the wake of Seymour's "Manifesto," New York National Guard General John A. Greene wrote that he hoped that a state draft could be avoided if the National Guard could be filled by volunteers, as the National Guard was intended to be the "bulwark and defense of law and order—of liberty and property; the guarantee of peace and safety to our citizens." Greene pointed to both the Second Amendment's protection of a "well regulated militia to be necessary to the security of a free State" and the New York constitution's provision "at all times" that the militia "be armed and disciplined and in readiness for service" as reflected that guarantee of peace and safety to the state and the people. *Arbitrary Arrests and Military Outrages—Seward and Lincoln "Bell" Played Out in New York*, DAYTON DAILY EMPIRE, July 22, 1864, at 2.

[96] Note that there were exceptions to this trend, particularly in the South. For instance, in his 1868 inaugural address, Republican Robert Kingston Scott, the first governor under South Carolina's 1868 Reconstruction Constitution, stated that the language of the second amendment should lead the state legislature to ask the War Department for half the standard quota of arms so as to ensure "obedience to the law." *See* Robert K. Scott, *Governor Scott's Message*, ANDERSON INTELLIGENCER, July 22, 1868, at 5–6. President Andrew Johnson also argued that the Reconstructions Act of 1867 were unconstitutional in that they interfered with his powers as commander in chief but also because they denied the right of states to protect their own citizens "contrary to the express declaration of the Constitution that 'a well-regulated militia being necessary to the security of a free state, the right of the people to keep and bear arms shall not be infringed.'" *See* Andrew Johnson, *Fourth Annual Message to Congress*, Dec. 8, 1868, *available at* https://millercenter.org/the-presidency/presidential-speeches/december-8-1868-fourth-annual-message-congress.

VI. Conclusion

Prior scholarly examinations of the legal history of the Second Amendment have examined early nineteenth-century court cases reflecting the individual and "civic" interpretations of the amendment, the common law and natural law history behind the amendment's language, and the history of legal regulation of firearms. The constitutional politics of the Second Amendment during the early republic and antebellum period, however, have been less often explored. This chapter argues that the constitutional politics of the period and into the American Civil War era show the consistent power, across ideological and sectional lines, of the "states power" or "civic" interpretation of the Second Amendment. This "civic" interpretation had a vision of the Second Amendment as both a federalism and popular sovereignty protection for states and "the people" against the intrusion of the federal government and the upholding of the "citizen soldier" ideal against the tyranny of standing armies.[97] The war itself and the politics of Reconstruction may have permanently relegated this traditional view to minority status, but only after its use by a loud opposition party to argue against the creation of a permanent standing army which national conscription represented.

---

[97] See also William A. Cook, Opinions and Practice of the Founders of the Republic or The Administration of Abraham Lincoln Sustained by the Sages and Heroes of the Revolution 10 (Washington, D.C., William H. Moore 1864) (arguing that the Second Amendment did not grant an "unrestricted right, an absolute guarantee to keep and bear arms" but instead, the "security of a free state of the government" was the *exclusive end for which the right has an existence* and thus government could seize arms purchased, carried, or kept "for a purpose or purposes inimical to the Government.").

5

Gun Laws in Early America

The Sometimes Contradictory Regulations of Gun Use in the Colonial South

Sally E. Hadden

I. Introduction

For Europeans who emigrated to North America in the seventeenth and eighteenth centuries, the woods surrounding their settlements appeared to teem with dangerous wildlife and multiple hazards. Where many species harmful to man had been hunted to extinction in Europe, the same was not true in early America. Panthers, bears, and other creatures that could attack humans ran unchecked in American forests not yet converted to farms, homesteads, and hamlets—the hallmarks of European habitation and civilized life. English colonists who knew little of hunting found themselves surrounded by an endless forest primeval, the exact opposite of where they thought humankind should live. Prevailing philosophy predicted that societies based upon hunting were meant to evolve into more civilized ones based upon agriculture.[1] Europeans looked down upon Native Americans who lived by hunting, regarding them as indolent and lazy, and now many English colonists discovered that their survival might depend upon those very skills.[2] Yet most immigrants lacked hunting talents, for sport hunting in Europe by the seventeenth century had largely become the preserve of elites, as wild animals grew scarce and nobles penned the remainder within their own game parks; hunting for subsistence varied widely by location. Though spiritual perils (to one's soul, to salvation) were never far from the minds of English colonists, menacing animals posed, at least at first, the highest risk to continued existence and called for firearms to lend some small degree of safety.

---

[1] Daniel J. Herman, *From Farmers to Hunters: Cultural Evolution in the Nineteenth-Century United States*, in 5 A Cultural History of Animals 50 (Linda Kalof & Brigitte Resl eds., 2008). On Enlightenment theories about the stages of society and connections between social progress and decay, *see* Drew McCoy, The Elusive Republic: Political Economy in Jeffersonian America 18–21 (1980).

[2] Stephen Aron, *Pigs and Hunters: "Rights in the Woods" on the Trans-Appalachian Frontier*, in Contact Points: American Frontiers from the Mohawk Valley to the Mississippi, 1750–1830, at 180 (Andrew Cayton & Fredrika Teute eds., 1998).

Early colonists kept guns close at hand to ward off foxes, cougars, and wolves, as well as to provide food from deer and other animals killed in the woods.

Animals approached early settlements by day or night, but those that prowled after dark did so at a more stressful time for the first European transplants. Darkness was not benign in settlers' minds. For the deeply religious, fear of the devil could turn nights forbidding; for those susceptible to folk tales, nighttime was best spent indoors, away from witches, demons, and creatures of temptation. Religious or not, colonists often viewed nights as menacing, and even staying indoors was no guarantee of safety—nightmares sprung from the deepest reaches of the subconscious spared no one.[3] The night cry of a wolf might have Virginians or Carolinians reaching for their Bibles, which provided a framework for thinking about such marauders. The humans in Old and New Testament stories often tended flocks of sheep, which wolves preyed upon for food. Negative wolf imagery abounded: wolves "in sheep's clothing" might deceive, while false prophets were no better than "ravening wolves." The faithful could count upon Christ, the Good Shepherd, to find them if they strayed and to fend off earthly predators.[4]

Whether animal or spiritual, dangers lurked abroad for European immigrants, yet their greatest fear was probably their fellow man—another reason to keep firearms at the ready. Native Americans might appear by stealth, bringing gifts and greetings or mayhem and destruction. Good relations between colonists and Native Americans could deteriorate quickly: the first instructions given to Jamestown settlers in 1606 warned against letting Native guides hold their European-made weapons for any reason, lest those firearms be carried away.[5] And the importation of African men and women as unfree workers, starting in the seventeenth century, added another layer of complexity when evaluating threats to personal safety. Slaves typically increased profits, particularly if they were skilled at hunting with guns, but arming slaves created the possibility of insurrections.

In the colonial world of Virginians and Carolinians, fear of the known and unknown caused lawmakers to craft legislation that might calm such anxieties, or merely recognize dangers without reducing them substantially. Some early laws restricting access to guns stemmed from White desires to prevent invasions by foreign powers or attacks by Native Americans. Meanwhile, the threats and opportunities posed by the natural world inspired legislators to create other

---

[3] PETER C. HOFFER, SENSORY WORLDS IN EARLY AMERICA 119, 126 (2003).
[4] JON T. COLEMAN, VICIOUS: WOLVES AND MEN IN AMERICA 41–42 (2004).
[5] THE OLD DOMINION IN THE SEVENTEENTH CENTURY: A DOCUMENTARY HISTORY OF VIRGINIA, 1606–1689, at 21 (Warren M. Billings ed., 1975) (citing *Instructions from the London Company to the First Settlers, November 1606*, 1 THE JAMESTOWN VOYAGES UNDER THE FIRST CHARTER, 1606–1609, at 49–54 (Philip L. Barbour ed., 1969)).

statutes that encouraged deer hunting, regulated wolf hunting, and revealed that slave owners continued to arm their own slaves to enhance their profits, regardless of local restrictions. The tendency of some masters to flout gun restrictions when it came to their own bondsmen generated new fears in the early South, that some owners were too lenient or unmindful of White security. State-mandated slave patrols came into being to punish slaves found with weapons if their masters would not.[6] Colonial attempts to regulate firearms were, therefore, not exclusively about protection, but encompassed trade and profits, notions about civilization, racism and fear—a complex web of connections that led to contradictory lawmaking. While such statutes sometimes failed badly, early laws reveal colonists' aspirations that settlers hoped to realize in a challenging New World.

II. Gun Regulation in the Colonial South

Fear of foreign invasion and Native attacks, as well as a general familiarity with militia service, caused English transplants to Virginia and the Carolinas to write many laws for individual armed preparedness.[7] Through the seventeenth and eighteenth centuries, peace alternated with war for the major European powers—repeated conflicts with the French, Spanish, and Dutch meant that English colonists had to be ready for attacks at any moment. A 1659 Virginia law even gives an indication of how much preparedness seemed reasonable to legislators: the statute mandated that all adult males be provided with "a fixt gunn two pounds of powder and eight pounds of shott at least" or else pay a fifty-pound tobacco fine to the county to be used for local defense.[8]

Given that early settlers rarely had military backgrounds, their ability with weapons can only be surmised. A sizeable number of indentured servants and colonists (especially those migrating from England's cities) would always be unfamiliar or less accomplished with weapons. Regular commentary on Virginians' deficiencies started crossing the Atlantic soon after the settlement of Jamestown. John Smith reported from Virginia in 1608 (describing a Native American raid) that of seventy-odd colonials fighting in the skirmish, some "tenne or twenty shot not knowing what to doe, nor how to use a Piece."[9] How often those early settlers

---

[6] SALLY E. HADDEN, SLAVE PATROLS: LAW AND VIOLENCE IN VIRGINIA AND THE CAROLINAS 6–40 (2003).

[7] The imitation of English laws and transplantation of Caribbean statutes to the North American mainland has been explored by many. *See* Jonathan Bush, *Free to Enslave: The Foundations of Colonial American Slave Law*, 5 YALE J.L. & HUMAN. 417 (1993); HADDEN, *supra* note 6, at 10–24.

[8] Act XXV, Provision to Bee Made for Ammunition, *in* 1 THE STATUTES AT LARGE; BEING A COLLECTION OF ALL THE LAWS OF VIRGINIA, FROM THE FIRST SESSION OF THE LEGISLATURE, IN THE YEAR 1619, at 525 (William Waller Hening ed., 1809).

[9] JOHN SMITH, A TRUE RELATION OF SUCH OCCURRENCES AND ACCIDENTS OF NOTE AS HATH HAPNED IN VIRGINIA SINCE THE FIRST PLANTING OF THAT COLONY, WHICH IS NOW RESIDENT IN

trained and how proficient they became in handling firearms remains speculative, but Virginia's swelling population meant that immigrants inexperienced with weapons continued to arrive. Even after training, laziness or a desire to return to "normal life" might undercut calls for military preparedness.[10] Colonists could not maintain permanent vigilance forever—other priorities intervened, and periods of lax law enforcement alternated with close adherence, depending upon how recently a Native American attack had taken place.[11] Regulations like the 1659 law mandated an individual's military readiness, a modest but essential goal given that some early colonies disappeared after violent raids, but whether the laws changed individual behavior cannot be determined. Ongoing reports to London suggest that local officials fought an uphill battle to keep Jamestown residents in a state of military readiness.

Colonies also required communal security measures, which became formalized with time and sufficient population growth. Virginia took nearly two decades to come up with official collective security measures, and finally in 1622 drew upon the English militia system as a model for defense, though with significant modifications.[12] Derelict and of limited effectiveness, the seventeenth-century English militia was "ill equipped, poorly trained and its musters widely evaded both by men and officers."[13] Nonetheless, the English militia provided a template for colonists, who adjusted the institution to fit North American circumstances: nearby elusive enemies, a widely dispersed population, and a near-total reluctance by the empire to help settlers defend themselves. Exact legal requirements in the colonies cannot always be determined, given the militia laws still extant. A number of the earliest militia laws, like South Carolina's from 1682 and 1685, are known only by their titles, not their content, which has been lost.[14] Whether the militia had any weapons at all varied dramatically by colony; in North Carolina, a 1729 report noted that the militia "had neither arms, ammunition, or fortifications."[15] Only rarely did militia fight as whole units: in South Carolina, nearly fifty years passed from settlement until the militia turned out as

THE SOUTH PART THEREOF, TILL THE LAST RETURNE FROM THENCE (1608), *reprinted in* NARRATIVES OF EARLY VIRGINIA 1606–1625: ORIGINAL NARRATIVES OF EARLY AMERICAN HISTORY 65 (Lyon G. Tyler ed., 1907).

[10] William L. Shea, To Defend Virginia: The Evolution of the First Colonial Militia, 1607–1677, at 36 (1975) (Ph.D. dissertation, Rice University) (on file with Rice University).
[11] *Id.*; Luther L. Gobbel, *The Militia of North Carolina in Colonial and Revolutionary Times*, 13 TRINITY COLLEGE HISTORICAL SOCIETY PAPERS 45 (1919).
[12] Shea, *supra* note 10, at 254–55.
[13] Theodore Jabbs, The South Carolina Militia, 1663–1733, at 7 (1973) (Ph.D. dissertation, University of North Carolina) (ProQuest).
[14] An Act for Settling the Militia, (1682) and (1685), *in* 1 THE LAWS OF THE PROVINCE OF SOUTH-CAROLINA, IN TWO PARTS. THE FIRST PART CONTAINING ALL THE PERPETUAL ACTS IN FORCE AND USE 1, 3 (Nicholas Trott ed., 1736).
[15] WILLIAM L. SAUNDERS, 23 COLONIAL RECORDS OF NORTH CAROLINA XIV (P.M. Hale ed., 1886).

a whole to fight in the Yamassee War. More often, portions of the militia would be mobilized for short periods of time.

Militia might protect against all such threats, but caution needs to be exercised when discussing militia in the colonial South. As noted military historian John Shy pointed out, scholars need to avoid thinking about the colonial militia as a static institution: their manpower, abilities, and effectiveness varied by location and throughout the colonial period. In seventeenth-century Southern colonies, population density warred with manpower and efficacy, for sprawling settlement patterns meant that militiamen might be scattered over great distances when danger appeared. As late as 1720, South Carolina leaders complained to the British Board of Trade that colonists did not live compactly enough for the militia to be reliable, much less successful.[16] A similar situation prevailed in many parts of Virginia and especially North Carolina, which had the smallest, most dispersed population of the three colonies and no militia until 1715, at the end of the Tuscarora War.[17] The overriding requirement to provide subsistence (and the secondary goal of profit seeking) meant that typical militiamen could well prioritize farming over security, particularly when danger seemed remote.[18]

Proximity to other imperial settlements on the continent presented ongoing hazards to new English outposts. The contest for colonial dominance in North America meant that France and Spain (with missions as close as Florida) or the Netherlands and Sweden (with communities near the Chesapeake and in the Caribbean) all posed risks to English settlements. The appearance offshore of an armed ship with warriors aboard it could threaten the very existence of English colonists who relaxed their vigilance. Memories of the 1670 Spanish raid on Charleston, barely six months after the settlement's founding, continued to haunt residents who remained wary of another attack, and they were right to be. Another came in 1686: the Spanish advanced to within twenty miles of Charleston. Following the outbreak of Queen Anne's War (1702–1713, known in Europe as the War of Spanish Succession), the French assaulted Charleston, as part of a joint operation with the Spanish in 1706. As historian Howard Peckham grimly remarked, "It was clear by this time that colony planting was far from a peaceful business."[19]

---

[16] John W. Shy, *A New Look at Colonial Militia*, 20 WM. & MARY Q. 175, 180 (1963).

[17] E. Milton Wheeler, *Development and Organization of the North Carolina Militia*, 41 N.C. HIST. REV. 307, 308 (1964). North Carolina's militia included all freemen sixteen to sixty, theoretically encompassing free African Americans living in the colony. An Act for the Better Regulating the Militia of this Government, *in* 23 COLONIAL RECORDS OF NORTH CAROLINA 29–31.

[18] Shy, *supra* note 16, at 175–77; Marvin L. Kay & William S. Price, *"To Ride the Wood Mare": Road Building and Militia Service in Colonial North Carolina, 1740–1775*, 57 N.C. HIST. REV. 361, 384 (1980).

[19] HOWARD PECKHAM, THE COLONIAL WARS, 1689–1762, at 15 (1964).

Imperial dangers might be anticipated, even planned for, but in the sixteenth and seventeenth centuries a new menace emerged: pirates and privateers. Virginians and Carolinians had to remain alert, for pirates routinely visited their shores, sometimes to trade, sometimes to loot.[20] Charleston, for a time, functioned as a haven for pirates, until London-based authorities pressed for their extermination at the end of the seventeenth century.[21] South Carolina's legislature passed additional laws about fortifying Charleston and building a public powder house to store ammunition. In 1704, fortifications encircled the town, protecting against threats from all directions.[22] North Carolinians knew pirates all too well into the early eighteenth century, as Blackbeard (Edward Teach) shifted from plundering to quiet living in Bath, before resuming his watery robberies in 1717–1718. Spanish privateers soon took his place in the 1740s.[23]

To the north, Virginians had reason to fear pirate attacks as well, but the proximity of Dutch settlements in Delaware and Maryland as well as the repeated appearance of Dutch merchant vessels gave rise to more pressing anxieties, so long as the Anglo-Dutch trade wars continued (on-again, off-again from 1652 to 1674). In the seventeenth century, the tobacco and slave trades regularly brought Dutch ships to Virginia's shores, but intermittent conflict meant that today's friendly ship captain might be tomorrow's violent adversary. Pirates presented precisely the same unpredictability. Sometimes they arrived with goods to exchange at cheap prices; sometimes they attacked.

Native Americans posed the same quandary: friend or foe? The armed Native in Figure 5.1 might be an ally or an aggressor.

Virginia's and South Carolina's proximity to foreign invaders as well as the occasional pirate prompted precautionary measures, but neighboring hazards caused even greater White anxiety. For the first colonists, the number and variety of Native tribes bordering their settlements must have seemed baffling, if not nerve-wracking, at times: in North Carolina, the Croatan, Hatteras, Pamlico, Tuscarora, Cherokee, Catawba, Waccamaw, Waxhaw, and Saponi vied with other tribal bands for dominance. In South Carolina, members of the Pee Dee, Chicora, Edisto, Santee, Yamassee, and Cherokee bands were but a few of the Native Americans new colonists might encounter only miles from Charleston. The Indians' nearness, as well as their qualities that Europeans perceived as alien and inferior, stimulated White fears about potential attacks. In Virginia, Native groups like the constituent members of the Powhatan confederacy crowded round the earliest European colonists, to the point that a 1643 law required every

---

[20] WALTER J. FRASER, CHARLESTON! CHARLESTON!: THE HISTORY OF A SOUTHERN CITY 11–15 (1990).
[21] MARK HANNA, PIRATE NESTS AND THE RISE OF THE BRITISH EMPIRE, 1570–1740 (2015).
[22] FRASER, *supra* note 20, at, 23.
[23] Gobbel, *supra* note 11, at 46.

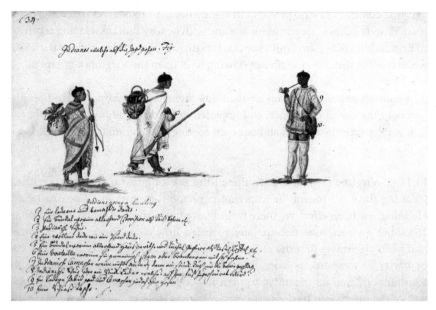

Fig. 5.1. Indians Going A-Hunting, from Philip von Reck's pencil drawings, catalog signature Ny kgl. Saml. 565, 4°, Copenhagen, Denmark: Royal Danish Library, http://www5.kb.dk/permalink/2006/manus/22/eng/25+verso/?var=. (Reproduced with permission from The Royal Library of Denmark, Manuscript Department (1736).)

family to bring a gun "with sufficient powder and shott" to each Sunday church service. Church wardens collected the reward of ten pounds in tobacco from forgetful churchgoers.[24]

Preventing attacks warred with settlers' instincts to seek profits in the New World, whether by growing tobacco in Virginia, harvesting naval stores in North Carolina, or planting rice and indigo in South Carolina. Tobacco fever had taken hold of the early Virginia settlers and nothing, not even hunger or personal danger, could shake it off. Yielding tidy profits, tobacco remained labor intensive, and many farmers planted it instead of sufficient foodstuffs; after all, food might be supplied through trade with Native Americans. Apparently, some

---

[24] Act XLI of 1642/43, in THE STATUTES AT LARGE; BEING A COLLECTION OF ALL THE LAWS OF VIRGINIA, FROM THE FIRST SESSION OF THE LEGISLATURE IN THE YEAR 1619, at 263 (William Waller Hening ed., 1823). South Carolina instituted a similar law in 1743. Both laws ran contrary to English statutes that provided that no man was to carry a weapon into church. An Act that Murthers and Felonies Done or Committed Within Any Lordship Marcher in Wales . . . , 26 Hen. 8, c. 6, § 3 (1534) (Eng.).

Virginia colonists saw no problem in selling firearms to Natives in exchange for food, despite years of intermittent warfare with nearby Indians. Having returned to England in 1609, John Smith spotted this disturbing trend as early as the 1620s while reading the correspondence flowing back from the Virginia settlement.

> It hath oft amazed me to understand how strangely the Salvages hath beene taught the use of our armes, and imploied in hunting and fowling with our fowling peeces [firearms], and our men rooting in the ground about Tobacco like Swine...[25]

In 1633, Virginia lawmakers prohibited the sale of guns to Native Americans; violating the edict meant life imprisonment and forfeiture of all possessions.[26] Had that law been effective, there would have been no need for its repetition in 1643, but a statute one decade later revealed how some ingenious Virginians had been circumventing the earlier law: legislators in 1643 prohibited the sale or barter of weapons, powder, and ammunition. To give the 1643 law teeth, legislators offered an incentive to turn in scofflaws: informants would receive half of the illegal gun trader's estate.[27] Even the threat of life imprisonment did not stop some colonists, however. Profit lured them into contrary practices, which lawmakers deplored: "[D]ivers persons do entertaine Indians to kill deare or other game, And do furnish the said Indians with peeces [firearms], powder and shott."[28]

After legislators banned the sale or barter of guns by law-skirting settlers, colonists turned to hiring Natives instead. This becomes apparent from the next round of firearm regulations. A 1654 Virginia law prohibited Whites from claiming that Native Americans were in their employ and allowed to use weapons, unless the Indian-White relationship was registered with the local county court.[29] Why would European settlers sell guns to Indians, or hire, arm,

---

[25] JOHN SMITH, CAPTAIN JOHN SMITH: A SELECT EDITION OF HIS WRITINGS 195 (Karen Kupperman ed., 2012) (citing JOHN SMITH, II THE GENERALL HISTORIE OF VIRGINIA, NEW-ENGLAND, AND THE SUMMER ISLES 284–85 (1624)).

[26] An Act that No Armes or Amunition be Sould to the Indians (1633), *in* 1 THE STATUTES AT LARGE; BEING A COLLECTION OF ALL THE LAWS OF VIRGINIA, FROM THE FIRST SESSION OF THE LEGISLATURE IN THE YEAR 1619, at 219 (William Waller Hening ed., 1823).

[27] Act XXIII of 1642, *in* 1 THE STATUTES AT LARGE; BEING A COLLECTION OF ALL THE LAWS OF VIRGINIA, FROM THE FIRST SESSION OF THE LEGISLATURE IN THE YEAR 1619, at 255 (William Waller Hening ed., 1823).

[28] *Id.*

[29] An Act concerning Imploying Indians with Guns (1654), *in* 1 THE STATUTES AT LARGE; BEING A COLLECTION OF ALL THE LAWS OF VIRGINIA, FROM THE FIRST SESSION OF THE LEGISLATURE IN THE YEAR 1619, at 391 (William Waller Hening ed., 1823). Northampton county court records suggest that Englishmen and Natives rarely followed these laws. HELEN C. ROUNTREE & THOMAS E. DAVIDSON, EASTERN SHORE INDIANS OF VIRGINIA AND MARYLAND 71 (1997).

and register them in the seventeenth century, given that Native attacks upon White settlements happened with regularity? Answer: hunting for profit.

For colonists, as for Native Americans, hunting and trade were intertwined.[30] The Lords Proprietors of Carolina recognized as much in 1681, when they reflected upon South Carolina's recent conflict with the Westoes. They were uncertain whether the battles had been motivated "upon a reall necessity" to preserve the colony or instead actually served the goals of "particular men by trade." Regardless, the Carolina Proprietors revealed their ultimate plan to subjugate the Westoes by making them dependent upon European trade goods—and should the Westoes not be pliable enough, others could be substituted. The Proprietors' design, even if not executed consistently, had a calculating logic.

> Furnishing a bold and warlike people with Armes and Ammunition and other things usefull to them . . . [would tie] them to soe strict a dependance upon us. . . that whenever that nation that we sett up shall misbehave . . . toward us, we shall be able whenever we please by abstaineing from supplying them with Ammunition . . . to ruine them.[31]

Trading firearms to the Indians could also create a buffer zone of security, such that more peaceful allies might provide early warnings about any potentially hostile Native American attacks.[32] Whether the English proprietors considered that groups like the Westoes might have alternative sources (Spanish, Dutch, or French) for powder, shot, and weapons is unknown, but Indians' eventual dependence upon European trade goods ultimately deprived them of the economic bargaining power to refuse every trade or alliance. In the colonial South, the trade good Europeans most wanted from Native Americans could only be obtained by hunting: animal skins.

In the colonial world, deerskins provided a ready trade good, convertible into English pots, cloth, ammunition, even alcohol by Native Americans.[33] Pelts from elk, moose, wildcat, beaver, mink, otter, and deer were all prized by Europeans for the warmth they imparted, and deer populations in the South were vast, dwarfing those of other creatures. Indeed, the supply of white-tailed deer seemed well-nigh inexhaustible. Biologists estimate that prior to European arrival in

---

[30] On Native American attitudes toward firearms in early America, *see* DAVID J. SILVERMAN, THUNDERSTICKS: FIREARMS AND THE VIOLENT TRANSFORMATION OF NORTH AMERICA (2016).

[31] 5 RECORDS IN THE BRITISH PUBLIC RECORD OFFICE RELATING TO SOUTH CAROLINA, 1710, at 115–18 (A.S. Salley ed., 1928).

[32] Shy, *supra* note 16, at 177.

[33] For a nuanced and sensitive reading of the multiple roles that hunting might play in colonial America, *see* Andrea L. Smalley, "The Liberty of Killing a Deer": Histories of Wildlife Use and Political Ecology in Early America (2005) (Ph.D. dissertation, Northern Illinois University) (on file with The Huskie Commons, Northern Illinois University).

the New World, North American deer numbered in the tens of millions.[34] In Europe, skins could be transformed into "hats, clothing, robes, and the coverings of trunks and boxes."[35] The abundance of deer and English demand for them meshed well with the desires of Indians to acquire goods only Europeans could provide, including those that had metal components. In a 1679 letter, naturalist John Banister explained how Native peoples in Virginia thirsted for new goods: "many Things which they wanted not before because they never had them are by that means become necessary both for their use & ornament."[36] Banister claimed they stood ready to trade beaver, otter, mink, wolf, and deer skins for "guns, gunlocks, powder, shot" and a variety of other European-made goods.[37] For Native Americans, trade provided a means to establish diplomatic ties and reciprocity in relationships, too. Seeking the best exchanges led Native groups to consider who would pay most for their goods. Groups like the Catawbas skillfully played off traders from Charleston against those from Virginia to gain the highest return on their skins in the early eighteenth century.[38]

Native Americans in the colonial South stood ready to provide European settlers with as many deerskins as they would trade for in the late seventeenth and early eighteenth centuries, so long as the trades included firearms. The Natives' shift in preference for European weapons over bows and arrows happened rapidly, within a few decades of Jamestown's settlement. Banister wrote in the early 1690s that Indians disdained unarmed Englishmen, whom they considered "fools." Failure to carry weapons would not occur to them "for they think themselves undrest & not fit to walk abroad, unless they have their gun on their shoulder, & their shot-bag by their side."[39] Cherokees in the Carolinas had largely converted to European weapons by 1725. English naturalist Mark Catesby, who visited the region in the 1720s, wrote that "there are very Few Indians ... that retain the use of bows and arrows."[40]

The shift from bow and arrow to firearms did little to change traditional hunting techniques among Native Americans, who used both types of weapons

---

[34] Andrea Smalley, *"They Steal Our Deer and Land": Contested Hunting Grounds in the Trans-Appalachian West*, 114 REG. KY. HIST. SOC'Y 306–07 (2016).

[35] CHARLES MCLEAN ANDREWS, 4 THE COLONIAL PERIOD OF AMERICAN HISTORY: ENGLAND'S COMMERCIAL AND COLONIAL POLICY 105 (1938).

[36] John Banister to Robert Morison, April 6, 1679, *reprinted in* JOSEPH EWAN & NESTRA EWAN, JOHN BANISTER AND HIS NATURAL HISTORY OF VIRGINIA 1678–1692, at 42 (1970).

[37] John Banister, *Of the Natives*, *reprinted in* JOSEPH EWAN & NESTRA EWAN, JOHN BANISTER AND HIS NATURAL HISTORY OF VIRGINIA 1678–1692, at 385 (1970).

[38] JAMES H. MERRELL, THE INDIANS' NEW WORLD: CATAWBAS AND THEIR NEIGHBORS FROM EUROPEAN CONTACT THROUGH THE ERA OF REMOVAL 82–83 (1989).

[39] EWAN & EWAN, *supra* note 37, at 382.

[40] TOM HATLEY, THE DIVIDING PATHS: CHEROKEES AND SOUTH CAROLINIANS THROUGH THE REVOLUTIONARY ERA 14 (1995) (citing Mark Catesby, *Of the Aborigines of Carolina and Florida* (ms. Royal Society, Decade I, #19, 13)). Hatley argued that by the time of the Yamassee War, "the majority of Cherokee men already owned the most costly trade item, a gun." *Id.* at 46.

to hunt deer. The traditional communal method of deer hunting relied upon using circles of fire in the winter to corral then kill the animals. Banister explained fire hunting this way: "A company go out & fire the Woods in a Circle of four or five miles compass, when they have compleated the Round, they step Ten or Twelve Paces in, each at his due distance, & put fire to the Leaves again, to accelerate the work." This process repeated "till the Circle be almost clos'd & they see their Game together," at which point "they fire upon them."[41] Colonials who accompanied Native Americans on fire hunts adopted the process and began using it themselves. Fire-hunting could easily lead to deer slaughter on a near wholesale basis. Given that fire posed a safety hazard and extreme loss of game might threaten food supplies, legislatures eventually passed laws against fire hunting, but not for many decades.[42] The deerskin trade remained too economically important to Europeans and Natives alike in the seventeenth and early eighteenth century to extinguish fire hunting altogether.

The extent of the deerskin economy meant that the potential for overhunting was ever present.[43] Anthropologist Charles M. Hudson posited that Native Americans were ready to "slaughter" deer "to the point that their prey became scarce."[44] Though the numbers of deerskins exported to Europe will never be fully enumerated, historians have determined that more than 50,000 deerskins per year were exported from Charleston alone in the early eighteenth century, rising to over 160,000 per year by mid-century. Combined with those exported from other seacoast towns, large herds would not last forever.[45] In 1764 alone, the southern colonies shipped over 800,000 pounds of deerskin to Europe.[46] Unrestrained killing of deer eventually depopulated the eastern portions of several colonies, though herds never reached the point of extinction.[47] What

---

[41] EWAN & EWAN, *supra* note 36, at 42–43.

[42] An Act to Prevent Hunting with a Gun, by Fire Light in the Night (1777), *in* WILLIAM L. SAUNDERS, 24 COLONIAL RECORDS OF NORTH CAROLINA 33. Section LXV fined any person twenty shillings for fire hunting, but mandated that Indians caught doing so have their weapons taken away. An Act for Settling the Titles and Bounds of Land, and for Preventing Unlawful Hunting and Ranging (1748), *in* 5 THE STATUTES AT LARGE; BEING A COLLECTION OF ALL THE LAWS OF VIRGINIA, FROM THE FIRST SESSION OF THE LEGISLATURE IN THE YEAR 1619, at 431 (William Waller Hening ed., 1819). The 1785 South Carolina statute is discussed *infra* at note 72 and accompanying text.

[43] For an overview, *see* KATHRYN E. BRAUND, DEERSKINS AND DUFFELS: THE CREEK INDIAN TRADE WITH ANGLO-AMERICA, 1685–1815 (1993).

[44] Charles M. Hudson, *Why the Southeastern Indians Slaughtered Deer*, *in* INDIANS, ANIMALS, AND THE FUR TRADE: A CRITIQUE OF KEEPERS OF THE GAME 162 (Shepard Krech ed., 1981).

[45] VERNER W. CRANE, THE SOUTHERN FRONTIER, 1670–1732, at 111–12 (1929); Robert M. Weir, *"Shaftesbury's Darling": British Settlement in The Carolinas at the Close of the Seventeenth Century*, *in* 1 THE OXFORD HISTORY OF THE BRITISH EMPIRE: THE ORIGINS OF EMPIRE: BRITISH OVERSEAS ENTERPRISE TO THE CLOSE OF THE SEVENTEENTH CENTURY 388 (Nicholas Canny ed., 1998).

[46] JAMES AXTELL, THE INDIANS' NEW SOUTH: CULTURAL CHANGE IN THE COLONIAL SOUTHEAST 48 (1997).

[47] Gregory Waselkov, *Introduction "Part Two: Politics and Economics,"* *in* POWHATAN'S MANTLE: INDIANS IN THE COLONIAL SOUTHEAST 132 (Peter Wood, Gregory Waselkov, & M. Thomas Hatley eds., 1989).

eventually replaced deerskins by the middle of the eighteenth century was the increasing importance of other trade commodities, including rice. For as long as Europeans would buy, however, Native Americans provided deerskins, seeking better prices where possible, to maximize the European trade goods they could demand, including guns.[48]

The valuable trade in skins gave Native peoples reason to war with one another or upon the enemies of English settlers. Native war goals encompassed not only capturing skins but also Indian slaves, to be sold to the English or used by the tribe in a number of other ways. By the mid-seventeenth century, attempts to capture hunting grounds or to acquire slaves encouraged the Westoes to make war on the Yuchis, Cherokees, and other Native groups deeper in the North American interior. After being armed by South Carolina authorities, the Westoes likewise made war upon Spanish settlements in Florida, seeking more slaves for the labor market in Carolina. By 1684, however, a band of South Carolina men took it upon themselves to attack the Westoes and drive them away from the colony, so that preference might be given to a different Native group. By the late 1680s, South Carolinians had begun trading with Creeks, who exchanged deerskins and slaves for cloth and guns; the Creeks and Yamassees captured skins and slaves while raiding Apalachee and Timucuan missions established by the Spanish in Florida.[49] The willingness of English colonists, at various times and places, to trade guns with Native Americans for goods or people, stands in broad contrast to the Spanish policy of not supplying muskets, powder, or shot to their Indian allies on the Spanish frontier (though Spaniards ignored these restrictions from time to time). This may explain why English colonists could find Native allies willing to raid Spanish outposts at great distances, while the Spanish had less success recruiting Indians to attack Charleston.[50]

The profits to be made by gun sales as well as the Indians' easy access to gun dealers elsewhere caused the Virginians, temporarily, to rethink their 1633 ban on selling Natives weapons. In 1659, Virginia's lawmakers reversed their earlier stance on not arming Indians, claiming that "neighbouringe plantations both of English and fforrainers do plentifully furnish the Indians with gunns, powder, & shott" and therefore Virginians should start profiting by doing the same. The "fforrainers" were nearby Dutch or Swedish traders in Delaware, who eventually left the area by 1664. With nearby competition in weapon sales substantially reduced, the Virginians promptly returned to restricting gun sales to Native

---

[48] Hudson argued that the eighteenth-century Indian had to do several things to increase his chances of survival, including "produce a commodity which was valuable enough to earn him some protection from English slavers." Hudson, *supra* note 44, at 169.

[49] Neal Salisbury, *Native People and European Settlers in Eastern North America, 1600–1783*, in 1 THE CAMBRIDGE HISTORY OF THE NATIVE PEOPLES OF AMERICA 424–25 (Bruce G. Trigger & Wilcomb E. Washburn eds., 1996).

[50] DAVID J. WEBER, THE SPANISH FRONTIER IN NORTH AMERICA 178 (1992).

peoples, but their efforts were in vain.[51] If Indians could not obtain what they wanted from Englishmen in Virginia, they would trade with others in the region; Marylanders' efforts to keep guns out of Native American hands had largely been abandoned by 1676, despite official statements to the contrary.[52] South Carolinians appear to have placed no restrictions on gun sales to Native peoples throughout this period.

Rivalry for hides led to tussles in forests over who had the right to use guns. In North America, deer came with no ownership labels attached—and the heavily forested area surrounding each settlement pitted hunters not only against wild animals but against each other in a competition that stretched for decades.[53] Struggles over gun ownership peppered the 1670s and 80s, as Native men appeared in Virginia courts to contest having their guns taken away improperly; in each case, judges ruled the gun seizures improper and ordered the weapons returned.[54] Virginia lawmakers tried to resolve these struggles once and for all when they passed "An Act to Prevent Indians Hunting and Ranging upon Patented Lands" in 1705, which permitted taking away a gun from a Native American if found upon land set aside for farming—but the law carved out exceptions for Pamunkeys, Chickahominies, or Natives living on the Eastern Shore, a caveat guaranteed to promote confusion.[55]

Hunting deer for their skins was only one path to making money with firearms for Native Americans and colonists. Hunting predators was another. Colonists' farms and settlements drew wolves with the lure of easily caught meals: wolves feasted upon a steady diet of domesticated animals like cattle, pigs, and chickens. Indeed, historian Timothy Silver has suggested that the wolf population in the Chesapeake *increased* after the introduction of colonists' livestock.[56] Multiple

---

[51] Free Trade with the Indians (1658/59), *in* 1 THE STATUTES AT LARGE; BEING A COLLECTION OF ALL THE LAWS OF VIRGINIA, FROM THE FIRST SESSION OF THE LEGISLATURE IN THE YEAR 1619, at 525 (William Waller Hening ed., 1819). The law permitting free trade in weapons was repealed in 1665. *See* An Act Prohibiting the Sale of Armes to the Indians (1665), *in* 2 THE STATUTES AT LARGE; BEING A COLLECTION OF ALL THE LAWS OF VIRGINIA, FROM THE FIRST SESSION OF THE LEGISLATURE IN THE YEAR 1619, at 215 (William Waller Hening ed., 1823). On the location of competing traders, *see* ROUNTREE & DAVIDSON, *supra* note 29, at 87.

[52] ROUNTREE & DAVIDSON, *supra* note 29, at 136. The authors considered Maryland's 1654 law against selling guns to Native Americans "a dead letter from the start." *Id.* at 294, n.31.

[53] *See* ROBERT B. MANNING, HUNTERS AND POACHERS: A SOCIAL AND CULTURAL HISTORY OF UNLAWFUL HUNTING IN ENGLAND, 1485–1640, at 76 (1993) (noting the legal doctrine that "wild beasts were *ferae naturae* and belonged to no man" and "that deer which 'have liberty to go at their pleasure' could not be stolen when they left their parks or forests"); P.B. MUNSCHE, GENTLEMEN AND POACHERS: THE ENGLISH GAME LAWS 1671–1831 (1981).

[54] ROUNTREE & DAVIDSON, *supra* note 29, at 72.

[55] An Act to Prevent Indians Hunting and Ranging upon Patented Lands (1705), *in* 3 THE STATUTES AT LARGE; BEING A COLLECTION OF ALL THE LAWS OF VIRGINIA, FROM THE FIRST SESSION OF THE LEGISLATURE, IN THE YEAR 1619, at 343 (William Walter Henning ed., 1812).

[56] Timothy Silver, *A Useful Arcadia: European Colonists as Biotic Factors in Chesapeake Forests*, *in* DISCOVERING THE CHESAPEAKE: THE HISTORY OF AN ECOSYSTEM 160–61 (Philip Curtin, Grace S. Brush, & George W. Fisher eds., 2001).

colonial governments placed bounties upon killing wolves to eradicate the marauders, and Virginia's legislature was no different.[57] An early statute offered one hundred pounds of tobacco as a reward to "what person soever" who killed a wolf.[58] A general 1656 law ambitiously attempted to "civilize" Indians through animal swapping, exchanging domesticated animals for wild ones: for every eight wolves' heads they brought in, Indians might receive a cow in return.[59] This would address two problems at once—rid settlements of the animal raiders, while introducing Native peoples to private property and sedentary farming. Well before Europeans offered bounties for wolves' heads, Indians knew how to kill the four-legged predators; killing wolves went hand in hand with trapping deer. Deer caught by snares or in pits offered wolves easy prey, and as they collected trapped deer, Native Americans remained alert to the possible presence of nonhuman hunters.

That Native Americans took advantage of the wolves' head reward system, and may have been given firearms to do so, becomes clear from a Virginia law passed in 1658. Entitled "Indians to Kill Wolves," the statute stipulated that "each county court" was to take whatever steps necessary to end the wolvish danger, "provided that they did not arm Native Americans with English guns."[60] This language suggests that prior to the law's passage, Indians had been supplied with firearms for that very purpose. Within a few years, horses were being taxed to pay for the wolves' head bounties that Natives collected.[61] Ten years later, Virginia's legislature revealed the economic chaos wrought by this open-ended incentive scheme: the number of bounties Indians sought for dead wolves had increased "to the insupportable burthen of the people"—meaning, they turned in so many heads for rewards that county taxes had skyrocketed as a result.[62] The new law

---

[57] New Englanders offered wolf bounties as early as 1644. Their lack of skill in wolf hunting caused them to also hire experienced hunters. COLEMAN, *supra* note 4, at 57–59.

[58] Act V (untitled, 1646), *in* 1 THE STATUTES AT LARGE; BEING A COLLECTION OF ALL THE LAWS OF VIRGINIA, FROM THE FIRST SESSION OF THE LEGISLATURE, IN THE YEAR 1619, at 328 (William Waller Hening ed., 1819).

[59] An Induction to the Acts concerning Indians (1655-6), *in* 1 THE STATUTES AT LARGE; BEING A COLLECTION OF ALL THE LAWS OF VIRGINIA, FROM THE FIRST SESSION OF THE LEGISLATURE, IN THE YEAR 1619, at 393, 395 (William Waller Hening ed., 1819).

[60] Indians to Kill Wolves (1657/58), *in* 1 THE STATUTES AT LARGE; BEING A COLLECTION OF ALL THE LAWS OF VIRGINIA, FROM THE FIRST SESSION OF THE LEGISLATURE, IN THE YEAR 1619, at 457 (William Walter Henning ed., 1819).

[61] Horses Tythable to Defray the Charges of Wolves' Heads (1662), *in* 2 THE STATUTES AT LARGE; BEING A COLLECTION OF ALL THE LAWS OF VIRGINIA, FROM THE FIRST SESSION OF THE LEGISLATURE, IN THE YEAR 1619, at 178 (William Waller Hening ed., 1810). In 1669, the legislature even introduced a quota system for each tribe to meet, in terms of wolves' heads delivered, but it included a bounty for additional heads delivered. Specifics giving numbers per tribe listed in An Act ffor Destroying Wolves (1669), *in* 2 THE STATUTES AT LARGE; BEING A COLLECTION OF ALL THE LAWS OF VIRGINIA, FROM THE FIRST SESSION OF THE LEGISLATURE, IN THE YEAR 1619, at 274 (William Waller Hening ed., 1810).

[62] Duplicity when it came to turning in wolves' heads (Natives collecting bounties in more than one place) led to tighter restrictions, as happened in New England. COLEMAN, *supra* note 4, at 61.

allowed county courts to set (and so reduce) bounties locally.[63] The prohibition seems not to have stopped Native Americans from hunting for profit—a 1691 law offered two hundred pounds of tobacco as a reward for "whoever" killed wolves using a gun.[64] Virginia law authorized payment to Native Americans, mulattoes, slaves, and anyone who killed wolves in 1748, and similar laws continued to be reenacted, though the reward might no longer be paid in tobacco but in local currency.[65] Bounties on wolves' heads, like the one used in Virginia, persisted far into the nineteenth century in many parts of North America.[66] As apex predators, wolves continued to threaten human settlements until humans decided to fight back.

Southern settlers of the seventeenth and eighteenth centuries perceived marauders like panthers, bears, crows, foxes, and wolves as vermin to be exterminated. The encouragement of farming led various colonies to attack the problem by offering bounties to whoever would destroy those predators. North Carolina's legislature enacted laws like Virginia and South Carolina's that required church wardens to pay bounties to slaves and Native Americans who killed wolves. A 1716 law offered a ten-shilling premium if wolves were killed with pits, five shillings if by gun; a similar statute in 1748 stipulated that ten shillings proclamation money be paid for every panther or wolf killed, whether the hunter "be Servant, Slave, or Indian."[67] Ten shillings at mid-century could purchase a piece of furniture, such as a bed, so the reward constituted a real prize. This North Carolina law, with slight variation in wording, would be re-enacted repeatedly through the 1760s, 1770s, and 1780s.[68]

Deer hunting had a direct impact on the wolf population and vice versa, while hunting both deer and wolf offered an alternative to farming for some colonists. Humans who killed deer for their skins but left carcasses behind may have increased the wolf population by offering easy fodder to feed their pups; Virginia began penalizing this practice by inquiring whether the person claiming a wolf bounty had also been deer hunting at the time.[69] Wolves grew up and formed

---

[63] An Act for Wolves Killed by Indians (1666), in 2 THE STATUTES AT LARGE; BEING A COLLECTION OF ALL THE LAWS OF VIRGINIA, FROM THE FIRST SESSION OF THE LEGISLATURE, IN THE YEAR 1619, at 87 (William Waller Hening ed., 1823).

[64] An Act Giving Reward for Killing of Wolves (1691), in 3 THE STATUTES AT LARGE; BEING A COLLECTION OF ALL THE LAWS OF VIRGINIA, FROM THE FIRST SESSION OF THE LEGISLATURE, IN THE YEAR 1619, at 47–48 (William Waller Hening ed., 1823).

[65] An Act for Giving a Reward for Killing Wolves (1748), in 6 THE STATUTES AT LARGE; BEING A COLLECTION OF ALL THE LAWS OF VIRGINIA, FROM THE FIRST SESSION OF THE LEGISLATURE, IN THE YEAR 1619, at 152 (William Waller Hening ed., 1819).

[66] Records from Vermont and Ohio's Western Reserve discussed in COLEMAN, supra note 4, at 83–86.

[67] An Act to Encourage the Destroying of Vermin (1716), in SAUNDERS, supra note 15, at 71; An Act for Destroying Vermin in this Province (1748), in SAUNDERS, supra note 15, at 288.

[68] SAUNDERS, supra note 15, at 617–18, 784–85, 914–15; WILLIAM L. SAUNDERS, 24 COLONIAL RECORDS OF NORTH CAROLINA XIV, at 33–34, 749–50, 476 (P.M. Hale ed., 1886).

[69] Smalley, supra note 34, at 312.

packs that could collaboratively hunt deer, as John Lawson reported while traveling through North Carolina in 1709: he heard wolves howling in the distance and then saw the results of a pack that had "torn a Deer in Pieces."[70] Predators like wolves had human imitators, who recognized that hunting deer and killing wolves might be a better way to earn money than scratching out a living on a subsistence farm. With the best farmland already claimed in many communities, men with no assets viewed deerskins and wolves' heads as a fast and relatively inexpensive way to generate cash.

North Carolina's dense woods and sparse settlement in the seventeenth and eighteenth centuries turned it into a magnet for the poor, the disaffected, and those inclined to roguishness, though all three colonies had "idle" people. Virginians or South Carolinians with few assets and fewer scruples migrated there and took advantage of the wolf bounties and deerskin profits to "live off the land." Of course, raiding a neighbor's farm for domesticated animals was not restricted to wolves or other predators: two-legged menaces also prowled the shadows. From the seventeenth century, Virginia's assembly tried to limit livestock thefts, to the point that restitution might be coupled with a few years as an indentured servant for those caught stealing, even if the animal taken had roamed freely rather than being penned up.[71] South Carolina's lawmakers eventually took up this concern after the Revolution; in 1785, they made it illegal for "idle and disorderly persons" to continue fire hunting, to attack deer or the "cattle or other stock of the good citizens" of the state. Violators faced a twenty-pound fine and three months in jail; slaves caught fire hunting off of their master's lands faced corporal punishment, usually up to forty lashes.[72]

Throughout the colonial period, slaves with guns provided protection and yet constituted a danger, too. Temporary laws enacted in 1672 by South Carolina's leading politicians ordered that, during possible attacks, slaves were to be left as a defensive force at the governor's home plantation—"the same being an outward place" some distance from Charleston—suggesting that they would be trusted enough to fight against Native Americans if an alarm happened.[73] Visitors to the colony remarked in the 1680s that enslaved people provided security as well as labor, for they fought against the Native Americans.[74] A 1696 South Carolina law required slave masters to inspect the cabins where enslaved families lived and

[70] JOHN LAWSON, A VOYAGE TO CAROLINA; CONTAINING THE EXACT DESCRIPTION AND NATURAL HISTORY OF THAT COUNTRY 67 (1709).
[71] VIRGINIA ANDERSON, CREATURES OF EMPIRE: HOW DOMESTICATED ANIMALS TRANSFORMED EARLY AMERICA 125–26 (2004).
[72] An Ordinance for the Preservation of Deer, and to Prevent the Mischiefs Arising from Fire-Hunting (1785), *in* 4 THE STATUTES AT LARGE OF SOUTH CAROLINA 719–20 (Thomas Cooper & David J. McCord eds., 1836).
[73] JOURNAL OF THE GRAND COUNCIL OF SOUTH CAROLINA, AUGUST 25, 1671–JUNE 24, 1680, at 36–37 (A.S. Salley ed., 1907).
[74] Jabbs, *supra* note 13, at 138.

seize any weapons found, but it's unknown how many took weapons away when Charleston remained threatened by rival colonies and Native Americans.[75]

With a White and Black population of roughly equal numbers in 1700 and the prospect looming of invasion by European enemies or attack by Native Americans, White South Carolinians took a series of unusual risks in the early 1700s. In 1703, lawmakers authorized masters to arm their "trusty slaves" if an enemy invasion appeared imminent: those who killed the enemy in battle would receive their freedom.[76] A South Carolina law in 1704 called for "one able slave armed with gunn or lance" to be trained for every White man in the militia.[77] Scholars familiar only with the threat of slave uprisings might be surprised that Carolina lawmakers required slaves to receive military training, but the shortage of White male colonists in early South Carolina virtually mandated it: east of the Appalachians, barely 3,800 Whites lived with 2,800 Africans they had enslaved, while roughly 7,500 Native Americans outnumbered both in 1700.[78] Failure to send a slave for militia duty "in time of alarms" would cost the master a five-pound fine. The 1704 law set no limits on how many slaves might be enrolled in South Carolina's militia, but a 1708 statute restricted the trained and armed bondsmen to a number less than the White militiamen.[79] Their dual race force made an impression on newcomers: Thomas Nairne, a Scots émigré to Charleston, noted that the colony's regiments of White militia were equaled by "a like number of Negro men slaves."[80] A 1712 modification acknowledged

---

[75] Governor Archdale's Laws, at 60–66 (1696), in 7 THE STATUTES AT LARGE OF SOUTH CAROLINA; EDITED, UNDER AUTHORITY OF THE LEGISLATURE 352–65 (Thomas Cooper & David J. McCord eds., 1836). Scholars relying upon Cooper and McCord's edition of laws—published in the nineteenth century—overlook many unpublished laws from this early period. For an overview of these omitted statutes, see CHARLES H. LESSER, SOUTH CAROLINA BEGINS: THE RECORDS OF A PROPRIETARY COLONY 1663–1721 (S.C. Dep't of Archives & Hist., 1995), which lists unpublished laws and where to find them.

[76] Acts Relating to the City of Charleston (1703), in 2 THE STATUTES AT LARGE OF SOUTH CAROLINA 33 (1836).

[77] An Act for Raising and Enlisting Such Slaves as Shall be Thought Serviceable to this Province in Time of Alarm (1704) and An Act for Enlisting Such Trusty Slaves as Shall be Thought Serviceable to This Province in Time of Alarm (1708), in 7 THE STATUTES AT LARGE OF SOUTH CAROLINA 347, 349. This imitated Barbadian practices, where many of the earliest South Carolinians hailed from: Barbadian law required White owners to send trusted slave men for military service. See Jabbs, supra note 13, at 33 (noting that how "the Barbadian militia performed well its task to overawe the resident blacks" and that "trusted slaves were even permitted to exercise with the militiamen during an alarm").

[78] Peter Wood, The Changing Population of the Colonial South: An Overview by Race and Region, 1685-1790, in POWHATAN'S MANTLE: INDIANS IN THE COLONIAL SOUTHEAST 38 (Peter Wood, Gregory Waselkov, & M. Thomas Hatley eds., 1989).

[79] An Act for Raising and Enlisting Such Slaves as Shall be Thought Serviceable to his Province in Time of Alarm and An Act for Enlisting Such Trusty Slaves as Shall be Thought Serviceable to This Province in Time of Alarm (1708), in 7 THE STATUTES AT LARGE OF SOUTH CAROLINA 347, 349.

[80] Governor and Council of South Carolina to the Lords Proprietors, Sept. 17, 1708, in 5 RECORDS IN THE BRITISH PUBLIC RECORD OFFICE RELATING TO SOUTH CAROLINA, 1701–1710, at 204 (A.S. Salley ed., 1947).

that slaves might be armed, but only in the immediate presence of their owners, suggesting that Whites had grown somewhat wary of providing firearms to the enslaved, who might point the guns not at invaders but at their presumptive owners. Enslaved individuals caught with guns off their masters' premises and beyond the control of their masters were to forfeit the guns.[81] "Trusty slaves" would be recruited for colony security in 1715 during the Yamassee War, in 1719 during "time of alarms," and again in 1739 when Spanish invasion seemed likely.[82] In the wake of the Stono rebellion, a comprehensive slave law passed in 1740 ended the practice of arming slaves for militia service.[83]

In these early South Carolina laws, a noticeable contradiction exists between Whites who trusted slaves with weapons and others who did not. In the same year that Carolinians ordered enslaved men into the ranks of the militia, South Carolina legislators also created a slave patrol system in 1704, designed to inspect slave cabins for weapons and prevent slave uprisings.[84] This 1704 law augmented the requirement from 1696 that slave masters search slave cabins for weapons, providing a state-sanctioned group to undertake the same work. A 1722 statute makes these contradictory indications even more obvious. Entitled "An Act for the Better Ordering and Governing of Negroes and Other Slaves," section four described "any slave so entrusted to keep a gun or cutlass" was required not to "lend it or suffer it to go out of his custody." At the same time, section six of the law mandated that an owner keep "all his guns and other arms" in a "room locked up" at all times, on pain of a three-pound penalty.[85] This seeming schizophrenia about whether enslaved people could be trusted while handling firearms continued for many years. In 1735, the legislature passed a law indicating that slaves were only to carry weapons abroad with written evidence of their masters' permission, but never on Sunday—suggesting that Sunday church services for Whites posed a time of particular vulnerability.[86]

---

[81] An Act for the Better Ordering and Governing of Negroes and Slaves (1712), *in* 7 THE STATUTES AT LARGE OF SOUTH CAROLINA 353.

[82] Benjamin Quarles, *The Colonial Militia and Negro Manpower*, 45 MISS. VALLEY HIST. REV. 649–50 (1959). In the wake of the Stono rebellion of 1739, the legislators reversed course and barred slaves from training in the militia. *Id*. An Act for the Enlisting Such Trusty Slaves as Shall be Thought Serviceable to This Settlement in Time of Alarms, and for Encouragement of Sailors to Serve the Same Against Our Enemies ... (1719), *in* 4 THE STATUTES AT LARGE OF SOUTH CAROLINA 108.

[83] An Act for the Better Ordering and Governing Negroes and Other Slaves in This Province (1740), *in* 7 THE STATUTES AT LARGE OF SOUTH CAROLINA 397.

[84] An Act to Settle a Patroll (1704), *in* 2 THE STATUTES AT LARGE OF SOUTH CAROLINA 254–55. Virginia's patrol came into existence in 1727, and North Carolina's in 1753. For details, *see* HADDEN, *supra* note 6, at ch. 1.

[85] 7 THE STATUTES AT LARGE OF SOUTH CAROLINA 373 (Thomas Cooper & David J. McCord eds., 1836).

[86] An Act for the Better Ordering and Governing Negroes and Other Slaves (1735), *in* 7 THE STATUTES AT LARGE OF SOUTH CAROLINA 385, 387.

Masters sometimes encouraged their enslaved men to hunt wolves for bounties or deer for profit, no matter where the animals led. A 1729 law in North Carolina emphasized that the eradication of wild animals was no excuse for violating private property. However: "Slaves being permitted to hunt or range with Dogs or Guns" had caused "great Damages," and any slave presuming to hunt must henceforth be accompanied by a White man. Violators could be given "a severe Whipping, not exceeding Forty Lashes" by the property owner and the master required to pay twenty shillings as well, if slaves were permitted to hunt on their own.[87] Of course, enslaved people might also be ordered to hunt deer by themselves, a situation recognized by lawmakers (many of whom were slave owners themselves). A 1738 Virginia law forbidding the hunting of deer in winter or by means of fire-hunting contained a specific clause about slaves hunting with guns: "[I]f any servant or slave, by command of his or her master, mistress, or overseer, shall, so hunt, shoot or kill" deer by fire hunting, then the master would be fined twenty shillings per deer killed. But if the bondsman "could not prove such command" then the penalty would be twenty lashes.[88] Slaves hunting in wintertime fit well with the typical calendar of planting in spring, harvesting in fall; winter was a fallow period for farmers, and slaves might be released more readily from farm work to go hunting for days at a time.

In time, as settlements grew more densely clustered, enslaved people living in eastern portions of the colonies would be governed more thoroughly by patrol law, enforced by slave patrols. Patrollers had the ability to remove any weapons found in slave cabins, whether or not a master permitted the individual slave to hunt or not. However, such regulations probably had little effect upon individuals living in the western parts of Virginia and the Carolinas, where patrols operated with less frequency and the proximity of Native Americans, wolves, and other dangers mandated that all go armed, lest they experience dangers that they could not protect themselves against.

III. Conclusion

White colonial settlers in Virginia and the Carolinas balanced many competing interests when deciding how much firearms should be regulated before the American Revolution. Some laws that they wrote mandated gun ownership, military preparedness, and militia training—edicts often ignored and weakly enforced. Other statutes attempted to regulate or even forbid the ownership

---

[87] An Additional Act to an Act, for Appointing Toll-Books, and for Preventing People from Driving Horses, Cattle, or Hogs, to Other Persons' Lands (1729), SAUNDERS, *supra* note 15, at 114.

[88] An Act for the Better Preservation of the Breed of Deer; and Preventing Unlawful Hunting, 5 STATUTES OF VIRGINIA 1738–1748, at 61.

of guns by Native Americans, laws the Natives themselves evaded repeatedly. Throughout this era, the lure of deerskin profits and the predatory hazards posed by wolves provided powerful counterweights to weapons regulations, encouraging the use of guns by all—unless they were vagrants, likely to pose a moral hazard to colonial settlement. Imperial threats as well as the possibility of violence at the hands of Native Americans also pushed South Carolina into requiring that slaves be armed with weapons and serve in the militia—at least for a few decades. The sometimes contradictory interplay of these laws makes it difficult to categorize early American gun law as purely protective against Native Americans, deliberately driven by imperial concerns, or entirely stimulated by greed. A mixture of many motives, these laws reveal the complexity of challenges faced by early American settlers attempting to tame the forest, its animals, and the people living there—including themselves.

6
To Brandish or Not to Brandish

The Consequences of Gun Display

Robert J. Spitzer

I. Introduction

In May of 2020, forty-six-year-old George Floyd, an African American, was arrested by police in Minneapolis for allegedly passing a phony $20 bill. After initially resisting, Floyd was handcuffed and pushed to the ground. One of the four officers on the scene kneeled on the back of Floyd's neck for roughly eight minutes. Despite his pleas and those of bystanders, the man suffocated and died on the scene. The event was recorded and seen by millions. The reaction was spontaneous nationwide outrage, and under the banner of the Black Lives Matter movement, organized several years earlier, protests spread like wildfire across the country. In fact, this sequence of events sparked an uncharacteristically rapid and decisive (if short-term) shift in public attitudes about policing and racism. Within weeks of the killing, a *Washington Post* poll reported that 69 percent of Americans agreed that Floyd's death represented a larger problem of police treatment of African Americans. This 69 percent support represented a tripling in that number compared with poll results from nine years earlier.[1] Six years earlier, after other police killings of unarmed Black men, 43 percent of the public agreed.[2] Other polls found similarly seismic shifts in opinion.[3]

One such post-Floyd killing protest was held in St. Louis on June 28, when a group of protesters marched on a private street called Portland Place to stage a protest at the home of the St. Louis mayor, who lived on the street. Entering through an unlocked gate, the protesters walked past another home, that of Mark

---

[1] Nolan McCaskill, *"A Seismic Quake": Floyd Killing Transforms Views on Race*, POLITICO, June 10, 2020, https://www.politico.com/news/2020/06/10/george-floyds-death-transforms-views-on-race-307515.

[2] Jacqueline Alemany, *Power Up: There's Been a Dramatic Shift in Public Opinion About Police Treatment of Black Americans*, WASH. POST, June 9, 2020, https://www.washingtonpost.com/news/powerpost/paloma/powerup/2020/06/09/powerup-there-s-been-a-dramatic-shift-in-public-opinion-over-police-treatment-of-black-americans/5edef042602ff12947e87b23/.

[3] Hannah Fingerhut, *Wide Shift in Opinion on Police, Race Rare in US Polling*, AP, July 2, 2020, https://apnews.com/8a0269689d3f981e8db1620adbde4b95.

Robert J. Spitzer, *To Brandish or Not to Brandish* In: *New Histories of Gun Rights and Regulation*. Edited by: Joseph Blocher, Jacob D. Charles, and Darrell A.H. Miller, Oxford University Press. © Oxford University Press 2023.
DOI: 10.1093/oso/9780197748473.003.0006

T. and Patricia N. McCloskey. Both are personal injury lawyers. As protesters walked past, the McCloskeys came outside of their palatial historic home, both carrying firearms, and standing on their property. Mr. McCloskey carried an AR-15 assault-style rifle; Mrs. McCloskey held a silver handgun with her finger on the trigger, which she pointed at the marchers. The McCloskeys claimed that the marchers had broken through the gate to the street, were trespassing on the private road, and had shouted threats and obscenities at them. Mr. McCloskey labeled the marchers "terrorists" and said, "I really thought it was storming the Bastille." Without the display of firepower, he insisted, "we'd be dead and the house would be burned."[4] For their part, the marchers said that they neither made nor posed any threat to the McCloskeys, that none of them stepped onto the McCloskeys' property, that they were simply passing his house on the way to their destination, and that the gate they entered was unlocked and open—all of which was confirmed by video footage and other accounts taken at the time. The protesters considered the private road trespass an act of civil disobedience, although locals report that such trespass on private roads by pedestrians is not uncommon.[5]

Shortly after the encounter, the McCloskeys were each charged with a felony count of unlawful use of a weapon by St. Louis Circuit Attorney Kim Gardner, who said, "[I]t is illegal to wave weapons in a threatening manner at those participating in nonviolent protest." Gardner proposed as a penalty that the couple complete a diversion program rather than face jail time. Gardner's allegation of wrongdoing against the McCloskeys was that they engaged in firearms "brandishing," succinctly defined by her statement. (Local police also seized the two guns in question.)[6] In October, a grand jury indicted them on felony charges of unlawful use of a weapon and evidence tampering.[7] In 2021, both pleaded

---

[4] Teo Armus & Kim Bellware, *St. Louis Couple Point Guns at Crowd of Protesters Calling for Mayor to Resign*, WASH. POST, June 29, 2020, https://www.washingtonpost.com/nation/2020/06/29/st-louis-protest-gun-mayor/.

[5] *Id.*; Rachel Rice & Kim Bell, *Couple Points Guns at Protesters Marching to St. Louis Mayor's Home to Demand Resignation*, ST. LOUIS POST DISPATCH, June 29, 2020, https://www.stltoday.com/news/local/crime-and-courts/couple-points-guns-at-protesters-marching-to-st-louis-mayor-s-home-to-demand-resignation/article_9edc57ed-c307-583f-9226-a44ba6ac9c03.html; Adam Weinstein, *Standing Their Ground in Well-Manicured Yards*, THE NEW REPUBLIC, June 29, 2020, https://newrepublic.com/article/158328/mark-patricia-mccloskey-st-louis-lawyers-guns-protesters; *Private Streets in Saint Louis*, URBANSTL, https://urbanstl.com/private-streets-in-saint-louis-t2397.html (last visited Feb. 8, 2023).

[6] Tom Jackman, *St. Louis Couple Who Aimed Guns at Protesters Charged with Felony Weapons Count*, WASH. POST, July 20, 2020, https://www.washingtonpost.com/nation/2020/07/20/st-louis-couple-who-aimed-guns-protesters-charged-with-felony-weapons-count/.

[7] Joel Currier, *Grand Jury Indicts Gun-Waving St. Louis Couple on Gun, Tampering Charges*, ST. LOUIS POST-DISPATCH, Oct. 6, 2020, https://www.stltoday.com/news/local/crime-and-courts/mccloskeys-lawyer-says-st-louis-couple-indicted-on-gun-tampering-charges/article_4b967366-e448-53fc-b718-c2741e45dc5d.html?utm_source=The+Trace+mailing+list&utm_campaign=d9dc14fa19-EMAIL_CAMPAIGN_2019_09_24_04_06_COPY_01&utm_medium=email&utm_term=0_f76c3ff31c-d9dc14fa19-69360165.

guilty: Patricia to misdemeanor harassment with a $2,000 fine, and Mark to fourth-degree assault with a $750 fine. They also agreed to give up the weapons they deployed in the encounter, although they did not lose their right to own firearms. When asked by the judge if he admitted putting people at risk, Mark replied, "I sure did your honor." Outside of the courthouse, however, he said, "I'd do it again." In August of 2021, Missouri's governor pardoned the couple.[8]

Several interrelated legal principles were immediately raised by those on both sides of the dispute, including so-called "stand your ground" laws that allow individuals to employ force, to the point of lethality, if confronted with a perceived threat in public places if they have a right to be where they are; the Castle doctrine, a related idea that people have no duty to retreat to protect their homes and property from intruders; open carry laws that make it legal to openly carry and display firearms in public; the Second Amendment, which by the reckoning of some protects a wide range of gun-related activities; and brandishing laws that criminalize the threatening display of weapons. In the case of Missouri, state gun laws are relatively lax. It has expansive stand-your-ground and Castle doctrine laws; open carry is allowed; and the state has a long gun-owning tradition. The state also has a brandishing law that defines as a criminal offense whenever anyone "[e]xhibits, in the presence of one or more persons, any weapon readily capable of lethal use in an angry or threatening manner."[9] In the modern era, nearly all states have some kind of brandishing law on the books. States without specific brandishing laws can still prosecute threatening behavior with a firearm under the categories of assault or menacing.[10]

The St. Louis case poses a contemporary exemplar of the complexities of gun-brandishing behavior. Yet the case is hardly unique. Since the start of 2020, when states and localities began to impose restrictive measures to combat the spreading COVID-19, protests sprang up in many states, often including armed protesters, who rankled against measures they considered excessive, draconian, and even a violation of fundamental freedoms. Armed protests and protesters, composed mostly of right-wing private militia groups and sympathizers, spread even more rapidly as Black Lives Matter protests continued into the summer of 2020. By one account, armed counterprotesters during this time appeared at anti-racism rallies in at least thirty-three states. Predictably, "the presence

---

[8] Jim Salter, *St. Louis Gun-waving Couple Pleads Guilty to Misdemeanors*, AP, June 17, 2021, https://apnews.com/article/michael-brown-st-louis-5d8c0dd118abef6df4a4214becd2f30a.
[9] *Missouri Revised Statutes Title XXXVIII. Crimes and Punishment; Peace Officers and Public Defenders § 571.030. Unlawful use of weapons—exceptions—penalties*, FINDLAW, https://codes.findlaw.com/mo/title-xxxviii-crimes-and-punishment-peace-officers-and-public-defenders/mo-rev-st-571-030.html; Chip Brownlee, *What Counts as Brandishing? When Is It Illegal?*, TRACE, July 2, 2020, https://www.thetrace.org/2020/07/armed-st-louis-missouri-couple-threat-brandishing-self-defense/.
[10] Brownlee, *supra* note 11.

of weapons at protests is ratcheting up tensions at a time when stress is high for protesters, counterprotesters and law enforcement alike." As this account observed: "Carrying a loaded firearm at a protest is an inherently dangerous situation."[11]

If asked why they carried guns, the armed protesters would surely respond that it is their right to do so. Strictly speaking, that is correct, since open gun carrying, including at public events, is legal in most states.[12] Moreover, in 2022, the Supreme Court ruled, for the first time in history, in *NYSRPA v. Bruen* that "the Second and Fourteenth Amendments protect an individual's right to carry a handgun for self-defense outside the home."[13]

In addition, gun activists view gun carrying as a positive action or symbol, based on motivations to "desensitize" or "normalize" the idea of gun carrying,[14] and also as an effort on their part to somehow keep the peace.[15] A Utah state legislator who introduced a bill in that state to expand public gun carrying justified the effort by saying, "Carrying openly causes lots of consternation for anti-gunners.... They see the weapon, wet their pants, and call the police. We're trying to eliminate the public consternation."[16]

To take a different example, a member of the extremist so-called "Boogaloo" movement gave a radio interview in 2020 in which he discussed his motivations for carrying a gun. He and others showed up at an otherwise peaceful rally in Las Vegas "armed to the teeth" and calling for the reopening of businesses and other services during the pandemic. The armed protester explained his actions by saying, "We're aware there's those that might be a little terrified of it. The point isn't to make people afraid, it's to show people and to bring up a dialogue."[17]

To cite another example, during a May 2020 armed protest in Michigan against strict state quarantining guidelines, one of the armed protesters, identified in a news report only as Mike S. of Detroit, said regarding the guns he and others were carrying that there was "obviously no intention to use it." Rather, he viewed

---

[11] Heath Druzin & Leigh Paterson, *Guns Are An Increasing Danger at Already Tense Protests*, GUNS & AM., July 30, 2020, https://gunsandamerica.org/story/20/07/30/guns-anti-police-violence-protests-aurora-colorado/; Joshua Partlow, *Politics at the Point of a Gun*, WASH. POST, July 28, 2020, https://www.washingtonpost.com/politics/2020/07/28/conservative-armed-militias-protests-coronavirus/.

[12] Alex Yablon, *The 36 States Where Local Officials Can't Ban Guns at Protests*, TRACE, Sept. 11, 2017, https://www.thetrace.org/2017/09/35-states-local-officials-cant-ban-guns-protests/.

[13] New York State Rifle & Pistol Association v. Bruen v. Bruen, 142 S. Ct. 2111 (2022).

[14] JENNIFER CARLSON, CITIZEN-PROTECTORS 129 (2015).

[15] A 2019 nationwide survey of over two thousand gun owners reported that about 8 percent of respondents said they owned guns "to exercise my constitutional rights, they give me a feeling of power." Michael B. Siegel & Claire C. Boine, *The Meaning of Guns to Gun Owners in the U.S.: The 2019 National Lawful Use of Guns Survey*, AM. J. PREVENTIVE MED., July 28, 2020, https://www.ajpmonline.org/article/S0749-3797(20)30239-7/fulltext.

[16] Mike Spies, *The Push to Allow Americans to Carry Concealed Guns Without Permits*, TRACE, Feb. 9, 2021, https://www.thetrace.org/2016/03/permitless-carry-states-west-virginia/.

[17] Leah Sottile, *The Chaos Agents*, N.Y. TIMES MAG., Aug. 23, 2020, at 42.

gun carrying at the public rally as a way to draw attention to "[c]onstitutional rights protesters are defending." Others at the rally strongly objected to the presence of guns at the event.[18] Another armed protester in Michigan who identified himself as part of a private militia group was described by a reporter as someone who "presents himself as an impartial guardian of the Bill of Rights."[19]

The fears of those who object to the presence of guns at public demonstrations were realized during a demonstration in Kenosha, Wisconsin, in August 2020 that was sparked by the August 23 police killing of a Black man who was shot by police seven times in the back. Film of the shooting enraged many, who took to Kenosha streets in unplanned protests that began peacefully, but that degenerated into mayhem. The moment attracted both protesters and armed counterprotesters. One of the latter, a seventeen-year-old from Illinois carrying an assault-style rifle, was interviewed on the street during the evening of August 25. When asked what he was doing in the midst of the disorder, he replied, "People are getting injured and our job [he and other armed individuals] is to protect this business [referring to a business that had been recently vandalized] and part of my job is to help people. If there's somebody hurt, I'm running into harm's way. That's why I have my rifle—because I can protect myself obviously, but I also have my med[ical] kit."[20] News accounts described him as a "police admirer." Shortly after the interview, the teenager shot three people, killing two of them. He was charged with murder, but found not guilty at trial. Open gun carrying without a license is legal in Wisconsin, but carriers must be at least eighteen.[21] This event was obviously not like the orderly protests previously described, but the intentions of the Kenosha shooter, as he described them, could be taken as honorable, even noble. Yet the end result was anything but that. We cannot know the shooter's true motivations, but the shooting could only have occurred by virtue of the fact that he was armed.

Regardless of the political or other motives of public gun carrying, such carrying is an act freighted with meaning and consequences. This simple fact is a central concern in the contemporary gun debate in America, but it is not a new concern, a fact reflected in early American law and earlier British law.

---

[18] Gus Burns, *Soggy Protesters Demand Michigan Gov. Whitmer End the Coronavirus "Lockdown,"* LiveMichigan, May 14, 2020, https://www.mlive.com/public-interest/2020/05/soggy-protesters-demand-michigan-gov-whitmer-end-the-coronavirus-lockdown.html.

[19] Luke Mogelson, *Nothing to Lose But Your Masks*, New Yorker, Aug. 24, 2020, at 38.

[20] @RichieMcGinniss, Twitter, Aug. 26, 2020, https://twitter.com/RichieMcGinniss/status/1298657958205820928.

[21] *17-Year-Old Arrested after 2 Killed During Unrest in Kenosha*, U.S. News & World Rep., Aug. 27, 2020, https://www.usnews.com/news/us/articles/2020-08-26/kenosha-police-3-shot-2-fatally-during-wisconsin-protests. Wisconsin also does not have a stand-your-ground law.

II. Myth and Reality in America's Gun Past

Thanks in large part to popular culture and American myth, a prevailing view of our gun past holds that gun laws and regulations are a product of modern American society and that in the nineteenth century and before, guns were widely owned and little regulated, if at all. Yet the opposite is true. Gun possession is as old as the country (though far less widespread than popular culture suggests), but so are gun laws. Indeed, from the earliest British settlements in America up to the start of the twentieth century, Americans enacted literally thousands of gun laws of every imaginable variety.[22] Among those many laws were measures pertaining to the brandishing, and in some cases the mere display, of firearms in public. These restrictions found roots in early British law. As gun law scholar Adam Winkler noted, "As long as people have been able to carry guns in public, there have been concerns about them terrorizing people."[23] Historian Saul Cornell concludes similarly, "The liberty interest associated with the right to arms was always balanced against the concept of the peace."[24] In fact, Cornell notes, under early British law the very act of riding armed "terrorized the King's subjects and therefore violated the peace." To do so "did not require any intentional act [i.e., no *mens rea* standard], or menacing behavior, to run afoul of the law; the mere act of arming itself was sufficient to trigger criminal prosecution...."[25] This principle, found in law from Britain in the Middle Ages to the present in the United States, has often been summarized as "going armed to the terror of the public."[26]

For example, in one of the most influential English legal handbooks that also served as a model for the development of American law dating to the early colonial period, Dalton's *Country Justice*, justices of the peace were granted broad powers to bind over individuals for a variety of violations of the King's Peace. Infractions included any who "go or ride armed offensively.... For these are accounted to be an Affray and Fear of the People, and a Means of the Breach of the Peace." Another section expressly said that the mere carrying of guns was

---

[22] Robert J. Spitzer, Guns across America: Reconciling Gun Rules and Rights 29–64 (2015).
[23] Dahlia Lithwick & Olivia Li, *Can You Bring a Gun to a Protest?*, Slate, Oct.17, 2017, https://slate.com/news-and-politics/2017/10/protests-might-be-one-place-you-cant-carry-guns.html.
[24] Saul Cornell, *The Right to Keep and Carry Arms in Anglo-American Law*, 80 Law & Contemp. Probs. 11, 14 (2017).
[25] Saul Cornell, *History, Text, Tradition, and the Future of Second Amendment Jurisprudence*, 83 Law & Contemp. Probs. 73, 82 (2020).
[26] Lithwick & Li, *supra* note 23. Mark Anthony Frassetto cites a number of British treatises and court cases that all confirm that "the simple possession of weapons was sufficient to turn a lawful gathering into an unlawful assembly." Neither violence nor the threat of violence need have occurred. Mark Anthony Frassetto, *To the Terror of the People: Public Disorder Crimes and the Original Public Understanding of the Second Amendment*, 43 S. Ill. U. L.J. 79 (2018).

an offense: "All such as shall go or ride armed (offensively) in Fairs, Markets or elsewhere; or shall wear or carry any Guns, Dag[ger]s or Pistols charged; any Constable, seeing this, may arrest them." The section ends with this: "And besides, it striketh a Fear and Terror into the King's Subjects."[27]

In American law, several prominent legal treatises adopted the British model. For example, the American edition of William Russell's *A Treatise on Crimes and Misdemeanors* from 1824 said, "[I]f a number of men assemble with arms, in terrorem populi [to the terror of the people], though no act is done, it is a riot."[28] The same standard was found in J.A.G. Davis's *On Criminal Law* (1838), James Stewart's version of *Blackstone's Commentaries* (1849), Francis Wharton's treatise, *Precedents of Indictments and Pleas* (1849), and Oliver Barber's *Treatise on the Criminal Law of the State of New York* (1852).[29]

In statutory law, two types of provisions penalized the mere public appearance of weapons (short of their actual use), including but not limited to firearms, in two circumstances: the brandishing of weapons—that is, to display them in a menacing or threatening manner—and the mere display of weapons. A 1642 provision in the colony of New Netherland (soon to be New York) said, "No one shall presume to draw a knife much less to wound any person, under ... penalty."[30] This reference did not mention firearms but allowed for penalties for merely drawing or displaying a weapon, even if no wounding occurred. Similarly, a 1786 Massachusetts law criminalized the mere assemblage of "any persons to the number of twelve, or more, being armed with clubs or other weapons." If they did not disperse within an hour of being warned, they could be subject to arrest.[31] That is, the mere appearance of such an armed assemblage was sufficient to justify legal action against them, although other provisions of the act penalized such groups who also behaved in a threatening manner.

These laws, it turns out, were common. Between the late 1600s and the early 1930s, a total of at least thirty-six colonies/states enacted laws that penalized weapons brandishing or display. Of these, twenty-one states criminalized weapons brandishing[32] by combining two elements: the display of the weapon

---

[27] MICHAEL DALTON, THE COUNTRY JUSTICE 380 (1727). The original version of Dalton's work dates to the early 1600s. *See* Cornell, *supra* note 24, at 18–21. Cornell traces these restrictions back to the British Statute of Northampton of 1328. It said in part that all subjects were bound to "bring no force in affray of the peace, nor to go nor ride armed by night nor by day." The law was enforced by the monarch's agents, who could arrest violators and cause them "to forfeit their armour to the King, and their bodies to prison at the King's pleasure."

[28] Frassetto, *supra* note 26, at 82.

[29] *Id.*, at 82–83.

[30] 1642 N.Y. Laws 33. This and all other colonial and state laws can be found at the Duke Center for Firearms Law digital archive of gun laws, https://firearmslaw.duke.edu/repository/search-the-repository/; Young v. Hawaii, 992 F.3d 765, 794–95 (9th Cir. 2021); Jonathan E. Taylor, *The Surprisingly Strong Originalist Case for Public Carry Laws*, 43 HARV. J.L. & PUB. POL'Y 347–56 (Spring 2020).

[31] 1786 Mass. Sess. Laws 87–88.

[32] VOLNEY E. HOWARD, THE STATUTES OF THE STATE OF MISSISSIPPI 676 (1840); 1854 Wash. Sess. Law 80; WILLIAM H.R. WOOD, DIGEST OF THE LAWS OF CALIFORNIA: CONTAINING ALL LAWS OF A

plus the manner of the display. For example, an 1840 Mississippi law said that "any person having or carrying any ... deadly weapon" who "shall, in the presence of three or more persons, exhibit the same in a rude, angry and threatening manner, not in self-defense" shall be subject to prosecution.[33] Note the two key elements: the "exhibit" or display of the weapon combined with doing so "in a rude, angry and threatening manner." The latter element brings to mind the perpetrator's *mens rea* or "guilty mind,"[34] revealing a criminal intent as invoked by the terms "rude, angry, and threatening." Of the twenty-one states with these laws, eleven used the identical "in a rude, angry and threatening manner" phrase; five used the word "threaten"; and the others used wording including "for the purpose of frightening or intimidating," "in a manner likely to cause terror," or simply "point."

A total of eighteen states enacted laws that penalized the mere display of firearms and other "deadly weapons."[35] (While a total of thirty-six states enacted one of these types of laws, three states—Indiana, New Mexico, and Wyoming—enacted both display and brandishing laws, for a total of thirty-nine laws in thirty-six states.) Several state laws in this category used the phrase "to point," as was true for a couple of laws in the brandish category, but the laws here had additional language that made clear that the intent of the person was irrelevant. An 1880 Georgia law, for example, made it a crime to "point or aim" a gun but added "loaded or unloaded,"[36] a distinction not made in the brandishing laws.

GENERAL CHARACTER WHICH WERE IN FORCE ON THE FIRST DAY OF JANUARY, 1858, AND PAGE 34, IMAGE 340 (1861); GEORGE W. PASCHAL, A DIGEST OF THE LAWS OF TEXAS: CONTAINING LAWS IN FORCE, AND THE REPEALED LAWS ON WHICH RIGHTS REST, ANNOTATED PAGE 1321, IMAGE 291 (VOL. 2, 1873); 1867 Ariz. Sess. Laws 21–22; 1868 Ark. Acts 218; DORSET CARTER, ANNOTATED STATUTES OF THE INDIAN TERRITORY (OKLAHOMA), SECOND SESSION OF THE FIFTY-FIFTH CONGRESS, PAGE 228, IMAGE 312 (1899); 1870 Id. Sess. Laws 21; 1873 Nev. Stat. 118; 1875 Ind. Acts 62; GEORGE W. COTHRAN, THE REVISED STATUTES OF THE STATE OF ILLINOIS, EMBRACING ALL LAWS OF A GENERAL NATURE IN FORCE JULY 1, 1883, PAGE 453, IMAGE 512 (1884); 1897 Wash. Sess. Laws 1956; LEBARON B. PRINCE, THE GENERAL LAWS OF NEW MEXICO 313 (1882); 1884 Wyo. Sess. Laws 114; 1885 Mont. Laws 74; 1897 Fla. Laws 59; 1931 Mich. Pub. Acts 670; Annotated Code of the State of Iowa, 1898 (1897); J.H. JOHNSTON, THE REVISED CHARTER AND ORDINANCES OF THE CITY OF BOONVILLE, MO. 91 (1881); JOHN PURDON, A DIGEST OF THE LAWS OF PENNSYLVANIA 250 (1860); 1925 W.Va. Acts 25–30.

[33] HOWARD, *supra* note 32.
[34] HENRY C. BLACK, BLACK'S LAW DICTIONARY 680 (1991).
[35] 1642 N.Y., *supra* note 30; 1686 N.J. Laws 289, ch. IX; 1692 Mass. Acts 10, 11–12; also 1786 Mass., *supra* note 31 (included Maine); 1699 N.H. Laws, 1, 1–2; 1786 Va. Acts 33, ch. 21; Francois Xavier Martin, A Collection of Statutes of the Parliament of England in Force in the State of North Carolina, 60–61 (Newbern 1792); 1801 Tenn. Pub. Acts 260, ch. 22; 1821 Me. Laws 285, ch. 73; 1880 Ga. Laws 151; Rev. Stats. of the State of Del., 333 (1852); 1883 Ind. Acts 1712; 1886 N.M. Laws 56; 1889 N.C. Sess. Laws 502; 1893 Or. Laws 29–30; WILLIAM L. MARTIN, THE CODE OF ALABAMA 171 (1897); BRUCE L. KEENAN, BOOK OF ORDINANCES OF THE CITY OF WICHITA, KANSAS 45 (1899); JOSIAH A. VAN ORSDEL, REVISED STATUTES OF WYOMING, PAGE 1252–1253, IMAGE 1252–1253 (1899); 1910 S.C. Acts 694.
[36] 1880 Ga. Laws 151.

Another law criminalized gun pointing "in jest or otherwise";[37] another added "with or without malice";[38] a fourth said "in fun or otherwise."[39] The thrust of these laws is that intent does not matter. The mere act of display is sufficient to warrant prosecution. Invariably, these laws made exceptions for justifiable arms carrying including weapons transport, travelers carrying weapons, law enforcement, the military, militias, and cases of self-defense.

To raise a final point about these laws, the weapons to which they referred included, with one exception, firearms, but also included certain named types of knives. While this may seem odd to contemporary readers, certain types of knives were widely used for interpersonal fighting. These named types of knives, including Bowie knives, Arkansas toothpicks, sword canes, swords, dirks, or other "deadly weapons" shared the trait of having long, thin blades that were favorites for fighting and were widely reviled for that reason. The very same list of firearms and knives was invariably included among those weapons barred from concealed carry in the colonies and states from the seventeenth through the start of the twentieth centuries. Indeed, by the start of the twentieth century, every state except one had enacted laws severely restricting or barring the concealed carrying of such weapons.[40] At the start of the 1980s, nineteen states still had no-carry laws on the books. By that point, however, the National Rifle Association began its effort in state legislatures to liberalize and repeal these strict anti-gun-carry laws.[41]

In addition to laws restricting concealed carry and brandishing, states commonly enacted time and place restrictions on gun carrying. These also stretched back to the seventeenth century, and restricted gun carrying in public places, at communal gatherings, schools, churches, circuses or shows, parades (if the weapons were loaded), in certain meeting places including legislative houses, at entertainments, on Sundays, or on election day. Separate measures commonly and strictly regulated firearm discharges.[42]

---

[37] Rev. Stats. of Del., *supra* note 35.
[38] 1893 Or. Laws 29–30.
[39] 1889 N.C. Sess. Laws 502.
[40] Robert J. Spitzer, *Gun Law History in the United States and Second Amendment Rights*, 80 LAW & CONTEMP. PROBS. 55, 63–67 (2017).
[41] ROBERT J. SPITZER, THE POLITICS OF GUN CONTROL 98–99 (8th ed. 2021).
[42] Spitzer, *supra* note 40, at 58–68; Robert J. Spitzer, *Guns Don't Belong Near Polling Places. Right Wingers Want Them There Anyway*, WASH. POST, Sept. 30, 2020, https://www.washingtonpost.com/outlook/2020/09/30/guns-polling-places-intimidation/.

III. The Modern Debate about Firearms Brandishing and Intimidation

This brings us to an important question: What happens when gun carrying intersects with public demonstrations? Considerable contemporary legal analysis has examined the relationship between free speech and arms carrying, generally framed as the intersection or collision of First and Second Amendment rights.[43] My purpose in this chapter is not to wade into that constitutional law question. The issue of weapons brandishing is a matter of criminal law,[44] and as the prior discussion illustrates, brandishing restrictions are deeply and firmly embedded in law dating back hundreds of years. (Analogously, Saul Cornell has pointed out that guns have been treated as a form of property for over three centuries.[45]) This legal tradition alone recognizes that weapons brandishing and even simple public weapons display when others are present is intimidating per se—by its very nature. First Amendment free speech considerations are about words (and occasionally expressive conduct). Gun carrying is about the human carrying of dangerous devices. By one account, "open [gun] carry is action, not speech."[46] Still, some of this writing addresses the focus of this chapter.

For example, Darrell A.H. Miller argues that "the presence of a gun in public has the effect of chilling or distorting the essential channels of a democracy—public deliberation and interchange. . . . A right to freely brandish firearms frustrates one of the very purposes of a constitution, which is 'to make politics possible.'"[47] Eugene Volokh takes issue with Miller's claim, calling it "speculation." His counterargument is that states with liberalized concealed carry firearms laws have shown no evidence of less free speech than those with strict carry laws, and thus gun carrying evinces no intimidation.[48] That argument, however, fails to address the fact and consequences of actual public gun

---

[43] For example: *see also* Darrell A.G. Miller, *Guns as Smut: Defending the Home-Bound Second Amendment*, 109 Colum. L. Rev. 1278 (2009); Eugene Volokh, *The First and Second Amendment*, 109 Colum. L. Rev. Sidebar 97 (2009); Darrell A.H. Miller, *A Short Reply to Professor Volokh*, 109 Colum. L. Rev. Sidebar 105 (2009); Eric M. Ruben, *Justifying Perceptions in First and Second Amendment Doctrine*, 80 Law & Contemp. Probs. 149 (2017); Katlyn E. DeBoer, *Clash of the First and Second Amendments*, 45 Hastings Const. L.Q. 333 (2018); Joseph Blocher & Bardia Vaseghi, *True Threats and the Second Amendment*, 48 J.L. Med. & Ethics 112 (2021); Michael C. Dorf, *When Two Rights Make a Wrong: Armed Assembly Under the First and Second Amendments*, 116 Nw. U. L. Rev. 111 (2021).

[44] Joseph Blocher et al., *Pointing Guns*, 99 Tex. L. Rev. 1173 (2021).

[45] Saul Cornell, *History and Tradition or Fantasy and Fiction: Which Version of the Past Will the Supreme Court Choose in NYSRPA v. Bruen?*, 49 Hastings Const. L.Q. 145 (2022).

[46] Gregory P. Magarian, *Conflicting Reports: When Gun Rights Threaten Free Speech*, 83 Law & Contemp. Probs. 172 (2020).

[47] Miller, *Guns as Smut*, supra note 43, at 1309–10.

[48] Volokh, *supra* note 43, at 102.

carrying. Only a small percent of people with gun carry licenses actually carry guns at any given time (and therefore a tiny percent of all adult Americans),[49] and the presence of guns must be visible and made known to others in a public setting in order for the consequences of gun display or brandishing to be felt. The question pertaining to brandishing is not whether the law allows gun carrying, but what people actually do, and under what circumstances. When visibly armed citizens appear in public, especially at a public demonstration or other event, it invariably makes news and raises alarm. The earlier examination of historical gun brandishing laws alone provides abundant evidence that public gun carrying engenders fear and that this has been universally understood for hundreds of years.

In modern times, the Black Panthers' armed protests in Sacramento, California, in 1967, armed protesters in Virginia while that state was considering new gun control laws in 2019 and early 2020, and armed demonstrators in numerous state capitals protesting strict quarantine measures in response to the COVID-19 pandemic in 2020 are but a few examples of the dismay and alarm that accompanied those actions and of the public attention these and other incidents received.[50] These incidents are not mere artifacts of subjective "perceptions" or "feelings," but predictable, even inevitable consequences arising from the visible presence of dangerous weapons in public places where others are gathered. Joseph Blocher and Bardia Vaseghi, for example, describe the vanishingly thin line between certain core Second Amendment conduct and torts and crimes like brandishing and assault.[51] Garrett Epps has argued similarly that gun carrying in a public context "is not like words or ideas. It [a gun] is an instrument of violence and death, and its display amid a crowd is a threat."[52]

As noted, our forebears well understood the inherently intimidating nature of weapons display. Two analogous examples will help illustrate how this is more than a matter of mere perception.

---

[49] Christopher Ingraham, *3 Million Americans Carry Loaded Handguns with Them Every Single Day, Study Finds*, WASH. POST, Oct. 19, 2017, https://www.washingtonpost.com/news/wonk/wp/2017/10/19/3-million-americans-carry-loaded-handguns-with-them-every-single-day-study-finds/. Three million divided by roughly 270 million adult Americans is a little over 1 percent. The consequences of concealed gun carry by definition center on its relationship to crime and safety, which is beyond the scope of this chapter. For more on that, *see* Spitzer, *supra* note 41, at 92–107.

[50] David Frum, *The Chilling Effects of Openly Displayed Firearms*, ATLANTIC, Aug. 16, 2017, https://www.theatlantic.com/politics/archive/2017/08/open-carry-laws-mean-charlottesville-could-have-been-graver/537087/.

[51] Blocher & Vaseghi, *supra* note 43.

[52] Garrett Epps, *Guns Are No Mere Symbol*, ATLANTIC, Jan. 21, 2020, https://www.theatlantic.com/ideas/archive/2020/01/guns-are-no-mere-symbol/605239/.

A. Police Interrogation and the Security Dilemma

In 1966, the Supreme Court ruled in *Miranda v. Arizona* that suspects being questioned while in police custody had to be informed of their constitutional rights, including the right to remain silent and to have the assistance of an attorney. The reason police were required to provide these "Miranda rights" to those being interrogated was because, as the Court said, "the very fact of custodial interrogation exacts a heavy toll on individual liberty" and "in-custody interrogation is inherently coercive."[53] Coerced confessions are by definition unreliable and a violation of the protection against self-incrimination. In other words, custodial interrogation, *by its very nature*, is inherently coercive, regardless of the good intentions or friendly demeanor of the police. The same can be said of the presence of guns in a political or public setting. The fact of gun carrying outweighs the stated intention of the carrier, no matter how benign or well intentioned.

Another analogy is found in international relations theory's "security dilemma." This bedrock principle states that the very steps nations take to protect themselves militarily from attack, through arming and fortification, has the perverse effect of ratcheting up the insecurity of other nations. Stated another way, "the means by which a state tries to increase its security decrease[s] the security of others."[54] As international relations expert John J. Mearsheimer observed, "the measures a state takes to increase its own security usually decrease the security of other states."[55] One need not doubt the desire of nations to avoid war and increase their own security to also understand that these good intentions are not sufficient. Intentions and perceptions, relatively speaking, do not matter, because they are eclipsed in the realities of nation-state relations by the factual consequences of military buildups. The same principle applies, with greater force and clarity, to nations that seek or acquire nuclear weapons. Nations like Iran and North Korea have pursued the possession of nuclear weapons, despite the economic and diplomatic costs of doing so, as a potent power resource—not by their use, but by their mere possession.[56] The same logic applies, on a much smaller scale, with firearms. In fact, a recent study confirms this very trend within the United States—escalating violence with a greater likelihood of lethal threats and deaths—in places where few or no restrictions on open gun carrying exist along

---

[53] Miranda v. Arizona, 384 U.S. 436, 455, 533 (1966).
[54] Robert Jervis, *Cooperation Under the Security Dilemma*, 30 WORLD POL. 167, 169 (Jan. 1978).
[55] JOHN J. MEARSHEIMER, THE TRAGEDY OF GREAT POWER POLITICS 36 (2014). *See also* BRUCE RUSSETT, THE PRISONERS OF INSECURITY (1983).
[56] MEARSHEIMER, *supra* note 55, at 129–30; JOSEPH S. NYE, UNDERSTANDING INTERNATIONAL CONFLICTS 61–63 (2009).

with expansive stand your ground laws that allow individuals to employ force, including lethal force, if they feel threatened in public places.[57]

In these instances, the objective circumstances and consequences of the actions taken outweigh the intentions (no matter how noble or even altruistic) of police practices and military policies of nations. The same can be said of the presence of guns in a public or political setting. The fact of gun carrying outweighs the stated intentions of the carrier, no matter how noble or sincere.

B. Gun Owners Know

Considerable evidence supports the proposition that some gun carriers have less than honorable motives. A 2019 nationwide survey of over two thousand gun owners lends inferential support for the proposition that at least some gun owners are drawn to guns precisely because firearms display in a public or political context is intimidating. The survey was designed to assess "the extent to which guns have a symbolic meaning to gun owners." For example, when asked the reason for their gun ownership, most cited personal defense and recreation; 7.9 percent, however, said "to exercise their constitutional rights or to give them a feeling of power." Even more to the point, 15.8 percent of respondents said that guns gave a feeling of "empowerment."[58] A recent study of the meanings given to guns by gun owners identified three distinct assessments of gun meaning: freedom, personal identity, and empowerment. This latter category identifies those who own guns "because they facilitate individual control over one's immediate environment," a sentiment consonant with guns as a source of intimidation, power, and empowerment.[59]

General public opinion data also supports the bifurcation of reactions to gun carrying. One the one hand, those who acquire guns for self-defense—mostly handguns—say that the guns give them a feeling of security or make them feel safer (even among gun owners, however, many oppose or are skeptical of public carrying).[60] Yet when others are asked their reactions to gun possession or gun carrying, the sentiments are invariably negative. For example, in a 2004 Gallup survey of Americans asking how safe they would feel in a "public place" that allowed the concealed carry of firearms, 65 percent said less safe, 25 percent more safe, and 8 percent no difference. When asked who they thought should be

---

[57] Guha Krishnamurthi & Peter Salib, *Small Arms Races*, 6/3/2022 U. CHI. L. REV. ONLINE 1 (2022).
[58] Siegel & Boine, *supra* note 15; JOAN BURBICK, GUN SHOW NATION 91–93 (2006).
[59] Tara D. Warner & Shawn Ratcliff, *What Guns Mean: Who Sees Guns as Important, Essential, and Empowering (and Why)?*, 91 SOC. INQUIRY 313, 332 (2021).
[60] David Hemenway, Sara J. Skolnick, & Deborah R. Azrael, *Firearms and Community Feelings of Safety*, 86 J. CRIM. L. & CRIMINOLOGY 121, 123 (Fall 1995); CARLSON, *supra* note 14, at 130.

allowed to carry concealed firearms in a public place, 44 percent said only "safety officials," 26 percent said only those with a "clear need," and 27 percent said private citizens.[61] A 2017 nationwide survey found even less support for public gun carrying, with between 17 and 33 percent of respondents saying that they favored public gun carrying in various listed public places, with large majorities expressing the opposing view.[62]

C. Hoplophobia Phobia

Some gun rights supporters have sought to belittle the sense of unease or fear of gun possession and carrying felt by others by invidiously labeling it "hoplophobia"—the supposedly irrational fear of guns (despite the clinical-sounding name, the term is not recognized by the American Psychiatric Association[63]). According to self-described "gun fanatic" and author Dan Baum, the term was coined in the 1960s by a military veteran, Jeff Cooper, who wrote on gun topics and taught gun safety. By Baum's account, the supposedly irrational fear of guns by non-gun owners explains why the latter focus on the gun as the culprit to explain terrible shootings. To gun owners, according to Baum, "imbuing an inanimate metal object with that kind of agency seems genuinely crazy," justifying the "phobia" label attributed to those leery of guns, as though such feelings were irrational or unjustifiable. To Baum, hoplophobia "is a pretty good way to delineate differences between what might be called the pro- and anti-gun camps."[64] Baum's comments are typical for those who seek to marginalize, delegitimize, or belittle the fears of non-gun owners.[65]

Baum's (and Cooper's) analysis fails on three grounds. First, it fails to recognize the fact, established here and as recognized in the law going back hundreds of years, that guns pose an inherent threat as soon as they come into contact with humans. The very rules of gun ownership, handling, and use that Baum touts verify this fact. The original five rules, expanded by others, and apparently developed by Cooper, are (or should be) well known to all gun owners: (1) all guns should be treated as though they were loaded; (2) never aim a gun at anything you are not willing to shoot; (3) one's finger should be kept off the trigger until the shooter is ready to shoot; (4) confirm the target and what might be behind it;

---

[61] *Guns*, GALLUP, https://news.gallup.com/poll/1645/guns.aspx.
[62] Julia A. Wolfson et al., *US Public Opinion on Carrying Firearms in Public Places*, 107 AM. J. PUB. HEALTH 929 (2017). Similar polling results date back decades. *See* Spitzer, *supra* note 41, at 106–07.
[63] Timothy Johnson, *Daily Caller Pushes Invented Psychological Disorder to Silence Victims of Gun Violence*, MEDIA MATTERS, May 2, 2013, https://www.mediamatters.org/national-rifle-association/daily-caller-pushes-invented-psychological-disorder-silence-victims-gun.
[64] DAN BAUM, GUN GUYS 151–52 (2013).
[65] SCOTT MELZER, GUN CRUSADERS 133–35 (2009).

and (5) keep control of the firearm.[66] Why treat these simple, inanimate objects with such extraordinary caution if they are simply "inanimate metal objects"? Refrigerators, for example, are inanimate metal objects, too, but hardly require similarly hyper-cautious treatment. The answer is obvious: guns are inherently and uniquely dangerous, a danger that is evident and universal when individuals carry them in a public setting. And while many other objects in daily life cause harm and death, all of them have other, manifest purposes. Guns have one and only one purpose.

The second problem with Baum's analysis is summarized by the "weapons instrumentality effect." This phrase refers to the independent effect of weapon type on crime and the likelihood of injury or death. No interpersonal weapon is more effective in causing injury or death than a gun, and none is easier to use. Numerous studies verify this simple fact, demonstrating, for example, that assaults with guns are five times more likely to result in death than knife assaults (the second most commonly used weapon). The successful completion of robberies is more likely when guns are used as compared with other weapons. Indeed, the mere presence of guns sometimes precipitates violence that would not otherwise occur. These findings extend to firearm homicide, suicide, and accident.[67] Further, emergency room physicians have long chronicled in great detail the uniquely devastating and destructive consequences of gunshot wounds on patients as compared with wounds from other sources or implements.[68]

The third problem is that the gun community knows perfectly well that public gun carrying is inherently intimidating. No better example is found than in the shifting positions of the nation's preeminent gun group, the National Rifle Association (NRA). The NRA has long been leery of open gun carrying in public, yet it had to act cautiously about the question for fear of alienating staunch gun people among its base. In a remarkably frank moment, it explained why in a post on its website in 2014:

---

[66] BAUM, *supra* note 64, at 151. With slight variations, these rules, sometimes expanded in number, are pretty much universal. *See also* NAT'L RIFLE ASS'N, NRA GUIDE TO THE BASICS OF PISTOL SHOOTING 3–8 (2009); Jessie Ann Bourjaily & Phil Bourjaily, *5 Gun Safety Basics to Practice and Pass On*, FIELD & STREAM, Oct. 30, 2019, https://www.fieldandstream.com/5-gun-safety-basics/.

[67] Spitzer, *supra* note 41, at 83–88. The instrumentality effect has been studied from both criminological and medical perspectives. It also explains why the American murder rate is far higher than that of other Western nations, even though our crime rates are otherwise about the same. Unlike other developed nations, guns are far more prolific in the United States and account for over half of all U.S. murders, central to understanding the far greater likelihood of death.

[68] For example, Yasser S. Selman, *Medico-legal Study of Shockwave Damage by High Velocity Missiles in Firearm Injuries*, 53 J. FAC. MED. BAGHDAD 401 (Oct. 2011); Leana Wen, *What Bullets Do to Bodies*, N.Y. TIMES, June 15, 2017, https://www.nytimes.com/2017/06/15/opinion/virginia-baseball-shooting-gun-shot-wounds.html?_r=0; Ryan Hodnick, *Penetrating Trauma Wounds Challenge EMS Providers*, J. EMERGENCY MED. SERVICES, Mar. 30, 2012, https://www.jems.com/patient-care/penetrating-trauma-wounds-challenge-ems/; Sarah Zhang, *What an AR-15 Can Do to the Human Body*, WIRED, June 17, 2016, https://www.wired.com/2016/06/ar-15-can-human-body/.

> Let's not mince words, not only is it [public open gun carrying] rare, it's downright weird and certainly not a practical way to go normally about your business while being prepared to defend yourself. To those who are not acquainted with the dubious practice of using public displays of firearms as a means to draw attention to oneself or one's cause, it can be downright scary. It makes folks who might normally be perfectly open-minded about firearms feel uncomfortable and question the motives of pro-gun advocates.[69]

The NRA rapidly backed away from this statement after angry reactions from some of its supporters, and it has maintained an official position that it supports open carry. Yet the concern it expresses is that of a political realist: people instinctively recoil from the presence of armed civilians in public, therefore impeding the gun rights cause. Far from normalizing the presence of guns, public carrying merely stokes fear and anxiety. The reason: such carrying is threatening per se, by its very nature.

Government officials have reported feeling the same intimidation when confronted with armed civilians in the seat of state government. At least eight states have laws allowing civilian gun carrying in capitol buildings. State legislators in three of those states have moved to restrict such carrying, and for the same reason: they all found such action intimidating when it actually occurred. In fact, Republican leaders in Michigan canceled several legislative sessions in 2020 because armed civilian gun carrying in their chambers was expected.[70]

IV. Conclusion

Whether public gun carriers admit it or not, gun carrying at public events or locations, like those described in this chapter, is by its nature intimidating. Indeed, firearms are carried precisely because they possess this trait.[71] This does not mean that guns in these settings will be fired—they rarely are—or that the carriers have nefarious intentions. But sometimes things go wrong.

In the summer of 2020, Portland, Oregon, was the scene of some of the most intense public demonstrations and counterdemonstrations of the Black Lives

---

[69] Timothy Williams, *N.R.A. Backs Away from Article Criticizing Advocates of Carrying Guns in Public*, N.Y. Times, June 4, 2014, https://www.nytimes.com/2014/06/05/us/nra-backs-away-from-criticism-of-open-carry-advocates.html.

[70] Jennifer Mascia, *"This Isn't Normal: Governing with Guns in the State House*, Trace, Oct. 31, 2020, https://www.thetrace.org/2020/10/michigan-missouri-washington-no-guns-inside-statehouse/.

[71] Robert J. Spitzer, *Why Are People Bringing Guns to Anti-quarantine Protests? To Be Intimidating*, Wash. Post, Aug. 27, 2020, https://www.washingtonpost.com/outlook/2020/04/27/why-are-people-bringing-guns-anti-quarantine-protests-be-intimidating/.

Matter movement. As protests continued, counterprotesters responded with increasing numbers. Some of them came armed with guns. In turn, some of the Black Lives Matter protesters began to do the same. The arrival of firearms escalated tensions—very much like arming escalations between nations discussed earlier. In short order, at the end of August, a self-identified member of Antifa (short for "anti-fascist"), a left-wing movement, allegedly shot and killed a member of a right-wing group called Patriot Prayer. Both men were armed with handguns. The alleged shooter, in turn, was tracked by the police, who then shot and killed him the next day in a nearby city as they attempted to arrest him. Police and witnesses said he displayed and fired his handgun, although that account has been disputed. Before being killed by the police, the man said in an interview that he was armed during the demonstration to provide "security." He explained his shooting of the other man by saying that he was defending himself and another man and that he "had no choice."[72]

Like the fatal shooting incident described at the start of this chapter, the participants stressed positive, even noble motives. But they represent the unspoken endpoint of weapons brandishing. Commenting on the escalating violence and presence of guns in Portland, former acting assistant U.S. Attorney General and now law professor Mary McCord said that the right to peaceful protest is trampled when "you have armed factions ideologically opposed to each other." Another observer referred to it as an "escalating arms race."[73] And the stakes of this problem have now been raised, perhaps dramatically, with the Supreme Court's 2022 decision in *NYSRPA v. Bruen*, in which the Court has now expanded the right of personal self-defense with guns into the public realm.

Recent writing has argued that guns have "agency," suggesting that they are not simply objects indistinguishable from other objects, but that "guns themselves might be active . . . they might have their own 'lives.'"[74] Whether this argument has merit or not, this chapter establishes that, as a matter of history, law, and behavior, public gun carrying, especially in a social or political context, transmits a universally understood message of intimidation. That message is utterly at odds with any notion of free speech and lawful expression in a democratic society. New Hampshire's Republican governor, Chris Sununu, would certainly agree. Re-elected to his post in 2020, he canceled the outdoor inauguration ceremony set for January 2021 because of armed protesters who dogged his trail after

---

[72] John Passantino et al., *Suspect in Fatal Portland Shooting of Right-Wing Activist Killed During Attempted Arrest, US Marshals Say*, CNN, Sept. 4, 2020, https://www.cnn.com/2020/09/04/us/portland-protest-suspected-killer/index.html; Chris Woodyard & Kevin McCoy, *"Arms Race": How the Portland Shooting Shows Protesters on the Right and the Left are Bringing Guns*, USA TODAY, Sept. 4, 2020, https://www.usatoday.com/story/news/2020/09/04/portland-shooting-how-protesters-right-and-left-may-arm-themselves-rallies/5723571002/.
[73] Woodyard & McCoy, *supra* note 72.
[74] THE LIVES OF GUNS 1 (Jonathan Obert, Andrew Poe, & Austin Sarat eds., 2019).

he ordered mandatory pandemic-related mask-wearing in public places. "For weeks," according to the governor, "armed protesters have increasingly become more aggressive, targeting my family, protesting outside my private residence, and trespassing on my property—an outdoor public ceremony simply brings too much risk."[75] In New Hampshire, as in many other places, weapons brandishing had again reared its ugly, undemocratic head.

---

[75] Kathy McCormack, *Governor Cancels Inaugural, Citing Mask Protests at His Home*, AP, Dec. 30, 2020, https://apnews.com/article/arrests-concord-coronavirus-pandemic-new-hampshire-74c5b e34db1e55a287b4b1da4bf89958.

7

THE LIFE SHE SAVES MAY BE HER OWN

THE RADICAL FEMINIST ARGUMENT FOR WOMEN'S GUN-ARMED SELF-DEFENSE

Mary Zeiss Stange

I. INTRODUCTION: A REASONABLE QUESTION?

We begin with a story and then a question. The story is about Yvonne Wanrow.[1] She is a young woman in her early thirties. Native American, born in Washington State. Married fresh out of high school, she and her husband had two children—a son and a daughter—before their marriage ended in divorce. She had ambitions to be a fashion designer and spent some time studying design in San Francisco, thanks to a relocation grant from the Bureau of Indian Affairs. After her young daughter's death from encephalitis, Yvonne and her husband briefly reunited; she bore another daughter, and the family moved to Portland, Oregon. The marriage once again failed, and she relocated with her children to Spokane, where she has family ties. It is in Spokane that her story will take a dark and complicated turn.

Wanrow's personal and family situation—like that of many "relocated" Native Americans—is complex. While she draws welfare and works at whatever odd jobs she can find, a friend named Shirley Hooper babysits Yvonne's children. Hooper has children of her own, and her seven-year-old daughter has contracted a sexually transmitted infection as the result of being molested by a man she refuses, apparently out of fear, to identify. Meanwhile, Shirley has been hearing someone prowling outside her home at night and has found evidence of an attempt to break in.

One summer day, Yvonne Wanrow's son is playing outside with Shirley Hooper's daughter, and a neighbor named William Wesler lures them into his house, with apparent intent to molest one or both of them. The children escape and run to Hooper's home. When she hears their story of what happened,

---

[1] The outlines of Yvonne Wanrow's story, relating to the events of Aug. 11, 1972, are widely available in the legal literature surrounding the case. My source for what follows is State v. Wanrow, 559 P.2d 548 (Wash. 1977).

Mary Zeiss Stange, *The Life She Saves May Be Her Own* In: *New Histories of Gun Rights and Regulation.* Edited by: Joseph Blocher, Jacob D. Charles, and Darrell A.H. Miller, Oxford University Press. © Oxford University Press 2023. DOI: 10.1093/oso/9780197748473.003.0007

Hooper calls the police to report the incident. Wesler shows up at about the same time as the police officers, shouting, "I didn't touch the kid. I didn't touch the kid." Hooper's daughter now identifies Wesler as the man who has sexually abused her. Wesler leaves the scene. Hooper wants him arrested, but the officers say they cannot do that until Monday morning, when the office is open and she can file the requisite forms.

Shirley Hooper then calls Yvonne Wanrow and tells her what has happened. Wanrow urges Shirley to pile Wanrow's children and her own into a taxi and come stay with her. But for some reason the police have told Shirley it would be too dangerous for her to leave home; she should stay and arm herself with a baseball bat so she could "conk him over the head" should Wesler succeed in re-entering the house. So Yvonne Wanrow takes a taxi to Shirley's place. The two women have a chat with Hooper's landlord, who confirms that her daughter was not the first child Wesler has molested and that he has been adjudged mentally ill. Indeed, Wesler has a local reputation for being dangerous to children.

As the night wears on, the two women become increasingly apprehensive about the prospect of Wesler's return. Yvonne calls her sister and brother-in-law, and they come to the house with their three children. All four adults remain awake, alert to any sound of Wesler's return. They are prepared for potential aggression. Yvonne Wanrow has a gun.

In the early morning hours, Wanrow's brother-in-law decides independently to go to Wesler's house and confront him as a pedophile. Wesler has company: he and a friend have been drinking heavily. They agree to go to Hooper's home, ostensibly in order to effect some sort of truce. As Wesler attempts to enter Hooper's home, she shouts at him to stay away. In the commotion that ensues, Yvonne Wanrow's three-year-old nephew wakes up crying. The drunken Wesler smiles at the small child and says, "My, what a cute little boy." He moves toward the child whose mother—Wanrow's sister—reacts with violent emotion. Tempers flare and considerable commotion ensues. At some point, Wesler approaches Yvonne Wanrow from behind, and she is startled to see him when she turns around. As if by reflex, she draws her handgun and shoots twice, killing Wesler and wounding his friend, who escapes.

Shirley Hooper calls 911 to report the shooting. At some point in the conversation, Yvonne Wanrow takes the phone from her. She confesses to the killing. She is not exactly calm, but she is far from hysterical. On the basis of this phone call, which has been recorded and will be used as evidence against her, as well as the fact that she shot and killed an unarmed man, Yvonne Wanrow is arrested for the murder of William Wesler.

Now comes the question—upon which the verdict will hinge: Was Yvonne Wanrow acting reasonably when she drew her pistol and pulled the trigger? In her 1973 trial, she argued the mitigating circumstance that she was acting in self-defense. That is, she believed herself and others present to be in mortal danger. Wanrow herself was disadvantaged by the fact that she had a broken leg, in a cast, and was on crutches. She *had* to act as she did. The all-Caucasian jury did not buy her argument and found her guilty of murder in the second degree and of first-degree assault. That verdict was immediately challenged; the case made its way to the Washington Supreme Court and was then remanded to the Spokane Superior Court for a retrial. Via a plea bargain, Wanrow's counsel, which included William Kunstler, arranged for her to plead guilty to manslaughter. She was sentenced to thirty years in prison, twenty-five of them suspended and the remaining five reduced to probation and community service.

After nearly a decade of litigious torture, Yvonne Wanrow's private hell was over. But her case would not only make, but change, the course of American legal history and practice relating to self-defense. This was all on account of the answer to that disarmingly simple question: Was Yvonne Wanrow acting reasonably when she shot and killed William Wesler? *State v. Wanrow* turned out to be a textbook case of all that was wrong—when issues of gender, race, and class were factored in—with conventional jury instructions regarding self-defense.

II. The Unreasonable "Reasonable Person"

There had, in fact, been numerous irregularities in Wanrow's original trial, but two stood out to the supreme court majority as particularly egregious. One was the use of Wanrow's telephone confession to the police operator as evidence against her. Wanrow had not been informed that the conversation was being recorded, nor did the law typically allow for such recordings to be admissible in court. So that recorded confession was fairly handily dismissed in the supreme court's ruling. It was the second flash point—how the jury had been instructed about the reasonableness of a claim of self-defense—that led the majority of the supreme court justices to dig deeper into the conventional legal theory regarding self-defense.

Any jury must depend upon guidance in the form of explicit instructions from the presiding judge to deliberate fairly the charges it is weighing. In Wanrow's case, the judge went with a pretty standard set of instructions regarding a claim of self-defense. The settled law was black and white when it came to a person's being in immediate danger of severe injury or death. But the gray areas warranted more detailed evaluation:[2]

---

[2] This and the quotations which follow are from the Washington Supreme Court's majority ruling, at 239–41.

> [W]hen there is no reasonable ground for the person attacked to believe that [h]is person is in imminent danger of death or great bodily harm, and it appears to [h]im that only an ordinary battery is all that is intended, and all that [h]e has reasonable grounds to fear from [h]is assailant, [h]e has a right to stand [h]is ground and repel such threatened assault, yet [h]e has no right to repel a threatened assault with naked hands, by the use of a deadly weapon in a deadly manner, unless [h]e believes, [a]nd has reasonable grounds to believe, that [h]e is in imminent danger of death or great bodily harm.[3]

Two things are immediately noteworthy about this passage. One is that its exemplary case is decidedly gendered male—not merely via pronominal reference but also by its reference to barehanded fisticuffs. In addition, it assumes that the person under real or potential attack must make a series of lightning-fast determinations as to the precise level of danger in which he finds himself, and—failing the threat of death or grievous bodily harm—he must, apparently, man up and take a beating, rather than resort to the unfair advantage a weapon might afford him.

The Washington Supreme Court majority found this instruction highly problematic in Wanrow's case. In part, there was the problem of social conditioning, or the lack thereof, when it came to women's ability to fend off violent male attacks. The justices wrote:

> In our society women suffer from a conspicuous lack of access to training in and the means of developing those skills necessary to effectively repel a male assailant without resorting to the use of deadly weapons. [The judge's instruction to the jury] does indicate that the "relative size and strength of the person involved" may be considered; however, it does not make clear that the defendant's actions are to be judged against her own subjective impressions and not those which a detached jury might determine to be objectively reasonable.[4]

It is at this juncture that the "reasonable person" enters the picture. Traditionally, judges would instruct juries to think in terms of what any "reasonable man"—a sort of jurisprudential Everyman—would do in a given situation. By the time of Wanrow's trials—the mid- to late-1970s—the phrasing had shifted to the "reasonable person." Of course, as the instructions regarding a fistfight illustrate, that person might be genderless in the abstract, but was still quite legally male.[5]

---

[3] *Id.* at 558.
[4] *Id.* (citation omitted).
[5] He was also legally Caucasian. The judge in Wanrow's original trial did not allow the defense to introduce expert testimony on the subject of what was then referred to as "battered women

Yet the jury's job is not to adopt the perspective of an abstract ideal, but rather to see through the experience of the defendant. That means, on the one hand, to take into meaningful account factual knowledge about a defendant's real or potential attacker: in Wanrow's case, the facts that Wesler was a known child molester, widely regarded as a dangerous person, had personally committed grievous harm recently to a young girl, and had threatened harm to her and another child that very day. The Washington Supreme Court majority concluded: "[T]he justification of self-defense is to be evaluated in light of [a]ll the facts and circumstances known to the defendant, including those known substantially before the killing."[6] In addition, the jury needed to comprehend Wanrow's situation relative to Wesler's:

> The impression created—that a 5' 4" woman with a cast on her leg and using a crutch must, under the law, somehow repel an assault by a 6' 2" intoxicated man without employing weapons in her defense, unless the jury finds her determination of the degree of danger to be objectively reasonable—constitutes a separate and distinct misstatement of the law and, in the context of this case, violates the respondent's right to equal protection of the law. The respondent was entitled to have the jury consider her actions in the light of her own perceptions of the situation, including those perceptions which were the product of our nation's "long and unfortunate history of sex discrimination."[7]

The appeal to equal protection under the law is the crucial point here. The justices concluded that until the injustices of a history of gender inequality are eradicated, "care must be taken to assure that our self-defense instructions afford women the right to have their conduct judged in light of the individual physical handicaps which are the product of sex discrimination. To fail to do so," they concluded, "is to deny the right of the individual woman involved to trial by the same rules which are applicable to male defendants."[8]

Of course, such denial of equal rights had long been a fact in the American common law tradition. To get at its roots, one must go back to Blackstone's *Commentaries on the Laws of England*, the compendium published in the

---

syndrome" and the concomitant subordination of women in American society, nor did he allow testimony on the social conditioning of Native Americans relative to the dominant White culture.

[6] State v. Wanrow, *supra* note 1, at 555.

[7] *Id.* at 558–59 (citation and quotation marks omitted).

[8] *Id.* at 559 (citation omitted). It is worth noting in this context that in her original trial, Wanrow's attorneys were not allowed to introduce information about anti-Native racism and the various ways in which Native Americans are disadvantaged in American society. The role of racism and sexism in the development of language surrounding "the reasonable person" is of major significance here. So, too, was the fact that her jury was all-White.

mid-eighteenth century that served as the foundational authority on British, and subsequently American, common law. When it came to the relative legal rights of males and females, Blackstone enshrined the doctrine of coverture, which gave total advantage to males, particularly those of dominant groups. Blackstone himself was merely theorizing legal, social, and ethical structures that, in their turn, had been centuries—in some cases millennia—in the making. Of course, in the English-speaking world, his imprimatur gave them that much more authority, moving into the modern period. But the material with which Blackstone had to work went back at least as far as Aristotle.

III. Women's Fundamental Inequality: An Old, Old Story

Given the limitations of space for this chapter, and perhaps just as fortunately, we may here suffice by summarizing, in fairly broad terms, the dominant ideas about appropriate gender relations that developed in the Western world and provided theoretical justifications for the structure of that world, directly impacting attitudes regarding women's self-defense. These ideas are as follows:

- From human prehistory forward, there appears to have been a presumption that tool manufacture and use was by and large the prerogative of men. This was especially the case when the tool in question could also function as a weapon.
- Women were, from ancient Greece forward, perceived to be both physiologically and intellectually inferior to men—in all respects, the weaker sex. They were therefore generally denied access to education, of both mind and body.
- The male's sphere of activity and influence was the world external to the home, the female's internal. Her primary role was to bear and raise the male's children.
- From ancient Israel came the idea of monotheism with the correlative idea of the centralization of power, on all levels and mutually reinforcing: one (male) god, one human ruler, the male as head of household. And what powers females had were largely subsumed by those of superior males. In John Milton's phrasing, "[He] for God only, [she] for God in him."[9]
- The male-headed heterosexual family (monogamous or polygamous, depending upon context) constituted the primary social unit.

---

[9] John Milton, Paradise Lost, bk. 4, l. 299.

- However else it might be defined in terms ranging from the romantic to the pragmatic, marriage was primarily a way of controlling and transferring property. Chief among a man's property were his wife or wives, his children, and (anciently) his slaves.

All of which brings us to Blackstone, for whom a major question at hand was that of the legal personhood of women. "Unattached" women had some rights: to property, to inheritance, to certain legal claims. But what about married women? Based upon centuries of precedent and his well-informed analysis of the legal facts of connubial life, Blackstone decided that "the very being or legal existence of the woman is suspended during the marriage, or at least is incorporated and consolidated into that of the husband: under whose wing, protection, and *cover*, she performs everything."[10] There can be in marriage only one person, and that person is the husband. The wife's identity—call it what you will: "suspended," "incorporated," or "consolidated"—is essentially that of a nonentity. In exchange for her husband's "protection," she renders services, sexual and otherwise. Coverture was a transactional understanding of gender relations within marriage, but the transaction was strictly, and irrevocably, a one-way affair. Nonconforming women risked being beaten into line by their husbands. The idea of "domestic chastisement" as an appropriate responsibility—indeed, a duty—for the husband-as-master was another key aspect of coverture, and one that can be traced back, historically, to the Inquisition.

In such a context, the legality of violence against women, and particularly sexual violence, was extremely problematic. Because sexual service was something the wife owed to the husband as part of her marriage contract, "marital rape" was necessarily a contradiction in terms. Logically, and legally, a husband could not rape his wife. And were another man to rape her, that act would constitute a crime against the husband, who was now, as it were, stuck with damaged property. Were the rape victim a daughter of his, and her attacker unmarried, things might be made right by marrying the daughter to her rapist. This twisted idea of making an "honest woman" out of a rape victim dated back to medieval Christian penitential literature. And it derives in large part from a traditional suspicion about female sexuality that is as old as the Lady Eve.

The male-dominated Western cultural tradition celebrates chastity and virginity because of a deeply intertwined mistrust, and accompanying fear, of unbridled female sexuality. We see it everywhere today: in the continuing penchant for blaming the victim in rape cases, in the political right's obsession with the

---

[10] Caroline Light, Stand Your Ground: A History of America's Love Affair with Lethal Force Self-defense 21 (2017) (quoting 1 W. Blackstone, Commentaries, *430 (1765)) (emphasis added).

control of women's reproductive lives and decisions, and most recently in the conservative backlash against the "Me Too" women's movement that took the nation more or less by surprise in late 2017.

The news, in the latter regard, was that women—of all walks of life and political affiliations—were finally, actively taking control of the discourse surrounding sexual abuses ranging from offensive and ill-conceived jokes to various degrees of sexual impropriety and assault. Something had changed in American law and society—something that Sir William Blackstone would neither approve nor understand. Nor would he have a legal theory to explain or contain this new spin on women's inviolable chastity as a form of self-defense.

But as new, and potentially transformative, as the "Me Too" movement appeared, it did not by any means happen overnight. The push for actively resisting male sexual aggression in all its forms actually began in earnest within radical second-wave feminism. And its primary theorists' focus was the question raised most pointedly, during that era, by Yvonne Wanrow's case: the question of the appropriateness of women's gun-armed, lethal force self-defense.

IV. "How Dare You Assume I'm Non-Violent?"

In her 1993 book *Fire with Fire,* Naomi Wolf—herself by no means a radical feminist—drew considerable heat from the liberal feminist sisterhood when, reflecting on a documented increase in the number of women buying firearms for self-defense, she advanced the following argument:

> I don't want to carry a gun or endorse gun proliferation. But I am happy to benefit from publicizing the fact that an attacker's prospective victim has a good chance of being armed. . . . Our cities and towns can be plastered with announcements that read, "A hundred women in this town are trained in combat. They may be nurses, students, housewives, prostitutes, mothers. The next woman to be assaulted may be one of these."[11]

Wolf was here reflecting upon trends in increasing female gun ownership and use over roughly the previous twenty years. Women's access to and use of firearms actually formed part of a much larger picture. It was clear that, as we approached the dawn of a new millennium, there were going to be some changes made in conventional gender roles and relationships across the board. Women were now entering previously male-dominated professions in record numbers, and

---

[11] Naomi Wolf, Fire with Fire: The New Female Power and How It Will Change the 21st Century 315 (1993).

they looked to be changing both the culture and the rules of those professions. Women possessed more disposable income than ever before, and when it came to marriage and family relationships, more women were going it on their own. Even among those who were in satisfying relationships with men, there was far less inclination to see those men as their saviors or protectors.

At the same time that these women were enjoying opportunities and freedoms largely unimagined by their mothers or grandmothers, the late twentieth century was experiencing a marked upsurge in violent crimes against women. Arguably, the more "liberated" a woman experienced her life to be, the more likely she was to live in a state of what sociologists Margaret Gordon and Stephanie Rigor called "the female fear": a pervasive and ever-present awareness of the potential of sexual assault, coupled with the negative social and economic consequences of this awareness.[12] It was against this backdrop that Wolf spun her fantasy of armed women taking up guns in defense of their neighborhoods, their sisters, themselves.

Perhaps not surprisingly, the quoted *Fire with Fire* passage was one of the most oft-quoted passages in reviews of Wolf's book—most of which, outside of the "hook and bullet" press, ranged from mixed to ambivalent when it came to Wolf's ideal of a "new power feminism."

Was the woman out of her mind? The editors of *Ms.* magazine certainly seemed to think so when they enlisted Ann Jones—herself the author of several books about violence against women, including *Women Who Kill*—to write a review of Wolf's book. Jones put Wolf down as a "popular, state-of-the-art, so-called feminist" with a fascination for the "pistol-packin' mamas" of the National Rifle Association. Of no small significance was the fact that, a mere three months earlier, Wolf had herself graced the cover of *Ms.* in an issue devoted to diversity in feminist thought. When it came to guns, diversity apparently had its limits. Indeed, it's fair to say that the liberal line of thinking that dominated so much of second-wave feminist theory and practice was universally opposed to the notion of women arming themselves—in self-defense or for pretty much any other reason. Guns were thoroughly associated with masculinity and, as in the line from Audre Lorde, quoted so often as to become a sort of mantra in feminist circles, one could not "dismantle the master's house" by using "the master's tools."[13]

Gun-slinging—even in imagination—was clearly behavior unbecoming for a card-carrying feminist. And yet, those same feminists who rejected firearms as symbols and tools of male power could be observed cheering wildly at the

---

[12] *See generally* Margaret T. Gordon & Stephanie Riger, The Female Fear: The Social Cost of Rape (1989).

[13] Audre Lorde, *The Master's Tools Will Never Dismantle the Master's House*, *in* The Glorious American Essay 775–78 (Phillip Lopate ed., 2020).

1991 film *Thelma & Louise*. Callie Khouri, that film's screenwriter, had quipped at the time that Thelma and Louise were not intended to be role models.[14] But they were provocative models of female power and feminist anger. The trick, of course, was not to take such fantasies literally.

Two years earlier, writing in *The Nation*, Ms. magazine cofounder Letty Cottin Pogrebin had struck a similar note. Writing in response to the popularity of Smith & Wesson's then recently reintroduced women's handgun, the LadySmith, Pogrebin observed that while "fantasies of female power and revenge may be seductive," women should resist them for their own good.[15] Guns designed for women were "neither pink nor cute." They could do serious damage; it was just best for women to stay away from them.

The interesting question here was, why? Pogrebin admitted that she had been "surprised" by her own gut reaction to the very idea of the LadySmith. "I'm for gun control and nonviolent conflict resolution," she wrote, "yet suddenly I imagined every woman armed, powerful and instantly equalized . . . POW—one less pervert; BANG—another rapist blown away . . . pistol-packin' mamas will fight back: ZAP—victims no more."[16] But then, Pogrebin recounts, she came to her liberal feminist senses and imagined "more likely scenarios" involving women and guns:

> *They shoot a lover or spouse in the heat of a quarrel, or are shot themselves.*
> *They are overwhelmed by a stronger assailant who turns the gun against them.*
> *Their child finds the gun and thinks it is a toy.*
> *They hear noises, panic, forget all safety instructions and shoot someone who is not an intruder.*
> *They overreact and shoot someone who could have been verbally restrained or pacified.*
> *They shoot when they could have chosen to escape.*
> *They shoot and harm an innocent bystander.*
> *Their gun discharges accidentally, or misfires.*
> *They get depressed and shoot themselves.*[17]

What is noteworthy about this gun-averse litany is the degree to which a major voice of second-wave feminism is here willing to accept—indeed, to promote—images of women that stress their instability and ineptitude, the likelihood that

---

[14] Larry Rohter, *The Third Woman of "Thelma and Louise,"* N.Y. TIMES, June 5, 1991, at C21, https://www.nytimes.com/1991/06/05/movies/the-third-woman-of-thelma-and-louise.html.

[15] MARY ZEISS STANGE & CAROL K. OYSTER, GUN WOMEN: FIREARMS AND FEMINISM IN CONTEMPORARY AMERICA 34 (2000), *quoting* Letty Cotton Pogrebin, *Neither Pink Nor Cute: Pistols for the Women of America*, THE NATION (1989).

[16] *Id.* at 35.

[17] *Id.*

they will panic or overreact, and make some sort of tragically stupid mistake. These are images of women that, in any other context, Pogrebin would have rightly and righteously been among the first to reject. Best, however, not to venture into that thorny territory. If the logic about the master's tools felt too uncomfortable when the subject was the possibility of women's possibly affirmative relationships with firearms, one could salve one's conscience by remembering that this was one area where the vast majority of Americans could agree with the majority of feminists. As Peggy Tartaro, the editor of *Women & Guns* magazine, had quipped about the question of a pro-gun feminism: in the popular perception of the general public, any gun-armed woman is "both Thelma *and* Louise on a very bad day, and dangerous to everyone within a 50-mile radius."[18]

Poor Naomi Wolf had made the mistake of taking the idea—if not entirely the fact—of gun-armed women seriously. She paid for it in the liberal feminist press, because that brand of feminism—and it was the dominant brand from the 1970s through the early 1990s—was concerned primarily with working within the system, ultimately to transform it. That meant coloring within certain lines that had been laid down by two centuries of liberal political philosophy.

However, there was another emergent wing of feminism that wanted not simply to dismantle the master's house, but to burn it down. In her hypothetical, based as it was in a real world of real women who were really buying firearms in apparently record numbers, Wolf had taken a pretty deep, if somewhat unintentional, dive into the radical feminist end of the pool.

Historians of the women's movement have most frequently characterized the radical feminists of the 1970s and '80s as a bunch of goddess-worshipping, politically lesbian, earth mothers. And so they were. They were also the activists who trained the spotlight on the fact that, as Adrienne Rich phrased it, "the woman's body is the terrain on which patriarchy is erected"; and sexual violence against women was key among the master's tools.[19] As legal scholars Don B. Kates and Carol Silver wrote, in light of radical activism, "musings about better solutions are of very little aid to a woman who is being strangled or beaten to death."[20] Not coincidentally, this was the generation of feminists who created the first rape crisis hotlines, domestic violence centers, and women's shelters. While some other feminists theorized about the necessary connection between theory and practice, these women lived that connection. As one of them, Catharine MacKinnon,

---

[18] *Id.* at 26 (emphasis added) (citation omitted).
[19] ADRIENNE RICH, OF WOMAN BORN: MOTHERHOOD AS EXPERIENCE AND INSTITUTION 55 (1976).
[20] GUNS IN AMERICA: A READER 372 (Jan E. Dizard, Robert Merril Muth, & Stephen P. Andrews eds., 1999).

has remarked: "It is common to say that something is good in theory but not in practice. I always want to say, then it is not such a good theory, is it?"[21]

Central to that theorizing was the patriarchal attack on, and control of, women's bodies. And the concomitant question: How are women to defend themselves? The answer seemed blindingly obvious: by any means necessary. And it is this theme that runs throughout the radical theorizing of the later twentieth century.

Catharine MacKinnon, for example, with regard to the rape of Muslim girls in Serbia by U.N. forces ostensibly there to protect them, observed:

> It pointedly poses a problem women have always had with male protection: who is going to watch the men who are watching the men who are supposedly watching out for us? Each layer of male protection adds a layer to violence against women. Perhaps intervention by a force of armed women should be considered.[22]

MacKinnon's colleague Andrea Dworkin struck a kindred note, but with more of a focus on women's learned helplessness and self-blame:

> Women don't understand self-defense the way men do—perhaps because sexual abuse destroys the self. We don't feel we have a right to kill, just because we are being beaten, raped, tortured and terrorized. We are hurt for a long time before we fight back. Then, usually, we are punished.[23]

In a trenchant essay titled "In Memory of Nicole Brown Simpson," Dworkin reflects, "You won't ever know the worst that happened to Nicole Brown Simpson in her marriage, because she is dead and cannot tell you. And if she were alive, remember, you wouldn't believe her."[24] Citing Malcolm X, Dworkin goes on to argue that, as the system protects batterers and punishes women who fight back against abuse, batterers must be stopped by any means necessary. Dworkin concludes that a battered woman has the right to stop the batterer "by law or force—before she's dead."[25] Writing before *Heller*, Dworkin continued:

---

[21] Catharine A. McKinnon, *From Practice to Theory, or What Is a White Woman Anyway?*, 4 YALE J.L. & FEM. 13, 13 (2015).

[22] *Rape, Genocide, and Women's Human Rights*, in VIOLENCE AGAINST WOMEN: PHILOSOPHICAL PERSPECTIVES 51 (Stanley G. French, Wanda Teays, & Laura M. Purdy eds., 1998).

[23] ANDREA DWORKIN, PORNOGRAPHY: MEN POSSESSING WOMEN, at xxiv (1981).

[24] Andrea Dworkin, *In Memory of Nicole Brown Simpson*, in LIFE AND DEATH: UNAPOLOGETIC WRITINGS ON THE CONTINUING WAR AGAINST WOMEN 41 (1997).

[25] *Id.* at 50.

She has a constitutional right to a gun and a legal right to kill if she believes she's going to be killed. And a batterer's repeated assaults should lawfully be taken as intent to kill.[26]

Dworkin is here following the same logic as had the Washington Supreme Court in its review of *Wanrow*. Women's self-defense involves a leap of imagination, and of self-definition, that is of profound importance. Women need to experience their lives and selves as worth fighting for, and themselves as willing and able to fight.

This of course means breaking some powerful, and deeply internalized, social and cultural taboos relating to women and violence. Radical activists Tara Baxter and Nikki Craft discovered this when they tried, and failed, to find a publisher for their co-authored review essay about the rabidly misogynistic novel *American Psycho*. The essay bore the wonderful title "There Are Other Ways of Taking Care of Bret Easton Ellis than Just Censoring Him ..." Editor after editor of feminist journals rejected it because it "focused on imagery and advocacy of violence by women against men,"[27] and "printing it might only escalate the violence pandemic among us." What Baxter and Craft were actually focusing on, of course, was the fundamental idea that women can, and should, take an aggressive role in their own self-protection against violent assault.

Baxter and Craft went on to argue more pointedly for women's arming themselves with guns. If a firearm could function as the quintessential symbol of male power, it might equally symbolize female resistance to male aggression. They began marketing buttons and t-shirts bearing messages like "So Many Men, So Little Ammunition," "Feminine Protection (accompanied by a picture of a gun)," "The Best Way to a Man's Heart Is Through His Chest," "How Dare You Assume I'm Non-Violent?," and a revision of the old Colt motto: "God created Man and Woman, Sam Colt Made Them Equal."

There remains the liberal feminist objection: Perhaps there may be times when a woman needs to resort to some form of violence to save herself or her loved ones from harm. But why can, or should, lethal force self-defense be construed as a feminist act?[28] The most cogent response to this question was provided by D.A. Clarke, in an oft-reprinted essay entitled "A Woman with a Sword: Some Thoughts on Women, Feminism, and Violence," originally published in 1993. Remarking that "[h]istorically, the prospect for peoples and cultures which avoid violence is not good," Clarke cogently argues that adopting a stance of nonviolent

---

[26] *Id.*
[27] Tara Baxter & Nikki Craft, *There are Better Ways of Taking Care of Bret Easton Ellis Than Just Censoring Him ...*, in MAKING VIOLENCE SEXY: FEMINIST VIEWS ON PORNOGRAPHY 245–53 (Diana E.H. Russell ed., 1993).
[28] This is essentially Ann Jones's argument against Wolf.

resistance is an empty gesture if the person or group making it is perceived as being incapable of genuine aggression in the first place.[29] Ironically, then, feminist nonviolence can only make sense as a political and ethical position to the extent that women are willing to engage in violent resistance against aggression. Clarke's rationale:

> If the risk involved in attacking a woman were greater, there might be fewer attacks. If women defended themselves violently, the amount of damage they were willing to do to would-be assailants would be the measure of their seriousness about the limits beyond which they would not be pushed. If more women killed husbands and boyfriends who abused them or their children, perhaps there would be less abuse. A large number of women refusing to be pushed any further would erode, however slowly, the myth of the masochistic female which threatens all our lives.[30]

If history is any indicator, the radical feminist argument goes, every woman at risk should be able to exercise her human right to self-defense, in whatever form that takes, and to count on support from her feminist sisters. The life she is fighting for, after all, is not simply her own.

V. Reasonable Women

It is no mere coincidence that Yvonne Wanrow's legal drama played itself out against the backdrop of such radical feminist assertions about women's ability—and their right—to resort, when circumstances warrant, to lethal force self-defense. Nor was it coincidental that her case attracted the attention of attorneys William Kunstler (who argued it) and Don B. Kates (who wrote about it). Kunstler had a well-deserved reputation for being, as the *New York Times* phrased it in his obituary, a "lawyer for social outcasts."[31] Kates's work on firearms law earned him the title, "The Johnnie Cochran of the Second Amendment." Kunstler's human rights work had led him to the Civil Rights South in the 1960s, where, for a time, Kates worked with him. These men were risk-takers, both in terms of the clients they represented and in the arguments they framed in defense of unpopular positions. And both recognized the direct connections between gender oppression and other, mutually reinforcing, forms of discrimination. Arguably, they

---

[29] Stange & Oyster, *supra* note 15, at 43.
[30] *Id.* at 44–45.
[31] David Stout, *William Kunstler, 76, Dies; Lawyer for Social Outcasts*, N.Y. Times, Sept. 5, 1995, at B6, https://www.nytimes.com/1995/09/05/obituaries/william-kunstler-76-dies-lawyer-for-social-outcasts.html.

went on to inspire a generation of younger legal minds, reasonable women and men, who are carving out new pathways toward genuine equality under the law. That said, we still have a long way to go on the road Yvonne Wanrow opened up for us.

The structural similarities between domestic violence and political oppression are clear and convincing. So too are the facts that in each case not only must women's lives be seen as worth fighting—and yes, even killing—for. For today's feminist jurists and equal rights activists, this means working to transform legal and social structures in such a way that "woman" becomes a name of a way of being fully human. Among other things, this means creating contexts wherein those experiences women share with one another—rooted in reproductive issues and in pervasive violence against women—will not be allowed to drift off the legal radar screen. It also means appreciating that change as massive as what the *Wanrow* case initiated, and that the "Me Too" movement carries forward, will necessarily be gradual and incremental.

But in the meantime—and given the pace of real social change, it promises to be a long meantime—every woman at risk should be able to exercise her human right to self-defense, in whatever form it takes, and to count on the support of her feminist sisters. The life she is fighting for is not simply her own. And the force she is fighting against is simultaneously as small as the man whose masculinity depends upon the rape and abuse of women and children, and as large as the state that continues to let him get away with it.

8
Historical Gun Laws Targeting "Dangerous" Groups and Outsiders

Joseph Blocher and Caitlan Carberry

I. Introduction

Then judge Amy Coney Barrett opened her dissent in *Kanter v. Barr* by identifying a historical principle underlying modern gun regulation: "History is consistent with common sense: it demonstrates that legislatures have the power to prohibit dangerous people from possessing guns."[1] She went on to suggest that dangerousness is the Second Amendment's exclusive limiting principle, such that "legislatures disqualified categories of people from the right to bear arms *only* when they judged that doing so was necessary to protect the public safety."[2]

This is a historically contestable position.[3] But *if* "dangerousness" is the operative principle for historically informed Second Amendment interpretation, how broadly does it sweep? In Barrett's terms, what do "history and tradition" tell us about the "scope of the legislature's power to take [the right to keep and bear arms] away?"[4] Answering that question means considering "a category simultaneously broader and narrower than 'felons'—it includes dangerous people who have not been convicted of felonies but not felons lacking indicia of dangerousness."[5] In her *Kanter* dissent (which argued that the federal felon prohibitor was unconstitutional as applied to a nonviolent felon), Judge Barrett focused on

---

[1] 919 F.3d 437, 454 (7th Cir. 2019) (Barrett, J., dissenting).
[2] *Id.* at 451 (Barrett, J., dissenting) (emphasis added).
[3] *See, e.g.*, Binderup v. Att'y Gen., 836 F.3d 336, 348 (3d Cir. 2016); United States v. Carpio-Leon, 701 F.3d 974, 980 (4th Cir. 2012) ("[F]elons 'were excluded from the right to arms' because they were deemed unvirtuous."); United States v. Yancey, 621 F.3d 681, 684–85 (7th Cir. 2010) ("[M]ost scholars of the Second Amendment agree that the right to bear arms was tied to the concept of a virtuous citizenry and that, accordingly, the government could disarm 'unvirtuous citizens.'"); United States v. Vongxay, 594 F.3d 1111, 1118 (9th Cir. 2010) (observing scholarly consensus "that the right to bear arms was 'inextricably . . . tied to' the concept of a 'virtuous citizen[ry]'"); United States v. Rene E., 583 F.3d 8, 15 (1st Cir. 2009) ("In the parlance of the republican politics of the time, these limitations were sometimes expressed as efforts to disarm the 'unvirtuous.'").
[4] *Kanter*, 919 F.3d at 452 (Barrett, J., dissenting).
[5] *Id.* at 454 (Barrett, J., dissenting).

the latter—felons who might not be dangerous. In this chapter, we focus on the former: non-felon groups disarmed because they were thought to be dangerous.

The historical evidence demonstrates that the "scope of the legislature's power" was quite broad, notwithstanding the fact that the founding generations applied that power to very different groups than law does today—both more narrowly (for example, by *not* disarming domestic abusers[6]) and more broadly.

We focus on two sets of historical gun laws that seem historically distant, but which the "dangerousness" approach makes relevant: laws regulating sales to Native Americans and laws regulating possession by those "disaffected to the cause of America." These groups—much more so than felons,[7] drug users, domestic abusers,[8] and other groups targeted by contemporary restrictions[9]—were subject to gun regulation by the founding generations, apparently based on the perceived threat they posed. Relying largely on the Repository of Historical Gun Laws, an online database maintained by the Center for Firearms Law at Duke Law School,[10] the second part of this chapter provides a historical overview of these laws, which have not received the same level of scholarly attention as some other historical prohibitions, such as those involving public carry or certain classes of arms.[11]

Comparing these historical laws to contemporary gun restrictions inevitably means reasoning by analogy—which is the centerpiece of the new Second Amendment methodology embraced by the Supreme Court in *New York State Rifle & Pistol Association v. Bruen*.[12] The Court held that "when the Second Amendment's plain text covers an individual's conduct . . . the government must demonstrate that the regulation is consistent with this Nation's historical tradition of firearm regulation."[13]

---

[6] Carolyn B. Ramsey, *Firearms in the Family*, 78 Ohio St. L.J. 1257, 1301 (2017).

[7] *See, e.g.*, United States v. Skoien, 614 F.3d 638, 650 (7th Cir. 2010) (en banc) (Sykes, J., dissenting) (noting that scholars "disagree about the extent to which felons . . . were considered excluded from the right to bear arms during the founding era" and that "[t]he historical evidence is inconclusive at best").

[8] *See, e.g., id.* at 642, 644 (discussing risk of future violence as a basis for denying domestic abusers access to firearms).

[9] 18 U.S.C. § 922(d) (2018) (enumerating classes of persons to whom it is unlawful to sell firearms, including anyone who is an "unlawful user of or addicted to any controlled substance" or who "has been convicted in any court of a misdemeanor crime of domestic violence").

[10] *Repository of Historical Gun Laws*, Duke Center for Firearms Law, https://firearmslaw.duke.edu/repository (last visited June 12, 2020).

[11] *See, e.g.*, Patrick J. Charles, *The Faces of the Second Amendment Outside the Home: History Versus Ahistorical Standards of Review*, 60 Clev. St. L. Rev. 1 (2012); David B. Kopel, *The History of Firearm Magazines and Magazine Prohibitions*, 78 Alb. L. Rev. 849 (2015).

[12] 142 S. Ct. 2111 (2022). As the majority recognizes—indeed, repeatedly emphasizes—application of its new methodology will come down not simply to identifying historical examples but to making analogies. Notably, the *Bruen* majority uses versions of the word "analogy" nearly thirty times.

[13] *Id.* at 2126.

The key step in analogical reasoning is identifying whether two things are *relevantly* similar,[14] a process that is hard—and perhaps even impossible—to fully articulate given the invisible abstractions and generalizations that underlie it.[15] Many scholars, including those sympathetic to broad gun rights, have noted some of the difficulties that arise when one looks for historical equivalents of modern laws.[16] But at the very least, a "dangerousness" approach to text, history, and tradition must mean identifying the groups that were disarmed on that basis either in the founding era or during Reconstruction.[17]

The third part of the chapter grapples with a question such regulations raise: What is to be done with the many historical laws that lack modern equivalents? Second Amendment historicism sometimes directs us to the family tree of gun laws in order to identify "lineal descendants" of particular guns or gun laws.[18] But what about the lines of regulation that died out for one reason or another?[19] Should embarrassing ancestors be cropped out of the historical picture entirely, or might they still have something to teach, in roughly the same way as *Dred Scott v. Sandford*[20] has been invoked to support the "individual right" reading of the Second Amendment?[21]

In some form or another, history is and will remain relevant to the question of whose access to guns can constitutionally be limited. Whether the answer to that question turns on a group's dangerousness,[22] virtuousness,[23]

---

[14] *See* Cass R. Sunstein, *On Analogical Reasoning*, 106 Harv. L. Rev. 744, 745 (1993).

[15] Frederick Schauer, *Analogy in the Supreme Court: Lozman v. City of Riviera Beach, Florida, 2013* Sup. Ct. Rev. 405, 422 (2014) (noting that people "draw their analogies... often without ever going to or even seeing the level of abstraction or generalization that... undergirds their judgments...."); *see also* Edward H. Levi, An Introduction to Legal Reasoning 2 (1949) ("The finding of similarity or difference is the key step in the legal process."); Lloyd L. Weinreb, Legal Reason: The Use of Analogy in Legal Argument 4–5 (2005); Scott Brewer, *Exemplary Reasoning: Semantics, Pragmatics, and the Rational Force of Legal Argument by Analogy*, 109 Harv. L. Rev. 923, 925 (1996).

[16] *See, e.g.*, Nelson Lund, *The Proper Role of History and Tradition in Second Amendment Jurisprudence*, 30 U. Fla. J.L. & Pub. Pol'y 1, 26 (2020).

[17] As with other incorporated rights, in cases involving challenges to state and local laws—which are subject to the Second Amendment through operation of the Fourteenth—the relevant era for historical analysis is arguably the 1860s rather than the late 1700s.

[18] Heller v. District of Columbia (*Heller II*), 670 F.3d 1244, 1275 (D.C. Cir. 2011) (Kavanaugh, J., dissenting) (quoting Transcript of Oral Argument at 77, District of Columbia v. Heller, 554 U.S. 570 (2008) (No. 07-290) (question of Roberts, C.J.)); *see also* Parker v. District of Columbia, 478 F.3d 370, 398 (D.C. Cir. 2007) (referring to "lineal descendant[s]" of firearms), *aff'd sub nom.* Heller, 554 U.S. 570.

[19] For an exploration of a similar theme, *see* Darrell A. H. Miller, *Second Amendment Traditionalism and Desuetude*, 14 Geo. J.L. & Pub. Pol'y 223 (2016).

[20] Dred Scott v. Sandford, 60 U.S. 393 (1857).

[21] Parker v. District of Columbia, 478 F.3d 370, 391 (D.C. Cir. 2007) (citing *Dred Scott*, 60 U.S. at 417), *aff'd sub nom.* District of Columbia v. Heller, 554 U.S. 570 (2008). *See also* Silveira v. Lockyer, 328 F.3d 567, 569 (9th Cir. 2003) (Kozinski, J., dissenting); United States v. Emerson, 270 F.3d 203, 228–29 (5th Cir. 2001).

[22] *Id.* at 454 (Barrett, J., dissenting).

[23] *See, e.g.*, Don. B. Kates Jr., *The Second Amendment: A Dialogue*, 49 Law & Contemp. Probs. 143, 146 (1986) ("[T]he right to arms does not preclude laws disarming the unvirtuous citizens (i.e., criminals) or those who, like children or the mentally unbalanced, are deemed incapable of virtue.").

either,[24] responsibility,[25] or some other principle is beyond the scope of this chapter. We assume that dangerousness was at least *one* reason why certain groups were disarmed. But whatever approach one takes, it is important to be clear about the historical record and the breadth of the government's power to regulate. For that, one must look to the laws that actually existed at the time of the founding, to which we now turn.

II. Regulations Targeting Dangerous Groups and Outsiders

Modern gun laws regulate—with varying degrees of severity—the who, what, when, where, and how of arms-bearing.[26] Our focus in this chapter is on "who" restrictions: those reaching a particular class of persons. Evaluating the constitutionality of such regulations through a historical lens provides a useful illustration of two contrasting approaches described earlier: one starting with contemporary prohibitions and looking for historical equivalents, and the other starting with historical prohibitions and considering their contemporary relevance.

In contemporary litigation, the two most prominent categories of "who" bans are those involving felons and the mentally ill. Felon cases, for example, make up about a quarter of post-*Heller* Second Amendment challenges,[27] so courts have understandably focused a great deal of attention on historical predecessors of the felon prohibitor. *Heller* described laws involving felons (and the mentally ill) as "longstanding" and therefore "presumptively lawful,"[28] and courts have overwhelmingly upheld them.[29] But the historical record as to these categories is not nearly as clear as one might suppose,[30] which means courts often look to a higher

---

[24] *See, e.g.*, Medina v. Whitaker, 913 F.3d 152, 158–59 (D.C. Cir. 2019) (suggesting that either dangerousness or lack of virtue could justify a ban), *cert. denied, sub nom.* Medina v. Barr, 140 S. Ct. 645 (2019).

[25] *See, e.g.*, United States v. Bena, 664 F.3d 1180, 1183 (8th Cir. 2011) (noting historical regulation of citizens who are not "responsible").

[26] *See* Eugene Volokh, *Implementing the Right to Keep and Bear Arms for Self-Defense: An Analytical Framework and a Research Agenda*, 56 UCLA L. Rev. 1443 (2009).

[27] Eric Ruben & Joseph Blocher, *From Theory to Doctrine: An Empirical Analysis of the Right to Keep and Bear Arms After* Heller, 67 Duke L.J. 1433, 1481 (2018) (noting that challenges to felon-in-possession statutes accounted for nearly a quarter of the roughly one thousand challenges studied).

[28] District of Columbia v. Heller, 554 U.S. 570, 626–27, 627 n.26 (2008).

[29] *See* Ruben & Blocher, *supra* note 27, at 1481 (noting that 99% of felon-in-possession challenges since *Heller* have failed).

[30] For a prominent skeptical conclusion, *see* C. Kevin Marshall, *Why Can't Martha Stewart Have a Gun?*, 32 Harv. J.L. & Pub. Pol'y 695, 708 (2009) ("Though recognizing the hazard of trying to prove a negative, one can with a good degree of confidence say that bans on convicts possessing firearms were unknown before World War I.").

level of generality when considering historical regulations: for laws regulating the dangerous or unvirtuous, for example.[31]

Once one starts to broaden the frame in that way—to look at the "who" regulations that actually appeared throughout history and not just those with straightforward contemporary equivalents—it is hard to avoid the central question: What groups *did* the framers think should be disarmed?

The Repository of Historical Gun Laws—whose coverage of such laws is substantial, but not comprehensive—provides a glimpse of the answer to that question and also illustrates the challenge of looking for direct analogies. Consider the category of felon, for instance. The first laws in the Repository that explicitly disarm felons do not appear until 1923.[32] These laws, one from California[33] and one from North Dakota,[34] prohibited felons (as well as "unnaturalized foreign born person[s]") from owning, possessing, or controlling any pistol or revolver. The California law also forbade the possession of any "other firearm capable of being concealed upon the person."[35]

At least with regard to the category of felon, approaching the Repository from a narrow, contemporary perspective yields limited results. Conversely, reversing the focus and considering the groups that earlier generations *did* specifically disarm provides a broader and perhaps more useful picture.

The Repository includes examples of laws limiting the sale of guns to classes of people as early as 1633.[36] Prior to 1776, such laws almost exclusively addressed Native Americans,[37] with some also restricting persons "inhabiting out of

---

[31] *Supra* notes 22-24.

[32] Because the Repository of Historical Gun Laws is not comprehensive, noting this fact is not intended to suggest that this was the first law of its type in existence. The lack of earlier laws in the Repository suggests that this type of law is relatively new but cannot conclusively prove as much.

[33] Act of June 13, 1923, ch. 339, § 2, 1923 Cal. Stat. 696.

[34] Act of Mar. 17, 1923, ch. 266, § 5, 1923 N.D. Laws 379, 380.

[35] Ch. 339, § 2, 1923 Cal. Stat. at 696.

[36] Ch. 58, § 2 (1663), Charters and General Laws of the Colony and Province of Massachusetts Bay 132, 133 (1814) (prohibiting the sale of guns to "Indian[s]" and "person[s] inhabiting out of this jurisdiction").

[37] *See, e.g.*, 1723 Conn. Acts 292 (forbidding prosecution of an action for guns or ammunition lent, sold or otherwise trusted to an "Indian"); Act of Nov. 21, ch. 4, § 3, 1757-68 Md. Acts 53 (forbidding the sale of gunpowder, shot, and lead to "Indian" women and "Indian" children and limiting the quantity of gunpowder, shot, and lead able to be sold to "Indian" men); Act of Aug. 4, 1675, 5 Records Of The Colony Of New Plymouth 173 (1856) (forbidding the sale, bartering, or giving, directly or indirectly, of "any gun or guns, or ammunition of any kind to any Indian or Indians"); Act of Mar. 31, 1639, 1639 N.Y. Laws 18-19 (expressly forbidding the sale of guns, powder, and lead to "Indians"); Act of Oct. 22, 1763, ch. 506, § 1, 1763 Pa. Laws 319-20 (forbidding the sale and exchange "with any Indian or Indians whatsoever" of "guns, gunpowder, shot, bullets, lead or other warlike stores without license"); Act of Jan. 22, 1677, 2 Records of the Colony of Rhode Island and Providence Plantations 560, 561 (1857) (ordering inhabitants to bring armed "Indians" without a "ticket" permitting passage with guns or ammunition before the governor or deputy governor); Act XVII, Acts of Jan. 6, 1639, 1639 Va. Acts 227 (repealing a 1637 act which made it a felony to barter with "Indians," and enacting a new law that trading with them for arms and ammunition is a felony).

this jurisdiction."[38] In 1776, following a recommendation by the Continental Congress,[39] Massachusetts,[40] Virginia,[41] and Pennsylvania[42] enacted laws disarming persons "disaffected to the cause of America" or who refused to take a loyalty oath or affirmation. Though these early laws might be distinguished on the basis that they predate the Second Amendment, *Heller* itself draws heavily on the seventeenth-century English Bill of Rights and Blackstone's *Commentaries on the Laws of England*,[43] and courts continue to debate the contemporary relevance of laws as old as the 1328 Statute of Northampton.[44] Their antiquity therefore does not necessarily rule them out, and they broadly share a common purpose: disarming groups of people thought to be dangerous.[45] The following sections offer a more in-depth analysis of the trends within each group.

A. Native Americans

Native Americans' access to guns was strictly regulated in the seventeenth, eighteenth, and nineteenth centuries. Historical accounts provide two dominant rationales for this regulation: (1) colonists were actively engaged in "a project

---

[38] Act of Dec. 1, 1642, Public Records of the Colony of Connecticut 79 (1850) (forbidding the sale or giving of guns, gunpowder, shot, lead, and military weapons to Indians, and requiring that persons "inhabiting out of this jurisdiction" have a license for such sale); Ch. 58, § 2, Charters and General Laws of the Colony and Province of Massachusetts Bay at 133 ("Nor shall any person sell, give or barter, directly or indirectly, any gun or guns, powder, bullets, shot, lead, to any Indian whatsoever, or to any person inhabiting out of this jurisdiction"); Duke of York's Laws, 1665–75, 1 Colonial Laws of New York from the Year 1664 to the Revolution 40–41 (1894) (forbidding the sale of guns, gunpowder, bullets, shot, and lead to both "Indian[s]" and those "inhabiting out of this Government" without a license); Charter To William Penn, And Laws Of The Province Of Pennsylvania, Passed Between The Years 1682 And 1700, at 32 (1879) (forbidding the sale of guns, gunpowder, bullets, shot, and lead to both "Indian[s]" and those "inhabiting out of this government" without a license).

[39] 4 Journals of the Continental Congress, 1774–1789, at 205 (Worthington Chauncey Ford ed., 1906) (recommending that colonies "cause all persons to be disarmed within their respective colonies, who are notoriously disaffected to the cause of America, or who have not associated, and shall refuse to associate, to defend, by arms, these United Colonies, against the hostile attempts of the British fleets and armies").

[40] Act of Mar. 14, 1776, ch. VII, 1775–76 Mass. Act 31–32, 35.

[41] Act of May 5, 1777, ch. 3, Va. Stat. 281–82 (1821).

[42] Act of June 13, 1777, ch. 756, §§ 2, 4, 1777 Pa. Laws 110, 111–13; *see also* Act of Apr. 1, 1778, ch. 796, §§ 1–3, 5, 10, 1778 Pa. Laws 238–39, 242, 244–45.

[43] District of Columbia v. Heller, 554 U.S. 570, 582, 593–94, 598, 608, 617, 626–27 (2008).

[44] *See, e.g.*, Wrenn v. District of Columbia, 864 F.3d 650, 659 (D.C. Cir. 2017); Moore v. Madigan, 702 F.3d 933, 936 (7th Cir. 2012).

[45] *See, e.g.*, Act of Aug. 4, 1675, 5 Records Of The Colony Of New Plymouth 173 (1856) ("[S]elling etc., of arms and ammunition to the Indians is very poisonous and destructive to the English. . . ."); Act of Mar. 31, 1779, ch. 836, §§ 4–5, 1779 Pa. Laws 346, 347–48 ("And whereas it is very improper and dangerous that persons disaffected to the liberty and independence of this state shall possess or have in their own keeping, or elsewhere, any firearms, or other weapons used in war, or any gun powder.").

of expropriating Native American land,"[46] a venture that was far more difficult when Native Americans were armed, and (2) disarmament was a way to protect against Native American attacks.[47] The latter concern is directly reflected in the language of some of the laws in the Repository. For instance, in 1656, New Netherland forbade the admission of armed Native Americans into the city "in order to prevent such dangers of isolated murders and assassinations."[48] The Colony of New Plymouth similarly forbade the selling of guns and ammunition to Native Americans because it was "very poisonous and destructive to the English."[49]

Restrictions targeting Native Americans were broadly phrased with regard to the types of weapons they reached, apparently including *all* guns within their scope.[50] Whether they prohibited possession or merely sale is a closer question. Most laws currently in the Repository concerning Native Americans restrict the *sale* of guns rather than possession, and thus directly governed the conduct of colonists. The Colony of Massachusetts enacted a law in 1633 that was typical of the time:

> And it is ordered, that no person whatsoever, shall . . . sell, give or barter, directly or indirectly, any gun or guns, powder, bullets, shot, lead, to any Indian whatsoever, or to any person inhabiting out of this jurisdiction: Nor shall any amend or repair any gun belonging to any Indian, nor shall [sic] sell any armor

---

[46] *See* Alexander Gouzoules, *The Diverging Right(s) to Bear Arms: Private Armament and the Second and Fourteenth Amendments in Historical Context*, 10 ALA. C.R. & C.L. L. REV. 159, 166 (2019).

[47] *See* Ann E. Tweedy, *"Hostile Indian Tribes... Outlaws, Wolves,... Bears... Grizzlies and Things Like That?" How the Second Amendment and Supreme Court Precedent Target Tribal Self-Defense*, 13 U. PA. J. CONST. L. 687, 697 (2011) ("Indian attacks were the primary reason that militias were initially formed, and throughout the colonial era, militias were understood to be necessary to protect against Indian attacks.").

[48] Act of July 1, 1656, 1656 N.Y. Laws 234–35; *see also* Act of Feb. 23, 1645, 1645 N.Y. Laws 47 (admonishing those who had sold guns, powder and lead to Indians "to the serious injury of this Country, the strengthening of the Indians and the destruction of the Christians").

[49] 5 Records Of The Colony Of New Plymouth at 173; *see also* Act of Mar. 31, 1639, 1639 N.Y. Laws 18–19 ("[M]any persons... have... presumed to sell to the Indians in these parts, Guns, Powder and Lead, which hath already caused much mischief.").

[50] *See, e.g.*, Ch. 58, § 2 (1633), Charters and General Laws of the Colony and Province of Massachusetts Bay 132, 133 (1814) ("And it is ordered, that no person whatsoever, shall . . . sell, give or barter, directly or indirectly, any gun or guns, powder, bullets, shot, lead, to any Indian whatsoever"). There is a possibility that pistols were not included within this prohibition, as pistols may not have broadly been understood to be a type of gun. The 1828 edition of Webster's *American Dictionary of the English Language*, which Justice Scalia cited in *Heller* when he defined "arms," "keep," "carry," and "militia," District of Columbia v. Heller, 554 U.S. 570, 581, 582, 584, 595 (2008), defined gun as "[a]n instrument consisting of a barrel or tube of iron or other metal fixed in a stock, from which balls, shot or other deadly weapons are discharged by the explosion of gunpowder. The larger species of guns are called cannon; and the small species are called muskets, carbines, fowling pieces, &c. *But one species of fire-arms, the pistol, is never called a gun.*" 1 NOAH WEBSTER, AN AMERICAN DICTIONARY OF THE ENGLISH LANGUAGE (1828) (emphasis added).

or weapons, upon penalty of ten pounds for every gun, armor or weapons so sold, given or bartered, five pounds for every pound of powder, forty shillings for every pound of shot or lead, and proportionately for any greater or lesser quantity.[51]

Though this statute forbade persons from selling, giving, or bartering guns to Native Americans, it implicitly acknowledged that Native Americans nevertheless possessed guns in its prohibition of "amend[ing] or repair[ing] any gun belonging to any Indian."[52]

Many of these early laws prohibited colonists from trading a variety of items with Native Americans, not just guns and firearms. In fact, the earliest statute in the Repository concerning Native Americans, which was enacted by Virginia in 1631, forbade *all* public and private trade with Native Americans.[53] The laws presently in the Repository, however, reflect an eventual shift in focus to weapons specifically. For instance, eight years after instituting a blanket prohibition on trade with Native Americans, Virginia enacted another statute specifying that "trading with [Native Americans] for arms and ammunition shall be felony, and for other commodities imprisonment at discretion of the Governor and Council."[54] Though the statute regulated trading of all commodities, the comparative penalties denote a particular emphasis on trade of arms and ammunition. Other laws from the same period regulated weapons beyond firearms, including one from 1665 in which the Colony of Connecticut banned repairing "any gun small or great belonging to any Indian" and forbade residents from making arrowheads.[55]

Initially, these laws carried rather severe punishments. From 1633 to 1645, all laws in the Repository that exclusively targeted the sale of arms to Native

---

[51] Ch. 58, § 2 (1633) Charters and General Laws of the Colony and Province of Massachusetts Bay 132, 133 (1814); *see also* Act of Dec. 1, 1642, Public Records of the Colony of Connecticut 79 (1850); Act of Oct. 22, 1763, ch. 506, § 1, 1763 Pa. Laws 319–20; Act X, Acts of Aug. 21, 1633, 1633 Va. Acts 219.

[52] Ch. 58, § 2, Charters and General Laws of the Colony and Province of Massachusetts Bay at 133; *see also* Public Records of the Colony of Connecticut at 79 (1850). Another element of this law is both representative and noteworthy: the apparent connection between Native Americans and those "inhabiting out of this jurisdiction." The grouping of these categories likely reflects the fact that many Native Americans were simply not within the jurisdictions of the colonies. *See generally* Yasu Kawashima, *Jurisdiction of the Colonial Courts over the Indians in Massachusetts, 1689–1763*, 42 NEW ENG. Q. 532 (1969). This would have implications both for the substance and justification of the laws. As to the former, while colonists could prohibit other colonists from selling guns to Native Americans, they were limited—as a legal, let alone practical, matter—in their ability to prohibit Native Americans from possessing them. As to the latter—the question of justification—the judicial status of Native Americans demonstrates that in addition to being considered dangerous they were simultaneously "outsiders."

[53] Act XLVI, Acts of Feb. 24, 1631, 1631 Va. Acts 173.
[54] Act XVII, Acts of Jan. 6, 1639, 1639 Va. Acts 227.
[55] Act of Dec. 1, 1642, Public Records of the Colony of Connecticut 79 (1850).

Americans punished violators with the penalty of death, forfeiture of their entire estate, or with the designation of felon,[56] which in the colonial period carried harsh consequences.[57] Sentencings appear to have eased over time, and the last law in the Repository to punish sale of firearms to Native Americans with death was enacted in 1675.[58] Following 1675, though some penalties were still severe,[59] they generally were limited to fines.[60] And beginning in 1676, the Repository suggests an increase in the number of laws that allowed for the sale of firearms and ammunition to Native Americans who possessed a license. Notably, all of the laws in the Repository from 1676 until the Revolutionary War either had an exception for sale of firearms by colonists to Native Americans with licenses or allowed a set amount of firearms or ammunition to be sold to Native Americans.[61]

Nevertheless, though the laws carried less severe penalties, regulations of Native Americans by and through restrictions on the conduct of colonists continued to be enacted leading up to and following the American Revolutionary War. In 1763, for instance, Maryland made it unlawful to give "any Indian Man... more than the Quantity of one Pound of Gun-powder, and Six Pounds of Shot or Lead, at any one Time."[62] Marylanders were also prohibited from giving "any Indian Woman or Child, any Gun-powder, Shot, or Lead, whatsoever."[63] That same year, Pennsylvania enacted a law that punished all who "directly or indirectly g[ave] to, s[old], barter[ed] or exchange[d] with any Indian or Indians

---

[56] Act of Mar. 31, 1639, 1639 N.Y. Laws 18–19; Act of Feb. 23, 1645, 1645 N.Y. Laws 47; see Act XXIII, 1642 Va. Acts at 255–56 (forfeiture of entire estate); Act XVII, 1639 Va. Acts at 227 (felony); Act X, Acts of Aug. 21, 1633, 1633 Va. Acts 219 (life imprisonment and forfeiture of all goods).

[57] Marshall, *supra* note 30, at 714–19.

[58] Act of Aug. 4, 1675, 5 Records Of The Colony Of New Plymouth 173 (1856).

[59] *See, e.g.*, Harry Toulmin, The Statutes of the Mississippi Territory, Revised and Digested by the Authority of the General Assembly Page 593, Image 612 (Natchez, 1807), available at The Making of Modern Law: Primary Sources (penalty of a sum not exceeding fifty dollars and imprisonment not exceeding thirty days); Act of Oct. 22, 1763, ch. 506, § 1, 1763 Pa. Laws 319–20 (penalty of five hundred pounds and thirty-nine lashes on the offender's bare back).

[60] *See, e.g.*, 1723 Conn. Acts 292 (persons who lend, sell, or otherwise trust "Indians" with guns or ammunition cannot prosecute any action to procure said gun or ammunition); Act of Nov. 21, ch. 4, § 3, 1757–68 Md. Acts 53 (forbidding sale of gunpowder, shot, and lead beyond the quantity of one pound of gunpowder, and six pounds of shot and lead, at any one time to an "Indian man," with a penalty of five pounds for every pound of gunpowder).

[61] *See, e.g.*, Ch. 4, § 3, 1757–68 Md. Acts at 53; Duke of York's Laws, 1665–75, 1 Colonial Laws of New York from the Year 1664 to the Revolution 40–41 (1894) (disallowing sale of guns, powder, and ammunition "without license first had and obtained under the governors [sic] hand and seal to any Indian whatsoever"); Charter To William Penn, And Laws Of The Province Of Pennsylvania, Passed Between The Years 1682 And 1700, at 32 (1879) (disallowing sale of guns, powder, and ammunition "without license first had and obtained under the Governor's hand and Seal, to any Indian whatsoever"); Act of Jan. 22, 1677, 2 Records of the Colony of Rhode Island and Providence Plantations 560, 561 (1857) (addressing "Indians" that "pass and repass on and off this Island, with guns and ammunition, *showing no ticket or order so to do*") (emphasis added).

[62] Ch. 4, § 3, 1757–68 Md. Acts at 53.

[63] *Id.*

whatsoever any guns, gunpowder, shot, bullets, lead or other warlike stores without license" with thirty-nine lashes on the violator's "bare back."[64]

In 1844, following the Revolutionary War and the enactment of the Second Amendment, no Missourian could "exchange or give, to any Indian, any horse, mule, gun, blanket, or any other article or commodity whatever, unless such Indian shall be traveling through the state" with a written permit from the proper authority or under the direction of an agent of the proper authority.[65] Similarly, in Oregon in 1853 it was unlawful for "any white citizen, or other person than an Indian, [to] sell, barter, or give to any Indian in this territory any gun, rifle, pistol or other kind of firearms, any powder, lead, percussion caps or other ammunition whatever."[66] Also during this period there existed at least some laws regulating citizens' procurement of firearms from Native Americans. For instance, in 1807, Mississippi prohibited all citizens from purchasing or receiving from Native Americans "in the way of trade or barter, a gun, or other article commonly used in hunting."[67] Violators were punished with a fee of up to fifty dollars and up to thirty days imprisonment.

Arms restrictions continued to govern sales to and by Native Americans at least until the middle of the nineteenth century. Then, during the American Revolutionary War, another group emerged as a primary target of disarmament: those "disaffected to the cause of America."

B. Disaffected to the Cause of America

In 1776, the Continental Congress recommended that the colonies disarm those who "are notoriously disaffected to the cause of America, or who have not associated, and shall refuse to associate, to defend, by arms, the United Colonies, against the hostile attempts of the British fleets and armies."[68] At least Massachusetts,[69] Virginia,[70] and Pennsylvania[71] followed the recommendation and enacted laws disarming men of military age who refused to take a loyalty oath. Given the timing of these enactments, scholars have presumed that their

---

[64] Ch. 506, § 1, 1763 Pa. Laws at 319–20.
[65] Act of Feb. 27, 1845, ch. 80, § 4, 1845 Mo. Laws 306.
[66] Act of Jan. 16, 1854, § 1, 1854 Or. Laws 257.
[67] Harry Toulmin, The Statutes of the Mississippi Territory, Revised and Digested by the Authority of the General Assembly Page 593, Image 612 (Natchez, 1807), available at The Making of Modern Law: Primary Sources.
[68] 4 JOURNALS OF THE CONTINENTAL CONGRESS, 1774–1789, at 205 (Worthington Chauncey Ford ed., 1906).
[69] Act of Mar. 14, 1776, ch. VII, 1775–76 Mass. Act 31–32, 35.
[70] Act of May 5, 1777, ch. 3, Va. Stat. 281–82 (1821).
[71] Act of June 13, 1777, ch. 756, §§ 2, 4, 1777 Pa. Laws 110, 111–13; see also Act of Apr. 1, 1778, ch. 796, §§ 1–3, 5, 10, 1778 Pa. Laws 238–39, 242, 244–45.

purpose was, as with the regulations disarming Native Americans, at least in part "to provide for internal security," as well as to limit arms ownership to those willing to bear arms for that security.[72]

Pennsylvania enacted at least two statutes mandating a loyalty oath and disarming those who declined to take it.[73] The first was enacted in 1777, and the disarmament provision read as follows:

> And be it further enacted by the authority aforesaid, That every person above the age aforesaid refusing or neglecting to take and subscribe the said oath or affirmation, shall during the time of such neglect or refusal, be incapable of holding any office or place of trust in this state, serving on juries, suing for any debts, electing or being elected, buying, selling or transferring any lands, tenements or hereditaments, *and shall be disarmed by the lieutenant or sublieutenants of the city or countries respectively.*[74]

This disarmament is particularly notable as Pennsylvania's constitution at the time strongly protected an individual right to bear arms.[75] And while the initial disarmament may not have been permanent,[76] in 1778 Pennsylvania amended the act to require all persons refusing to take the oath to deliver their arms to the state.[77] After delivery, they were not permitted to "carry any arms about [their] person or keep any arms or ammunition in [their] house or elsewhere" on pain of forfeiture.[78]

Massachusetts similarly passed a law in 1776 requiring "every male person above sixteen years of age" to take an oath of loyalty.[79] Those who refused were

---

[72] Saul Cornell, *Commonplace or Anachronism: The Standard Model, The Second Amendment, and the Problem of History in Contemporary Constitutional Theory*, 16 CONST. COMMENT. 221, 228–29 (1999) ("Gun ownership in Pennsylvania was based on the idea that one agreed to support the state and to defend it against those who might use arms against it. Only citizens who were willing to swear an oath to the state could claim the right to bear arms."). The content of these acts, in particular the "Test Acts" in Pennsylvania, actually extended beyond disarmament and also "barred citizens who refused to take the oath from voting, holding public office, serving on juries, and transferring real estate." *Id.*

[73] Ch. 756, §§ 2, 4, 1777 Pa. Laws at 111–13; Ch. 796, §§ 1–3, 5, 10, 1778 Pa. Laws at 238–39, 242, 244–45; *see* Cornell, *supra* note 72, at 228–29.

[74] Ch. 756, § 4, 1777 Pa. Laws at 112–13 (emphasis added).

[75] PA. CONST. OF 1776, Decl. of Rights, art. XIII ("That the people have a right to bear arms for the defence of themselves and the state."); *see also* Marshall, *supra* note 30, at 724 (similarly noting the strength of Pennsylvania's contemporaneous arms provision).

[76] There is no prohibition against purchasing new arms following a violator's disarmament, and the regulation only applied "during the time of such neglect or refusal" to take the loyalty oath. *See* Ch. 756, §§ 2, 4, 1777 Pa. Laws at 111–13.

[77] Ch. 796, § 5, 1778 Pa. Laws at 242.

[78] *Id.*; *cf.* Saul Cornell & Nathan DeDino, *A Well Regulated Right: The Early American Origins of Gun Control*, 73 FORDHAM L. REV. 487, 506 (2004) ("Such a broad provision effectively eliminated the opportunity for someone to violently protest the actions of the Pennsylvania government or defend himself with a firearm.").

[79] Act of Mar. 14, 1776, ch. VII, 1775–76 Mass. Act 31–32.

disarmed of "all such arms, ammunities and warlike implements, as by the strictest search can be found in his possession or belonging to him."[80] Unlike Pennsylvania's amended provision, the enactment did not clearly state that those disarmed were precluded from purchasing new arms.[81] It also included at least one important exception: Quakers' religious preferences were accommodated, and they were exempted from the oath required of other men.[82] Instead, Quakers were required to make a different declaration, one which did not contravene their religious beliefs.[83]

It has been argued that these Revolutionary laws were "enacted in the darkest days of an existential domestic war" and thus "one must proceed with caution in using . . . [them] as evidence of the scope of the Second Amendment."[84] Yet even after the "extraordinary period"[85] of the American Revolution, Massachusetts continued to disarm political dissidents. For instance, following Shays' Rebellion, Massachusetts permitted those who had taken up arms against the state to obtain a pardon if they swore allegiance to the state and delivered their arms to a justice of the peace.[86] For a span of three years they were required to keep the peace and, as with the 1777 Pennsylvania law,[87] were disqualified from serving as jurors or holding office in the state (among other restrictions).[88] These disqualifications were removed if they exhibited "plenary evidence of their having returned to their allegiance, and kept the peace, and that they possess[ed] an unequivocal attachment to the government."[89] Similar limitations would emerge in many places in the aftermath of the Civil War. In Kansas, as late as 1868, no person who

---

[80] *Id.*

[81] *See id.*; Marshall, *supra* note 30, at 724 (observing that the Pennsylvania law in 1777 "read more like forfeiture laws than disabilities").

[82] Ch. VII, 1775–76 Mass. Act at 35.

[83] *Id.*; *see also* Cornell & DeDino, *supra* note 80, at 507 ("[T]he right for a Quaker to practice his religion outweighed the state's interest in its preferred test of allegiance. The right to bear arms, however, did not outweigh the state's interest in maintaining security through disarmament of those considered dangerous to the state. Instead, the state's interest in public safety dominated.").

[84] Marshall, *supra* note 30, at 725 ("[T]he arms disabilities cannot be isolated from their context as part of a wholesale stripping of a distrusted group's civil liberties."); *but see* Cornell, *supra* note 78, at 228 ("Both the timing and language of the [Pennsylvania] Acts suggests that they were not simply an emergency measure enacted during time of war, but a reflection of a particular republican ethos that was antithetical to modern liberal ideas about rights.").

[85] Cornell & DeDino, *supra* note 78, at 507.

[86] Act of Feb. 16, 1787, ch. VI, 1787 Mass. Acts 555.

[87] Act of June 13, 1777, ch. 756, § 4, 1777 Pa. Laws 110, 112–13.

[88] Ch. VI, 1787 Mass. Acts 555; *see also* Cornell & DeDino, *supra* note 78, at 508 ("The nature of the other disqualifications that went along with disarmament only underscores the civic character of the right to bear arms. Those seeking pardon were not robbed of a right to free speech or free exercise of their religion, rights indisputably associated with individuals. Instead, the penalties deal more with the rights and obligations associated with a citizen's duty to society.").

[89] Ch. VI, 1787 Mass. Acts 555; *but cf.* Binderup v. Att'y Gen., 836 F.3d 336, 348 (3d Cir. 2016) ("There is no historical support for the view that the passage of time or evidence of rehabilitation can restore Second Amendment rights that were forfeited").

had "ever borne arms against the government of the United States" could carry a pistol "or other deadly weapon" within the limits of the state.[90]

Such wholesale disarmament of groups perceived to be dangerous outsiders were in some ways reminiscent of laws enacted in England to disarm Catholics at the end of the seventeenth century.[91] The English Bill of Rights recognized "[t]hat the Subjects which are Protestants may have Arms for their Defence suitable to their Conditions and as allowed by Law."[92] That same year also saw "An Act for the Better Secureing the Government by Disarming Papists and Reputed Papists," which explicitly disarmed Catholics:

> Bee it further enacted and declared That noe Papist or reputed Papist soe refuseing or makeing default as aforesaid shall or may have or keepe in his House or elsewhere or in the Possession of any other person to his use or at his disposition any Arms Weapons Gunpowder or Ammunition (other then such necessary Weapons as shall be allowed to him by Order of the Justices of the Peace at their Generall Quarter Sessions for the defence of his House or person).[93]

As in the United States a century later, the targeted group's disarmament "was part of a wholesale stripping of rights and privileges."[94] Both contexts also required a loyalty oath that "was effectively a naturalization oath" in which the person renounced allegiance to the political opposition; "[t]o refuse it was to declare oneself a resident alien... and, given the war, a resident enemy alien."[95] One key distinction between the disarmament of Catholics in this provision and the disarmament of "those disaffected to the cause of the United States," however, is that even those who refused to take the oath in England were able to keep arms that were found necessary "for the defense of house and person."[96] That exception is not enumerated in the American laws currently in the Repository—and expressly denied in some.

Historical laws disarming disaffected groups thus have a long lineage stretching all the way back to England and at least imply an understanding of the right to keep and bear arms that allowed for disarmament of large segments of the

---

[90] Ch. 31, art. 9, § 282 (1868), 1 General Statutes of the State of Kansas 329 (1876) (disarming "[a]ny person who is not engaged in any legitimate business, any person under the influence of intoxicating drink, and any person who has ever borne arms against the government of the United States").

[91] See Marshall, *supra* note 30, at 721 ("[T]he stated principle supporting the disability [in England] was cause to fear that a person, although technically an English subject, was because of his beliefs effectively a resident enemy alien liable to violence against the king.").

[92] 1 W. & M., Sess. 2, c. 2, § 1 (1688).

[93] 1 W. & M., Sess. 1, c. 15 (1689).

[94] Marshall, *supra* note 30, at 724.

[95] *Id.* at 723–25.

[96] 1 W. & M. ch. 15.

population. Several courts and scholars have in fact cited these laws as evidence that founding-era governments disarmed groups for public safety reasons,[97] notwithstanding the fact that those specific laws would be unconstitutional today for various reasons. On other hand, ignoring them entirely would mean cutting out a fairly sizeable portion of the very laws that the framers thought to be desirable and constitutional. What guidance might they offer, then, is the question to which we now turn.

III. Takeaways and Caveats

What relevance might these laws have under *Bruen*'s "historical tradition" test? One obvious answer is "none whatsoever." Legal interpretation does, after all, sometimes require choices between competing lines of authority, whether of precedent or regulatory tradition.[98] Just as we would not look to the founding era's Sedition Act for guidance about the scope of the First Amendment, so too should we avoid defining the scope of the Second Amendment based on a set of laws that we would today clearly reject. For example, scholars have cataloged some of the ways in which gun laws historically targeted African Americans.[99] However, while we might find such outdated laws altogether irrelevant, we can alternatively look to them as a lesson that gun regulations, especially those targeting particular classes of persons, should be closely scrutinized for discriminatory motive and violations of Equal Protection.[100]

Whether or not such laws would violate modern Fourteenth Amendment doctrine, they might also be relevant to the issues that matter for Second Amendment analysis, including the breadth of the government's power to regulate guns. Answering that question means considering the array of gun regulations at the founding (or in the mid 1800s for state and local laws), even those whose specific targets are no longer relevant, desirable, or even constitutional. One might accept the historical principle that the government can

---

[97] *See, e.g.*, Nat'l Rifle Ass'n of Am., Inc. v. Bureau of Alcohol, Tobacco, Firearms, & Explosives, 700 F.3d 185, 200 (5th Cir. 2012).

[98] Consider in this respect the Ninth Circuit panel decision in *Peruta v. County of San Diego*, which recognized that "in a broad sense ... every historical gloss on the phrase 'bear arms' furnishes a clue of that phrase's original or customary meaning," but that "historical interpretations of the right's scope are of varying probative worth" depending on how well they mesh with *Heller*. 742 F.3d 1144, 1155 (9th Cir. 2014), *overruled on rehearing en banc*, 824 F.3d 919 (9th Cir. 2016); *see* Jud Campbell, *Natural Rights, Positive Rights, and the Right to Keep and Bear Arms*, 83 Law & Contemp. Probs. 31 (2020).

[99] *See, e.g.*, Robert J. Cottrol & Raymond T. Diamond, *The Second Amendment: Toward an Afro-Americanist Reconsideration*, 80 Geo. L.J. 309, 338 (1991).

[100] *Kanter*, 919 F.3d 437, 458 n.7 (Barrett, J., dissenting) ("It should go without saying that such race-based exclusions would be unconstitutional today.").

regulate persons whose legal status serves as a proxy for dangerousness—felons or those convicted of domestic violence crimes, for example—without accepting the framers' conclusions about how that principle applies—to Native Americans, for example.[101] *If* the Second Amendment demands rigorous historical analysis, as *Heller* arguably suggests,[102] let alone analysis based *solely* on text, history, and tradition,[103] then it is hard to justify ignoring these unseemly laws, which after all help demonstrate the "principles" the framers thought relevant.[104] To disregard them in favor of the more reassuring laws disarming violent criminals risks, as Justice Scalia famously put it in another context, "looking over a crowd and picking out your friends."[105]

In other words, one can accept that the framers denied firearms to groups they thought to be particularly dangerous (or unvirtuous, or irresponsible) without sharing their conclusion about which groups qualify as such. Indeed, that bridge has long since been crossed, though only in one direction. By disarming specific groups (domestic violence offenders, for example,[106] or users of controlled substances) that the framers did not, modern lawmakers are—appropriately enough—expressing disagreement with the state of gun regulation in the late 1700s. The historical approach resolves that gap through analogical reasoning: by suggesting that our modern prohibition is based on a principle that the framers endorsed, even if they did not apply it to drug users.[107] But to fully understand the scope of the regulatory authority the framers thought they had, one must

---

[101] *See* Jack M. Balkin, *Abortion and Original Meaning*, 24 CONST. COMMENT. 291, 292 (2008) (offering "an argument for the right to abortion based on the original meaning of the constitutional text as opposed to its original expected application"); *see also* SOTIRIOS A. BARBER & JAMES E. FLEMING, CONSTITUTIONAL INTERPRETATION: THE BASIC QUESTIONS 84–91 (2007) (discussing the difficulties of "narrow" or "concrete" originalism); PATRICK J. CHARLES, HISTORICISM, ORIGINALISM AND THE CONSTITUTION: THE USE AND ABUSE OF THE PAST IN AMERICAN JURISPRUDENCE (2014) (describing "historical guidepost" approach to use of history in constitutional interpretation and applying it to the Second Amendment).

[102] District of Columbia v. Heller, 554 U.S. 570, 591 (2008).

[103] Heller v. District of Columbia (*Heller II*), 670 F.3d 1244, 1276 (D.C. Cir. 2011) (Kavanaugh, J., dissenting).

[104] As then judge Brett Kavanaugh put it in *Heller II*, arguing for adoption of a "text, history, and tradition" approach to Second Amendment questions: "The constitutional principles do not change (absent amendment), but the relevant principles must be faithfully applied not only to circumstances as they existed in 1787, 1791, and 1868, for example, but also to modern situations that were unknown to the Constitution's Framers." Heller v. District of Columbia (*Heller II*), 670 F.3d 1244, 1275 (Kavanaugh, J., dissenting).

[105] ANTONIN SCALIA, A MATTER OF INTERPRETATION: FEDERAL COURTS AND THE LAW 36 (1997). Justice Scalia borrowed the phrase from Judge Harold Leventhal of the D.C. Circuit.

[106] The common law gave husbands a "right of chastisement" until at least the mid-1800s. Reva Siegel, *"The Rule of Love": Wife Beating as Prerogative and Privacy*, 105 YALE L.J. 2117, 2121–42 (1996).

[107] *See, e.g.*, United States v. Bena, 664 F.3d 1180, 1183 (8th Cir. 2011) (analogizing § 922(g)(8) to "longstanding" gun regulations approved in *Heller*, and finding it consistent with "a common-law tradition that permits restrictions directed at citizens who are not law-abiding and responsible").

actually consider the gun laws that they *did* pass, even if we would reject those laws (perhaps for other constitutional reasons) today.

One caveat is that while we interpreted the laws targeting Native Americans and those disaffected to the cause of America as regulations of people perceived to be dangerous, they could in the alternative be understood as regulations of people who are "outsiders." The inclusion of persons "inhabiting out of this jurisdiction" in several of the statutes cited above supports such an understanding. However, as already noted, at least some of the statutes explicitly referred to the alleged dangerous character of Native Americans, and the disarmament of apparently disloyal colonists was in the midst of the Revolutionary War. It is hard to imagine that safety was not at least a partial consideration.

IV. Conclusion

To return to the questions with which we began: What power does the government have to deny guns to groups of people thought to be dangerous? How and on what basis are such restrictions consistent with the Second Amendment? These questions were not unknown to earlier generations of Americans, though the targets of the restrictions were different: Native Americans, the "disaffected," and even nonresidents and noncitizens. What can we learn from historical laws that targeted those groups?

When historical analysis begins with contemporary laws denying firearms to particular categories of persons, it almost always leads to a narrow focus on historical analogs of laws targeting felons or the mentally ill. This is for two reasons: One, those laws are important as a matter of modern practice. And two, they are widely accepted as constitutional.

What if, instead, we considered things from the framers' perspective? We need not accept their conclusions, of course, in order to care about their premises—their *reasons* for believing certain gun laws to be constitutional. If they thought that gun laws were constitutional so long as they targeted groups of people thought to be dangerous, then arguably that reason is what matters, not the groups to which they affixed that label. This kind of comparison seems to be exactly in keeping with *Bruen*'s direction that historical and modern gun laws be compared based on how they are or were "justified."[108]

To be clear, the lessons here can be instructive in a cautionary way—not only with regard to the groups that were wrongly subject to disarmament in the past but also the potential malleability of a "dangerousness" principle. In particular, the historical record shows an inclination to disarm those who were considered

---

[108] *Bruen*, 142 S. Ct. at 2132–33.

threats to public safety and the political order. Whether and how history can provide guidance with regard to the targets of contemporary prohibition—felons and domestic abusers, for example—is a broader question of constitutional interpretation. But understanding the full historical record, and the breadth of the government's historical power, is a crucial first step.

9
Strange Bedfellows

Racism and Gun Rights in American History and Current Scholarship

Brennan Gardner Rivas

I. Introduction

A common adage is that "politics makes strange bedfellows." The same can be true of scholarship. In recent years, some authors on the front lines of ethnic studies and antiracism have found some common ground with the advocates of expansive gun rights. In cataloging the effects of systemic racism and illuminating the deeply biased nature of American culture and public policy, their attention has turned to gun laws and the Second Amendment.[1] For centuries, according to one such scholar, these laws have "maintained hierarchies of race, gender, disability, nationality, class, and sexuality."[2] More than that, according to others, "the gun" has "demarcated the borders of exclusion"[3] in America and "served as a tool of white privilege, forever linked to a history of violence and oppression."[4] These bold statements perch themselves atop the research of gun rights scholars who have cobbled together a portfolio of publications that, taken collectively, condemn gun control as an inherently racist undertaking.[5]

---

[1] *See, e.g.*, Roxanne Dunbar-Ortiz, Loaded: A Disarming History of the Second Amendment (2018); Carol Anderson, The Second: Race and Guns in a Fatally Unequal America (2021).

[2] Gabriel Arkles, *Gun Control, Mental Illness, and Black Trans and Lesbian Survival*, 42 Sw. L. Rev. 855, 865 (2013).

[3] Pratheepan Gulasekaram, *Guns and Membership in the American Polity*, 21 Wm. & Mary Bill Rts. J. 619, 620 (2012).

[4] Angela R. Riley, *Indians and Guns*, 100 Geo. L.J. 1675, 1680 (2012).

[5] *See generally* Clayton E. Cramer, *The Racist Roots of Gun Control*, 4 Kan. J.L. & Pub. Pol'y (1995); Kevin Yuill, *"Better Die Fighting against Injustice than to Die Like a Dog": African-Americans and Guns, 1866–1941*, in A Cultural History of Firearms in the Age of Empire 211 (Karen Jones, Giacomo Macola, & David Welch eds., 2013); Stephen P. Halbrook, Freedmen, the Fourteenth Amendment, and the Right to Bear Arms, 1866–1876 (1998); David B. Kopel, The Truth about Gun Control (2013). The best scholarship in this vein is the collaborative work of Robert J. Cottrol and Raymond T. Diamond. *See The Second Amendment: Toward an Afro-Americanist Reconsideration*, 80 Geo. L.J. 309 (1991) [hereinafter *Afro-Americanist Reconsideration*]; *Never Intended to Be Applied to the White Population: Firearms Regulation and Racial Disparity—The Redeemed South's Legacy to a National Jurisprudence?*, 70 Chi.-Kent L. Rev. 1307 (1995) [hereinafter *Never Intended*].

As is true with gun rights scholarship in general, there are serious flaws in methodology and argumentation in many of the published works concerning the matrix of race, weapons, and bearing arms. Some of the claims are irresponsible to the point of fraudulence. For instance, Clayton Cramer has asserted that Thomas Dodd, chairman of the U.S. Senate subcommittee that drafted the 1968 Gun Control Act, modeled the legislation on Nazi gun policies that ultimately disarmed German Jews. The alleged "smoking gun" evidence was Dodd's decision to include in the official record translations of certain Nazi firearm regulations that went into effect in the 1930s.[6] In fact, Dodd commissioned the translations from the Library of Congress and included them in the subcommittee's record because spokespersons for the National Rifle Association (NRA) were trying to kill Dodd's bill by falsely associating its proposed policies with Nazism. Cramer's article insinuating that Dodd, a prosecutor at the Nuremberg trials, might have been inspired by Nazi policies has been cited in scholarly works.[7] The inference that gun regulation in America might make this country vulnerable to totalitarianism lives on in Stephen Halbrook's *Gun Control and the Third Reich*, the inspiration for which the author attributes to contemporaneous reports on Dodd's subcommittee hearings.[8]

Other claims, particularly those of Robert Cottrol and Raymond Diamond, are less outrageous but no less misleading. At times they engage in cherry-picking by examining only those laws that specifically mention racial groups. The presentation of African Americans' and Indigenous Americans' experiences with weapons is important because some laws, particularly during the antebellum nineteenth century, targeted non-White racial groups. But this small body of racially discriminatory statutes does not accurately represent the wide spectrum of gun and weapon regulations in American history and should not be deployed to malign all gun control efforts as detrimental to people of color.[9] Another

---

[6] Cramer, *supra* note 5, at 21–22. While admitting that Dodd was "an aggressive prosecutor of civil rights violations" and "not a Nazi," Cramer still asserts that "it would not be surprising if Dodd found it convenient to adapt a law that had already proved its efficacy at disarming a minority group." *Id.* at 22.

[7] *See, e.g.*, Yuill, *supra* note 5, at 217 n.14; CHARLES E. COBB JR., THIS NONVIOLENT STUFF'LL GET YOU KILLED: HOW GUNS MADE THE CIVIL RIGHTS MOVEMENT POSSIBLE 193 (2015); John C. Lenzen, *Liberalizing the Concealed Carry of Handguns by Qualified Civilians: The Case for "Carry Reform,"* 47 RUTGERS L. REV. 1503, 1509 n.22 (1995).

[8] *See* STEPHEN P. HALBROOK, GUN CONTROL AND THE THIRD REICH: DISARMING THE JEWS AND "ENEMIES OF THE STATE" (2013). *See also* STEPHEN P. HALBROOK, GUN CONTROL IN NAZI-OCCUPIED FRANCE: TYRANNY AND RESISTANCE (2018); STEPHEN P. HALBROOK, THE SWISS AND THE NAZIS: HOW THE ALPINE REPUBLIC SURVIVED IN THE SHADOW OF THE THIRD REICH (2006). On Dodd's committee hearings as Halbrook's inspiration, *see* Eric Heyl, *The Day the Holocaust Began*, TRIBLIVE, Dec. 7, 2013, https://archive.triblive.com/news/the-day-the-holocaust-began/.

[9] Cottrol and Diamond research "the connections between racial conflict in American history and the evolution of the notion of the right to bear arms in American constitutionalism." *Never Intended*, *supra* note 5, at 1307–08. It is, therefore, unsurprising that they tend to focus on southern statutes that applied to enslaved men and women, free Blacks, and Freedpeople. However, when that scholarship portrays current gun control efforts as tantamount to Black disarmament by saying, "a society with a

common tactic is to dismiss gun control by associating it with the horrors of racial slavery and the violence of Reconstruction. But this straw-man argument ignores important facts, like the existence of concealed-carry prohibitions in the antebellum South that targeted White men and the nullity of postbellum Black Codes after the ratification of the Fourteenth Amendment in 1868.[10] A still more slippery approach involves distraction. After being presented with examples of Black armed resistance to heinous racial violence, readers forget that the besieged African Americans in question had access to weapons, knew how to use them, and frequently succeeded in countering the immediate threat through the force of arms.[11] In fact, after the revolutionary changes of Reconstruction, which conferred upon them citizenship and civil rights, Black Americans thwarted White supremacist attempts to disarm them; when they have taken up weapons in the post-emancipation period, it has been as a form of armed resistance against a hostile society that threatened them with violence while simultaneously denying them the protection of the law.[12]

---

dismal record of protecting a people [African Americans] has a dubious claim on the right to disarm them," *Afro-Americanist Reconsideration*, *supra* note 5, at 361, it becomes a form of cherry-picking.

[10] Cottrol and Diamond focus on weapon regulations enacted in the South during the "eras of Reconstruction and Redemption," *Never Intended*, *supra* note 5, at 1309, to ascertain what legislators intended by these statutes, yet they do not provide any political, social, or even legislative history of them. *See id.* at 1307–11, 1324–35. *See also* Yuill, *supra* note 5, at 217–22; Cramer, *supra* note 5, at 18–21.

[11] Cottrol and Diamond finish their "Afro-Americanist Reconsideration" of the Second Amendment by examining the "ignored" history of armed self-defense by African Americans in the twentieth century. In this final section of a paper that concludes with the specter of Black disarmament, they provide countless examples of African Americans using weapons to defend themselves from murderous Whites. *See Afro-Americanist Reconsideration*, *supra* note 5, at 351–58. The authors claim, "When blacks used firearms to protect their rights, they were often partially successful but were ultimately doomed." *Id.* at 353. This statement aptly describes *some* of the examples provided, wherein African Americans received brutal retaliation for engaging in armed self-defense; but it does not account for others, like the Deacons for Defense and similar groups whose arms and numbers successfully warded off White attacks during the civil rights era.

[12] Undoubtedly there have been isolated instances of the legal or forcible disarmament of some African Americans, but the constitutional protections of the Fourteenth Amendment have prevented the reappearance of racially discriminatory weapon regulations. Interestingly, Cottrol and Diamond briefly mention an 1891 Tennessee case wherein the disarmament of a Black militia unit resulted in a lynching; for reasons that remain unclear, they relegate this damning piece of evidence to a footnote. *See id.* at 354 n.243. There is a robust and growing literature on Black Americans' use of armed resistance during the twentieth century. Authors highlight the ubiquity and usefulness of firearms among some members of the Freedom Movement. These authors generally align Black armed resistance with empowerment and "insurgent political action," AKINYELE OMOWALE UMOJA, WE WILL SHOOT BACK: ARMED RESISTANCE IN THE MISSISSIPPI FREEDOM MOVEMENT 7 (2013), rather than expansive gun rights or repeal of weapon regulations. *See also, e.g.*, SIMON WENDT, THE SPIRIT AND THE SHOTGUN: ARMED RESISTANCE AND THE STRUGGLE FOR CIVIL RIGHTS (2007); LANCE HILL, THE DEACONS FOR DEFENSE AND JUSTICE: ARMED RESISTANCE AND THE CIVIL RIGHTS MOVEMENT (2005). One exception is Charles Cobb, who mentions "an ironic similarity" between the Black Codes and current supporters of gun control, though he does not explain the connection. Cobb, *supra* note 7, at 42.

Though some claims made by gun rights scholars are fallacious, we should not move on from the topic without further inquiry. To do so would be ceding the field to the strange bedfellows of gun rights and ethnic studies scholars who have simplified the ways in which racism relates to weapon regulation and the bearing of arms. This is an important issue deserving of intense scrutiny, careful analysis, and extreme caution.[13]

The enterprise of regulating the possession, transportation, and use of dangerous weapons is not an inherently racist one. It predates racial slavery in the Americas and aligns with one of the most fundamental responsibilities of civil government—to protect people and property. In a similar vein, the development of weapon regulation policies in the United States has not been universally detrimental to people of color. Rather, there are some notable examples of gun control policies designed specifically to protect racial minorities from a violent and well-armed White majority. None of this denies that race has been and continues to be an important part of our country's history when it comes to weapons and armed violence; persistent and pernicious anti-Black racism has been especially problematic in the enforcement of gun regulations by police during the twentieth century. But race as a crucial *part* of the story should not be mistaken for racism as the *whole* story.

II. Race and Militia Laws

The proper starting place for a study of race and the right to bear arms is the militia. Militia laws were some of the first weapon-related statutes to be enacted by colonial legislatures, and they became an important part of national defense and local policing, as well as the shared power within the federal system. At many points throughout American history, race has been intricately bound up with them because the privileges and obligations of citizenship tended to be reserved for White men.

It is easy to see how racial difference and membership within the body politic intersected from the beginning of the Anglo-European colonial enterprise in North America. The first opponents against whom colonial militiamen took up arms were neighboring Indigenous communities—separate, sovereign, and

---

[13] The question of how racial animus has affected the development and enforcement of gun regulations throughout American history has become a prominent point of discussion among Second Amendment scholars. Numerous briefs filed on behalf of New York State Rifle & Pistol Association (NYSRPA) in the recent case, *NYSRPA v. Bruen*, 142 S. Ct. 2111 (2022), relied upon a supposed connection between racism and gun control to overrule New York's longstanding handgun licensing program. The justices did not wade deeply into those waters, but *Bruen*'s call to focus on historical analogs in future firearm cases means that it will likely become even more significant in the coming years.

sometimes hostile nations. Even when colonies maintained military alliances with Indian groups, service in the militia was the responsibility of the free men of the colony, most of whom were White. One of the earliest militia laws in American history, from Virginia in 1640, ordered "heads of families" to accumulate sufficient arms for the men of their households, and they were exempted from provisioning weapons for their slaves.[14] Some historians interpreted this law to prohibit Black Virginians from owning weapons, but it is important to note that some of the householders subject to its dictates were themselves free Blacks.[15] The participation of free Black men in colonial and later state militias varied over time and by location. There was a general trend toward racial exclusion as the eighteenth century progressed, though emergencies prompted governments to put domestic security ahead of race discrimination. Occasionally states included them even in the antebellum nineteenth century (as North Carolina did through 1812), while others merely refrained from excluding them.[16]

After emancipation and the conclusion of the Civil War, the racial composition of the militia became a divisive political and cultural issue. For the defeated Confederates, the prospect of men formerly held in bondage organizing into state-sanctioned militias and drilling in the public square was unconscionable. Bearing arms in service to the state and community had long been a marker of citizenship and manliness that most White southerners believed Freedmen to be incapable of.[17] This atmosphere of White suspicion led several southern states to drag their feet on enrolling Freedmen into state militias, even under Republican governments that supported Black suffrage and civil rights. Informal militia groups emerged, though, and Republican leadership in other former Confederate states had no qualms about Black militia service.[18] But Democratic-leaning southerners responded to the elevation of the Republican Party and Black men by forming Klan chapters that functioned as White

---

[14] I have emulated historians of colonial Virginia by assigning this law to 1640 rather than 1639. For an abridged version, *see* Act X of Jan. 6, 1639, *in* 1 THE STATUTES AT LARGE; BEING A COLLECTION OF ALL THE LAWS OF VIRGINIA, FROM THE FIRST SESSION OF THE LEGISLATURE, IN THE YEAR 1619, at 226 (William Waller Hening ed., 1823). For a full transcription, *see Acts of the General Assembly, 1639-40*, 4 WM. & MARY Q. 145, 147 (1924).

[15] T. H. BREEN & STEPHEN INNES, "MYNE OWNE GROUND": RACE AND FREEDOM ON VIRGINIA'S EASTERN SHORE, 1640–1676 21–25 (25th anniv. ed. 2004).

[16] WINTHROP JORDAN, WHITE OVER BLACK: AMERICAN ATTITUDES TOWARD THE NEGRO, 1550–1812, at 411–12 (2d ed. 2012).

[17] On the importance of race and gender to militia service, *see* CAROLE EMBERTON, BEYOND REDEMPTION: RACE, VIOLENCE, AND THE AMERICAN SOUTH AFTER THE CIVIL WAR (2013).

[18] Informal groups arose, particularly around the Loyal League. *See* ERIC FONER, RECONSTRUCTION: AMERICA'S UNFINISHED REVOLUTION 283–84 (1988). On the dangers of raising Black militia units, *see id.* at 438–40; RICHARD WHITE, THE REPUBLIC FOR WHICH IT STANDS: THE UNITED STATES DURING RECONSTRUCTION AND THE GILDED AGE, 1865–1896, at 305–06 (2017). Even Mississippi, whose Republican government had refrained from passing any militia law for fear of racial violence, changed course in 1875 when their demise was imminent. *See* UMOJA, *supra* note 12, at 14–16.

paramilitaries dedicated to disarming Freedmen. At the local level across the South, Reconstruction was frequently undone by small-scale race wars in which these White militias outgunned their Black opponents and used their superior firepower to control the outcome of an upcoming election.[19] For the most part, the end of Reconstruction signaled the end of Black militia participation; some segregated Black units remained in the southern states but usually for ceremonial rather than defense purposes.[20]

III. Colonial and Antebellum Weapon Regulations

Militia laws are central to the meaning of the Second Amendment and the act of "bearing arms" in American history, but they are actually irrelevant to the longstanding practice of regulating the possession, use, and transportation of dangerous weapons. Militia laws focused on arming eligible citizens with military-grade equipment, so those excluded from militia service were not automatically barred from owning or using weapons. The more appropriate precedent for modern gun control efforts rests in the Anglo-American common law tradition, which authorized local officials to detain and penalize people who engaged in unacceptable or threatening behavior like carrying weapons in public.[21] As American legislatures became more prone to the enactment of statutes, this authority evolved into laws that limited which weapons could be carried in public, when, and by whom.

The earliest of these written statutes targeted persons deemed suspicious or untrustworthy, particularly Indians and slaves. Laws prohibiting the trade of arms and ammunition to hostile Indian tribes functioned as commonsense security policy. Illicit trade with Native groups was a persistent problem in the colonial backcountry as well as frontier states, and Americans were not the only ones attempting to control what kind of weaponry their Indigenous enemies had access to.[22] Where Indians might pose a threat to the White community from the outside, slaves posed one from within. After decades of exponential growth of an enslaved population, Slave Codes emerged in the early eighteenth century and remained a fixture in southern law through the Civil War. The weapon-related provisions within these sweeping codes discouraged free people from providing arms to slaves and punished enslaved men and women for hunting or carrying

---

[19] FONER, *supra* note 18, at 436–44.
[20] *See, e.g., Colored Encampment Attracts Many People*, AUSTIN STATESMAN, July 22, 1903, at 3.
[21] Saul Cornell, *The Right to Keep and Carry Arms in Anglo-American Law: Preserving Liberty and Keeping the Peace*, 80 LAW & CONTEMP. PROBS. 11, 27–28 (2017).
[22] For example, the Spanish in New Mexico tried to prevent Comanches from obtaining high quality arms. *See* PEKKA HÄMÄLÄINEN, THE COMANCHE EMPIRE 41, 189, 383 n.9 (2008).

weapons without permission. In most cases, slave owners retained wide latitude to arm their slaves as needed on their own property or with their express authorization.[23] Postbellum Black Codes tried to replicate this discretionary arming of a subjugated Black labor force, but they proved unenforceable after the ratification of the Fourteenth Amendment in 1868.

Of those antebellum laws that affected the free population, the racially motivated ones concerned free Blacks—a group believed by most White southerners to be untrustworthy and liable to lead a slave revolt. The general practice among slave states was to require licensure for free Blacks to possess or carry weapons. Those seeking licenses usually had to be "house keepers" or "house holders," meaning that they lived independently even if they did not own property. Upon application, local officials could grant temporary gun licenses that had to be renewed (often on an annual basis). The status of free Blacks under law differed from one colony or state to the next and often changed over time. Older states on the Atlantic seaboard generally had sizeable free Black populations and therefore tended to enact harsher regulations than their more westerly counterparts. Furthermore, the mounting crisis over slavery prompted some states to become increasingly stringent in their efforts to control free Blacks' access to arms. The most extreme example of this trend was Delaware, which went from allowing gun licenses for "free negroes and free mulattoes" in 1832[24] to threatening free Blacks in possession of arms with sale into servitude in 1863.[25] But despite the draconian policies in mid-nineteenth-century Delaware, such was not the norm in the South (which generally required licensure), let alone the United States as a whole. On the southwestern frontier was Texas,

---

[23] Most of these statutes provided exceptions for enslaved persons to carry weapons, such as on the property of a master or mistress, with appropriate permission, or in the presence of a White person. Only rarely did they completely prohibit slaves from carrying weapons. One example is a Virginia law from 1792. See An Act of Dec. 17, 1792, ch. 103, § 8, in A COLLECTION OF ALL SUCH ACTS OF THE GENERAL ASSEMBLY OF VIRGINIA, OF A PUBLIC AND PERMANENT NATURE, AS ARE NOW IN FORCE 187 (1803). Slave Code provisions concerning weapons were frequently complex, listing numerous exceptions. The South Carolina code from 1740 is demonstrative in this regard. See An Act for the Better Ordering and Governing Negroes and Other Slaves in this Province, § 23, 1731–43 S.C. Acts 168. When Mississippi enacted a total ban on slaves carrying weapons in 1799, A Law for the Regulation of Slaves, 1799 Miss. Laws 113, the legislature swiftly amended it to allow for exceptions within a master's discretion, An Act Respecting Slaves, § 4, 1804 Miss. Laws 90–91. The 1799 law seems to make no provision for free Blacks to possess firearms, but that is inaccurate. A proviso to the law can be found in SARGENT'S CODE: A COLLECTION OF THE ORIGINAL LAWS OF THE MISSISSIPPI TERRITORY ENACTED 1799–1800 BY GOVERNOR WINTHROP SARGENT AND THE TERRITORIAL JUDGES 44 (1939).
[24] An Act to Prevent the Use of Fire Arms by Free Negroes and Free Mulattoes and for Other Purposes, ch. 176, § 1, 1832 Del. Laws 180; An Act of Feb. 28, 1843, ch. 501, § 1, 1843 Del. Laws 552. Delaware's licensure policy allowed free Blacks "a gun or fowling piece" and presumably omitted the remaining prohibited weapons: "pistol, sword or any warlike instruments whatsoever."
[25] An Act in Relation to Free Negroes and Mulattoes, ch. 305, § 7, 1863 Del. Laws 332. The 1863 law was likely a response to the Emancipation Proclamation, which rendered the future of slavery in unionist Delaware uncertain. It mandated a fine of ten dollars, and anyone unable to pay even after a period in jail would "be sold to pay the fine and cost, for any period not exceeding seven years."

which barred free Blacks from militia service but permitted them to own and use whatever weapons they wanted.[26] Though an example of leniency in comparison to other southern states, the Texan approach reflected the general rule across the nation, including most northern states.[27]

Though these racially motivated laws affecting Indians, enslaved people, and free Blacks illustrate an acute awareness among early Americans of the potential danger of arms in the hands of non-White people, they do not represent the full spectrum of weapon regulations in the antebellum era, let alone the broad sweep of American history. Regulations pertaining to the safe storage and transportation of arms and ammunition reach back to the seventeenth century. During the eighteenth century, several colonies and states enacted regulations that limited the carrying of weapons in public. Hunting laws in Pennsylvania and New Jersey forbade carrying a gun beyond the confines of one's own property.[28] Statutes elsewhere explicitly stated what had long been encompassed within the authority of local justices of the peace under English common law—to apprehend and punish people who went armed in public areas.[29]

The enterprise of regulating public carry by state-level statute really took off during the antebellum nineteenth century. There are several reasons for this. First, innovations in technology and transportation rendered ever more handheld weapons available for purchase, which posed a serious threat to the security of fast-growing market towns and commercial centers. Second, a southern custom of men carrying weapons in public had developed by the early nineteenth century. Though the origins of this practice remain unclear, its effects do not.[30] By the 1810s, there were enough southern men tucking away dangerous weapons in their clothing and canes that their proclivity toward violence

---

[26] Brennan Gardner Rivas, The Deadly Weapon Laws of Texas: Regulating Guns, Knives, and Knuckles in the Lone Star State, 1836–1930, at 36 (May 2019) (Ph.D. dissertation, Texas Christian University) (on file with the Texas Christian University Library System).

[27] In most northern states, the closest thing to a race-based gun law was the exclusion of enslaved men and free Blacks from militia service. Massachusetts granted an "exemption" for "negros" like that extended to ministers, disabled persons, and local officials. An Act for Regulating the Militia, § 12, 1693–94 Mass. Acts 50. See also An Act for Regulating the Militia of the State of New York, ch. 33, 1778 N.Y. Laws 62; An Act to Organize and Discipline the Militia and Volunteer Militia, ch. 120 § 8, in THE PUBLIC STATUTES OF THE STATE OF MINNESOTA, 1849–1858, at 799 (1859).

[28] An Act of Apr. 21, 1760, ch. 456 § 6, 1759–70 Pa. Laws 229; An Act for the Preservation of Deer, and Other Game, and to Prevent Trespassing with Guns, ch. 540, § 10, 1763–75 N.J. Laws 346.

[29] See, e.g., An Act of Jan. 29, 1795, ch. 2, 1795 Mass. Laws 436; An Act for Preventing and Suppressing of Riots, Routs and Unlawful Assemblies, ch. 12, § 1, 1749–51 Mass. Acts 339. The question of what types of public carry were permissible under common law has been the subject of much debate. The work of Saul Cornell presents a compelling argument that carrying weapons in public was, in most circumstances, considered a disturbance of the peace and punishable by law. See Cornell, supra note 21.

[30] Recent scholarship demonstrates that this was, for the most part, a regional custom not derived from English practice. See Eric M. Ruben & Saul Cornell, Firearm Regionalism and Public Carry: Placing Southern Antebellum Case Law in Context, 125 YALE L.J. F. 121, 125 (2015), 124–28; Never Intended, supra note 5, at 1318–19; RANDOLPH ROTH, AMERICAN HOMICIDE 218 (2009).

endangered civil society in many communities. The popularity of dueling among southerners likely contributed to their willingness to settle differences via impromptu fights in which one or both combatants resorted to using hidden knives, pistols, and sword-canes.[31] Prohibitions against concealed weapons followed apace, reaching eight southern states by 1839.[32] Louisiana declared in 1813 that "any person who shall be found with any concealed weapon ... shall on conviction thereof before any justice of the peace, be subject to pay a fine."[33] Arkansas prescribed a fine and jail time for "[e]very person who shall wear any pistol, dirk, butcher or large knife, or a sword in a cane, concealed as a weapon, unless upon a journey."[34]

A third factor in the rise of laws like these during the antebellum era relates to state legislatures switching their focus from private bills to generally applicable laws.[35] The result was a barrage of statute-writing in the first half of the nineteenth century, some of it aimed at clarifying which elements of English common law still applied in the states. For this reason, many public carry laws—particularly those enacted earlier or in northern states—repeated traditional common law language and required violators to post a peace bond.[36] In 1795, Massachusetts empowered justices of the peace to "cause to be staid and arrested" all who (among other things) "ride or go armed offensively, to the fear or terror of the good citizens." Each offender had to "find sureties for his keeping the Peace" or remain in jail indefinitely.[37] Maine, formerly part of Massachusetts, used identical verbiage in a similar 1821 statute.[38] By 1836, Massachusetts had adopted even more explicit language by declaring "[i]f any person shall go armed with a dirk, dagger, sword, pistol, or other offensive and dangerous weapon, without reasonable cause ... he may ... be required to find sureties for keeping the peace."[39]

---

[31] CLAYTON E. CRAMER, CONCEALED WEAPONS LAWS OF THE EARLY REPUBLIC: DUELING, SOUTHERN VIOLENCE, AND MORAL REFORM (1999).

[32] These included Kentucky (1813), Louisiana (1813), Tennessee (1821), Florida (1835), Georgia (1837), Arkansas (1837), Virginia (1838), and Alabama (1839). Tennessee (1821) and Georgia (1837) laws were broad enough to prohibit open carriage as well, but they did not withstand judicial scrutiny and were subsequently altered.

[33] An Act against Carrying Concealed Weapons, and Going Armed in Public Places in an Unnecessary Manner § 1, 1812 La. Acts 172.

[34] An Act of Feb. 26, 1838, ch. 103, § 17, in THE REVISED STATUTES OF THE STATE OF ARKANSAS 587 (1838).

[35] Farah Peterson, Statutory Interpretation and Judicial Authority, 1776–1860, at 97–99 (2015) (Ph.D. dissertation, Princeton University) (on file with the Princeton University Library system).

[36] This language dates to the Statute of Northampton. See Cornell, supra note 21, at 18–19, 22, 24; Statute of Northampton, 2 Edw. 3, c. 3 (1328) (Eng.). Examples of this phrasing, related to the separate offense of affray, include Virginia (1786), Massachusetts (1795), Tennessee (1801), and Delaware (1852).

[37] An Act of Jan. 29, 1795, ch. 2, 1795 Mass. Laws 436.

[38] An Act of Mar. 15, 1821, ch. 76, § 1, 1821 Me. Laws 285.

[39] Ch. 134, § 16, in THE REVISED STATUTES OF THE COMMONWEALTH OF MASSACHUSETTS 750 (Theron Metcalf ed., 1836).

This Massachusetts model was replicated in six northern states prior to the Civil War.[40]

At a time when American jurists and litigants sought clarity from the law, it is sensible to conclude that legislators wrote statutes spelling out more clearly what they understood the common law on public carry to mean in light of the profound political and technological changes that had taken place following 1776. That sectional differences spawned regional divergences in policy is neither surprising nor a compelling reason to accept the more lenient southern approach as a national standard. What northern and southern public carry laws had in common was their affirmation of states' authority to regulate (if not prohibit) the public carrying of weapons in sweeping and flexible ways without running afoul of the national or state constitutions. The importance of this point is worth emphasizing. During the period of most strident pro-slavery virulence, when some four million Black persons were enslaved in this country, the overwhelming majority of arms regulations *were* intended to be applied to the general population—which in most of the settled sections of America, was White.

IV. Regulating Weapons during Reconstruction

When the Civil War drew to a close, chaos and disorder prevailed in much of the South. It was unclear whether Confederate officials, even at the state and local levels, would be prosecuted as traitors to the United States, and bands of Confederate soldiers often caused disruption while traveling home from wartime service. The Confederates' wounded pride spawned horrifying bloodshed, and long-suppressed tensions between planter and bondsman, unionist and secessionist, erupted in shocking outbursts of violence. Some municipalities confronted this situation by enacting ordinances that restricted the carrying of arms within city or town limits. This was a notable and important step because charters issued by state legislatures during the antebellum period tended to vest local governments with vague powers like "[preserving] the peace, comfort, cleanliness and salubrity of said City." These nebulous phrases offered municipal leaders a degree of flexibility in meeting unforeseen challenges. For instance, Galveston, Texas—the site of a chaotic surrender by Confederate General Edmund Kirby-Smith's army—banned concealed weapons within city limits in 1865 even though the city charter did not specifically authorize the municipal government to do so, and the ban defied state jurisprudence.[41] The city received a

---

[40] Ruben & Cornell, *supra* note 30, at 132.
[41] *Proceedings of the City Council*, FLAKE'S BULLETIN, Dec. 28, 1865, at 2. *See also* Brad R. Clampitt, *The Breakup: The Collapse of the Confederate Trans-Mississippi Army in Texas, 1865*, 108 Sw. HIST. Q. 498 (2005)

new charter the following year which stated unequivocally the city government's power "to regulate the carrying of weapons, and prevent the carrying of the same concealed."[42]

It was during this same time period that postbellum Black Codes made their brief appearance in the law books of the South. Secession and emancipation created fundamental legal problems that the states of the former Confederacy urgently needed to resolve. New state constitutions initiated the process of readmission to the Union, though under the terms laid out by Abraham Lincoln and Andrew Johnson, Black suffrage was not a requirement. Deeper than the questions of honoring wartime bond issuances and whether Black men would vote was the crucial question of how to transform a racial hierarchy into a biracial society of equal citizens. The first southerners to rewrite postwar constitutions preferred to recreate the former than confront the reality of the latter, so the governments created under their auspices enacted Black Codes. Of primary importance were laws affecting laborer-employer relations and the custody of legal minors, but the codes touched upon nearly all aspects of economic and social life—including the possession of guns. In 1865, Mississippi declared "no freedman, free Negro, or mulatto" except those in U.S. military service or properly licensed "shall keep or carry firearms of any kind," and other states followed suit.[43] The intention of the law was clear: freedmen without firearms would be defenseless, while those who chose to take up arms would be committing an arrestable offense. When the Black Codes' glaring violations of basic rights inflamed the Republican-dominated U.S. Congress, states still in the process of drafting new legislation and constitutions used race-neutral language to accomplish the same goal.

The brazenness of the postbellum southern politicians elicited a strong response from the U.S. Congress, which was controlled by the Radical faction of the Republican Party. Congressional Reconstruction began in 1867 and compelled seceded states to restart the readmission process with new requirements to provide for Black suffrage and respect the civil rights of Freedmen. To put these changes into effect, most states in the former Confederacy had to write yet new constitutions and create yet new civil governments. These constitutional conventions and governments tended to be controlled by a fledgling, biracial Republican Party in the South that not only recruited Black voters but committed itself to protecting them. By and large, Republicans and Freedmen believed that the best way to accomplish this task was to disarm the public sphere (especially polling places) and form loyal militias that included Freedmen. For this reason, several state constitutions drafted during congressional Reconstruction either

---

[42] An Act to Re-Incorporate the City of Galveston, tit. 4, § 27.13 (1866), *in* 5 THE LAWS OF TEXAS, 1822–1897, at 1540 (H.P.N. Gammel ed., 1898).

[43] An Act to Punish Certain Offenses Therein Named, and for Other Purposes, ch. 23, 1865 Miss. Laws 165.

broadened the scope of protected arms-bearing to remove prior race-based restrictions or explicitly affirmed the authority of the state legislature to regulate deadly weapons. Arkansas began the readmission process in 1864 under Lincoln's Ten Percent Plan,[44] and the constitution drafted that year reserved the right to bear arms and therefore participate in the militia to "the free white men of the state" for "their common defence."[45] However, when Republicans mandated a new constitution that reflected the racial egalitarianism of the party, the 1868 document declared that "citizens," a term by then embracing both races, had a right to "keep and bear arms for their common defense."[46] Florida Republicans did much the same in their 1868 constitution, which declared a right to bear arms for "the people" rather than the "free white men" of the state.[47] These altered constitutional protections opened the door to Black participation in state militias that might defend Republican governments and their supporters.[48]

Another trend that occurred among some southern states during Reconstruction was the introduction of explicit legislative power to regulate deadly weapons. Georgia's first three constitutions, which governed the state from independence to secession, omitted any mention of a right to bear arms. That trend changed with the constitution of 1861, which adopted part of the Second Amendment by saying, "The right of the people to keep and bear arms shall not be infringed."[49] This standard of repeating all or part of the Second Amendment remained a feature of Georgia constitutions in 1865, 1868, and 1877.[50] In an effort to bring the public wearing and carrying of weapons within the purview of state regulation, the Republican document (1868) added the proviso, "but the general assembly shall have power to prescribe by law the manner in which arms may be borne."[51] This innovation in Georgia's constitutional

---

[44] FONER, *supra* note 18, at 35–36. Under Lincoln's Ten Percent Plan, seceded states could be readmitted once 10 percent of the eligible voters had sworn allegiance to the United States. This wartime Reconstruction process did not mandate that states provide for Black suffrage and therefore fell by the wayside as Republicans became increasingly committed to enforcing Black rights.

[45] ARK. CONST. of 1864, art. II, § 21.

[46] ARK. CONST. of 1868, art. I, § 5. On the biracial nature of citizenship and voter qualification in Arkansas, *see also* art. VIII, § 2.

[47] *Compare* FLA. CONST. of 1868, Decl. of Rights, § 22, *with* FLA. CONST. of 1838, art. I, § 21. The Florida constitution of 1865 did not include bearing arms in its Declaration of Rights, possibly out of racial animus and controversy surrounding the composition of the state militia. *See* FLA. CONST. of 1865., Decl. of Rights. Cottrol and Diamond note the pattern of changing language in state constitutions. *See Never Intended, supra* note 5, at 1325–26. An absence of historical context prompts them to impute racist motives to these changes when, in fact, the opposite is the case.

[48] On the political complexity of race and militia laws during Reconstruction, *see* EMBERTON, *supra* note 17.

[49] GA. CONST. of 1861, art. I, § 6.

[50] GA. CONST. of 1865, art. I, § 4; GA. CONST. of 1868, art. I, § 14; GA. CONST. of 1877, art. I, §1.22. The wording of the 1877 document remains unchanged: "The right of the people to keep and bear arms shall not be infringed, but the General Assembly shall have power to prescribe the manner in which arms may be borne."

[51] GA. CONST. of 1868, art. I, § 14.

law was not undertaken by the forces of White supremacy but by the men who supported a biracial convention that would enshrine Black suffrage and promote education for all children; delegates of that same convention expressed their gratitude to Major General George Meade for his controversial removal of Governor Charles J. Jenkins as an impediment to Reconstruction.[52] The architect of the proviso was none other than Amos T. Akerman, an ardent defender of Black suffrage who went on to lead the Justice Department during the Ku Klux Klan trials.[53] Though debates about their ultimate motives are not extant, the policies of the convention and the government created by its constitution paint a picture of men seeking the restoration of peace in a war-ravaged state, not a creatively subtle way to disarm Black Georgians. The trajectory of constitutional change in Texas followed the pattern set in Georgia, with authorization of legislative regulation initiated by Republicans in 1869[54] and reiterated by Democrats in the subsequent constitution of 1876.[55]

Texas provides an especially intriguing and insightful case study regarding racism and gun control. Due to the geographic size of the state, U.S. Army soldiers and Freedmen's Bureau agents could not establish the firm military presence needed to combat the endemic racial and political violence. Though all sides could agree that something should be done to curtail the "wretchedly abused" right to carry arms at all times and places, Texas Democrats preferred a tax on pistols worn in public, while the biracial Republican Party sought a blanket prohibition of all public carrying.[56] Republicans controlled the state government from 1869 to 1874, and during that time they prohibited the carrying of all "deadly weapons" in public with few exceptions; the legislation followed the Massachusetts model that had gained traction in some northern states decades earlier, but the penalty entailed jail time or a fine rather than a peace bond. Democrats chafed under this law and even included it in a list of grievances against the Republican governor which they delivered to the U.S. Congress. But Texas Republicans felt quite the opposite, noting that "[t]he Democrats are sullen and angry because the firearm bill has robbed rowdies of their six-shooters, their bowie knives and their sword canes; let us continue to disarm rowdies and murderers, to stop bloody affrays, and to thus oppose the

---

[52] Meade removed Jenkins on January 13, 1868, and members of the convention (several days later) adopted a resolution praising "the course he has pursued in regard to Reconstruction." *See* JOURNAL OF THE PROCEEDINGS OF THE CONSTITUTIONAL CONVENTION OF THE PEOPLE OF GEORGIA 162 (1868).

[53] On Akerman, *see* LOU FAULKNER WILLIAMS, THE GREAT SOUTH CAROLINA KU KLUX KLAN TRIALS, 1871–1872, at 43–45, 101 (1996).

[54] TEX. CONST. of 1869, art. I, § 13.

[55] TEX. CONST. of 1876, art. I, § 23.

[56] This quotation comes from the gubernatorial message of James W. Throckmorton. H.R. JOURNAL, 11th Regular Sess. 199–200 (Tex. 1866).

Democracy."[57] Republicans constituted a demographic minority in Texas, so their grip on state politics was tenuous at best. They recognized that any allowance of deadly weapons in public, even those carried openly, would leave them outgunned by Democrats and vulnerable to intimidation. The actions of Texas Republicans offer us a striking example of gun control as a way of attacking White supremacy and protecting Black Americans.[58]

When taken collectively, the arms-related policies of southern states in the aftermath of the Civil War tell a more complicated story than the one usually propounded by opponents of gun control. Black Codes were the fleeting anomaly within a larger context of racial egalitarianism that defined the spirit, if not the lived experience, of the Reconstruction era. Constitutional changes paved the way for Black militia service and assembled the necessary framework for weapon laws that might disarm the public sphere. These two policies were corollaries to an overall strategy of protecting Republicans and Freedmen; by no other means could the atmosphere of intimidation and violence perpetuated by the former Confederates be obliterated. Furthermore, the work of Reconstruction-era legislatures pertaining to public carry laws stands as evidence that American lawmakers of both political parties and both races thought that weapon regulation was permissible under their state constitutions and the Second Amendment.

As Reconstruction fell apart in the states of the former Confederacy, Democratic governments returned to power and began restoring White supremacy by disassembling much of the Republicans' programs created over the past decade. Laws pertaining to elections, public accommodations, and education were overtly discriminatory and created a clear regional pattern of legally disempowering Black Americans. Democratic action regarding deadly weapon laws, however, did not fit a pattern. In some states, like Tennessee, the politics of race seem to have played some role in policy changes during the Gilded Age. After moderate Republicans had banned "publicly or privately [carrying] a dirk, swordcane, Spanish stiletto, belt or pocket pistol or revolver," Democrats added weapons associated with Black men to the prohibited list.[59] For other states,

---

[57] *A Good Lesson*, HOUSTON DAILY UNION, June 30, 1871, at 2.

[58] On weapon policy in Reconstruction-era Texas, *see* Brennan Gardner Rivas, *An Unequal Right to Bear Arms: State Weapons Laws and White Supremacy in Texas, 1836–1900*, 121 SW. HIST. Q. 284 (2018); Rivas, *supra* note 26, at 41–83. Other states may provide similar stories. For instance, a coalition of moderate Republicans and former Democrats defeated Tennessee's Radical Republicans in 1869 and enacted a strict weapon law in 1870. This might initially seem to support the Cottrol and Diamond hypothesis that Reconstruction-era gun laws were covertly racist; however, the decision by lame-duck Radicals to bar weapons from public events shows that Republicans representing Black voters believed such laws to be important. *See* An Act to Amend the Criminal Laws of the State, ch. 22, §§ 1–2, 1869–70 Tenn. Pub. Acts 23.

[59] An Act of Jan. 6, 1870, ch. 41, § 2, 1869–70 Tenn. Pub. Acts 55. Razors became prohibited concealed weapons in 1879. An Act of Mar. 27, 1879, ch. 186, § 1, 1879 Tenn. Pub. Acts 231. *See also* Brennan Gardner Rivas, *The Problem with Assumptions: Reassessing the Historical Gun Policies of Arkansas and Tennessee*, SECOND THOUGHTS BLOG, Jan. 20, 2022, https://firearmslaw.duke.edu/

though, the end of Reconstruction meant little or no change. After Georgia's sweeping 1837 prohibition against keeping or selling most pistols had been struck down by the state's high court, the legislature adopted a concealed carry law that remained largely unaltered until the twentieth century.[60] Texas judges affiliated with both political parties affirmed the constitutionality of their comprehensive deadly weapon law in light of state constitutions adopted in 1869 and 1876.[61]

Between 1877 and 1900, a host of weapon regulations took shape across the country; from Rhode Island to Alaska and Montana to Arizona, state and territorial governments sought to restrict the presence of weapons in public spaces. Some, like West Virginia and Arizona, emulated the approach of Massachusetts, Texas, and others that prohibited openly borne and concealed pistols, knives, and metal knuckles with few exceptions.[62] But most public carry laws from the closing decades of the nineteenth century applied only concealed weapons. Though it might be tempting to interpret these laws as evidence of widespread social acceptance of carrying pistols and knives openly, such a conclusion would be a mistake. In fact, Americans generally disdained the presence of unnecessary weapons in the public sphere. Though northeastern public opinion acquiesced to the idea that a pistol might be an essential accoutrement for cowboys and western folk, the people living in the trans-Mississippi West thought them incongruous with "the proper costume of a gentleman."[63] The booming market towns of the West were filled with forward-thinking risk-takers whose dearly held middle-class values condemned such behavior.[64]

2022/01/the-problem-with-assumptions-reassessing-the-historical-gun-policies-of-arkansas-and-tennessee/.

[60] *See* Nunn v. State, 1 Ga. 243 (1846). 1 CODE OF THE STATE OF GEORGIA § 4413 (1861); An Act to Preserve the Peace and Harmony of this State, and for Other Purposes, tit. 15 § 1, 1870 Ga. Laws 421; §§ 347–48, *in* 6 PARK'S ANNOTATED CODE OF THE STATE OF GEORGIA 233 (Orville Augustus Park et al. eds., 1914). Georgia adopted licensure for carrying pistols in 1910.

[61] Mark Anthony Frassetto, *The Law and Politics of Firearms Regulation in Reconstruction Texas*, 4 TEX. A&M L. REV. 95, 113–21 (2016).

[62] An Act of Offenses against the Peace, ch. 148, § 7, 1891 W. Va. Code 915; An Act Defining and Punishing Certain Offenses against the Public Peace, § 1, 1889 Ariz. Sess. Laws 16. Western governments, like Arizona, often restricted weapons solely in established towns.

[63] Editorial, *Out of Style in Texas*, WACO DAILY EXAMINER, Aug. 26, 1884, at 4, *reprinted from* N.Y. SUN.

[64] On the middle-class mentality of Great Plains residents, *see* ROBERT R. DYKSTRA, THE CATTLE TOWNS (1968); Robert R. Dykstra, *To Live and Die in Dodge City: Body Counts, Law and Order, and the Case of* Kansas v. Gill, *in* LETHAL IMAGINATION: VIOLENCE AND BRUTALITY IN AMERICAN HISTORY 211 (Michael A. Bellesiles ed., 1999); MARK R. ELLIS, LAW AND ORDER IN BUFFALO BILL'S COUNTRY: LEGAL CULTURE AND COMMUNITY ON THE GREAT PLAINS, 1867–1910 (2007). On the radicalism and modernism of agrarian movements more generally, *see* ELIZABETH SANDERS, ROOTS OF REFORM: FARMERS, WORKERS, AND THE AMERICAN STATE, 1877–1917 (1999); CHARLES POSTEL, THE POPULIST VISION (2007).

V. Conclusion

If post-Reconstruction changes to state policies on public arms-carrying do not easily conform to a pattern of racial discrimination, they do follow the development of progressivism during the latter nineteenth century.[65] Technological innovations led to greater availability of cheap revolvers and introduced new products, like toy pistols, metal knuckles, and slingshots. Meanwhile, railroad construction and growing newspaper readership revolutionized the transportation and advertising of consumer goods—including pistols. Policymakers across the country proposed innovative solutions to the unforeseeable problems posed by these deadly weapons, from occupation taxes and sales taxes to prohibitions and cumbersome licensing procedures.[66] This is a story of progressive reform inseparable from the rise of the regulatory state, not one of veiled racism. The strange bedfellows of gun rights and ethnic studies scholars are correct to see race bound up with gun regulations, even if their assessment of that relationship is overblown. Racism moves from periphery to center when we consider the enforcement of gun laws since about 1900. Originally intended to be color-blind, these regulations became tools of social control during the era of Jim Crow. An in-depth study of the Texas deadly weapon law asserts that discriminatory enforcement developed over time as the Republican Party ceased to be a force in local politics. In sample counties surveyed, persons arrested for "unlawful carrying" initially reflected the racial demographics of the county in question. Around 1890, however, African Americans came to represent a disproportionate number of violators; the racial gap only widened over time such that by 1920 nearly everyone arrested for carrying arms was Black or Mexicano. The rise of discriminatory enforcement in Texas overlapped with the collapse of the Republican Party locally.[67] Events in other states likely followed a similar trajectory in which loss of political voice through disfranchisement mechanisms and White population growth left racial minorities vulnerable to mistreatment by local authorities.[68]

Selective enforcement of penal laws like this one created an evidentiary foundation for progressive sociologists and statisticians to criminalize persons of color by falsely associating them with lawbreaking. This criminalization process occurred during the height of progressivism and seemingly proved that Black men and women were the problem, not their treatment within American

---

[65] Rebecca Edwards, *Politics, Social Movements, and the Periodization of U.S. History*, 8 J. GILDED AGE & PROGRESSIVE ERA 463 (2009).

[66] PATRICK J. CHARLES, ARMED IN AMERICA: A HISTORY OF GUN RIGHTS FROM COLONIAL MILITIAS TO CONCEALED CARRY 161–65 (2018).

[67] Rivas, *supra* note 26, 164–95.

[68] At this time, Texas remains the only case study that can inform scholarly conclusions on this subject.

society.[69] Rather than decry the laws themselves as the problem, the strange bedfellows who see racism in gun control efforts would be better served by focusing on the inequitable enforcement of gun laws over the past century and more. Such an approach would put them shoulder to shoulder with the antiracist scholars[70] who have illuminated the ways in which well-meaning government policies have, especially through policing, reinforced anti-Black racism.

[69] *See generally* KHALIL GIBRAN MUHAMMAD, THE CONDEMNATION OF BLACKNESS: RACE, CRIME, AND THE MAKING OF MODERN URBAN AMERICA (2010).
[70] *See generally* IBRAM X. KENDI, STAMPED FROM THE BEGINNING: THE DEFINITIVE HISTORY OF RACIST IDEAS IN AMERICA (2016); ELIZABETH HINTON, FROM THE WAR ON POVERTY TO THE WAR ON CRIME: THE MAKING OF MASS INCARCERATION IN AMERICA (2016).

10

A Brief Overview of Gun Registration in U.S. History

Genesa C. Cefali and Jacob D. Charles

I. Introduction

Modern opponents of gun regulations tend to maintain a special antipathy for laws mandating the registration of firearms.[1] These laws generally allow the government to keep information about guns and their owners. Although the purposes for registration vary, California's statute describes its law as designed to "assist in the investigation of crime, the prosecution of civil actions by city attorneys . . . , the arrest and prosecution of criminals, and the recovery of lost, stolen, or found property."[2] Such laws may also have an incentive effect on gun owners, by discouraging risky loans or sales. After all, if guns are tied to owners, then a recovered crime gun ought to reveal its prior lawful owner.

Despite any potential benefits, gun-rights proponents worry that registration will lead to firearm confiscation, and to potentially worse outcomes.[3] As one opponent writes: "Registration. Confiscation. Extinction. Each step makes the next step much easier."[4] Based in part on these concerns, Congress expressly

---

[1] Bernard E. Harcourt, *On Gun Registration, the NRA, Adolf Hitler, and Nazi Gun Laws: Exploding the Gun Culture Wars (A Call to Historians)*, 73 Fordham L. Rev. 653 (2004) ("Say the words 'gun registration' to many Americans—especially pro-gun Americans, including the 3.5 million-plus members of the National Rifle Association ('NRA')—and you are likely to hear about Adolf Hitler, Nazi gun laws, gun confiscation, and the Holocaust.").

[2] Cal. Penal Code § 11106(a)(1)(D); Daniel W. Webster et al., *Relationship Between Licensing, Registration, and Other Gun Sales Laws and the Source State of Crime Guns*, 7 Inj. Prevention 184, 184 (2001) ("Mandatory registration makes it easier to trace guns used in crime to their last known legal owner, and to investigate possible illegal transfers.").

[3] Dean Weingarten, *Gun Registration Is Gun Confiscation—Updated 2019 Edition*, Ammoland, Sept. 10, 2019, https://www.ammoland.com/2019/09/gun-registration-is-gun-confiscation-updated-2019-edition/#axzz68UCTsjub (declaring that "[o]nce your guns are required to be registered, they are, in effect, already confiscated"); *see also* Stephen P. Halbrook, *The Empire Strikes Back: The District of Columbia's Post-Heller Firearm Registration System*, 81 Tenn. L. Rev. 571, 574 (2014) ("It is no secret that, while not inevitable, registration facilitates confiscation, and that it has occurred in some of the darkest pages of history."); Dave Kopel, *The Catastrophic Consequences of Gun Registration*, Dave Kopel, https://davekopel.org/2A/catastrophic-consequences-gun-registration.html (last visited June 16, 2022) ("[G]un registration is very good for one thing—confiscation.").

[4] Kopel, *supra* note 3.

prohibited a national gun registry in the 1986 Firearm Owners Protection Act.[5] (Since 1934, however, federal law has required comprehensive registration for a small category of firearms, including machineguns and short-barrel rifles and shotguns.[6]) As of 2021, six states and the District of Columbia required some or all guns to be registered; eight states barred such registries by law.[7]

In modern litigation over the scope of the Second Amendment, courts, scholars, and litigants increasingly look to history to guide the inquiry. Indeed, according to Justice Brett Kavanaugh, "Gun bans and gun regulations that are longstanding . . . are consistent with the Second Amendment individual right. Gun bans and gun regulations that are not longstanding or sufficiently rooted in text, history, and tradition are not consistent with the Second Amendment individual right."[8] He concluded that comprehensive registration schemes were not longstanding and would therefore have struck down a District of Columbia law so requiring. In its 2022 decision, *New York State Rifle & Pistol Association v. Bruen*, the Supreme Court vindicated Justice Kavanaugh's view: history is now the benchmark for constitutionality of gun laws.[9]

Our analysis in this chapter suggests that registration laws in fact enjoy a robust historical pedigree, though *Bruen* does tend to discount evidence from the twentieth century as coming too late. By 1933, twenty-two states—almost half of those then admitted—had enacted some form of registration scheme for firearms or ammunition.[10] As we discuss in more detail in section III, these laws vary along several different dimensions. Some directed gun sellers to

---

[5] 18 U.S.C. § 926(a)(3) ("No such rule or regulation prescribed after the date of the enactment of the Firearm Owners' Protection Act may require that records required to be maintained under this chapter or any portion of the contents of such records, be recorded at or transferred to a facility owned, managed, or controlled by the United States or any State or any political subdivision thereof, nor that any system of registration of firearms, firearms owners, or firearms transactions or dispositions be established.").

[6] *National Firearms Act Division*, BUREAU OF ALCOHOL, TOBACCO, FIREARMS AND EXPLOSIVES, https://www.atf.gov/resource-center/fact-sheet/fact-sheet-national-firearms-act-nfa-division (last visited June 14, 2022) (describing how the Bureau of Alcohol, Tobacco, Firearms and Explosives' National Firearms Act Division "maintains the National Firearms Registration and Transfer Record (NFRTR), the central registry for all items regulated under the NFA. More than 3 million items are currently registered in the NFRTR, which dates back to the enactment of the NFA in 1934.").

[7] See *Registration*, GIFFORDS LAW CENTER TO PREVENT GUN VIOLENCE, https://giffords.org/lawcenter/gun-laws/policy-areas/owner-responsibilities/registration (last visited June 8, 2022) (scroll to "Summary of State Law" subheading) (documenting state laws barring state or local government entities from creating registries).

[8] Heller v. District of Columbia, 670 F.3d 1244, 1285 (D.C. Cir. 2011) (Kavanaugh, J., dissenting); *see also id.* at 1271 ("[C]ourts are to assess gun bans and regulations based on text, history, and tradition, not by a balancing test such as strict or intermediate scrutiny.").

[9] New York State Rifle & Pistol Association, Inc. v. Bruen, 597 U.S. ___ (2022).

[10] Arkansas (1923); California (1917); Connecticut (1918, 1923); Georgia (1866, 1921); Hawaii (1925, 1927, 1933); Illinois (1881, 1931); Indiana (1925); Michigan (1913, 1925, 1927); Minnesota (1933); Mississippi (1900); Montana (1918); New York (1911); North Carolina (1919); Ohio (1933); Oregon (1917); South Carolina (1934); South Dakota (1933); Texas (1931); Virginia (1926, 1934); West Virginia (1925); Wisconsin (1933); Wyoming (1933). *See* App. 1 for full citations.

collect information; others required individuals to report it themselves. But each mandated the creation of government-accessible data linking a gun to its owner in just the ways that critics denounce. That is the core of what we consider a registration law.[11]

We distinguish, and for the rest of this chapter set aside, two other types of laws that are conceptually similar to registration laws. Early militia laws mandated that citizens eligible for militia service acquire and bear certain types of firearms. These laws generally empowered government officials to inspect such arms and provided penalties for arms that failed to meet government standards; they were, in that sense, quite intrusive. Although non-militia private arms were not subject to such official oversight, the guns kept at home during this period were vastly different from the private arsenals gracing suburbanite gun safes today—or even of the last hundred years. The early militia inspection laws illustrate governmental authority to control, in some manner and to some extent, information about the arms possession of the majority of the arms-bearing population. But since these laws had different aims and ends, we do not discuss them further in this chapter.

Second, although firearm registration laws are similar to firearm licensing laws, we keep the two separate here to clarify the analysis. One key difference is in the object of regulation: "Licensing requirements mandate that gun owners meet certain standards or pass certain tests before owning guns or using them in particular ways. . . . Registration requirements, by contrast, require registration of individual guns."[12] We are focused on the laws that regulate the gun, not its owner. To be sure, one of the ways registration laws have worked historically is by mandating that owners file certain paperwork concerning their weapons. In this sense, they regulate the gun *by* regulating the owner; but, in registration laws, the lethal instrument is still the focal point.

Section II provides an overview of some of the earliest laws we recognize as modern registration laws, drawn from the Duke Repository of Historical Gun Laws. We focus on the intrusiveness of the laws and the pushback (or not) that they appear to have received. Section III turns to analyze early registration laws on several important dimensions, including the types of arms they regulated and the information they collected. Finally, section IV provides some brief reflections on how this history may factor into current debates over modern registration laws.

---

[11] Our definition is broad. It would count the current federal requirement that federal firearms licensees—like gun stores—keep information linking the gun to the purchaser. The 1986 restrictions on the centralizing of this data, however, sets this law apart from its historical counterparts. We find no such express restrictions in the laws in this chapter.

[12] *Heller*, 670 F.3d at 1291 (Kavanaugh, J., dissenting).

II. Overview of Early U.S. Gun Registries

As far back as 1866, Georgia enacted a firearm tax that required the owner of every plantation within several specified counties to report, under oath, the number of guns, pistols, muskets, and rifles over three on their plantations.[13] Although this law differed greatly from later registration schemes, it falls prey to the same objections that modern commentators invoke against contemporary registries: the government had in its hands the information on where guns were located and how many guns belonged to each covered owner. If registration enables quick confiscation on the way to tyrannical rule, then Georgia's law ought to have invoked quite an alarm. We have not found such outrage in the historical record.

Following the Civil War, civilian firearms, especially concealable ones, came under increasing government scrutiny. In 1881, Illinois enacted one of the first modern firearm registries we have found, which it directed toward gun dealers.[14] The statute declared:

> All persons dealing in deadly weapons, hereinbefore mentioned, at retail within this State shall keep a register of all such weapons sold or given away by them. Such register shall contain the date of the sale or gift, the name and age of the person to whom the weapon is sold or given, the price of the said weapon, and the purpose for which it is purchased or obtained. The said register shall be in the following form: [Form of Register]. Said register is to be kept open for inspection of the public, and all persons who may wish to examine the same may do so at all reasonable times during business hours. . . .[15]

The registry provision was part of a broader deadly weapons law that, as the *Chicago Tribune* contemporaneously noted, worked "a complete revision of the old law, touching not only the carrying of concealed weapons, but placing proper restrictions around their disposition, and absolutely prohibiting their sale to minors."[16] The law was motivated by concerns over the common carrying and threatening display of concealable weapons; the legislator who introduced the bill and shepherded it through passage was convinced this more "stringent"

---

[13] *See* An Act to Authorize the Justices of the Inferior Courts of Camden, Glynn, and Effingham Counties to Levy a Special Tax for County Purposes, and to Regulate the Same, No. 41, §§ 1–2, 1866 Ga. Laws 27, 27–28 (requiring the owners to "render, upon oath, a full return of every . . . gun, pistol, musket, or rifle so held or kept"); *see also* Brian Sawers, *Race and Property After the Civil War: Creating the Right to Exclude*, 87 Miss. L.J. 703, 743–44 (2018) (discussing racist use of the law).

[14] *See* 1 Annotated Statutes of the State of Illinois in Force 771, para. 90 (Merritt Starr & Russell H. Curtis eds., 1885).

[15] *Id.*

[16] *Deadly Weapons*, Chi. Daily Trib., June 3, 1881, at 9.

regulation was needed to get "to the root of the evil."[17] The goal of the registration provision, wrote the *Tribune*, "was presumably to enable the police authorities to control the sale of revolvers particularly, and to give them a clew to the purchaser in the event of the weapon being found when a murderer escaped."[18] But, just days after it went into effect, the paper was already criticizing the registration requirement because it could be so easily be evaded with a false name.[19] Because the law mandated that the registries be open to public inspection, the *Tribune* surveyed several retailers, reporting that, in one store, three of the five purchasers had listed "Fourth of July" as the reason for purchasing a revolver.[20]

In the early twentieth century, the proliferation of firearms, increased mobility, and immigration created new concerns that led to increased state action attempting to deal with crime.[21] In 1918, Montana passed a comprehensive firearm registration law, appropriately titled "An Act Providing for the Registration of All Fire Arms and Weapons . . ."[22] The law required, in relevant part:

> [E]very person within the State of Montana, who owns or has in his possession any fire arms or weapons shall make a full, true, and complete verified report upon the form hereinafter provided to the sheriff of the County in which such person lives, of all fire arms and weapons which are owned or possessed by him or her or are in his or her control, and on sale or transfer into the possession of any other person such person shall immediately forward to the sheriff of the County in which such person lives the name and address of that purchaser and person into whose possession or control such fire arm or weapon was delivered.[23]

The law covered every firearm—long guns as well as handguns—and required owners to personally register those weapons with the government. Yet in spite of the intrusiveness of such a law on the Western frontier, initial response appears to have been muted. Writing contemporaneously in the *Daily Missoulian*, the

---

[17] *Id.*

[18] *Sale of Pistols: How the New Law Is Observed*, CHI. DAILY TRIB., July 7, 1881, at 8; *see also* People v. Davies, 354 Ill. 168, 179 (1933) ("By means of this register the name of the purchaser of the weapon may be determined, thus in many cases affording a valuable clue to the detection of the person guilty of the violation of the criminal law.").

[19] *Sale of Pistols: How the New Law Is Observed*, CHI. DAILY TRIB., July 7, 1881, at 8.

[20] *Id.*

[21] New York's 1911 Sullivan Act, which required licensing for handgun owners, also instituted a broad registration requirement that gun dealers had to maintain.

[22] An Act Providing for the Registration of All Fire Arms and Weapons and Regulating the Sale Thereof and Defining the Duties of Certain County Officers and Providing Penalties for a Violation of the Provisions of this Act, ch. 2, 1918 Mont. Laws 6.

[23] *Id.* § 1, at 6.

editors observed that "[t]he law was made primarily to make it less easy for the disturbing elements to get possession of dangerous weapons."[24] "Every good citizen," the paper suggested, "will lose no time after the blanks have been furnished in obeying the law, and he should also make it his business to see that others obey."[25] Why worry about registering arms if they were employed for lawful purposes, the paper suggested. Just six weeks later, the paper reported that nine thousand Missoula residents had registered arms.[26]

A newspaper serving Glasgow, Montana, described the new law for readers and, as an aid for gun owners, listed the registration agents appointed by the county sheriff for receiving the required reports.[27] Confirming the ubiquity of firearms in this part of the country, the paper observed that this new law was one "that hits practically every citizen in the state of Montana."[28] It also warned readers that the registration deadline was two weeks away, and the law made failure to register one's arms a misdemeanor.[29] Other reports suggest that "[l]ate [c]omers" were still registering weapons past the deadline; "[s]ome of them said they have been out in the hills and could not get in in time."[30]

There was some predictable pushback, however. In a letter to the editor published in the *Butte Daily Bulletin* in June 1919, a reader complained about the law in terms familiar to a modern follower of contemporary gun debates.[31] Under the title, "Register the Pick Handles," the author derided law enforcement's concern with the number of firearms in Butte and ridiculed a report that authorities had "contemplated a search for unregistered guns."[32] Law enforcement had better things to do than search for unregistered firearms, he suggested.[33] Plus, "if the object of registering guns is to keep some check upon the dangerous proclivities of the obstreperous, why neglect the little item of pick handles?"[34] Pick handles, along with clubs, knives, and all sorts of weapons, could be dangerous in the wrong hands and used to injure and kill. What about all those implements? The writer concluded that all "these pick handles should be gathered up at once," for

---

[24] *Gun Toting*, DAILY MISSOULIAN, Mar. 6, 1918, at 6.
[25] *Id.*
[26] *9,000 Missoulians Register Weapons: No Attempt Made as Yet to Catalogue Arms*, DAILY MISSOULIAN, Apr. 21, 1918, at 5 (reporting that although the names were all alphabetized, the local law enforcement authorities had not started to catalog the weapons of each owner).
[27] *Citizens Must Register Guns: All Fire Arms and Weapons of Every Nature Must Be Registered with Sheriff*, GLASGOW COURIER, Mar. 8, 1918, at 1.
[28] *Id.*
[29] *Id.*
[30] *Alibis and Weapons Offered to Sheriff: Late Comers Have Excuses for Tardiness*, DAILY MISSOULIAN, Apr. 9, 1918, at 2.
[31] Brian Seawell, Letter to the Editor, *Register the Pick Handles*, BUTTE DAILY BULL., Jan. 18, 1919, at 3.
[32] *Id.*
[33] *Id.*
[34] *Id.*

"[l]eft lying about among ignorant, ruthless, rebellious, bolshevik-contaminated workingmen, they constitute a grave menace to the stability of the established order."[35] In other words, guns don't kill people, people do.

The Montana law aimed, as both supporters and critics acknowledged, at those who might misuse weapons, and it appears also to have been motivated in part from concerns arising during World War I. The law was repealed three years later in 1921, but the reasons for that repeal are not altogether clear.[36]

Another comprehensive registration regime from this period is a 1923 Arkansas law, titled "An Act to regulate the Ownership of Pistols and Revolvers."[37] It declared:

> Any person having in his possession or custody any pistol or revolver, shall within 60 days from the approval of this Act, present such firearm to the county clerk of the county, where he resides, and it shall be the duty of the said county clerk to enter upon a separate record provided for that purpose, the name, age, place of residence, and color of the party, together with the make, calibre and number of said pistol or revolver.[38]

Unlike the Montana law, Arkansas's focused narrowly on what was then a nationwide concern for gun violence: concealable weapons, like the handgun. Just like in Montana, the Arkansas statute required each individual owner to present their handguns to a local government official and provide personal information about himself and his weapon.

This law, too, was short-lived. A 1926 article in the *American Bar Association Journal* reported that "[t]his law was found so impracticable in enforcement that it was later repealed."[39] It lasted for just a few years. Although the cause of the impracticability is not described in the article, in the days when paper records were the only way to track ownership, it is not hard to understand why an avalanche of paperwork would become impractical for underresourced local governments and law enforcement authorities. There was also pushback from citizens. As an Arkansas legislator said during hearings on a federal registration scheme, the law "was so unpopular that at last the legislature repealed it."[40]

---

[35] *Id.*
[36] David B. Kopel, *Background Checks for Firearms Sales and Loans: Law, History, and Policy*, 53 HARV. J. ON LEGIS. 303, 344 (2016).
[37] An Act to Regulate the Ownership of Pistols and Revolvers, No. 430, 1923 Ark. Acts 379.
[38] *Id.* § 1, at 379.
[39] Charles V. Imlay, *The Uniform Firearms Act*, 12 A.B.A. J. 767, 768 (1926).
[40] *National Firearms Act: Hearings on H.R. 9066 Before the H. Comm. on Ways & Means*, 73rd Cong. 15 (1934) (statement of Rep. Claude A. Fuller, Member, H. Comm. on Ways & Means).

A final early example is the registration requirement in Michigan's 1927 law.[41] It expanded on an earlier attempt several years before to register all handguns in the state.[42] It provided:

> [A]ny person within this state who owns or has in his possession a pistol as defined in this act, shall ... present such weapon for safety inspection to the commissioner or chief of police of such city or village [or to the county sheriff]. Any person owning or coming into possession of a pistol after [November 1, 1927,] shall forthwith present such pistol for safety inspection in the manner provided in this section. A certificate of inspection shall thereupon be issued in triplicate on a form provided by the commissioner of public safety, containing the name, age, address, description and signature of the person presenting such pistol for inspection, together with a full description thereof; the original of such certificate shall be delivered to the registrant; the duplicate thereof shall be mailed to the commissioner of public safety and field and indexed by him and kept as a permanent official record for a period of six years, and the triplicate of such certificate shall be retained and filed in the office of said sheriff, or commissioner or chief of police, as the case may be.[43]

As one expert put it in testimony before the U.S. Senate, Michigan's law was, as far as he knew, "the first effort made to bring about the effective control of privately armed persons unknown to the authorities."[44]

In 1934, the federal government itself considered, and came very close to passing, a nationwide registration scheme for all firearms except standard rifles and shotguns. Eventually, however, handguns were removed from the legislation and only "gangster" weapons—machine guns, short-barrel rifles and shotguns, and silencers—were part of the registration regime. And nearly no one thought these weapons would be registered in any appreciable number. Rather, as the U.S. Department of Justice backers of the bill said, the registration requirement would provide an effective way to prosecute dangerous criminals who possessed unregistered guns but whose other crimes might have been too hard to prove.[45]

---

[41] An Act to Regulate and License the Selling, Purchasing, and Possessing and Carrying of Certain Firearms..., No. 372, § 9, 1927 Mich. Pub. Acts 887, 891.

[42] An Act Providing for the Registration of the Purchasers of Guns, Pistols, Other Fire-arms and Silencers for Fire-arms and Providing a Penalty for Violation, No. 250, §§ 1–2, 1913 Mich. Pub. Acts 472, 472 (requiring that retail dealers of guns, pistols, other firearms, and silencers for firearms, keep a register recording identifying information).

[43] § 9, 1927 Mich. Pub. Acts at 891.

[44] *To Regulate Commerce in Firearms: Hearings on S. 885, S. 2258, S. 3680 Before a Subcomm. of the S. Comm. on Commerce*, 73rd Cong. 43 (1934) (statement of Dr. Frederick L. Hoffman).

[45] *National Firearms Act: Hearings on H.R. 9066 Before the H. Comm, on Ways & Means*, 73rd Cong. 92 (1934) (statement of Joseph B. Keenan, Assistant Att'y Gen., U.S. Dep't of Just.).

As this overview illustrates, intrusive registration schemes are not a novel phenomenon. The earliest comprehensive regimes were implemented more than a century ago. And they did not lead to widespread abuse, let alone lead inexorably to confiscation and tyrannical rule. Even absent court intervention, local constituencies were able to effectively fight for the repeal of laws that were considered too burdensome, administratively inconvenient, or simply ineffective. While this section highlighted a few of these older laws, section III turns to the details of how early registration laws were structured and administered.

III. The Framework of Regulation

Section II focused on a few of the oldest and most comprehensive registration schemes, but those were by no means the only ones. In fact, as we have noted, by 1933 nearly half the states had enacted some form of registration scheme for firearms or ammunition.[46] If licensing schemes are included in this calculus, the number jumps to at least two-thirds of the states.[47]

This section drills down into the details of the registration laws. It first discusses in subsection A the statutory design of historical registration laws, focusing on the types of arms required to be registered and the personal identifying information required. Although registration laws most commonly targeted handguns, some registration laws reached long guns, and others narrowly targeted machine guns. Moreover, the personal identifying information required by these registration laws was fairly extensive. Subsection B discusses the administration of these registration schemes. The majority of these schemes were registers of sales kept by firearm dealers. A substantial portion of the registration schemes required individual owners to report firearms they possessed.

A. Statutory Design

This subsection focuses on the design of these historical firearm regulations as a whole, exploring the types of arms regulated and the type of information required.

1. Types of Arms
The majority of historical registration statutes applied only to handguns—pistols, revolvers, and other concealable firearms. The language of such laws

---

[46] *See* App. 1 for full citations of these laws.
[47] *See* App. 2 for full citations of these laws.

would typically run as follows: "Every person in the business of selling, leasing, or otherwise transferring a pistol, revolver or other firearm, *of a size capable of being concealed upon the person* . . . shall keep a register . . . ."[48]

The early twentieth century saw a greater frequency of registration laws that targeted concealable weapons.[49] Some, no doubt, were advocated for on less than benign grounds. For example, a 1905 editorial in the *New York Times* urged a very strict handgun licensing law, which "would prove corrective and salutary in a city filled with immigrants and evil communications, floating from the shores of Italy and Austria-Hungary."[50] Moreover, the enactment of national Prohibition under the Eighteenth Amendment in 1919 aggravated the problem of gun crime, when organized-crime groups smuggled alcohol and competed for territory.[51] Coming after President William McKinley's assassination in 1901, concerns about concealable firearms and violence were widespread.

Although laws requiring the registration of long guns were not as common, they certainly did exist. Several laws in the late nineteenth and early twentieth century expressly required registration of long guns. Such statutes explicitly listed types of long guns among the firearms to which the statutes applied. For example, the 1866 Georgia statute required plantation owners to report "muskets" and "rifles," in addition to pistols.[52] Similarly, Montana's 1918 registration statute applied to "all fire arms and weapons,"[53] defining firearms as "any revolver, pistol, shot gun, [or] rifle."[54] The detailed descriptions of weapons in Wyoming's 1933 registration scheme was even broader. Retail dealers were required to record "all

---

[48] An Act . . . to Control and Regulate the Possession, Sale and Use of Pistols, Revolvers and Other Firearms Capable of Being Concealed Upon the Person . . . , ch. 1098, § 2, 1931 CAL. STAT. 2316, 2317 (emphasis added).

[49] *See, e.g.*, An Act Prohibiting the Manufacture, Sale, Possession, Carrying, or Use of any Blackjack, Slungshot, Billy, Sandclub, Sandbag, Metal Knuckles, Dirk, Dagger or Stiletto, and Regulating the Carrying and Sale of Certain Firearms, and Defining the Duties of Certain Executive Officers, and Providing Penalties for Violation of the Provisions of this Act, ch. 377, § 5, 1917 Or. Sess. Laws 804, 805–06 (declaring that "[e]very person in the business of selling, leasing or otherwise transferring a pistol, revolver, or other firearm *of a size which may be concealed upon the person* . . . shall obtain a legal register") (emphasis added).

[50] *See Concealed Pistols*, N.Y. TIMES, Jan. 27, 1905, at 6.

[51] *Id.*; *see also* NPR Staff, *Prohibition-Era Gang Violence Spurred Congress to Pass First Gun Law*, NPR (June 30, 2016, 4:25PM), https://www.npr.org/2016/06/30/484215890/prohibition-era-gang-violence-spurred-congress-to-pass-first-gun-law (explaining that Prohibition fueled an increase in organized crime, which was part of the 1920s and 1930s gun violence epidemic).

[52] An Act to Authorize the Justices of the Inferior Courts of Camden, Glynn, and Effingham Counties to Levy a Special Tax for County Purposes, and to Regulate the Same, No. 41, §§ 1–2, 1866 Ga. Laws 27, 27–28.

[53] An Act Providing for the Registration of All Fire Arms and Weapons and Regulating the Sale Thereof and Defining the Duties of Certain County Officers and Providing Penalties for a Violation of the Provisions of this Act, ch. 2, § 1, 1918 Mont. Laws 6, 6.

[54] *Id.* § 8, at 9.

firearms" in their "Firearms Register," and identify whether the firearm was "automatic, a revolver, a single shot pistol, a rifle, a shot gun or a machine gun."[55]

Some registration statutes heavily implied application to long guns, although the laws did not explicitly state as such. For example, Michigan's 1913 registration statute applied to "guns, pistols, other fire-arms and silencers for fire-arms."[56] The broad range of items to which the statute applied—including even silencers—implies that long guns were incorporated into the registration scheme.[57] Hawaii's 1927 registration statute featured even broader language. Retail dealers were required to register "any firearm or any ammunition, capable of causing death or inflicting great personal injury."[58] With such a broad definition, the statute likely included long guns as well as pistols. Hawaii's 1933 registration law required registration of *firearms of any description*, "whether usable or unusable, serviceable or unserviceable, modern or antique," as well as the registration of ammunition "of any kind or description."[59] The act defined "firearm" as "any weapon, the operating force of which is an explosive."[60]

In the 1920s and 1930s, state lawmakers became more concerned with the spreading use and possession of machine guns.[61] While some states reacted by placing outright bans on machine guns,[62] other states passed laws that mandated registration of machine guns.[63] Some states struck a middle ground, banning possession of machine guns for all but certain classes of individuals, like police

---

[55] An Act Relating to the Registering and Recording of Certain Facts Concerning the Possession and Sale of Firearms by all Wholesalers, Retailers, Pawn Brokers, Dealers and Purchasers, Providing for the Inspection of Such Register, Making the Violation of the Provisions Hereof a Misdemeanor, and Providing a Penalty Therefor, ch. 101, § 1, 1933 Wyo. Sess. Laws 117, 117.

[56] An Act Providing for the Registration of the Purchasers of Guns, Pistols, Other Fire-arms and Silencers for Fire-arms and Providing a Penalty for Violation, No. 250, § 1, 1913 Mich. Pub. Acts 472, 472.

[57] Moreover, the 1828 edition of the American Dictionary of the English Language (which Justice Scalia cited in *District of Columbia v. Heller*) defines "gun" broadly, which implies that the term "gun" includes long guns. *See* Catie Carberry, *What's in a Name? The Evolution of the Term "Gun,"* SECOND THOUGHTS: A BLOG FROM THE CENTER FOR FIREARMS LAW AT DUKE UNIVERSITY (July 24, 2019), https://sites.law.duke.edu/secondthoughts/2019/07/24/whats-in-a-name-the-evolution-of-the-term-gun (defining a "gun" as any "instrument consisting of a barrel or tube of iron or other metal fixed in a stock, from which balls, shot, or other deadly weapons are discharged by the explosion of gunpowder.... *But one species of fire-arms, the pistol, is never called a gun*.").

[58] Small Arms Act, No. 206, § 18, 1927 Haw. Sess. Laws 209, 213.

[59] An Act Regulating the Sale, Transfer, and Possession of Firearms and Ammunition..., No. 26, § 3, 1933 Haw. Sess. Laws 35, 36–37.

[60] *Id.* § 2, at 36.

[61] For example, Texas in 1933 passed an "anti-machine gun law," the rationale for which was "[t]he fact that there are many gangsters purchasing machine guns in Texas, causing a menace to the citizenry of Texas," which created "an emergency." *See* An Act Defining "Machine Gun" and "Person"; Making It an Offense to Possess or Use Machine Guns...., ch. 82, § 6, 1933 Tex. Gen. Laws 1st Called Sess. 219, 220.

[62] *See id.* §§ 2–3, at 219 (banning the possession, use, sale, and gift of machine guns).

[63] For example: Illinois (1931), South Dakota (1933), Wisconsin (1933), Ohio (1933) (the statute speaks in terms of "licensing" as opposed to "registration"; however, a new permit was required for each gun, which makes the statute more analogous to a registration scheme), Virginia (1934).

officers,[64] and then requiring those certain individuals to register their machine guns.[65]

These statutes typically defined machine guns as firearms from which more than two shots[66] could be discharged automatically with a single pull of the trigger.[67] The registration schemes that states enacted for these firearms varied: some states required that dealers keep registries of machine guns sold by them,[68] other states required individual reporting by machine gun owners,[69] and some states required both.[70]

In short, although the majority of historical registration statutes targeted pistols, revolvers, and other concealable firearms, registration statutes that targeted long guns were not unheard of.

---

[64] When states restricted machine gun ownership to certain classes of individuals, these enumerated individuals had occupations that either held some sort of peacekeeping function or some element of danger. *See, e.g.*, 1934 An Act Regulating the Use and Possession of Machine Guns, No. 731, § 5, 1934 S.C. Acts 1288, 1288–89 ("The provisions of this Act [i.e., the banning of machine guns] shall not apply to the army, navy, or marine corps of the United States, the National Guard, and organizations authorized by law to purchase or receive machine guns from the United States, or from this State, and the members of such corps. National Guard and organizations while on duty or at drill, may possess, carry and transport machine guns, and, *Provided, further,* That any peace officer of the State, counties, or political sub-division thereof[,] State Constable, member of the Highway patrol, railway policemen, warden, superintendents, headkeeper or deputy of any State prison, penitentiary, workhouse, county jail, city jail, or other institution for the detention of persons convicted or accused of crime, or held as witnesses in criminal cases, or persons on duty in the postal service of the United States, or common carrier while transporting direct to any police department, military or naval organization, or person authorized by law to possess or use a machine gun, may possess machine guns when required in the performance of their duties[.]").

[65] For example: Minnesota (1933), South Carolina (1934). *See* App. 1 for full citations.

[66] For example, Wisconsin determined that machine gun applied to firearms that could shoot "more than two shots" automatically "by a single function of the firing device," whereas South Carolina defined machine guns as an instrument "capable of automatically discharging more than *eight* cartridges successfully without reloading." *See* Uniform Machine Gun Act, ch. 164, WIS. STAT. tit. 16 § 164.01 (1933) (emphasis added).

[67] *See, e.g.*, An Act Defining "Machine Gun" and "Person"; Making It an Offense to Possess or Use Machine Guns. . . . , ch. 82, § 1, 1933 Tex. Gen. Laws 1st Called Sess. 219, 219 (defining "machine gun" as "a weapon of any description by whatever name known, loaded or unloaded, from which more than five (5) shots or bullets may be automatically discharged from a magazine by a single functioning of the firing device").

[68] *See, e.g.*, An Act to Regulate the Sale, Possession, and Transportation of Machine Guns, § 4, 1931 Ill. Laws 452, 453 ("Every manufacturer or merchant shall keep a register of all machine guns manufactured or handled by him. . . .").

[69] *See, e.g.*, An Act Regulating the Use and Possession of Machine Guns, No. 731, § 5, 1934 S.C. Acts 1288, 1288–89 ("Within thirty days of the passage of this Act every person permitted by this Act to possess a machine gun or immediately after any person is elected to or appointed to any office or position which entitles such person to possess a machine gun, shall file on the office of the Secretary of State on a blank to be supplied by the Secretary of State on application therefor, an application. . . .").

[70] *See, e.g.*, An Act Relating to Machine Guns, and to Make Uniform the Law with Reference Thereto, ch. 206, §§ 7–8, 1933 S.D. Sess. Laws 245, 246–47 ("Every manufacturer shall keep a register of all machine guns manufactured or handled by him. . . . Every machine gun now in this state adapted to use pistol cartridges of 30 (.30 in. or 7.63 mm.) or larger caliber shall be registered in the office of the Secretary of State, on the effective date of this act, and annually thereafter.").

2. Information Kept in Registries

Registries collected a substantial amount of personal information, which was included alongside information on the firearm being purchased or reported. Most of these registration laws were relatively searching in their inquiries. For example, the 1881 Illinois law, likely one of the oldest ones on the books, required not only the name and age of the purchaser but also "the purpose for which [the deadly weapon was] purchased or obtained."[71] Illinois was not the only state that inquired into the purpose for purchase.[72]

State registries often also made searching inquiries into the characteristics of the purchaser. New York's 1911 Sullivan Act required not only name, age, and residence of the purchaser but also his occupation.[73] Registries also made detailed records of the purchaser's appearance. For example, the 1918 Montana law described previously in section II required the possessor's age, height, skin color, eye color, and hair color, among other reporting requirements.[74] Some citizens objected to such revealing disclosures. One particular anecdote from Montana is worth quoting at length from an April 13, 1918, news story in the *Daily Missoulian*, "All Because She Wouldn't Tell Her Age":

> Yesterday was the last day allowed for registering guns, and the last person to appear at the sheriff's office was a middle-aged woman, who announced that she would like to register a revolver which she possessed.
>
> Deputy Clemens in a matter-of-fact manner took the number and make of the gun and the name of the woman. All went well until he asked her in what year she was born. When the query was made there was no response and a painful silence followed. Deputy Clemens looked up from his writing in surprise and found the woman surveying him with an attitude of scorn and defiance.
>
> "You know, madam, it is customary—," he began, but he got no further. "I don't see where my age has anything to do with the business, and I hope you don't think that I am not of age," she snapped.

---

[71] 1 Annotated Statutes of the State of Illinois in Force 771, para. 90 (Merritt Starr & Russell H. Curtis eds., 1885) (emphasis added).

[72] *See* Sale of Firearms, ch. 331, Conn. Gen. Stat. § 2678 (1918) ("No person, firm or corporation engaged in the business of selling or exchanging firearms of any description shall ... sell or exchange any pistol or revolver[] without making record of such sale immediately thereafter in a book kept for that purpose only, such record to state the name, address and occupation of the purchaser and the *purpose for which purchased*....") (emphasis added).

[73] Sullivan Act, ch. 195, § 2, 1911 N.Y. Laws 442, 444–45 (requiring retail dealers keep a register of purchasers of firearms that can be concealed on the person; *see also* An Act Providing for the Registration of All Fire Arms and Weapons and Regulating the Sale Thereof and Defining the Duties of Certain County Officers and Providing Penalties for a Violation of the Provisions of this Act, ch. 2, §§ 1, 3, 8, 1918 Mont. Laws 6, 6–7, 9 (requiring occupation as well). *See* App. 1 for form of register.

[74] The other requirements include: the jurisdiction of which the possessor is a citizen, the possessor's place and date of birth, and the possessor's occupation. §§ 1–2, 1918 Mont. Laws at 6.

Deputy Clemens surveyed the gray hair of the woman and noted a number of lines on her face and assured himself that he did not. However, the wording of the law was plain and he persisted—at least he attempted to explain.

"If you want me to register this gun, all right," she declared angrily, "but if you want my age you won't get it."

"Madam, the law says you must give the date of your birth and I didn't write the law or pass it," he replied and turned to his work without further comment.

After almost 20 minutes reflection the applicant, seeing that Deputy Clemens was not going to weaken, said:

"Well I guess it won't do you any good to know my age anyway. I was born in '75."

Deputy Clemens finished filling out the registration slip without further comment.[75]

Not everyone, then, was sanguine about disclosing what the law required. But, as this anecdote reveals, the mandate to register guns seemed to generate less opposition than the details involved.

Montana's registries were not the only ones to go into such detail: Oregon's 1917 registration law required the same identifying information.[76] And Arkansas' 1923 pistol registration law functioned more as a hybrid registration-licensing scheme, which required not only standard identifying information—"the name, age, place of residence, and color of the party"[77]—but the subsequent licensing application required consideration of the possessor's moral character.[78] In assessing an applicant's moral character, authorities considered, among other factors, the applicant's occupation.[79] While the identifying information that Arkansas required is typical for a historical registration scheme, the requirement of good moral character is akin to modern restrictions on concealed carry licensing.[80]

---

[75] *All Because She Wouldn't Tell Her Age*, DAILY MISSOULIAN, Apr. 13, 1918, at 6.

[76] *See* An Act Prohibiting the Manufacture, Sale, Possession, Carrying, or Use of any Blackjack, Slungshot, Billy, Sandclub, Sandbag, Metal Knuckles, Dirk, Dagger or Stiletto, and Regulating the Carrying and Sale of Certain Firearms, and Defining the Duties of Certain Executive Officers, and Providing Penalties for Violation of the Provisions of this Act, ch. 377, § 5, 1917 Or. Sess. Laws 804, 805–06 (requiring "name of purchaser, permanent resident, temporary residence, age, occupation, height, color of skin, color of eyes, color of hair and signature of purchaser").

[77] An Act to Regulate the Ownership of Pistols and Revolvers, No. 430, § 1, 1923 Ark. Acts 379, 379.

[78] *See id.* § 2, at 379–80 ("Any person so registering as provided in section 1 of this Act, shall then make application for a license or permit, which said application shall be passed upon by a board consisting of the sheriff, county judge and county clerk of said county whose duty it shall be to consider the application and if the applicant be a person of good moral character, whose conduct, past record and occupation is such as to prove to said board that he is a person of good character....").

[79] *Id.*

[80] *See, e.g.*, West Virginia's 1882 handgun licensing scheme. Act of Mar. 24, 1882, ch. 135, § 1, 1882 W. Va. Acts 421, 421–22 ("[I]f upon the trial of an indictment for carrying any such pistol . . . the

In all, the majority of registration laws required an in-depth personal profile of the purchaser.[81] Often, registries collected personal identifying information such as the purchaser's full name, address, occupation, nationality, and date of sale.[82] Some collected an even more detailed personal profile, requiring characteristics like the purchaser's age, height, skin color, eye color, hair color, and signature.[83] A few registries required the purchaser to state the reason for his purchase.[84]

Not only did state registries keep detailed information about the purchaser or possessor, but they also kept detailed information about the firearm being purchased or possessed. Illinois' 1881 law asked for the "kind and description of weapon." Oregon's 1917 law required "the date of sale, name of maker, number (if any), caliber."[85] Other states also sought information as specific as marks of identification on the gun.[86] Montana's 1918 registration statute featured functionally the same requirements. The registration form demanded the manufacturer's

defendant shall prove to the satisfaction of the jury that he is a quiet and peaceable citizen, of *good character and standing in the community* in which he lives ... the jury shall find him not guilty.") (emphasis added).

[81] *See, e.g.*, An Act Relating to the Registering and Recording of Certain Facts Concerning the Possession and Sale of Firearms by all Wholesalers, Retailers, Pawn Brokers, Dealers and Purchasers, Providing for the Inspection of Such Register, Making the Violation of the Provisions Hereof a Misdemeanor, and Providing a Penalty Therefor, ch. 101, 1933 Wyo. Sess. Laws 117 (requiring the dealer to record the manufacturer name of the firearm, the person or firm from whom the firearm was acquired, the date of acquisition, the manufacturer's number, the color, caliber, whether it was new or secondhand, whether it was automatic, a revolver, a single-shot pistol, a rifle, a shotgun, or a machine gun, the name of the purchaser, and the date of sale).

[82] *See, e.g.*, An Act to Regulate the Possession and Sale of Pistols, Revolvers and Guns; to Provide a Method of Licensing Those Carrying Such Weapons Concealed; and to Provide Penalties for Violations of Such Regulations, No. 313, § 7, 1925 Mich. Pub. Acts 473, 474 (requiring every purchaser of a pistol, revolver, or gun to give the seller a statement containing his full name, address, occupation, nationality, and the date of sale, among other information about the firearm).

[83] *See, e.g.*, An Act Prohibiting the Manufacture, Sale, Possession, Carrying, or Use of any Blackjack, Slungshot, Billy, Sandclub, Sandbag, Metal Knuckles, Dirk, Dagger or Stiletto, and Regulating the Carrying and Sale of Certain Firearms, and Defining the Duties of Certain Executive Officers, and Providing Penalties for Violation of the Provisions of this Act, ch. 377, § 5, 1917 Or. Sess. Laws 804, 805–06 (requiring in the registry "name of purchaser, permanent resident, temporary residence, age, occupation, height, color of skin, color of eyes, color of hair and signature of purchaser").

[84] *See, e.g.*, 1 ANNOTATED STATUTES OF THE STATE OF ILLINOIS IN FORCE 771, para. 90 (Merritt Starr & Russell H. Curtis eds., 1885) (requiring "[s]uch register shall contain ... the purpose for which [the deadly weapon] is purchased or obtained").

[85] *See* § 5, 1917 Or. Sess. Laws at 805–06.

[86] *See, e.g.*, An Act Relating to and Regulating the Carrying, Possession, Sale or Other Disposition of Firearms Capable of Being Concealed Upon the Person; Prohibiting the Possession, Carrying, Manufacturing and Sale of Certain Other Dangerous Weapons and the Giving, Transferring and Disposition Thereof to Other Persons Within this State; Providing for the Registering of the Sales of Firearms; Prohibiting the Carrying or Possession of Concealed Weapons in Municipal Corporations; Providing for the Destruction of Certain Dangerous Weapons as Nuisances and Making it a Felony to Use or Attempt to Use Certain Dangerous Weapons Against Another, ch. 145, § 7, 1917 CAL. STAT. 221, 222–23 (requiring "the time of sale, the date of sale, the name of the salesman making the sale, the place where sold, the make, model, manufacturer's number, caliber *or other marks of identification on such pistol, revolver or other firearm*") (emphasis added).

name, the manufacturer's number, the caliber, and the manufacturer's series. Few other registration schemes varied significantly from this baseline.[87] If registration schemes varied, they varied in the direction of requiring more information.[88] Wyoming's 1933 registration statute required not only manufacturer's number, color, and caliber, but whether the firearm "is new or second hand, whether it is automatic, a revolver, a single shot pistol, a rifle, a shot gun or a machine gun."[89]

B. Administration of Registries

Retail dealers were usually tasked with creating and overseeing registries, but not always. Some earlier forms of registries, primarily those for taxation purposes,[90] were administered by state officials, as opposed to retail dealers. For example, Mississippi's 1900 statute tasked the clerk of the board of supervisors of each county to assess the number of guns and pistols in their respective counties.[91]

Moreover, some states enacted mandatory reporting for private citizens who owned firearms. Georgia's 1866 statute—although for taxation purposes[92]— required the owner of every plantation to personally report, under oath, every "gun, pistol, musket, or rifle" over three.[93] Similar mandatory reporting laws cropped up in the early twentieth century. Montana's 1918 registration law required every person who owned firearms within the state of Montana to make a report to the county sheriff of his respective county.[94] While Montana only

---

[87] See, e.g., An Act to Regulate the Possession and Sale of Pistols, Revolvers and Guns; to Provide a Method of Licensing Those Carrying Such Weapons Concealed; and to Provide Penalties for Violations of Such Regulations, No. 313, § 7, 1925 Mich. Pub. Acts 473, 474 (requiring "the date of sale, the caliber, make, model and manufacturer's number of the weapon").

[88] Compare An Act to Authorize the Justices of the Inferior Courts of Camden, Glynn, and Effingham Counties to Levy a Special Tax for County Purposes, and to Regulate the Same, No. 41, §§ 1–2, 1866 Ga. Laws 27, 27–28 (requiring that "the owner of every plantation . . . shall be required to render, upon oath, a full return of every dog, gun, pistol, musket, or rifle so held or kept"), with An Act Regulating the Sale, Transfer, and Possession of Firearms and Ammunition . . . , No. 26, § 4, 1933 Haw. Sess. Laws 35, 37–38 (requiring "the make, style, caliber, and number").

[89] An Act Relating to the Registering and Recording of Certain Facts Concerning the Possession and Sale of Firearms by all Wholesalers, Retailers, Pawn Brokers, Dealers and Purchasers, Providing for the Inspection of Such Register, Making the Violation of the Provisions Hereof a Misdemeanor, and Providing a Penalty Therefor, ch. 101, § 1, 1933 Wyo. Sess. Laws 117, 117.

[90] See, e.g., §§ 1–2, 1866 Ga. Laws at 27–28. The statute's caption explicitly states that its purpose is to levy a special tax for county purposes. Also, the text clarifies that the tax is $1 per every gun over three, and then requires a report of such guns so that the possessors are held responsible for the tax.

[91] See An Act to Amend Chapter 32 of the Acts of 1894 Relating to Personal Assessment Rolls, ch. 49, § 1, 1900 Miss. Laws 51, 51–52.

[92] See §§ 1–2, 1866 Ga. Laws at 27–28.

[93] See id.

[94] See An Act Providing for the Registration of All Fire Arms and Weapons and Regulating the Sale Thereof and Defining the Duties of Certain County Officers and Providing Penalties for a Violation of the Provisions of this Act, ch. 2, §§ 1, 3, 8, 1918 Mont. Laws 6, 6–7, 9.

required that residents send in their verified report to the sheriff,[95] Arkansas's 1923 registration law required persons to physically present their firearms to the county clerk.[96] Despite the pushback to Arkansas' law, Arkansas was not the only state to enact in-person reporting. Michigan in 1927 also required persons to physically present their firearms to the chief of police or sheriff for safety inspection.[97]

Some states' reporting requirements targeted private sales and transfers of firearms between individuals. For example, Montana's 1918 registration scheme included a provision requiring the transferor to forward the name and address of the transferee to the sheriff of the county in which the transferee lives.[98] Similarly, in 1918, Connecticut required that any person who sold a pistol or revolver to forward to the local authorities a statement containing the purchaser's name and address, as well as identifying the firearm sold.[99] Michigan's 1925 private transfer statute was much more detailed in its requirements.[100] Before the firearm could be delivered, the state mandated that the purchaser sign and deliver a statement containing both personal and firearm identifying information to the seller.[101] The seller was then tasked with forwarding a copy of the statement to both the chief of police and the secretary of state, while also keeping a

---

[95] Hawaii in 1933 also required a similar mail-in reporting system. Every person within the territory was required to register his firearm with the chief of police or county sheriff within ten days of the passage of the act. The Bureau of Crime Statistics provided the registration forms, and county sheriffs collected and forwarded copies of the completed registration forms back to the Bureau of Crime Statistics. *See* An Act Regulating the Sale, Transfer, and Possession of Firearms and Ammunition..., No. 26, § 3, 1933 Haw. Sess. Laws 35, 36–37.

[96] *See* An Act to Regulate the Ownership of Pistols and Revolvers, No. 430, § 1, 1923 Ark. Acts 379, 379.

[97] *See* An Act to Regulate and License the Selling, Purchasing, and Possessing and Carrying of Certain Firearms..., No. 372, § 9, 1927 Mich. Pub. Acts 887, 891.

[98] § 1, 1918 Mont. Laws at 6.

[99] Sale of Dangerous Weapons; Notice, ch. 331, CONN. GEN. STAT. § 6372 (1918). I assume that this statute targets private sales and transfers between individuals because Connecticut concurrently enacted another registration statute that applies to retail dealers. *See* Sale of Firearms, ch. 137, CONN. GEN. STAT. § 2678 (1918) ("No person, firm or corporation engaged in the business of selling or exchanging firearms of any description shall ... sell or exchange any pistol or revolver, without making a record of such sale immediately thereafter in a book kept for that purpose only....").

[100] Michigan enacted two registration statutes, one in 1913 and one in 1925. The 1913 registration statute applied to "[e]very person, firm or corporation ... selling at retail guns, pistols, other fire-arms and silencers for fire-arms." The 1913 statute's plain language required retail dealers to keep a registry available for police review. On the other hand, the 1925 statute (discussed in-text here) is broad in application. "No person shall deliver or otherwise transfer" a gun unless following the requirements of the act. The only explicit restriction on this broad scope is that the act does not apply "to sales at wholesale." Thus, the act applies to any person except wholesale dealers. Because of the statute's lack of mention of retail dealers, combined with the preexisting 1913 statute targeting retail dealers, the statute was likely intended to target private sales between individuals. *See* App. 1 for citations.

[101] An Act to Regulate the Possession and Sale of Pistols, Revolvers and Guns; to Provide a Method of Licensing Those Carrying Such Weapons Concealed; and to Provide Penalties for Violations of Such Regulations, No. 313, § 7, 1925 Mich. Pub. Acts 473, 474.

copy.[102] Noncompliance with the law was subject to either fine, imprisonment, or both.[103]

Hawaii's private transfer statute, enacted in 1927, featured even stricter requirements.[104] As a baseline, the statute required the purchaser to sign and deliver to the seller a statement containing both personal identifying information and firearm-identifying information.[105] Similar to Michigan's scheme discussed previously in this section, the seller then signed and mailed a copy to both the territory treasurer and to the county sheriff.[106] In addition, Hawaii required that the transferor have no reasonable cause to believe that the transferee committed a crime of violence.[107] Further, the statute required a waiting period: the seller could not transfer the firearm on the day that the application to purchase and the statement by the purchaser were made.[108]

Still, the majority of registration laws focused on sales by retail dealers. Such registration laws, despite spanning several states,[109] were relatively similar. The laws required retail dealers of firearms to keep a record of all sales of firearms, and each entry in the record included the identifying information of both the purchaser and the firearm as described in section III.A.2.[110] Further, these registration laws generally required the registries be open to inspection by authorities.[111] Some states required dealer registries to be open to the general public for inspection.[112]

---

[102] Id.

[103] Id.

[104] Hawaii, like Michigan, has a concurrent statute that explicitly regulates dealers. See Small Arms Act, No. 206, § 22, 1927 Haw. Sess. Laws 209, 215 ("Wherever any person, firm, corporation, copartnership, dealing in or keeping for sale firearms or ammunition, shall make a sale of any firearms or ammunition or shall in any manner dispose of the same to any person, it shall be the duty of such person, firm, corporation, copartnership, promptly to make an official written report of said transaction and to include therein such information as shall satisfy the requirements of this chapter.").

[105] See id. § 9, at 211 ("Before a delivery be made the purchaser shall sign in triplicate and deliver to the seller a statement containing his full name, address, occupation, race, nationality, color and place of birth, the date of sale, the caliber, make, model, and manufacturer's number of the weapon, and stating that he has never been convicted of a crime of violence.").

[106] Id.

[107] Id.

[108] Id.

[109] Illinois (1881), New York (1911), Michigan (1913), Oregon (1917), California (1917), Connecticut (1918), North Carolina (1919), Virginia (1926), Texas (1931), California (1931), Wyoming (1933), among others. See App. 1 for full citations.

[110] See, e.g., Sullivan Act, ch. 195, § 2, 1911 N.Y. Laws 442, 444–45.

[111] For example, Michigan's 1913 statute required the register to be open to the inspection "of all peace officers at all times." An Act Providing for the Registration of the Purchasers of Guns, Pistols, Other Fire-arms and Silencers for Fire-arms and Providing a Penalty for Violation, No. 250, §§ 1–2, 1913 Mich. Pub. Acts 472, 472.

[112] To illustrate, Illinois' 1881 registration statute provided "[s]aid register is to be kept open for inspection of the public, and all persons who may wish to examine the same may do so at all reasonable times during business hours." 1 ANNOTATED STATUTES OF THE STATE OF ILLINOIS IN FORCE 771, para. 90 (Merritt Starr & Russell H. Curtis eds., 1885).

Despite the focus on individual retail dealers, these laws did feature centralizing components. State authorities generally provided the registration form that retail dealers used.[113] For example, the text of the 1881 Illinois registration statute detailed the form that registries were to take. Illinois was not the only state to do so.[114] Further, states often required that retail dealers forward the registration forms they collected to state authorities. For example, California's 1917 registration statute required that, on the day of sale, the dealer send a duplicate of the registration form to the chief of police or county sheriff of the dealer's jurisdiction.[115] Texas similarly mandated that dealers mail a copy of their registration forms to the State Adjutant General's Department.[116] Although ostensibly for taxation purposes,[117] Virginia required retail dealers to report information about the purchasers and their firearms to the county treasurer once per month.[118]

Registration schemes were generally wide in their application: they required registration for every purchase from a retail dealer. For example, North Carolina's 1919 registration law required that "*each and every dealer* in pistols, pistol cartridges, and other weapons . . . shall keep an accurate record of *all sales thereof*."[119] Similarly, the 1913 Michigan registration law directed that the retail dealer should keep a register "of *each and every* purchaser" of guns, pistols, and other firearms.[120] However, wholesale dealers were usually exempted from these registration regimes.[121]

---

[113] Both Oregon and California's 1917 registration laws tasked the state printer with providing registration forms to dealers.

[114] *See* App. 1 for California (1917), Montana (1918), and Hawaii (1925).

[115] *See* An Act Relating to and Regulating the Carrying, Possession, Sale or Other Disposition of Firearms Capable of Being Concealed Upon the Person; Prohibiting the Possession, Carrying, Manufacturing and Sale of Certain Other Dangerous Weapons and the Giving, Transferring and Disposition Thereof to Other Persons Within this State; Providing for the Registering of the Sales of Firearms; Prohibiting the Carrying or Possession of Concealed Weapons in Municipal Corporations; Providing for the Destruction of Certain Dangerous Weapons as Nuisances and Making it a Felony to Use or Attempt to Use Certain Dangerous Weapons Against Another, ch. 145, § 7, 1917 CAL. STAT. 221, 222–24.

[116] *See* Occupation Tax on Sale of Pistols, ch. 267, § 3, 1931 Tex. Gen. Laws 447, 447 ("Each such dealer shall keep a permanent record of all such pistols bartered, leased, or otherwise disposed of . . . . [A] copy of this record shall be mailed to and filed for record with the State Adjutant General's Department. This filing to be made each three (3) months.").

[117] The act's caption calls for improving "a license tax on pistols and revolvers," regulating the sale thereof, and providing that "the proceeds of such tax shall be used for the establishment of a diseased and crippled children's hospital." An Act to Improve a License Tax on Pistols and Revolvers; to Regulate the Sale Thereof and of Ammunition Therefor; and to Provide that the Proceeds of Such Tax Shall be Used for the Establishment of a Diseased and Crippled Children's Hospital, ch. 158, §§ 1–9, 1926 Va. Acts 285, 285–87.

[118] *See id.* § 2.

[119] An Act to Regulate the Sale of Concealed Weapons in North Carolina, ch. 197, § 5, 1919 N.C. Pub. Laws 397, 398–99 (emphasis added).

[120] An Act Providing for the Registration of the Purchasers of Guns, Pistols, Other Fire-arms and Silencers for Fire-arms and Providing a Penalty for Violation, No. 250, § 1, 1913 Mich. Pub. Acts 472, 472 (emphasis added).

[121] *See* Sullivan Act, ch. 195, § 2, 1911 N.Y. Laws 442, 444–45 (laying out the dealer registration scheme and then clarifying that it did "not apply to wholesale dealers").

Unlike concealed carry laws, most registration schemes did not appear to exempt police officers, sheriffs, and other similarly situated public officials.[122]

This discussion of the administrative details of the laws underscores how intrusive and comprehensive they could be. Registries often asked for minute personal information, occasionally demanded individual reporting, and frequently either centralized such data or opened it to public inspection. None of them remotely led to efforts to confiscate private arms.

IV. LESSONS FOR MODERN DEBATES

In the days before electronic recordkeeping and instantaneous communication, it is easy to see why these laws—even those that sought to be comprehensive—could turn out to be less effective than their proponents intended. But states kept enacting them nonetheless. Although our historical overview stops in the early 1930s, registration schemes did not. That history, as we have discussed, is becoming an increasingly important part of the legal debates surrounding the Second Amendment's right to keep and bear arms.

Some opponents invoke not just prudential arguments against registration schemes but also claim such laws are unconstitutional. History and tradition are now dispositive in the constitutional calculus. And even if it were not dispositive, courts have often placed special emphasis on historical analysis in Second Amendment cases.[123]

Because of this focus, the registration laws laid out in sections II and III carry important implications for current Second Amendment doctrine. After *Heller*, the federal circuit courts largely applied a two-step inquiry to questions arising under the Second Amendment.[124] First, courts asked whether the challenged law burdened conduct protected by the Second Amendment.[125] If it did not, the Second Amendment was not implicated.[126] If it did, courts asked whether the

---

[122] For an example of a common exception to a statute prohibiting concealed carry, see CODE OF VIRGINIA: WITH THE DECLARATION OF INDEPENDENCE AND THE CONSTITUTION OF THE UNITED STATES; AND THE CONSTITUTION OF VIRGINIA tit. 52, § 3780 (1887) ("If any person carry about his person, hid from common observation, any pistol ... he shall be fined ... : *Provided*, that this section shall not apply to any police officer, town or city sergeant, constable, sheriff, conservator of the peace, or collecting officer, while in the discharge of his official duty.").

[123] JOSEPH BLOCHER & DARRELL A.H. MILLER, THE POSITIVE SECOND AMENDMENT: RIGHTS, REGULATION, AND THE FUTURE OF *HELLER* 127 (2018); see Tyler v. Hillsdale Cty. Sheriff's Dep't, 837 F.3d 678, 687 (6th Cir. 2016) (en banc) (acknowledging that "*Heller*'s analytical structure and its conclusions command resort to historical evidence in determining the scope of the Second Amendment").

[124] SARAH HERMAN PECK, CONG. RSCH. SERV., R44618, POST-HELLER SECOND AMENDMENT JURISPRUDENCE 12 (2019).

[125] *Id.*

[126] *Id.*

challenged law survived under an approximation of intermediate scrutiny.[127] Under that test, the challenged law must be substantially related to an important government interest.[128]

Although *Bruen* displaced the two-part framework in favor of a history-only test, a registration scheme could be analyzed through the two-step framework. First, a court could find that the historical pedigree of firearm registration schemes may indicate that such a scheme does not burden Second Amendment conduct. Courts generally require a strong showing of historical basis for the law to succeed at the first step, and this chapter demonstrates a rich history.[129] Second, if a court nonetheless found that a firearm registration law burdened Second Amendment conduct, such a law could still likely succeed under intermediate scrutiny. A modern registration scheme would likely be designed to promote public safety and prevent gun violence.[130] Although this chapter is focused on history and not empirics, the components of a registration scheme, like requiring personal identifying information or periodic reporting by gun owners, could be found to be related to promoting public safety. Such information and reporting may help law enforcement in tracing crime guns and thus solving more crimes, and it imposes little burden on gun owners.

A modern registration scheme might even fit within a categorical exception to the Second Amendment laid out by *Heller*,[131] which *Bruen* does not seem to have unsettled. The federal courts have struggled to reconcile these "presumptively lawful" exceptions to the Second Amendment with the developing two-step framework,[132] but they may be more useful under *Bruen*'s history-only test. A modern registration scheme might be a longstanding condition or qualification on the commercial sale of firearms, by reference to its historical analogs. Requiring retail dealers to record personal identifying information and to forward such information to law enforcement authorities appears to be a longstanding qualification on the commercial sale of firearms.

---

[127] *Id.* at 12–13.
[128] Kwong v. Bloomberg, 723 F.3d 160, 168 (2d Cir. 2013).
[129] *See, e.g., Tyler*, 837 F.3d at 687 (refusing to give *Heller*'s categorical ban on possession of firearms by the mentally ill conclusive effect because the statute at issue lacked a "historical pedigree").
[130] *See, e.g., Kwong*, 723 F.3d at 168 (observing that the New York state handgun licensing statute at issue was designed to promote public safety and prevent gun violence, and that such interests were not only substantial but compelling).
[131] *See* District of Columbia v. Heller, 554 U.S. 570, 626–27 (2008) ("[N]othing in our opinion should be taken to cast doubt on longstanding prohibitions on the possession of firearms by felons and the mentally ill, or laws forbidding the carrying of firearms in sensitive places such as schools and government buildings, or laws imposing conditions and qualifications on the commercial sale of arms.").
[132] *See id.* at 627 n.26 ("We identify these presumptively lawful regulatory measures only as examples; our list does not purport to be exhaustive.").

Under *Bruen*'s approach, regulatory measures on firearms are constitutional if they have a historical analog, which shows such measures were within the historical understanding of the scope of the Second Amendment right.[133] The historical registration schemes discussed here provide a firm historical basis for a modern registration law—*over twenty-two* states enacted some form of registration scheme. Still, this claim is subject to reasonable debate. For one, many of these registration laws were enacted in the early twentieth century, well past the 1791 and 1868 markers. Further, the analogical value of such historical registration laws depends on the level of abstraction with which they are viewed.[134] *Bruen* itself suggested that twentieth-century laws were not probative of original public meaning, but they may still be usefully viewed as continuations of efforts to deal with the problems of (especially) concealable firearms that proliferated after the Civil War.

Regardless of the result of a court's inquiry, the historical registration statutes laid out in this chapter can inform Second Amendment analysis moving forward. If nothing else, these statutes remind us that regulation surrounding firearm ownership is anything but novel.

---

[133] *See* Heller v. District of Columbia, 670 F.3d 1244, 1280 (D.C. Cir. 2011) (Kavanaugh, J., dissenting) (claiming that "the scope of the right [in *Heller*] was determined by text, history, and tradition, and such longstanding laws were within the historical understanding of the scope of the right").

[134] For example, then judge Kavanaugh "distinguish[ed] registration requirements imposed on gun *owners* from record-keeping requirements imposed on gun *sellers*." *Id.* at 1292.

Appendix 1

Citation for note 46 ("by 1933 over twenty-two states had enacted some form of registration scheme for firearms or ammunition"):

- Arkansas (1923): An Act to Regulate the Ownership of Pistols and Revolvers, No. 430, §§ 1–4, 1923 Ark. Acts 379, 379–80 (requiring persons having pistols and revolvers to present such firearm to the county clerk for registration and requiring such persons to apply for a license to possess the firearm);
- California (1917): An Act Relating to and Regulating the Carrying, Possession, Sale or Other Disposition of Firearms Capable of Being Concealed Upon the Person; Prohibiting the Possession, Carrying, Manufacturing and Sale of Certain Other Dangerous Weapons and the Giving, Transferring and Disposition Thereof to Other Persons Within this State; Providing for the Registering of the Sales of Firearms; Prohibiting the Carrying or Possession of Concealed Weapons in Municipal Corporations; Providing for the Destruction of Certain Dangerous Weapons as Nuisances and Making it a Felony to Use or Attempt to Use Certain Dangerous Weapons Against Another, ch. 145, §§ 7–8, 1917 Cal. Stat. 221, 222–24 (requiring every person in the business of selling firearms capable of being concealed on the person to keep a register of sales);
- Connecticut (1918): Sale of Firearms, ch. 137, CONN. GEN. STAT. § 2678 (1918) (requiring any person engaged in the business of selling or exchanging firearms to keep a register);
- Connecticut (1918): Sale of Dangerous Weapons; Notice, ch. 331, CONN. GEN. STAT. § 6372 (1918) (requiring any person who sells a pistol or revolver to, within twenty-four hours after the delivery of such weapon, give written notice to the chief of police of the city);
- Connecticut (1923): An Act Concerning the Possession, Sale, and Use of Pistols and Revolvers, ch. 252, 1923 Conn. Pub. Acts 3707 (requiring a permit to sell pistols and revolvers at retail and requiring retail dealers to keep registries which are forwarded to the chief of police);
- Georgia (1866): An Act to Authorize the Justices of the Inferior Courts of Camden, Glynn, and Effingham Counties to Levy a Special Tax for County Purposes, and to Regulate the Same, No. 41, §§ 1–2, 1866 Ga. Laws 27, 27–28 (requiring a report of every gun, pistol, musket, or rifle over three, on which the state placed a tax);
- Georgia (1921): Explosives, Use of Regulated, No. 160, § 1, 1921 Ga. Laws 247, 248 (requiring the registration of any person doing business in explosives);

- Hawaii (1925): 1 Revised Laws of Hawaii §§ 2136–47 (1925) (requiring any person in possession of a firearm or ammunition to report to the county clerk, among other regulations);
- Hawaii (1927): Small Arms Act, No. 206, §§ 9, 12, 17, 1927 Haw. Sess. Laws 209, 210–13 (requiring that any transfer of pistols or revolvers be accompanied by a letter forwarded to the sheriff with the transferee's personal identifying information, among other regulations);
- Hawaii (1933): An Act Regulating the Sale, Transfer, and Possession of Firearms and Ammunition . . . , No. 26, §§ 1–16, 1933 Haw. Sess. Laws 35, 35–40 (requiring any person possessing a firearm or ammunition to register with the chief of police or county sheriff, among other regulations);
- Illinois (1881): 1 ANNOTATED STATUTES OF THE STATE OF ILLINOIS IN FORCE 771, ¶ 90 (Merritt Starr & Russell H. Curtis eds., 1885);
- Illinois (1931): An Act to Regulate the Sale, Possession, and Transportation of Machine Guns, § 4, 1931 Ill. Laws 452, 453 (requiring registration of machine guns);
- Indiana (1925): An Act to Regulate and Control the Possession, Sale, and Use of Pistols, and Revolvers in the State of Indiana, to Provide Penalties, and for Other Purposes, ch. 207, § 9, 1925 Ind. Acts 495, 497–98 (requiring dealers to keep a register of pistols and revolvers sold);
- Michigan (1913): An Act Providing for the Registration of the Purchasers of Guns, Pistols, Other Fire-arms and Silencers for Fire-arms and Providing a Penalty for Violation, No. 250, §§ 1–2, 1913 Mich. Pub. Acts 472, 472 (requiring that retail dealers of guns, pistols, other firearms, and silencers for firearms must keep a register recording identifying information);
- Michigan (1925): An Act to Regulate the Possession and Sale of Pistols, Revolvers and Guns; to Provide a Method of Licensing Those Carrying Such Weapons Concealed; and to Provide Penalties for Violations of Such Regulations, No. 313, § 7, 1925 Mich. Pub. Acts 473, 474 (requiring individual buyers and sellers of firearms to record personal identifying information and forward it to law enforcement agencies);
- Michigan (1927): An Act to Regulate and License the Selling, Purchasing, and Possessing and Carrying of Certain Firearms . . . , No. 372, § 9, 1927 Mich. Pub. Acts 887, 891 (requiring individuals who own or have in their possession a pistol to present such pistol to the county authorities for safety inspection and registration);
- Minnesota (1933): An Act Making It Unlawful to Use, Own, Possess, Sell, Control, or Transport a "Machine Gun," as Hereinafter Defined, and Providing a Penalty for the Violation Thereof, ch. 190, 1933 Minn. Laws 231 (creating an exception to the ban on possessing machine guns for law enforcement officials and other various enumerated groups, provided such

excepted individuals register such possession with the Bureau of Criminal Apprehension);
- Mississippi (1900): An Act to Amend Chapter 32 of the Acts of 1894 Relating to Personal Assessment Rolls, ch. 49, § 1, 1900 Miss. Laws 51, 51–52 (requiring the clerk of the board of supervisors of each county to record the number of guns over one and the number of pistols);
- Montana (1918): An Act Providing for the Registration of All Fire Arms and Weapons and Regulating the Sale Thereof and Defining the Duties of Certain County Officers and Providing Penalties for a Violation of the Provisions of this Act, ch. 2, §§ 1, 3, 8, 1918 Mont. Laws 6, 6–7, 9 (requiring any person in possession of any firearms or weapons to make a report to law enforcement authorities);
- New York (1911): Sullivan Act, ch. 195, § 2, 1911 N.Y. Laws 442, 444–45 (requiring retail dealers keep a register of purchasers of firearms that can be concealed on the person);
- North Carolina (1919): An Act to Regulate the Sale of Concealed Weapons in North Carolina, ch. 197, § 5, 1919 N.C. Pub. Laws 397, 398–99 (requiring dealers to keep a record of sales of pistols, including identifying information);
- Ohio (1933): An Act . . . Relative to the Sale and Possession of Machine Guns, 1933 Ohio Laws 189 (requiring those who are exempted from the ban on machine guns to register such machine guns);
- Oregon (1917): An Act Prohibiting the Manufacture, Sale, Possession, Carrying, or Use of any Blackjack, Slungshot, Billy, Sandclub, Sandbag, Metal Knuckles, Dirk, Dagger or Stiletto, and Regulating the Carrying and Sale of Certain Firearms, and Defining the Duties of Certain Executive Officers, and Providing Penalties for Violation of the Provisions of this Act, ch. 377, § 5, 1917 Or. Sess. Laws 804, 805–06 (implementing a dealer registry for all purchases of firearms that can be concealed on the person);
- South Carolina (1934): An Act Regulating the Use and Possession of Machine Guns, No. 731, §§ 1–6, 1934 S.C. Acts 1288, 1288–89 (requiring those exempted from the ban on machine guns to register such machine guns);
- South Dakota (1933): An Act Relating to Machine Guns, and to Make Uniform the Law with Reference Thereto, ch. 206, §§ 1–8, 1933 S.D. Sess. Laws 245, 245–47 (requiring all who possess machine guns to register, and requiring retail dealers to keep registries of machine gun purchases);
- Texas (1931): Occupation Tax on Sale of Pistols, ch. 267, § 3, 1931 Tex. Gen. Laws 447, 447 (requiring retail dealers to keep registries of sales of firearms);
- Virginia (1926):, An Act to Improve a License Tax on Pistols and Revolvers; to Regulate the Sale Thereof and of Ammunition Therefor; and to Provide that the Proceeds of Such Tax Shall be Used for the Establishment of a

Diseased and Crippled Children's Hospital, ch. 158, §§ 1–9, 1926 Va. Acts 285, 285–87 (requiring retail dealers to keep registries of pistols and revolvers);
- Virginia (1934): An Act to Define the Term "Machine Gun"; to Declare the Use and Possession of a Machine Gun for Certain Purposes a Crime and to Prescribe the Punishment Therefor . . . , ch. 96, §§ 1–7, 1934 Va. Acts 137, 137–39 (requiring manufacturers and dealers to keep a register of all machine guns manufactured or handled by them);
- West Virginia (1925): An Act . . . Providing for the Granting and Revoking of Licenses and Permits Respecting the Use, Transportation, and Possession of Weapons and Fire Arms . . . , ch. 3, 1925 W.Va. Acts 1st Extraordinary Sess. 24, 30–31 (although the act does not explicitly mention "registers," the act requires a licensing scheme in which the machine guns' identification number must be certified to the superintendent of public safety);
- Wisconsin (1933): Uniform Machine Gun Act, ch. 164, WIS. STAT. § 164.01 (1933) (requiring manufacturers and retail dealers of machine guns to register);
- Wyoming (1933): An Act Relating to the Registering and Recording of Certain Facts Concerning the Possession and Sale of Firearms by all Wholesalers, Retailers, Pawn Brokers, Dealers and Purchasers, Providing for the Inspection of Such Register, Making the Violation of the Provisions Hereof a Misdemeanor, and Providing a Penalty Therefor, ch. 101, 1933 Wyo. Sess. Laws 117 (establishing a Firearm Register to be kept by dealers, requiring identifying information).

Appendix 2

Citation for note 47 ("If licensing schemes are included in this calculus, the number jumps to over two-thirds of the states"):

- Alabama (1892): License Taxes; from Whom and for What Businesses Required; Prices; County Levy, ALA. CODE § 4122 (1897) (requiring a license and tax for dealers in pistols or pistol cartridges);
- Arkansas (1923): see App. 1;
- California (1917): see App. 1;
- Connecticut (1918, 1923): see App. 1;
- Delaware (1909): House Joint Resolution Providing for Increase in Non-Resident Gunners License Fee, ch. 271, 1909 Del. Laws 577 (increasing the license fee for non-Delaware resident personal use of firearms);
- Florida (1893): An Act to Regulate the Carrying of Firearms, ch. 4147, §§ 1–4, 1893 Fla. Laws 71, 71–72 (requiring a license and a fee "to carry or own a Winchester or other repeating rifle");
- Georgia (1910): 6 PARK's ANNOTATED CODE OF THE STATE OF GEORGIA 1914 § 348(a)–(d), at 234 (Orville A. Park ed.) (1915) (requiring a license to carry a pistol or revolver on the person);
- Hawaii (1925, 1927, 1933): see App. 1;
- Illinois (1881, 1931): see App. 1;
- Maryland (1876): 1 REVISED CODE OF THE PUBLIC GENERAL LAWS OF THE STATE OF MARYLAND, WITH THE CONSTITUTION OF THE STATE 173 (Lewis Mayer et al. eds., 1879) (requiring a license granted by the court to shoot at wild water fowl from a sink-box or sneak-boat);
- Massachusetts (1920): Sale of Firearms, MASS. GEN. LAWS ch. 140, §§ 121–31 (1921) (requiring approval from the licensing board in a town to obtain a license to sell, rent, or lease firearms);
- Michigan (1913, 1925, 1927): see App. 1;
- Minnesota (1888): HARRY TOULMIN, ORDINANCES OF THE CITY OF ST. PAUL, FROM MAY, 1887, TO JULY, 1889, at 89–91 (1889) (available at The Making of Modern Law: Primary Sources) (requiring a license and fee for merchants in gunpowder);
- Mississippi (1900): see App. 1;
- Missouri (1899): Mo. REV. STAT § 7457 (1899) (requiring a permit from the clerk of the county court or the mayor of St. Louis to keep explosives);
- Montana (1918): see App. 1;
- Nebraska (1895): An Ordinance Regulating and Prohibiting the Use of Fire-arms, Fire-works, and Cannon in the City of Lincoln . . . Prescribing Penalties for Violation of the Provisions of This Ordinance, and Repealing Ordinances in Conflict Herewith, REV. ORDINANCES OF THE CITY OF

LINCOLN, NEB. art. 16, para. 787, § 6 (1895) (authorizing the Mayor in the City of Lincoln to grant licenses to carry concealed weapons; the licenses required the name, age, occupation, and residence of the person to whom granted);

- New Hampshire (1917): An Act for the Regulation of the Sale and Use of Explosives and Firearms, ch. 185, § 6, 1917 N.H. Laws 727, 728–29 (requiring a permit application for foreigners to possess any firearm of any description);
- New Jersey (1902): An Act to Require Non-residents to Secure Licenses before Hunting or Gunning within the State of New Jersey and Providing Penalties for Violation of Its Provisions, ch. 263, § 1, 1902 N.J. Laws 780, 780–81 (requiring a license for nonresidents to hunt);
- New York (1911): see App. 1;
- North Carolina (1919): see App. 1;
- North Dakota (1923): Pistols and Revolvers, ch. 266, § 8, 1923 N.D. Laws 379, 380–81 (allowing the police or county sheriff to issue a license for concealed carry if the applicant has good reason);
- Ohio (1884): 4 SUPPLEMENT TO THE REVISED STATUTES OF THE STATE OF OHIO 633 (James M. Williams ed., 3d ed. 1884) (requiring a license and fee for vendors of gunpowder, as well as a license and fee for all keepers or owners of gunpowder magazines);
- Oregon (1917): see App. 1;
- Pennsylvania (1903): An Act Requiring non-resident hunters, and unnaturalized, foreign born, resident-hunters, to procure a license before hunting in the Commonwealth . . . , No. 136, §§ 1–2, 1903 Pa. Laws 178, 178–79 (requiring a license for foreigners to hunt);
- South Carolina (1893): An Act to Amend an Act Entitled "An Act to Provide for A License for the Sale of Pistols or Pistol Cartridges Within the Limits of this State," No. 309, § 2, 1893 S.C. Acts 426, 426–27 (allowing counties to issue licenses and charge license fees for the sale of pistol and pistol cartridges);
- Texas (1931): see App. 1;
- Utah (1905): An Act for the Protection of Fish, Game, and Birds . . . , ch. 118, § 30, 1905 Utah Laws 188, 197 (requiring a license for foreigners to hunt);
- Virginia (1926): see App. 1;
- Washington (1911): An Act Relating to the Carrying of Firearms, Requiring Licenses of Certain Persons, and Fixing a Penalty for the Violation Thereof, ch. 52, 1911 Wash. Sess. Laws 303 (requiring a license for a foreigner to possess any shotgun, rifle, or other firearm);
- West Virginia (1925): see App. 1;
- Wisconsin (1933): see App. 1;
- Wyoming (1933): see App. 1.

11
Historical Militia Law, Fire Prevention Law, and the Modern Second Amendment

Mark Anthony Frassetto

I. Introduction

In *New York State Rifle and Pistol Association v. Bruen*, the U.S. Supreme Court placed the history of gun regulation at the center of the Second Amendment analysis.[1] In a majority opinion, written by Justice Clarence Thomas, the Court struck down a provision of New York's public carry licensing law that required applicants for permits to show "proper cause" before being issued a permit.[2] In the process, the Court rejected the two-part framework for deciding Second Amendment cases which had been unanimously adopted by the lower federal courts. Under this now rejected approach, courts first looked to history and then applied the tiers of constitutional scrutiny.[3] The Court instead applied a new analytical framework focused on the text and history of the Second Amendment.[4] This new framework makes the Duke Center for Firearms Law's Repository of Historical Gun Laws an indispensable tool for identifying and understanding the scope of constitutionally acceptable gun regulation.[5]

In the pre-*Bruen* two-part framework, the historical analysis had focused largely on gun regulations which, like present-day gun laws, were enacted with

---

[1] N.Y. Rifle & Pistol Assoc. v. Bruen, 142 S. Ct. 2111 (2022). The author is Deputy Director of Second Amendment History and Scholarship at Everytown Law. The views expressed in this chapter are solely those of the author and do not necessarily represent the views of Everytown for Gun Safety. The author would like to thank Garrett Lance for his excellent research assistance. He would also like to thank Prof. Joseph Blocher, Prof. Darrell Miller, Prof. Jake Charles, Prof. Saul Cornell, and Brittany Frassetto for their comments and suggestions. Thank you as well to the Duke Center for Firearms Law for organizing this project and its students for their excellent work editing and revising this chapter. All mistakes remain the author's.
[2] *Id.* at 2122.
[3] *Bruen*, 142 S. Ct. at 2126.
[4] *Id.* at 2131.
[5] *See, e.g.*, United States v. Marzzarella, 614 F.3d 85, 89 (3d Cir. 2010) (establishing two-part framework).

Mark Anthony Frassetto, *Historical Militia Law, Fire Prevention Law, and the Modern Second Amendment* In: *New Histories of Gun Rights and Regulation*. Edited by: Joseph Blocher, Jacob D. Charles, and Darrell A.H. Miller, Oxford University Press. © Oxford University Press 2023. DOI: 10.1093/oso/9780197748473.003.0011

the purpose of reducing the risk of violent crime—laws regulating carrying guns in public, regulating especially dangerous weapons, and prohibiting firearms possession by felons and minors.[6]

This chapter will address a different category of historical gun regulations that were not intended to directly prevent crime but instead to accomplish other goals. Specifically, this chapter will discuss historical militia laws and laws intended to prevent fires and explosions. Such laws imposed obligations and burdens on gun owners that were at least as stringent as many modern gun regulations but were widely accepted and deemed necessary for the functioning of a safe and secure state. These laws providing historical analogies for many modern gun regulations include requiring firearms registration, responsible firearms storage, restrictions on large capacity magazines, and firearms training before purchasing a gun or carrying one in public.

Although these historical laws were rarely addressed by federal courts in Second Amendment cases in the pre-*Bruen* era, *Bruen* changes that analysis. Under *Bruen*, lower courts are instructed to consider whether the historical and modern regulations impose a "comparable burden" and are "comparably justified." In other words, a historical regulation imposed for a different purpose than a modern regulation but that imposes a comparable burden would support the constitutionality of the modern regulation.

Section II of this chapter will briefly discuss the *Bruen* framework for deciding Second Amendment cases. Section III will address the scope of militia regulation and fire prevention laws during the founding period and in the nineteenth century. Section IV will analyze how courts have previously considered (or not considered) these historical regulations and will discuss why such regulations should be considered an essential part of the history of gun regulation, particularly under the *Bruen* framework. Finally, section V will draw some conclusions.

II. THE *BRUEN* SECOND AMENDMENT FRAMEWORK

In *Bruen*, the Supreme Court upended the Second Amendment framework that had uniformly been adopted by the lower federal courts over the fourteen years since *District of Columbia v. Heller*.[7] In the pre-*Bruen* two-part framework, courts first looked to whether a challenged regulation fell within the scope of the Second Amendment as defined by an analysis of the right's text, history,

---

[6] *See, e.g.*, Peruta v. Cnty. of San Diego, 824 F.3d 919 (2016); Heller v. District of Columbia (*Heller II*), 670 F.3d 1244 (D.C. Cir. 2011) (Kavanaugh, J., dissenting); Nat'l Rifle Ass'n v. Bureau of Alcohol, Tobacco, Firearms and Explosives, 700 F.3d 185 (5th Cir. 2012).

[7] *Bruen*, 142 S. Ct. at 2131.

and tradition.[8] If a regulation did fall within the historical scope of the Second Amendment, a court would then apply one of the tiers of constitutional scrutiny, either intermediate or strict, depending on how significantly the regulation burdened the right.[9] Under this framework, the lower courts upheld a wide variety of gun regulations, while striking down a few outlier laws.[10]

In *Bruen*, the Supreme Court adopted a new framework focused on the Second Amendment's text and history. Under this framework, courts will first look at whether "the Second Amendment's plain text covers an individual's conduct."[11] This step will likely focus on Justice Scalia's textual analysis of the Second Amendment in *District of Columbia v. Heller*.[12] In *Heller*, the Court summarized the Second Amendment's text as protecting an "individual right to possess and carry weapons in case of confrontation."[13]

If a challenged regulation does fall within the plain text of the Second Amendment, courts then consider whether the regulation is "consistent with the Nation's historical tradition of firearm regulation."[14] This analysis can be viewed as having two stages. At the first stage, a court asks whether there was a tradition of "distinctly similar historical regulation[s]" aimed at the same "general societal problem."[15] This essentially asks whether there is a historical tradition of very similar regulations which were adopted to address essentially the same problem as a modern regulation.

If a court fails to find a "distinctly similar historical regulation," it then moves on to the second stage of the historical analysis and asks whether there is a historical tradition of analogous regulations.[16] At this step, a court analyzes whether a historical regulation is "relevantly similar" to the challenged modern gun regulation.[17] This analysis includes "how and why the regulations burden a law-abiding citizen's right to armed self-defense."[18] In other words, the court considers "whether modern and historical regulations impose [a] comparable burden on the right of armed self-defense and whether that burden is comparably justified."[19] The modern regulation need not be "a dead ringer for historical

---

[8] For an excellent explanation of the two-step framework and why it makes sense, *see* Brief of Second Amendment Law Professors as Amicus Curiae in Support of Neither Party, *New York State Rifle and Pistol Ass'n v. City of New York*, 139 S. Ct. 939 (No. 18-280).

[9] *See Marzzarella*, 614 F.3d at 89; *see also Nat'l Rifle Ass'n*, 700 F.3d at 195.

[10] *See generally* Giffords Law Center, *Post-Heller Litigation Summary*, available at https://giffords.org/lawcenter/gun-laws/litigation/post-heller-litigation-summary/ (last visited July 20, 2022).

[11] *Bruen*, 142 S. Ct. at 2126.

[12] 554 U.S. 570, 579–92 (2008).

[13] *Id.* at 592.

[14] *Bruen*, 142 S. Ct. at 2126.

[15] *Id.* at 2131.

[16] *Id.* 2131–32.

[17] *Id.* at 2132.

[18] *Id.* at 2133.

[19] *Id.* at 2133.

precursors," but courts should also not uphold "every modern law that remotely resembles a historical analogue."[20] Courts may also use the provisions identified as presumptively lawful in *Heller* as analogies for modern regulations without independently showing a historical tradition of similar regulations during the relevant historical period.[21]

The historical regulations discussed in this chapter are relevant at stage two of the *Bruen* historical analysis. They are not "distinctly similar historical regulation[s]" aimed at the same "general societal problem."[22] Instead, they are laws that impose a "comparable burden on the right of armed self-defense" and are "comparably justified."[23] Historical militia laws and anti-fire laws imposed burdens on the right to keep and bear arms that were oftentimes more severe than modern gun regulations; however, they did so to address different but extremely important issues of the time. Modern gun laws impose similar burdens on Second Amendment rights and are aimed at addressing new, but equally weighty, concerns. Under the *Bruen* framework, these historical laws provide historical analogies that are relevant and, in many cases, will be decisive in deciding Second Amendment cases.

III. Historical Militia and Fire Laws

A. Historical Militia Laws

The text of the Second Amendment—"A well regulated militia, being necessary for the security of a free state, the right of the people to keep and bear arms, shall not be infringed"—closely ties the individual right identified by the Supreme Court in *Heller* to the need for state militias.[24] At the founding, the militia was deemed a necessity to "execute the Laws of the Union, suppress insurrections and repel invasions."[25] The Second Amendment was ratified specifically in response to provisions in the original Constitution, which authorized Congress "to provide for the organizing, arming, and disciplining, the Militia" and for governing militia members "employed in the Service of the United States."[26] Authority was

---

[20] *Id.* at 2133.
[21] *Id.* at 2133.
[22] *Id.* at 2131.
[23] *Id.* at 2133.
[24] U.S. Const. amend. II.
[25] U.S. Const. art. I, § 8, cl. 16. *See also* Patrick J. Charles, Armed in America: A History of Gun Rights from Colonial Militias to Concealed Carry 76 (2018) (discussing eighteenth-century militia law preambles which described the purpose of state militias); Saul Cornell, A Well-Regulated Militia: The Founding Fathers and the Origins of Gun Control in America (2006).
[26] U.S. Const. art. I, § 8, cls. 15–16. *See also* Akhil Amar, The Bill of Rights: Creation and Reconstruction 54 (1998); Noah Shusterman, Armed Citizens: The Road from Rome to

specifically delegated to the states to "appoint[] officers and train[] the militia" as long as the training met the baseline requirements laid out by Congress.[27] However, many feared that "the federal government would use the militia clauses to disarm the citizenry"[28] or to assert total federal authority over the militia, leaving states defenseless against tyranny.[29]

The militias of the founding era were unique to the time and place of the colonial United States.[30] Their existence and central role in early American society were the culmination of an Anglo-American civic-republican legal tradition which believed standing armies inevitably led to despotism and citizen militias were an essential defense of liberty.[31] In practice, militias were central because they provided the only financially viable means for the relatively poor American colonies and states to protect against foreign invasion, internal insurrection, revolts by enslaved persons, and attacks by American Indians resisting settler expansion.[32] The militia also provided a bulwark against federal usurpation. As Hamilton wrote in *The Federalist No. 46*, "[t]he existence of subordinate governments, to which the people are attached, and by which the militia officers are appointed, forms a barrier against the enterprises of ambition, more insurmountable than any which a simple government of any form can admit of."[33] To further these objectives, both the states and the federal government passed laws for the organization and training of state militias.[34]

During both the colonial period and the early republic, most states enacted laws establishing a state militia.[35] These laws defined the membership of the

THE SECOND AMENDMENT 187 (2020); ADAM WINKLER, GUN FIGHT: THE BATTLE OVER THE RIGHT TO BEAR ARMS IN AMERICA 107–08 (2013).

[27] U.S. CONST. art. I, § 8, cl. 16.
[28] WINKLER, *supra* note 26, at 108.
[29] *See* SHUSTERMAN, *supra* note 26; AMAR, *supra* note 26; BERNARD BAILYN, THE IDEOLOGICAL ORIGINS OF THE AMERICAN REVOLUTION 340 (1992).
[30] *See generally* SHUSTERMAN, *supra* note 26 (discussing the intellectual, ideological, and historical sources that culminated in the ratification of the Second Amendment).
[31] *See id.* at 180; AMAR, *supra* note 26, at 53–54.
[32] *See* SHUSTERMAN, *supra* note 26, at 195.
[33] THE FEDERALIST NO. 46 (Alexander Hamilton); one could reasonably doubt Hamilton's sincerity in this view given his support for developing a standing army. *See* SHUSTERMAN, *supra* note 26, at 193 (quoting Hamilton: "the steady operations of war against a regular and disciplined army can only be successfully conducted by a force of the same kind").
[34] *See generally Repository of Historical Gun Laws*, DUKE CENTER FOR FIREARMS LAW, https://firearmslaw.duke.edu/repository/search-the-repository/ (noting the various militia regulations); JOSEPH BLOCHER & DARRELL A.H. MILLER, THE POSITIVE SECOND AMENDMENT: RIGHTS, REGULATION, AND THE FUTURE OF HELLER 21–22 (2018).
[35] *See, e.g.*, An Act for the Regulating, Training, and Arraying of the Militia, ch. 22, § 11, 1778 N.J. Laws 42, 45 (establishing a state militia); An Act for Forming and Regulating the Militia, 1779 Vt. Sess. Laws 57, 59 (same). *See also* Robert H. Churchill, *Gun Regulation, the Police Power, and the Right to Keep Arms in Early America: The Legal Context of the Second Amendment*, 25 LAW & HIST. REV. 139, 161 (2007) (noting that "Early American militia laws prohibited the use of guns on the day of muster . . . required militiamen and other householders to bring their guns to the muster field twice a year so that militia officers could record which men in the community owned guns [and] [s]ome

militia, the weapons a militiaman was required own, and the regular training militiamen were required to undergo.[36] Militia laws oftentimes required extensive recordkeeping of the training undergone by militiamen and the weapons they brought to muster.[37] In some cases, this recordkeeping went as far as requiring militia officials to do a house-by-house census of people's weapons.[38] It is worth noting at the outset that these laws were often more aspirational than real. Firearms ownership and militia participation were never universal even among the limited group required to participate in militia service.[39] That said, for a substantial minority of the population and the vast majority of people with full citizenship, militia service would have imposed a variety of costly and time-consuming burdens, many of which are more burdensome than the present-day gun laws currently being challenged for violating the Second Amendment.[40]

To put things in more concrete terms, in New Jersey in 1778, a White male farmer[41] would have been required to "keep himself furnished with a good musket, well fitted with a bayonet, [and] steel ramrod" or "a rifle gun . . . and a tomahawk."[42] If the farmer was like a lot of his fellow citizens, he might have bent the rules and used a fowling piece, a type of shotgun, rather than the mandated musket and bayonet, which would have been less useful in his day-to-day

colonies authorized door-to-door surveys of gun ownership."); SHUSTERMAN, *supra* note 26, at 186 (noting "Congress's right to maintain a minimum level of standards binding for each state").

[36] *Id.*; *see generally Repository of Historical Gun Laws*, *supra* note 34. The author plans to submit additional militia statutes for eventual inclusion in the Repository as well.
[37] *See, e.g.*, An Act for Regulating of the Militia, ch. 3, §§ 1, 5, 1693 Mass. Acts 48 ("[A]ll male persons from sixteen years of age to sixty, (other than such as are herein after excepted), shall bear arms, and duly attend all musters and military exercises of the respective troops and companies where they are listed."); An Act in Addition to the Several Acts of This Province for Regulating the Militia, ch. 12, 1757 Mass. Acts 51 ("[The captain] shall make a strict enquiry into the state of the arms and ammunition of his Company.").
[38] An Act for the Regulating, Training, and Arraying of the Militia, ch. 22, § 11; An Act for Regulating the Militia of the Province of Maryland (Act, May 22, 1756), *available at* https://archive.org/details/backgroundsofsel25unit/page/84/mode/2up.
[39] Kevin M. Sweeney, *Firearms Ownership and Militias in Seventeenth and Eighteenth Century England and America*, Table 3.8, *in* A RIGHT TO BEAR ARMS?: THE CONTESTED ROLE OF HISTORY IN CONTEMPORARY DEBATES ON THE SECOND AMENDMENT 54, 66, tbl.3.8. (Jennifer Tucker, Barton C. Hacker, & Margaret Vining eds., 2019) (showing militia participation rates between 46% and 95% and percentage of foot soldiers armed between 14% and 88%. Participation rates and percentage armed also seem to have been inversely correlated.).
[40] *See, e.g.*, Maryland Shall Issue v. Hogan, 353 F.Supp.3d 400, 405 (D. Md.) (discussing a challenge to Maryland's requirement that handgun purchasers first undergo training); Yukutake v. Conners, 554 F.Supp.3d 1074, 1091 (D. Haw.) (holding that Hawaii's requirement that newly registered handguns be inspected by the chief of police violates the Second Amendment).
[41] The law excluded from service members of Congress, the state legislature, judges, ministers, professors, ferry operators, sheriffs, constables, and enslaved people. An Act for the Regulating, Training, and Arraying of the Militia, ch. 22, § 11.
[42] *Id.*

activities.[43] If he could not afford a gun, the state would take one from a wealthier neighbor who would be reimbursed if the gun was not returned.[44]

Our farmer would then be required to attend musters with his company nine times per year and "spend the Remainder of the Day in Training and Exercise."[45] This training was likely in line with rules developed in 1777 and 1778 at Valley Forge by Baron Friedrich von Steuben and formalized the next year in his *Regulations for the Order and Discipline of the Troops of the United States*.[46] Failure to attend these musters would result in fines, progressively tiered based on rank.[47] At these musters, the farmer would be required to present his gun and supplies for inspection and then to engage in training as a company. Twice a year, the company's commanding officer was required to report on the state of the company's arms and equipment.[48] Beyond that, once every four months, a militia sergeant would come to the farmer's home to "examin[e] the State of his Arms, Accoutrements, and Ammunition; of which said Serjeant shall make exact Report to [the commanding officer of the company]."[49]

As a militia member, the farmer could be deployed by his officers or the governor to suppress any "invasion, insurrection, sedition or alarm."[50] He could also be called out to guard the state's borders or be deployed to assist another state or the newly formed United States in its ongoing war with England.[51] However, deployments with the militia were limited to one month, except in the case of an ongoing invasion or insurrection within the state.[52]

Other states had different standards, and the burdens imposed on militia members were calibrated by state legislatures and militia leaders depending on the level of threat a colony faced. The Minutemen in Lexington and Concord trained multiple times a week, while at other times militias trained as rarely as once a year.[53] That said, across founding-era history, "[c]olonial law required

---

[43] Lindsay Schakenbach Regele, *A Different Constitutionality for Gun Regulation*, 46 HASTINGS CONST. L.Q. 523, 524 (2019).

[44] An Act for the Regulating, Training, and Arraying of the Militia, ch. 22, § 35.

[45] An Act for the Regulating, Training, and Arraying of the Militia, ch. 22, §§ 14–15, 1778 N.J. Laws 42, 45.

[46] FRIEDRICH WILHELM VON STEUBEN, REGULATIONS FOR THE ORDER AND DISCIPLINE OF THE TROOPS OF THE UNITED STATES (1779).

[47] An Act for the Regulating, Training, and Arraying of the Militia, ch. 22, §§ 14–15, 1778.

[48] *Id.* at § 10.

[49] *Id.* at § 13. Maryland's 1756 law required militia officers to "make d[i]ligent Search and Enquiry" in their districts and to report "what Number of Arms and what Quantity of Ammunition they ... discover and the Condition and kind of such Arms and Ammunition and who shall be possessed thereof distinctly in Writing," and it required "all and every Person" to produce their arms and ammunition on demand for this recording, on penalty of a five pound (roughly $1,200) fine. An Act for Regulating the Militia of the Province of Maryland (May 22, 1756), *available at* https://archive.org/details/backgroundsofsel25unit/page/84/mode/2up.

[50] An Act for the Regulating, Training, and Arraying of the Militia, ch. 22, § 21.

[51] *Id.* at §§ 19, 20.

[52] *Id.* at § 23.

[53] *See* SHUSTERMAN, *supra* note 26, at 158 ("The Provincial Congress's suggestion was [to train] 'three times a week, and oftener, as opportunity may offer.'"); An Act for Establishing a Militia Within

almost all free men to participate in regular military training, with their own arms, for much of their adult lives."[54] This differed from the situation in England, Ireland, and the British Caribbean, where militia service was limited to a "trained band" selected for the members' martial ability, but more importantly for their political loyalty.[55]

When Congress exercised its power under the Militia Clauses and enacted the Militia Act in 1792, it made clear that all militiamen were expected to train with their firearms. The act required all "free, able-bodied white male citizens" between the ages of eighteen and forty-five to enroll in the militias, equip themselves with, among other tools of the trade, "a good musket or firelock," and "appear so armed, accoutered and provided, *when called out to exercise* or into service."[56] The militiamen were required to be trained in military discipline as provided in Baron von Steuben's military training manual, which Congress had adopted as a national standard in 1779.[57] Each militia brigade was also required to appoint a "brigade-inspector to attend the regimental and battalion meeting of the militia composing their several brigades, during the time of their being under arms, to inspect their arms, ammunition and accoutrements."[58] These inspectors were required to keep records of the units' weapons and training and make reports to the state's adjutant general, who would forward the records to the state governor and the president.[59] While the importance of the militia waned in the nineteenth century, the Militia Act technically remained in effect until the creation of the National Guard in 1903.[60]

Cumulatively, these militia regulations imposed substantial burdens and obligations on militia members of the founding era. The government intervened in decisions about what gun a person bought, checked up on the gun's upkeep

---

the State, §§ 1, 5–6, 1782 Del. Acts 1, 3 (requiring militia units to train "once in every month" except for three and militia battalions to train twice per year); An Act to Amend and More Effectually Put In Force For The Time Therein Limited, The Act Entitled An Act For The Regulation Of The Militia Of This State, 1791 S.C. Acts 16 (requiring training three times per year); 19 THE COLONIAL RECORDS OF THE STATE OF GEORGIA 350–51 (2018) (requiring militia companies to train up to six times per year); An Act for Raising Troops for the Protection of the Inhabitants of Davidson County, ch. 1, § 11, 1786 N.C. Sess. Laws 407, 411 (requiring each captain to "instruct [his militia company] in the necessary exercises and maneuvers" four times per year, as each colonel was, but once per year); An Act to Regulate the Militia, ch. 25, 1786 N.Y. Laws 220, 222 (requiring "every able bodied male person being a citizen" to "rendezvous four times in every year, for the purpose of training, disciplining, and improving in martial exercises").

[54] Churchill, *supra* note 35, at 141.
[55] *Id.* at 145–46.
[56] Militia Act of May 8, 1792, ch. 33, § 1, 1 Stat. 271, 271, *repealed* by Dick Act of 1903, ch. 196, § 25, 32 Stat. 775, 780.
[57] *Id.* at § 7; 13 JOURNALS OF THE CONTINENTAL CONGRESS, 1774–1789, at 384 (W. Ford ed., 1904).
[58] Militia Act of May 8, 1792, at § 10.
[59] *Id.*
[60] Dick Act of 1903, ch. 196, § 25, 32 Stat. 775, 780.

and functionality, recorded the guns people owned, and regulated how often they trained with it. While these laws were intended to further different objectives than modern gun laws—maintaining a sufficient force to protect the colony or state from foreign invasion, insurrection, or criminal activity, rather than pure crime prevention—they still provide useful historical analogies for modern gun laws. Would the founders have accepted a law requiring a gun be inspected by government authorities upon initial purchase? Requiring a gun be registered with the local government? Mandating training? If we look to founding-era militia laws as relevant historical analogs, then the answer to each of these questions is yes.

B. Historical Firearms Regulations Intended to Prevent Fires

Fires were a horrifying specter in the eighteenth- and nineteenth-century urban world.[61] Before the widespread use of modern building materials, smoke detectors, sprinkler systems, and professional, highly capable firefighting corps, major cities were routinely gutted by conflagration.[62] Much of London burned in 1666.[63] Boston burned in 1711, 1760, and 1872.[64] New York went up in flames in 1776, 1835, and 1845.[65] New Orleans in 1788 and 1794.[66] Chicago burned in 1871 on the same night a forest fire centered in Peshtigo, Wisconsin, ignited a firestorm that killed twenty-five hundred people.[67] Because of this threat, laws at the time gave state and local governments broad powers to take action to prevent fires.[68] For example, cities could destroy people's homes or businesses without having to pay compensation, often by blowing them up, to create a fire break to

---

[61] JILL LEPORE, NEW YORK BURNING: LIBERTY, SLAVERY AND CONSPIRACY IN EIGHTEENTH CENTURY MANHATTAN 42 (2005) (noting that "fire was the greatest danger facing an early modern city").

[62] Id.

[63] *The Great Fire of London*, LONDON FIRE BRIGADE, https://www.london-fire.gov.uk/museum/history-and-stories/the-great-fire-of-london/ (last visited May 19, 2022).

[64] *Boston History Before 1859*, BOSTON FIRE HISTORICAL SOCIETY, https://bostonfirehistory.org/boston-history-before-1859/ (last visited May 19, 2022); *Great Boston Fire of 1872*, BOSTON FIRE HISTORICAL SOCIETY, https://bostonfirehistory.org/fires/great-boston-fire-of-1872/ (last visited May 19, 2022).

[65] Amy Zerba, *Notable Fires in the New York City Area*, N.Y. TIMES, June 20, 2014, https://cityroom.blogs.nytimes.com/2014/06/20/notable-fires-in-the-new-york-city-area/.

[66] Sally Reeves, *French Quarter Fire and Flood*, NEW ORLEANS FRENCH QUARTER, https://www.frenchquarter.com/elements/ (last visited May 19, 2022).

[67] Encyclopedia Britannica, online edition, *available at* https://www.britannica.com/event/Chicago-fire-of-1871 (last visited May 19, 2022); Kim Estep, *The Peshtigo Fire*, NATIONAL WEATHER SERVICE (May 19, 2022, 1:13 PM), https://www.weather.gov/grb/peshtigofire (reprinted from the *Green Bay Press-Gazette*).

[68] *See generally* WILLIAM NOVAK, THE PEOPLE'S WELFARE: LAW AND REGULATION IN NINETEENTH CENTURY AMERICA (1996).

stop fires from spreading.[69] In fact, "[a]t the common law every one [including private individuals] had the right to destroy real and personal property, in cases of actual necessity, to prevent the spreading of a fire, and there was no responsibility on the part of such destroyer, and no remedy for the owner."[70]

The state's police power to enact fire prevention laws extended to regulating ammunition and firearms.[71] Historically, virtually every jurisdiction heavily regulated the possession, transportation, sale, and manufacture of gunpowder to prevent fires and explosions and regulated the shooting of guns in public both to protect against unintentional shootings and fires caused by gunshots.[72]

1. Gunpowder Regulations

American colonies and later states enacted laws requiring gunpowder above a certain quantity to be stored in a public storehouse and requiring any gunpowder stored at a home or in a business to be stored in specific ways.[73] In Massachusetts, gunpowder could not be stored with other weapons.[74] In New Hampshire, it had to be stored in a secured tin canister.[75] In New York, it had to be stored in jugs or canisters, none of which could hold more than seven pounds.[76] Pennsylvania required gunpowder to be stored on the top floor of a house, and in Rhode Island, gunpowder had to be stored in a tin powder flask.[77]

These laws were not challenged under the Second Amendment or state Second Amendment analogs.[78] Instead, the limited number of challenges related to whether regulating gunpowder storage fell within the state police power or whether storing gunpowder in cities represented a per se nuisance. The best example of these challenges came from a case in New York and its fiery aftermath.

[69] See generally Mugler v. Kansas, 123 U.S. 623, 666 (1887) (discussing how government actions to regulate the use of property under the police power do not require compensation).
[70] Bowditch v. Boston, 101 U.S. 16, 18 (1879); Stone v. Mayor of New York, 25 Wend. 157, 162 (N.Y. 1840) (noting that "it is lawful to raze a house to the ground to prevent the spreading of a conflagration"); Respublica v. Sparhawk, 1 Dall. 357, 362 (Pa. 1788) ("It is a rule, however, that it is better to suffer a private mischief, than a public inconvenience; and the rights of necessity, form a part of our law.... Houses may be razed to prevent the spreading of fire, because for the public good.").
[71] See Repository of Historical Gun Laws, supra note 34 (category: "transportation, storage, firing").
[72] Id.; see also LEPORE, supra note 61, at 46 (describing dangers of extinguishing a fire in a building housing "gunpowder, hay, pitch, tar, resin, and turpentine").
[73] See, e.g., An Act in Addition to the Several Acts Already Made for the Prudent Storage of Gun-Powder Within the Town of Boston, ch. 13, 1783 Mass. Acts 218 (prohibiting storing loaded guns); An Act to Prevent the Keeping of Large Quantities of Gun-Powder in Private Houses in Portsmouth, and for Appointing a Keeper of the Magazine Belonging to Said Town, 1786 N.H. Laws 383–84; An Act to Prevent the Danger Arising from the Pernicious Practice of Lodging Gun Powder in Dwelling Houses, ch. 28, 1784 N.Y. Laws 627; Act of Apr., 1782, ch. 9, § 42, 1782 Pa. Laws 41; Act of Dec. 6, 1783, ch. 1059, § 1, 11 Pa. Stat. 209; Act of June 28, 1762, 1762 R.I. Pub. Laws 130, 132.
[74] Act of Mar. 7, 1782, ch. 9, 1782 Mass. Acts 116, 119.
[75] An Act to Prevent the Keeping of Large Quantities of Gun-Powder in Private Houses in Portsmouth, § 1, 1786 N.H. Laws 383, 384.
[76] Act of Apr. 13, 1784, ch. 28, 1784 N.Y. Laws 627, 627.
[77] Ch. 9, § 42, 1782 Pa. Laws at 41; 1762 R.I. Pub. Laws at 132.
[78] See McDonald v. City of Chicago, 561 U.S. 742 (2010).

People v. Sands was an 1806 case in which the operators of a gunpowder storage house appealed a conviction for "keeping a nuisance" by operating a storage house in Brooklyn.[79] In *Sands*, the court applied a negligence standard to the nuisance question, looking to whether the facility posed an actual danger to public safety.[80] The court took judicial notice that the facility was

> a brick building, constructed for the storing of powder, and secured by conductors, and every usual guard against accidents.... The danger of a magazine exploding when properly built and secured is remote indeed.... [O]nly one witness was produced who had ever heard of such an event, and that but once.[81]

The court overturned the conviction by a 2–1 vote, finding that "it is not unlawful... to keep gunpowder in a magazine properly constructed and secured, though the same be near to dwelling-houses, and a public street; but that if, by negligence, or want of care, it becomes dangerous, the owner may be indicted."[82] However, an unusual footnote followed the court's analysis about the safety of storing powder in the city:

> It so happened that [six months later] the very powder magazine in question, with above 400 quarter casks of powder in it, blew up. By the explosion the windows of the church, and of several dwelling-houses, were broken to pieces, but no lives were lost.[83]

After the *Sands* court's policy judgments blew up in its face, courts generally treated the storage of gunpowder in populated areas as a per se nuisance.[84] One Tennessee court made clear that the nuisance abated was not just the potential danger of an explosion but also the constant fear of an explosion faced by nearby residents.[85]

---

[79] People v. Sands, 1 Johns. R. 78, 78 (N.Y. Sup. Ct. 1806).
[80] *Id.*
[81] *Id.*
[82] *Id.* at 88.
[83] *Id.* at 84, n. 1.
[84] *See* Myers v. Malcolm, 6 Hill 292, 292 (N.Y. 1844); Cheatham v. Shearon, 31 Tenn. 213, 214–15 (Tenn. 1851); Bradley v. People, 56 Barb. 72, 72–73 (N.Y. 1866) (using a standard closer to that of *Sands*); Wier's Appeal, 74 Pa. 230, 230 (1873); Heeg v. Licht, 80 N.Y. 579, 579 (N.Y. 1880) (rejecting *Sands* standard and finding gunpowder storage in populated areas is per se nuisance).
[85] *Cheatham*, 31 Tenn. at 216. For an excellent discussion of why mitigating perceptions of danger are an important government interest, *see* Eric Ruben, *Justifying Perceptions in First and Second Amendment Doctrine*, 80 Law & Contemp. Probs. 149 (2017).

Throughout the early nineteenth century, states and municipalities required gunpowder be safely stored.[86] This regulation did not just occur through nuisance law as in *Sands*, but widely through criminal sanctions for improperly storing gunpowder.[87] Again, several of these statutes limited the quantities of gunpowder that individuals could store, ranging from the fairly low, such as Connecticut, which limited residents to one pound of gunpowder, to the quite high, such as Kentucky, which allowed no more than one hundred pounds in any one building.[88] Regulations concerning the manner in which gunpowder could be stored continued to be passed as well. In Salem, Massachusetts, gunpowder was permitted only if it was "well secured in tight casks or canisters," and in Cincinnati, Ohio, individuals were permitted only "twenty-five pounds, to be divided into six equal parts."[89] States also often regulated the transportation of gunpowder, requiring it to be clearly labeled, protected from stray embers, and secured in casks.[90]

After the enactment of the Fourteenth Amendment, numerous states either further strengthened existing rules or imposed new regulations governing the safe storage of gunpowder and other hazardous materials.[91] All told, then, of the forty-eight states in the Union in the early twentieth century (Alaska and Hawaii did not become states until 1959), at least forty-seven had laws regulating the safe storage of gunpowder or firearms by individuals.[92]

---

[86] *See Repository of Historical Gun Laws, supra* note 34 (category: "storage"); *see also* BLOCHER & MILLER, *supra* note 34, at 20.

[87] *Id.*

[88] PORTLAND, ME., REV. ORDINANCES ch. 13, §§ 1–4 (1848) (mandating one pound only); ST. LOUIS, MO., REV. ORDINANCES ch. 22, §§ 1–5 (1828) (mandating thirty pounds); CINCINNATI, OH., REV. ORDINANCES §§ 1–4, at 57–58 (1835) (mandating twenty-five pounds); PITTSBURGH, PA., REV. ORDINANCES ch. 2, § 1 (1816) (mandating thirty pounds); R.I. Pub. Laws 1798–1813, 85, § 2 (mandating twenty-eight pounds); COLUMBIA, S.C., REV. ORDINANCES no. 57 (1823) (mandating fifty pounds).

[89] JOSEPH BARLOW FELT OSGOOD, THE CHARTER AND ORDINANCES OF THE CITY OF SALEM, TOGETHER WITH THE ACTS OF THE LEGISLATURE RELATING TO THE CITY: COLLATED AND REVISED PURSUANT TO AN ORDER OF THE CITY COUNCIL 67–68 (1853); CINCINNATI, OH., REV. ORDINANCES §§ 1–4, at 57–58 (1835) (mandating twenty-five pounds).

[90] LAWS, STATUTES, ORDINANCES AND CONSTITUTIONS, ORDAINED, MADE AND ESTABLISHED, BY THE MAYOR, ALDERMEN, AND COMMONALTY, OF THE CITY OF NEW YORK, CONVENED IN COMMON-COUNCIL, FOR THE GOOD RULE AND GOVERNMENT OF THE INHABITANTS AND RESIDENTS OF THE SAID CITY (1763); MERCER BEASLEY, REVISION OF THE STATUTES OF NEW JERSEY 263 (1877).

[91] *See* Act of Mar. 8, 1866, § 2, 1868 Pa. Laws 319, 321 (empowering local govt. to regulate gunpowder); Act of Mar. 29, 1869, art. 4, § 10, 1869 Ill. Laws 13, 17 (same); Act of Mar. 14, 1863, § 15, 1869 Mich. Pub. Acts 2d Reg. Sess. 156, 158 (same); An Act to Amend and Reduce into One the Several Acts in Reference to the Town of Princeton, art. 5, § 14, 1869 Ky. Acts 481, 481 (same).

[92] *See* Brief of Amicus Curiae Everytown for Gun Safety in Support of Defendant's Motion to Dismiss or for Summary Judgment at 13, Johnson v. Lyon, 406 F.Supp.3d 651 (W.D. Mich.) (No. 2:17-cv-00124-PLM-TPG). Arizona does not have any gunpowder storage regulations listed in the Repository of Historical Gun Laws.

2. Regulations on Firing Guns in Public

Similarly, laws regulating firing guns in public were nearly universal during the founding period, the nineteenth century, and largely to the present day. The Repository of Historical Gun Laws lists 201 examples, but those are just a subset of the essentially omnipresent regulations.[93] There were multiple motivations for laws prohibiting gun discharge: during the colonial period, when guns were used to alert residents of an Indian attack, robbery, or fire, prohibitions on firing were intended to prevent false alarm;[94] others were intended to ensure respect for the Sabbath;[95] and others were intended to prevent unintentional shootings.[96] Most relevant for this chapter, many were intended to prevent fire and were often combined with prohibitions on shooting other flammable objects like fireworks.[97] These laws continued to be enacted and re-enacted during Reconstruction, the turn of the twentieth century, and the early twentieth century.[98] Still today, the vast majority of jurisdictions continue to regulate and prohibit firing guns in populated areas.[99]

Together, these laws imposed significant regulation on the storage and transportation of firearms ammunition and the firing of weapons in urban areas. While historically these laws were primarily intended to prevent fires, their modern-day equivalents such as responsible firearms storage requirements and prohibitions on firing guns in populated areas seek to prevent children from

---

[93] See Repository of Historical Gun Laws, supra note 34 (category: "firing").

[94] See E.B. O'CALLAGHAN, LAWS AND ORDINANCES OF NEW NETHERLAND, 1638–1674 (1868); THE GENERAL LAWS AND LIBERTIES OF CONNECTICUT, 1672–1714 (1673).

[95] The Sabbath to Be Kept Holy, 1657 Va. Acts 432, 434. These kinds of laws are not purely historical. Pennsylvania did not repeal its prohibition on hunting on Sundays until 2020. See Amber Gerard, *First Firearms Deer Season That Allows Sunday Hunting Begins in Pennsylvania*, WGAL.COM (Nov. 28, 2020), https://www.wgal.com/article/first-firearms-deer-season-that-allows-sunday-hunting-begins-in-pennsylvania-nov-2020/34810105.

[96] EDWARD LIVINGSTON, LAWS AND ORDINANCES, ORDAINED AND ESTABLISHED BY THE MAYOR, ALDERMEN, AND COMMONALTY OF THE CITY OF NEW-YORK, IN COMMON-COUNCIL CONVENED, FOR THE GOOD RULE AND GOVERNMENT OF THE INHABITANTS AND RESIDENTS OF SAID CITY 83–84 (1803).

[97] ORDINANCES ORDAINED AND ESTABLISHED BY THE MAYOR & CITY COUNCIL OF THE CITY OF NEW ORLEANS 68 (1817) ("No person shall hereafter be permitted to fire or discharge any gun, pistol, fowling piece or firearm, nor to discharge or let off any rocket, cracker, squib or other fire-works, in any street, court yard, lot, walk or public way, within the city or suburbs."); ALEXANDER EDWARDS, ORDINANCES OF THE CITY COUNCIL OF CHARLESTON, IN THE STATE OF SOUTH-CAROLINA, PASSED SINCE THE INCORPORATION OF THE CITY 289 (1802) (similar).

[98] See Repository of Historical Gun Laws, supra note 34 (category: "firing," time period: 1863–1936).

[99] See, e.g., ALA. CODE § 13A-11-61.3(g)(11) (2022) (generally preempting local gun regulation but not prohibiting "a municipality from regulating the discharge of firearms within the limits of the municipality or a county from exercising any authority it has under law, to regulate the discharge of firearms within the jurisdiction of the county"); COLO. REV. STAT. § 30-15-302 (2022) (permits counties to regulate the discharge of firearms in areas with an average population of at least 100 persons per square mile); GA. CODE ANN. § 16-11-173(e) (2015) ("Nothing contained in this Code section shall prohibit municipalities or counties, by ordinance or resolution, from reasonably limiting or prohibiting the discharge of firearms within the boundaries of the municipal corporation or county.").

accessing guns, reduce the risk of firearms theft, and reduce the risk of unintentional shootings from irresponsible gun use.[100] Differences aside, the burdens imposed on gun owners today would not seem novel to people of the founding era or nineteenth century.

IV. Case Law Addressing Historical Militia and Fire Laws

As in the previous section, there is a long history of virtually every state regulating the conduct of gun owners to further non-crime prevention goals. These laws represent important historical analogies for modern gun laws requiring training, registration, responsible storage, and potentially restrictions on magazine capacity. They imposed burdens on gun owners comparable to or, in several cases, substantially more stringent than modern gun laws and were clearly deemed acceptable by the founding generation.

In the decade-plus of Second Amendment litigation before *Bruen*, the very limited number of federal courts to consider historical militia and fire prevention laws have generally not been receptive to their relevance. These cases are no longer precedential and the ongoing relevance of their analysis is doubtful. The history-focused framework the Supreme Court adopted in *Bruen* explicitly calls for considering laws that imposed an analogous historical burden, even if adopted for a different purpose. That said, pre-*Bruen* case law provides insights into some of the arguments—albeit, now incorrect—that will likely ensue in post-*Bruen* cases about using historical gun laws aimed at objectives other than crime reduction.

The clearest discussion of the issue comes in a dissenting opinion written by then judge, now Justice, Brett Kavanaugh in *Heller v. District of Columbia* (*Heller II*), a case challenging the District of Columbia's firearms licensing and registration laws, as well as its prohibition on assault weapons and large-capacity magazines.[101] In *Heller II*, the District sought to analogize its requirement that handguns be registered to the kinds of historical militia inspection and recordkeeping requirements discussed previously in section III.A—although the District made this argument in a fairly perfunctory manner in the pre-Repository world.[102] Judge Kavanaugh rejected the historical relevance of these

---

[100] Lower storage requirements would also likely have imposed burdens on the ammunition a person could have readily available that were akin to modern restrictions on magazine capacity. *See generally* Charter and By-Laws of the City of New Haven, New Haven, Conn. (1848) (limiting residents to one pound of gunpowder in their home); The Revised Ordinances of the City of Portland (1848) (same).

[101] Heller v. District of Columbia (*Heller II*), 670 F.3d 1244, 1293 (D.C. Cir. 2011) (Kavanaugh, J., dissenting).

[102] *Id.*

laws and noted that he would have ended his inquiry there and found a Second Amendment violation without applying any of the traditional tiers of constitutional scrutiny.

Kavanaugh rejected militia laws as historical analogs for two reasons. The first was that "early militia laws applied only to militiamen, not to all citizens."[103] Kavanaugh believed that because the militia inspection requirements applied only to White men in a certain age range and excluded women, it was not a viable comparison.[104] This is an odd criticism. While men over a certain age may no longer have been required to participate in the active militia, they would have been required to abide by mandatory militia requirements during the earlier years of their lives. They also likely would have still been subject to arms-keeping requirements and, in many states, would have been subject to gun censuses or, in times of crisis, gun impressment.[105]

It is even more dubious why women being excluded from militia inspection requirements would make militia requirements irrelevant to modern gun laws. At the time of the founding, women would have generally been excluded from the body politic.[106] Most women would not have "owned" any firearms or, in a legal sense, any property at the time, as the property of married women was placed under their husbands' control and they themselves were considered wards of their husbands.[107] Similarly, unmarried women and men who had not yet established their own households would have been considered wards of their fathers.[108] The only women who would have been considered "owners" of firearms were widows—whose firearms may well have been accounted for if they had sons eligible for militia service—and single adult women living alone.[109] The laws' exclusion of these relatively small groups of female firearms owners seems like an odd reason to reject the relevance of universally adopted founding-era gun laws.

Another important exclusion unmentioned in Judge Kavanaugh's dissenting opinion is the exclusion of enslaved persons, free Blacks, and American Indians from militia service.[110] But again, to an even greater degree than women, the horrific injustices of the founding and antebellum eras held these groups to be outside of the body politic.[111] Further, most American Indians were not

---

[103] *Id.*
[104] *Id.*
[105] Churchill, *supra* note 35, at 141–44 (discussing how keeping arms was a practice incumbent on every member of the "body politic").
[106] Mary B. Norton, *The Constitutional Status of Women in 1787*, 6(1) LAW & INEQ. 7 (1988).
[107] *Id.*
[108] *Id.* at 8.
[109] *Id.*
[110] *See generally Repository of Historical Gun Laws, supra* note 34 (category: "race and slavery based").
[111] The most egregious example is obviously the Dred Scott Case, in which Chief Justice Taney found Black people are "not included, and were not intended to be included, under the word 'citizens'

citizens of the United States until 1924. At the founding, they would have been considered more akin to citizens of a foreign nation than members of the body politic.[112] The historical scope of a right should be analyzed based on the rights and responsibilities of those who enjoyed full citizenship, not those with limited or no rights.

More substantively, Judge Kavanaugh's second reason for rejecting the analogy between firearms inspection laws and the District's challenged laws was because "militia members were required to submit for inspection only one or a few firearms, not all of their firearms."[113] Kavanaugh described these laws as "*not registration of firearms, but rather simply to ensure that the militia was well-equipped.*"[114] As a matter of history, this analysis is incomplete. As discussed previously in section III.A, gun censuses and recordkeeping requirements were sometimes used to take account of all the weapons in a given area to help determine an area's real military capacity.[115] The District's brief, which was written before the creation of resources such as the Duke Repository, did not clearly convey this reality.[116]

It is worth noting that, while Judge Kavanaugh's rejection of militia laws as a relevant historical analog was somewhat dubious, he did at least consider them before rejecting them on the merits. This implies that had Judge Kavanaugh believed the burdens imposed were more analogous to the District's registration law—rather than a "far cry from a registration requirement for all firearms"—he would have viewed them as a relevant historical analog even though they were intended to further the goals of the militia rather than protect against the misuse of firearms.[117]

Judge Kavanaugh's willingness to consider non-criminal law historical analogs is contrary to the Seventh Circuit's view in Ezell v. City of Chicago, a case challenging Chicago's prohibition on firing ranges within the city. Judge Diane Sykes, writing for a panel of the Seventh Circuit, rejected the relevance of historical laws prohibiting the shooting of guns in cities because they "had clear fire suppression purposes [and therefore] do not support the proposition that target practice at a

---

in the Constitution, and can therefore claim none of the rights and privileges which that instrument provides for and secures to citizens of the United States." *Scott v. Sandford*, 60 U.S. 393, 404 (1857).

[112] *See* Indian Citizenship Act of 1924, Pub. L. No. 68-175, 43 Stat. 253 (1924) (codified as amended at 8 U.S.C. § 1402(b) (2012)).
[113] Heller v. District of Columbia (*Heller II*), 670 F.3d 1244, 1293 (D.C. Cir. 2011) (Kavanaugh, J., dissenting).
[114] *Id.*
[115] *See* discussion *supra* section III.A.
[116] *See* Brief for Appellees, Heller v. District of Columbia, 670 F.3d 1244 (D.C. Cir. 2011) (No. 10-7036).
[117] *See Heller II*, 670 F.3d at 1293 (Kavanaugh, J., dissenting).

safely sited and properly equipped firing range enjoys no Second Amendment protection whatsoever."[118]

Similarly, in *Yukutake v. Connors*, the District of Hawaii rejected consideration of historical militia inspection laws in a case challenging a law requiring firearms purchasers to have their weapons inspected by police as part of the registration process.[119] The court said that the "purpose and scope of these colonial-era militia laws are too dissimilar" to the challenged law to meet the longstanding requirement.[120] The District of Hawaii also pointed out that the law would not have applied to everyone; instead it "applied only to militiamen."[121]

Finally, in *Jackson v. City & County of San Francisco*, a challenge to a San Francisco law that required firearms be locked up when not in a person's immediate possession, a panel of the Ninth Circuit refused to consider historical anti-fire gunpowder storage regulations as relevant analogs.[122] The panel found: "The fact that states historically imposed modest restrictions on the storage of gunpowder, a dangerous and highly flammable substance, does not raise the inference that the Second Amendment is inapplicable to regulations imposing restrictions on the storage of handguns."[123] The panel further found that because "*Heller* rejected the probative value of this evidence," meaning historical gunpowder storage laws, the panel could not rely on such laws now.[124] Rejecting the historical arguments for the law's validity, the *Jackson* court then moved onto the second step of the two-part framework and upheld the constitutionality of the law under intermediate scrutiny.[125]

The Jackson Court's reliance on *Heller* to reject consideration of gunpowder storage laws is misguided. It is true that Justice Scalia rejected the analogy of gunpowder storage laws to laws completely prohibiting handgun possession, saying:

> The other laws Justice Breyer cites are gunpowder-storage laws that he concedes did not clearly prohibit loaded weapons, but required only that excess gunpowder be kept in a special container or on the top floor of the home. Nothing about those fire-safety laws undermines our analysis; they do not remotely burden the right of self-defense as much as an absolute ban on handguns.[126]

---

[118] Ezell v. City of Chicago, 651 F.3d 684, 706 (7th Cir. 2011).
[119] Yukutake v. Connors, 554 F.Supp.3d 1074 (D. Haw. 2021).
[120] *Id.*, at 1087.
[121] *Id.*
[122] *See* Jackson v. City & County of San Francisco, 746 F.3d 953, 962 (9th Cir. 2014).
[123] *Id.* at 963.
[124] *Id.*
[125] *Id.* at 964–65.
[126] District of Columbia v. Heller, 554 U.S. 570, 632 (2008) (citations omitted).

However, the Supreme Court went on to say that rejecting this analogy in the context of laws completely prohibiting the possession of functional firearms does not "suggest the invalidity of laws regulating the storage of firearms to prevent accidents."[127] Thus, far from rejecting the probative value of historical gunpowder storage laws, the Supreme Court seemed to implicitly accept the analogy of such laws to modern firearms storage laws.

Collectively, these cases are not especially supportive of using militia and fire prevention laws as historical analogies justifying modern gun regulations, but pre-*Bruen*, there was some justification for this approach. Courts that could not find a nearly identical historical analogy to the challenged modern regulation—particularly with respect to purpose—could nonetheless uphold the modern regulation under the pre-*Bruen* tiers of constitutional scrutiny analysis. In three of the cases—*Ezell*, *Yukutake*, and *Jackson*—the courts went on to consider the laws under one of the traditional tiers of constitutional scrutiny, and in *Jackson*, the court upheld the modern regulation. The Supreme Court's *Bruen* framework expressly requires looking for historical analogies that are not "dead ringers" for modern laws and removes the tiers of constitutionality scrutiny analysis altogether. Thus, under the *Bruen* framework, courts must conduct a broader and more thorough analysis of historical analogs going forward. Historical regulations regarding militias and fire prevention are an important and relevant part of such analysis.

V. Conclusions

New York State Rifle and Pistol Association v. Bruen placed history at the center of the Second Amendment analysis. Courts are instructed to decide Second Amendment challenges based on the Second Amendment's text, as well as on the history of weapons regulation. This analysis clearly does not require a precise match between the objectives behind modern and historical regulations. Instead, courts can and should consider the comparable burden of modern and historical regulations, even if motivated by different goals. Under this standard, historical militia and fire prevention laws provide important and relevant historical analogies for modern gun regulations. Such laws, which existed in the founding era and in the nineteenth century, were at least as burdensome as modern regulations regarding firearms storage, training, and registration. These laws, therefore, provide the exact type of historical support that *Bruen* requires courts to consider.

---

[127] *Id.* at 632.

12

ABOLITION, ARMED SELF-DEFENSE, AND FIREARMS REGULATION IN ANTEBELLUM AMERICA

THE ENFORCEMENT OF SURETY LAWS IN BOSTON

Saul Cornell

I. INTRODUCTION

The complex connections between race and the right to bear arms in American history have generated considerable scholarly interest in recent years.[1] Two rival narratives have emerged from this debate. Some scholars have argued that gun control has invariably been tainted by racism for most, if not all, of American history.[2] Gun regulations in this account have been cast as a tool to perpetuate White racial hegemony. Alternatively, other scholars have maintained that the Second Amendment is itself racist.[3] According to this view, the Second Amendment has been used to arm militias that were created to police slave populations and wage genocidal warfare against tribal peoples.

Each of these narratives contains elements of truth, but each is overly simplistic and ignores the historical complexity of the relationship between race and guns in the period between the adoption of the first state arms bearing provisions during the American Revolution (1776) and the Civil War (1861).[4] In particular, neither narrative captures the shifting historical dynamics governing race and firearms regulation in the years before the Civil War. Indeed, the most recent scholarship on race and guns suggests that even Southern slave owners, the group that enacted the most wide-ranging racially discriminatory bans on gun

---

[1] *See generally* ADAM WINKLER, GUNFIGHT: THE BATTLE OVER THE RIGHT TO BEAR ARMS IN AMERICA (2013).

[2] NICHOLAS JOHNSON, NEGROES AND THE GUNS: THE BLACK TRADITION OF ARMS (2014).

[3] *See, e.g.*, CAROL ANDERSON, THE SECOND: RACE AND GUNS IN A FATALLY UNEQUAL AMERICA (2021); ROXANNE DUNBAR-ORTIZ, LOADED: A DISARMING HISTORY OF THE SECOND AMENDMENT (2018).

[4] Brian Delay, *A Misfire on the Second Amendment*, 47 REVS. IN AM. HIST. 319 (2019).

ownership, were forced to adopt a flexible attitude toward race and firearms because of the military threats posed by rival European powers and hostile tribal populations.[5] Although laws disarming slaves and free Blacks were adopted early in the colonial period, there were also moments in Southern history when the planter class accepted that it was necessary to arm Blacks so that they might help defend against more pressing threats. In short, if one looks at the entire course of American history and analyzes the impact of guns and gun regulation on race, dynamism—not stasis—is the defining feature of this history. Put another way, there was no single understanding of the Second Amendment and its many state analogs when it came to race. Nor was there a uniform approach to firearms regulation. Gun laws and gun rights could be deployed in the service of equality or to perpetuate stark inequalities.[6]

No serious legal historian familiar with modern historical scholarship would presume to generalize about the connections between race and law without acknowledging the profound regional diversity that characterized early American law. Similarly, no historian acquainted with this wide-ranging body of scholarship would argue that gun rights and gun regulation stood outside of the dynamic processes of change that transformed American life in the decades following the adoption of the Second Amendment.[7] The early nineteenth century was a period of tremendous ferment and legal change. The unraveling of the Founders' republican vision of law and the emergence of a more democratic, individualistic, and starkly racist understanding of constitutionalism during the Jacksonian period was one part of this process of change, but it was hardly the only area of American law marked by change and contestation. The expansion of slavery into the new territories acquired by America and the demands of abolitionists for an immediate end to slavery agitated American law and suffused nearly every aspect of American life, including constitutional culture.[8]

Although there is a rich and impressive historiography covering abolitionism, including discussions of abolitionism and violence,[9] little of this scholarship has informed the academic or jurisprudential debate over the history of the Second Amendment and gun regulation. The absence of such discussion is problematic because abolitionists played an important role in transforming ideas about the

---

[5] Sally Hadden, *Gun Laws in Early America: The Sometimes Contradictory Regulations of Gun Use in the Colonial South*, in NEW HISTORIES OF GUN RIGHTS AND REGULATION: ESSAYS ON THE PLACE OF GUNS IN AMERICAN LAW AND SOCIETY (Joseph Blocher, Jacob D. Charles, & Darrell A.H. Miller eds., 2023).

[6] SAUL CORNELL, A WELL-REGULATED MILITIA: THE FOUNDING FATHERS AND THE ORIGINS OF GUN CONTROL IN AMERICA (2006).

[7] GERALD LEONARD & SAUL CORNELL, THE PARTISAN REPUBLIC (2019).

[8] Ariela Gross, *Slavery, Anti-Slavery and the Coming of the Civil War*, in 2 THE CAMBRIDGE HISTORY OF LAW IN AMERICA: THE LONG NINETEENTH CENTURY (1789–1920), at 280 (Michael Grossberg & Christopher Tomlins eds., 2008).

[9] JAMES BREWER STEWART, ABOLITIONIST POLITICS AND THE COMING OF THE CIVIL WAR (2008).

right to bear arms and the scope of the law of self-defense in American thought. As was true for much of the history of abolitionism, this story was complex and was often marked by contention, not consensus.[10]

At the dawn of the nineteenth century, abolitionists were divided between proponents of gradual and immediate emancipation. By the 1830s, support for incremental reform had collapsed, replaced by a more militant phase of abolitionism devoted to the cause of immediatism: the belief that slavery was so evil it had to be abolished without regard to prudential concerns.[11] Despite an intensification of rhetoric and activism, many abolitionists continued to embrace nonviolence as the preferred method to achieve their goal.[12] By the middle of the century, within two decades of the emergence of immediatism in the 1830s, calls for peaceful change were largely supplanted by more militant strains of abolitionist thought. The transformation of abolitionism was facilitated by several developments. The rise of more militant pro-slavery ideology, increased violence against abolitionists and free Blacks outside of the South, and a more aggressive federal fugitive slave policy. The increasing prominence of Black abolitionists in the movement also facilitated this change because of the rising threat of rogue slave catchers capturing and enslaving free people of color outside of the South.[13] By the 1850s, many abolitionists had come to believe that the rifle had usurped the Bible as the tool to end slavery: moral suasion gave way to calls for armed resistance.[14]

II. THE RADICAL ABOLITIONIST CRITIQUE OF SOUTHERN GUN CULTURE: THE PISTOL AND LASH

Massachusetts Senator Charles Sumner was one of the most eloquent opponents of slavery in American public life in the pre–Civil War era. His impassioned speech during the violent struggles over slavery in Kansas in the 1850s, "The Crime Against Kansas," galvanized the nation. Indeed, the speech led one irate Southern congressman, Preston Brooks, to attack the Massachusetts Senator on the floor of Congress with a cane. Trapped beneath his Senate desk, Sumner rose up, tore his Senate desk loose from the bolts securing it to the floor, and collapsed in a bloody heap. The caning of Sumner was a brutal assault that

---

[10] CORNELL, *supra* note 6.
[11] On prudentialism as a modality of American legal argument, *see* PHILIP BOBBITT, CONSTITUTIONAL FATE: THEORY OF THE CONSTITUTION 61 (1982). For a thoughtful discussion of legal prudentialism in the context of the Second Amendment, *see* Neil S. Siegel, *Prudentialism in McDonald v. City of Chicago*, 6 DUKE J. CONST. L. & PUB. POL'Y 16 (2010).
[12] STEWART, *supra* note 9.
[13] MANISHA SINHA, THE SLAVE'S CAUSE: A HISTORY OF ABOLITION (2016).
[14] *Id.*

shocked abolitionists and drew praise from defenders of slavery.[15] In his discussion of the plight of anti-slavery forces in Kansas Sumner reminded the Senate that "[t]he rifle has ever been the companion of the pioneer, and, under God, his tutelary protector against the red man and the beast of the forest."[16] Sumner praised pioneers bearing muskets in "The Crime Against Kansas" speech, linking their actions with the ideas of manifest destiny.[17] Having conjured up the mythic image of a lone pioneer, gun in hand, conquering the West. Sumner added: "Never was this efficient weapon more needed in just self-defense, than now in Kansas, and at least one article in our National Constitution must be blotted out, before the complete right to it can in any way be impeached."[18] The guns of a well-regulated militia, long guns, were linked with American progress. The dispossession of tribal peoples and the spread of American civilization were thus inextricably linked with firearms.

Sumner's vision of the Second Amendment has figured prominently in discussion of the right to bear arms.[19] What has drawn less interest among Second Amendment scholars was his denunciation of the proliferation of pistols and other easily concealable weapons. If the rifle was tied to a heroic narrative of American conquest, concealed weapons were linked to the evils of slavery.[20] To understand abolitionist views of the connection between the right to bear arms and regulation one must acknowledge both dimensions of Sumner's attitude toward guns.

In *Heller*, Justice Scalia erroneously claimed that the Founding era militia depended on citizens bringing whatever guns were in common use to muster.[21] In fact, as recent scholarship has conclusively demonstrated, this claim was not only false but was the mirror image of historical reality. Although some Americans did bring whatever weapon was at hand to muster, the goal of

---

[15] For a discussion of the incident and the larger impact of slavery on violence in Congress, *see* JOANNE B. FREEMAN, THE FIELD OF BLOOD: VIOLENCE IN CONGRESS AND THE ROAD TO CIVIL WAR (2018).

[16] CHARLES SUMNER, THE CRIME AGAINST KANSAS. THE APOLOGIES FOR THE CRIME. THE TRUE REMEDY. SPEECH OF HON. CHARLES SUMNER, IN THE SENATE OF THE UNITED STATES, 19TH AND 20TH MAY, 1856, at 64 (Boston, John P. Jewett & Co. 1856).

[17] On race and manifest destiny, *see* REGINALD HORSMAN, RACE AND MANIFEST DESTINY: THE ORIGINS OF AMERICAN RACIAL ANGLO-SAXONISM (1981).

[18] SUMNER, *supra* note 16, at 64. On the myth of the lone pioneer in Western history, *see* Stephen Aron, *Lessons in Conquest: Towards a Greater Western History*, 63 PAC. HIST. REV. 125 (1994).

[19] For a good example of the use and abuse of Sumner's writings by pro-gun activists, *see* David B. Kopel, *The Second Amendment in the Nineteenth Century*, 1998 BYU L. REV. 1359, 1446–48 (1998).

[20] N.Y. TRIB., May 23, 1856, at 4. *Speech of Hon. C. Sumner*, CONG. GLOBE, App., 34th Cong. 1st Sess. 529 (May 20, 1856). Butler explained his intention in a response to Charles Sumner, delivered after Sumner's "Crime against Kansas Speech." *Speech of A.P. Butler*, CONG. GLOBE, Appendix, 34th Congress, 1st session June 13, 1856, at 1093.

[21] District of Columbia v. Heller, 554 U.S. 570, 624 (2008). The only authority Scalia cited for this proposition was *United States v. Miller*, 307 U.S. 174 (1939), a case he himself attacked for its shoddy history.

American policy was to discourage Americans from doing so and force them to acquire the types of weapons the government believed were essential to the creation of a well-regulated militia. Guns that furthered the goal of a well-regulated militia enjoyed the greatest constitutional protection in early America, and guns that were of modest military value, weapons, best suited to assault, affray, and murder enjoyed minimal protections.[22]

The different legal treatment of easily concealable pistols and guns suitable for a militia, an important distinction in early American law, also influenced the way abolitionists approached the right to bear arms. This distinction emerges clearly in the thought of Charles Sumner. His discussion of pistols and bowie knives—two types of easily concealed weapons—were closely associated with slavery and its brutal system of labor discipline and punishment. If muskets and rifles conjured up images of heroic pioneers, avatars of American liberty, easily concealed weapons were cast as the embodiment of all the ills wrought by slavery.

> In those portions of our country where it is supposed essential to personal safety to go armed with pistols and bowie-knives, mortal affrays are so frequent as to excite but little attention, and to secure, with rare exceptions, impunity to the murderer; whereas, at the North and East, where we are unprovided with such facilities for taking life, comparatively few murders of the kind are perpetrated.[23]

Sumner's account of America's divergent gun cultures became a staple in abolitionist literature and culture—for leading abolitionist Southern culture was synonymous with despotism, a corrupt and oppressive legal order maintained by the rule of the pistol and the lash. Modern scholarship has vindicated much of Sumner's account. The South was more violent and homicidal during this period of American history.[24] Recent scholarship has also shown how distinctive regional legal cultures emerged in early America and firearms regulation was no exception to this process.[25]

---

[22] Kevin M. Sweeney, *Firearms, Militias, and the Second Amendment*, in THE SECOND AMENDMENT ON TRIAL: CRITICAL ESSAYS ON *DISTRICT OF COLUMBIA V. HELLER* 310 (Saul Cornell & Nathan Kozuskanich eds., 2013). *See also* Saul Cornell, *History and Tradition or Fantasy and Fiction: Which Version of the Past will the Supreme Court Choose in NYSRPA v. Bruen?*, 49 HASTINGS CONST. L.Q. 145 (2022).

[23] CHARLES SUMNER, EXTRACTS FROM "THE TRUE GRANDEUR OF NATIONS": AN ORATION 25 (Kessinger Publishing LLC 2010) (1846).

[24] For unreliable ahistorical accounts of sureties that ignore the role of the justice of the peace as conservators of the peace, *see* David B. Kopel & George A. Mocsary, *Errors of Omission: Words Missing from the Ninth Circuit's* Young v. State of Hawaii, 2021 U. ILL. L. REV. ONLINE 172, 175–76 (2021).

[25] On the importance of early American regional differences in the evolution of the common law, *see generally* David Konig, *Regionalism in Early American Law*, in 1 THE CAMBRIDGE HISTORY OF LAW IN AMERICA: EARLY AMERICA (1580–1815), at 144 (Michael Grossberg & Christopher Tomlins

Although Justice Scalia had few qualms about generalizing American legal attitudes based on the views of a small coterie of slave-owning judges in the antebellum era, most historians would find such an approach deeply problematic. There is little doubt that a more expansive conception of gun rights emerged in parts of the Slave South.[26] But it is equally indisputable that a different model of firearms regulation emerged in Massachusetts and spread to other parts of the nation, and eventually to some parts of the Slave South.[27] This alternative "Free State Model" used sureties of the peace and good behavior to enforce the peace.[28] The erroneous claim that surety of the peace laws allowed individuals to carry arms, unless a specific individual came forward to demand a peace bond, turns Founding-era history on its head. The purpose of these laws was to achieve the opposite goal: limit armed travel in public to a narrow range of situations.[29]

Gun rights advocates have approached Anglo-American law as if little changed between the Glorious Revolution and the American Civil War.[30] A proper understanding of the evolving meaning of self-defense and the changing legal response to the potential threat posed by the emergence of cheap, reliable, and easily concealed weapons is essential to making sense of the legal history of this period. The common law model of conserving the peace inherited from England was rooted in the face-to-face communal practices of early modern England's

---

eds., 2008); Lauren Benton & Kathryn Walker, *Law for the Empire: The Common Law in Colonial America and the Problem of Legal Diversity*, 89 CHI.-KENT L. REV. 937 (2014).

[26] Eric M. Ruben & Saul Cornell, *Firearm Regionalism and Public Carry: Placing Southern Antebellum Case Law in Context*, 125 YALE L.J. F. 121 (2015).
[27] *Id. Cf.* District of Columbia v. Heller, *supra* note 21.
[28] On the idea of a Massachusetts Model, *see* JOSEPH BLOCHER & DARRELL A.H. MILLER, THE POSITIVE SECOND AMENDMENT: RIGHTS, REGULATION, AND THE FUTURE OF *HELLER* 30–31 (2018). Given that this model spread to other states outside of the Slave South, it is more properly understood as a "Free States Model" rather than the Massachusetts Model. I would like to thank historian James Oakes for suggesting this refinement of my earlier formulation of this idea.
[29] MICHAEL DALTON, THE COUNTREY JUSTICE: CONTAINING THE PRACTICE OF THE JUSTICES OF THE PEACE AS WELL IN AS OUT OF THEIR SESSIONS 194 (London, John Streater, James Flesher & Henry Twyford 1666) ("[I]f he hath broken (or forfeited) his recognizance by breach of the peace, the Justices of Peace may and ought to bind him anew, and by better sureties, for the safety of the person in danger. . . ."). The notion that sureties allowed one to continue to continue to engage in antisocial behavior makes little legal, logical, or historical sense. This claim is an invention of modern gun rights activists and has no foundation in the historical record; on the distortion of sureties in modern gun rights scholarship, *see* Patrick J. Charles, *The Invention of the Right to "Peaceable Carry" in Modern Second Amendment Scholarship*, U. ILL. L. REV. ONLINE 195 (2021). Sureties were also used to address issues such as uttering "menacing speeches" and "whore mongers" and "common drunkards." For an elaboration of the role of peace bonds and good behavior bonds in Anglo-American law, *see generally* STEVE HINDLE, THE STATE AND SOCIAL CHANGE IN EARLY MODERN ENGLAND, C. 1550–1640, at 99–101 (2000); and LAURA F. EDWARDS, THE PEOPLE AND THEIR PEACE: LEGAL CULTURE AND THE TRANSFORMATION OF INEQUALITY IN THE POST-REVOLUTIONARY SOUTH 105–06 (2009).
[30] Eugene Volokh, *The First and Second Amendments*, 109 COLUM. L. REV. SIDEBAR 97, 101 (2009) (reading developments in the antebellum South backward into earlier English and American history erroneously).

rural communities.[31] Until the rise of modern police forces in the nineteenth century, this community-based model of policing dominated on both sides of the Atlantic.[32] As conservators of the peace, justices of the peace, sheriffs, and constables maintained their traditional authority to enforce the peace, including the power to preemptively disarm, bind over with sureties of the peace or good behavior, and imprison those who violated the prohibition on armed travel.[33]

The importance of this tradition was underscored in the Massachusetts case of *Commonwealth v. Leach*.[34] The case addressed the question of how much of the traditional power accorded justice of the peace under common law had been absorbed into Massachusetts law. The case affirmed that the statutes enacted during the reign of Edward III bestowing extensive powers on justices of the peace had been fully absorbed into the state's common law, including the wide-ranging authority to detain, disarm, and bind to the peace any individual who traveled armed outside of the recognized exemptions.[35]

Massachusetts law expanded gun rights well beyond traditional English common law view, but it stopped short of the modern libertarian vision of gun rights. The approach taken by Massachusetts in this effort to rationalize their law was built on the landmark decision on the scope of legal self-defense, *Commonwealth v. Selfridge*, a case that changed the course of American criminal law and its view of armed self-defense.[36] By failing to understand the role of *Selfridge* in the history of the evolution of American self-defense law, gun rights advocates and their scholarly allies have warped early American criminal law almost beyond recognition, and therefore failed to grasp the significance of developments in Massachusetts and the emergence of the "Free States Model."[37]

Under English common law there was no good cause or imminent threat exception that allowed individuals to preemptively carry arms to defend against

---

[31] *See generally* STEVE HINDLE, THE STATE AND SOCIAL CHANGE IN EARLY MODERN ENGLAND 1550–1640 (Rab Houston & Edward Muir eds., 2000).

[32] LAURA F. EDWARDS, THE PEOPLE AND THEIR PEACE: LEGAL CULTURE AND THE TRANSFORMATION OF INEQUALITY IN THE POST-REVOLUTIONARY SOUTH 100 (2009). For examples of unreliable historical accounts of sureties and the role of the justice of the peace as conservators of the peace, *see* Kopel & Mocsary, *supra* note 24.

[33] CORNELL, *supra* note 6.

[34] Commonwealth v. Leach, 1 Mass. 59, 60–61 (1804).

[35] *See id.*

[36] Commonwealth v. Selfridge, 2 Am. St. Trials 544 (Mass. 1806). Retreat, not stand your ground, was the legal requirement under English common law. The notable exception to this rule was the "castle doctrine" covering deadly force in the home against intruders. *See* Semayne's Case (1604), 77 Eng. Rep. 194, 195 (KB). *See generally* Darrell A.H. Miller, *Self-Defense, Defense of Others, and the State*, 80 LAW & CONTEMP. PROBS. 85 (2017). On Selfridge's importance to the American law of self-defense, *see* RICHARD MAXWELL BROWN, NO DUTY TO RETREAT: VIOLENCE AND VALUES IN AMERICAN HISTORY AND SOCIETY (1991); Eric Ruben, *An Unstable Core: Self-Defense and the Second Amendment*, 108 CAL. L. REV. 63, 84–86 (2020).

[37] *See* Reply Brief for Petitioners, N.Y. State Rifle & Pistol Ass'n v. Bruen, 142 S. Ct. 2111 (Oct. 14, 2021) (No. 20-843).

a specified threat. Massachusetts built on *Selfridge*'s new reasonable fear standard.[38] According to the *Selfridge* standard, if an individual had a reasonable fear of serious injury or death, a specified threat, arming preemptively was now legal.[39] The new approach to arming in cases of specified need was an important break with English law, but it was not a total rejection of the entire common law approach to limiting armed travel. It would be hard to overstate the significance of *Selfridge* to American law. *Selfridge* recognized that the traditional communal enforcement of the peace that shaped English law was itself insufficient in the changed circumstances of the early American republic. The world of the Founders had been replaced by the one chronicled by Tocqueville in *Democracy in America*.[40] The right of self-defense as articulated in *Selfridge* reflected the growth of a new, more individualistic conception of armed self-defense, an approach that recognized the need to arm in situations in which an individual could not depend on neighbors or the law for protection.[41] Charles Sumner's characterization of his state's limits on public carry accurately captured the new model of firearms regulation that gained ground in the antebellum period in much of the young republic, particularly outside the Slave South.[42]

III. Surety Laws and the Rise of the Free States Model: Reforming the American Law of Self-Defense

Massachusetts codified its new approach to firearms regulation in two distinct provisions of the revised Massachusetts criminal code adopted in the 1830s. The first provision reaffirmed the right of any person to seek a peace bond against any individual who threatened the peace, but now recognized a good cause exception for armed travel.

> If any person shall go armed with a dirk, dagger, sword, pistol, or other offensive and dangerous weapon, without reasonable cause to fear an assault or other injury, or violence to his person, or to his family or property, he may, on

---

[38] The impact of Selfridge on criminal reform in Massachusetts is evident. REPORT OF THE PENAL CODE OF MASSACHUSETTS 22 (1844).
[39] On the significance of Selfridge, see FRANCIS WHARTON, A TREATISE ON CRIMINAL LAW OF THE UNITED STATES 259 (Arkrose Press 2015) (1846).
[40] George Kateb, *Democratic Individualism and Its Critics*, 6 ANN. REV. POL. SCI. 275, 293 (2003).
[41] Daniel Breen, *Parson's Charge: The Strange Origins of Stand Your Ground*, 16 CONN. PUB. INT'L L.J. 41, 70–73 (2017).
[42] Cornell, *supra* note 22.

complaint of any person having reasonable cause to fear an injury, or breach of the peace, be required to find sureties for keeping the peace....[43]

Massachusetts law also expressly reaffirmed the broad powers of justices of the peace to maintain the peace even in cases in which no individual brought forward a complaint.

> Every justice of the peace, within his county, may punish by fine, not exceeding ten dollars, all assaults and batteries, and other breaches of the peace, when the offence is not of a high and aggravated nature, and cause to be stayed and arrested all affrayers, rioters, disturbers and breakers of the peace, and all who go armed offensively, to the terror of the people, and such as utter menaces or threatening speeches, or are otherwise dangerous and disorderly persons.[44]

The mechanism for enforcing the new approach was a traditional common law tool, sureties of the peace or good behavior. Under common law, any justices of the peace or any member of the community could have an individual bound to the peace. The payment of a peace bond was intended to enforce the prohibition on armed travel in public, absent a good cause. Such laws did not function as a de facto license to carry, a claim made by some gun rights advocates that is wholly invented and has no foundation in the historical record.[45] In fact, as the statute's text makes clear, the reasonable cause standard applied to the exception, not to the rule, limiting armed travel in public.[46] The plain meaning of the statutes and the long history of how sureties of the peace functioned under Anglo-American law make it clear that these laws aimed to discourage the practice of "habitual carry."[47] The absurdity of the countervailing gun rights view of these laws is ably illustrated if one notes that sureties were also issued to prohibit individuals from uttering "menacing speeches" or engaging in "whore mongering." If the anachronistic gun-rights reading of these texts was correct, then any individual could continue to utter menacing speeches and pay for illicit sex as long as they paid

---

[43] Of Proceedings to Prevent the Commission of Crime, ch. 134, § 16, REVISED STATUTES OF THE COMMONWEALTH OF MASSACHUSETTS 748, 750 (1836).

[44] Of Justices of the Peace, ch. 85, § 24, REVISED STATUTES OF THE COMMONWEALTH OF MASSACHUSETTS 526, 529 (1836).

[45] In his reply brief in *NYSRPA v. Bruen*, Paul Clement repeated this false claim, which is little more than a gun rights fantasy. According to Clement's erroneous account, the surety laws "required a magistrate to find 'reasonable cause' that someone had demonstrated a propensity to *misuse* a firearm to cause 'injury, or breach the peace,' before a surety could be demanded to *continue* carrying it." Reply Brief, *supra* note 37, at 11. This was not how sureties functioned under Anglo-American law. *See* HINDLE, *supra* note 29.

[46] *See* Of Proceedings to Prevent the Commission of Crime, ch. 134, § 16, REVISED STATUTES OF THE COMMONWEALTH OF MASSACHUSETTS 748, 750 (1836).

[47] For the best account of the English tradition of sureties, *see* HINDLE, *supra* note 29, at 94–114. On the American use of sureties, *see* EDWARDS, *supra* note 32, at 96.

their peace bond, an absurd contention that also has no foundation either text or history. The only justification for traveling armed under the Massachusetts law was the existence of a specified threat. In fact, violators of the law not only faced the prospect of being bound to the peace but they were liable to further fine or jail time if they traveled armed.

> All persons, arrested for any of the said offences, shall be examined by the justice, before whom they are brought, and may be tried before him, and if found guilty, may be required to find sureties of the peace, and be further punished by fine as before provided; or, when the offence is of a high and aggravated nature, they may be committed or bound over, for trial before the court of common pleas, or other court having jurisdiction of the case.[48]

The key innovation in the new regulatory scheme implemented in Massachusetts in the 1830s was the express recognition of a good cause exception for cases where a specific threat existed. Grounded in a new and distinctly American view of self-defense that emerged in the first decade of the nineteenth century, more than a decade after the adoption of the Second Amendment and decades after the Massachusetts state constitution first linked the right to bear arms with a corresponding right to keep those arms needed to meet the public obligation to defend the state, the new framework for limiting public carry acknowledged a right to arm preemptively if a specified threat existed. In contrast to the extremely limited scope of the right of self-defense and arming under English common law, the new model was a significant expansion of gun rights.[49] Although this new conception falls far short of the extreme libertarian vision at the core of the modern gun rights movement, it is important not to smuggle modern ideological assumptions into an assessment of what the law was in the 1830s. The new criteria adopted by Massachusetts no longer was based on where and when one traveled, the key factors underlying the common law's approach to determining if self-defense was legitimate, but now recognized the subjective psychological beliefs of the person threatened and their reasonable fears of harm. Traditionally, prosecutions under common law for criminal behavior seldom required establishing a modern form of subjective *mens rea*.[50] Instead,

---

[48] Of Justices of the Peace, ch. 85, § 25, REVISED STATUTES OF THE COMMONWEALTH OF MASSACHUSETTS 526, 529 (1836).

[49] One of the leading commentators on the common law, William Hawkins, was emphatic that arming oneself could not be justified or "excuse[d]," by claiming "that such a one threatened him, and that he wears for the safety of his person from his assault." 1 WILLIAM HAWKINS, A TREATISE OF THE PLEAS TO THE CROWN 136 (London, Eliz. Nutt 1716). On *Selfridge's* role in changing the course of American law, *see* BROWN, *supra* note 36; CORNELL, *supra* note 6, at 116–17.

[50] Guyora Binder & Robert Weisberg, *What Is Criminal Law About?*, 114 MICH. L. REV. 1173, 1183 (2016); Miller, *supra* note 36, at 85.

the common law inferred the necessary evil intention from the prohibited act itself. The reforms included in the new approach first developed in Massachusetts and adopted the emerging subjective psychological standard that gained traction in early nineteenth-century American law. The addition of this principle made the expanding "Free States Model" consistent with the broader Enlightenment goals of criminal law reform in the early republic.[51] The new legal paradigm did not sanction habitual public carry: it expanded the right to travel armed in a limited fashion by recognizing the new reasonableness standard premised on the existence of a specified and concrete threat that justified arming oneself in public.[52]

Leading jurists in Massachusetts echoed Sumner's characterization of their state's law. One of the best sources for understanding the public meaning of the Massachusetts law, a statute that provided a template for so many other antebellum states is a commentary on criminal law authored by one of the nation's most respected jurists in pre–Civil War America, Peter Oxenbridge Thacher.[53] Lawyers and judges in antebellum America were familiar with a legal maxim drawn from Lord Coke that "great regard, in the exposition of statutes ought to be paid to, the construction that sages of the law, who lived about the time."[54] Few jurists in Massachusetts better fit the category of "sage of the law" than Thacher. Indeed, Judge Thacher's reputation extended well beyond Massachusetts; he

---

[51] On the role of Enlightenment thought, particularly Scottish Enlightenment thought, in legal reform in antebellum America, *see* Susanna L. Blumenthal, *The Mind of a Moral Agent: Scottish Common Sense and the Problem of Responsibility in Nineteenth-Century American Law*, 26 LAW & HIST. REV. 99, 104–05 (2008). For anachronistic gun rights interpretations of this history, *see* Clayton E. Cramer & David B. Kopel, *"Shall Issue": The New Wave of Concealed Handgun Permit Laws*, 62 TENN. L. REV. 679, 694–96 (1995). For a more scholarly treatment of this issue, *see generally* Jacob D. Charles, *Securing Gun Rights by Statute: The Right to Keep and Bear Arms Outside the Constitution*, 120 MICH. L. REV. 581 (2022).

[52] *See generally* Saul Cornell, *The Long Arc of Arms Regulation in Public: From Surety to Permitting, 1328-1928*, 55 U.C. DAVIS L. REV. 2547 (2022).

[53] The dominant model of originalism, public meaning originalism focuses on how an ideal, legally knowledgeable reader at the time would have understood the words of the text. For a useful guide to originalist theory, *see generally* Keith E. Whittington, *Originalism: A Critical Introduction*, 82 FORDHAM L. REV. 375 (2013). Critiques of originalism are legion. For historical critiques of originalist methodology, *see generally* Saul Cornell, *Reading the Constitution, 1787–91: History, Originalism, and Constitutional Meaning*, 37 LAW & HIST. REV. 821 (2019); Jonathan Gienapp, *Historicism and Holism: Failures of Originalist Translation*, 84 FORDHAM L. REV. 935 (2015); Jack Rakove, *Tone Deaf to the Past: More Qualms about Public Meaning Originalism*, 84 FORDHAM L. REV. 969 (2015). For other critiques, *see generally* FRANK B. CROSS, THE FAILED PROMISE OF ORIGINALISM 112–15 (2013); Stephen M. Griffin, *Rebooting Originalism*, 2008 U. ILL. L. REV. 1185, 1186–91 (2008).

[54] E. FITCH SMITH, COMMENTARIES ON STATUTE AND CONSTITUTIONAL LAW AND STATUTORY AND CONSTITUTIONAL LAW CONSTRUCTION 739 (New York, Banks, Gould & Co. 1848). Coke's legal maxim regarding the importance of consulting the sages of the law when interpreting statutes was familiar to lawyers and judges in the early Republic. *See id.* On Smith's significance to antebellum legal culture, *see* WILLIAM D. POPKIN, STATUTES IN COURT: THE HISTORY AND THEORY OF STATUTORY INTERPRETATION 69–70 (1999). Modern gun rights advocates have ignored this rule, substituting their own ahistorical reading of the law in place of the views of the leading criminal jurists of period. *See generally* NICHOLAS JOHNSON ET AL., FIREARMS LAW AND THE SECOND AMENDMENT: REGULATION, RIGHTS, AND POLICY (3d ed. 2021).

was recognized by members of the antebellum legal community to be one of the nation's leading experts on criminal law. Contemporaries praised him for his "thorough knowledge of the criminal law and its practical application."[55]

Thacher explained the meaning of his state's prohibition on armed travel in an influential grand jury charge that was reprinted as a pamphlet and was deemed sufficiently important to be published separately in the press. *The American Review*, an influential Whig magazine, singled out the publication of a collection of Judge Thacher's cases and grand jury charges as a major contribution to American law. Praising the judge's "high character as a magistrate," the review remarked that Thacher "was not only known to the profession in New England, but his published charges to grand juries, and occasional reports of important cases tried before him, had made him known throughout the country."[56] Gun rights advocates have either ignored or dismissed the relevance of Thacher's commentary on his state's law, casting his authoritative explication of the text as little more than empty verbiage uttered on a largely meaningless ceremonial occasion.[57] In fact, grand jury charges were not simply greetings but were an important civic occasion in antebellum America because they gave the "sages of the law" an opportunity to expound and elucidate important legal concepts to the public.[58] Jury charges offer one of the clearest illustrations of the way judges in the antebellum era would have interpreted the Massachusetts statute prohibiting armed travel absent a good cause.[59]

Thacher's reading of his own state's laws on public carry left no room for interpretive confusion: "In our own Commonwealth [of Massachusetts]," he reminded members of the grand jury "no person may go armed with a dirk, dagger, sword, pistol, or other offensive and dangerous weapon, without reasonable cause to apprehend an assault or violence to his person, family, or property."[60] This approach

---

[55] Horatio Woodman, Reports of Criminal Cases, Tried in the Municipal Court of the City of Boston, Before Peter Oxenbridge Thacher, Judge of that Court, from 1823 to 1843, at v (Forgotten Books 2018) (1845).

[56] 3 Am. Rev.: Whig J. Pol., Literature, Art & Sci. 222–23 (1846) (reviewing Horatio Woodman, Reports of Criminal Cases, Tried in the Municipal Court of the City of Boston, Before Peter Oxenbridge Thacher, Judge of that Court, from 1823 to 1843 (Boston, Charles C. Little & James Brown 1845)); *see* Woodman, *supra* note 55, at v.

[57] The decision of gun rights advocates to disregard Thacher's interpretation of his own state's law violates both the accepted rules of legal historical method and the relevant rules of statutory construction well known to judges and lawyers in antebellum America. *See* Johnson et al., *supra* note 54, at 79–80.

[58] The phrase "sages of the law" was frequently used by legal commentators from Coke to Kent. *See, e.g.*, James Kent, 1 Commentaries on American Law 463 (New York, O. Halsted 1826) (describing law reports as faithful records containing "true portraits of the talents and learning of the sages of the law"). On Coke's instantiation of the concept in Anglo-American law, *see* Wilfrid Priest, *History and Biography, Legal and Otherwise*, 32 Adel. L. Rev. 185, 188 (2011).

[59] On the role of grand jury charges in this period of American legal history, *see* Dennis Hale, The Jury in America: Triumph and Decline 93–98 (2016); Joshua Glick, Comment, *On the Road: The Supreme Court and the History of Circuit Riding*, 24 Cardozo L. Rev. 1753, 1754 (2003).

[60] Peter Oxenbridge Thacher, Two Charges to the Grand Jury of the County of Suffolk for the Commonwealth of Massachusetts, at the Opening of Terms of the

to gun regulation limited public carry to situations in which an individual faced a specified threat. It was a significant expansion of the right of self-defense beyond the limits of the common law, but it was not, as modern gun rights advocates have mistakenly urged, an endorsement of habitual carry.[61]

Nor was Thacher the only distinguished Massachusetts jurist to characterize his state's ban on armed travel as a general prohibition absent a specified threat. Other jurists in Massachusetts echoed his account of the law. Among the clearest expression of this view was a statement by the presiding judge in case that caused a minor stir at the time. The Snowden case involved the prosecution of two African American abolitionists for violating the state's law on public carry. A relatively minor footnote in the history of abolitionism, the case featured prominently in Justice Thomas's majority opinion in *NYSRPA v. Bruen*.[62] Unfortunately, the account of the case the opinion relied upon was deeply flawed, both as a matter of history and of law.[63] Indeed, the erroneous account of the Snowden case serves as a yet another warning about the continuing dangers posed by law office history in Second Amendment jurisprudence.[64]

IV. THE SNOWDEN CASE AND THE PROBLEM OF ANTEBELLUM GUN LAW ENFORCEMENT: VIOLENCE AND ABOLITIONISM IN PRE-CIVIL WAR BOSTON

Abolitionist politics heated up after Congress adopted the Compromise of 1850. The most controversial provision of the law strengthened the Fugitive Slave Act (1793), it greatly expanded the powers of the federal government to apprehend escaped slaves in the North. Federal marshals and bounty hunters

---

MUNICIPAL COURT OF THE CITY OF BOSTON ON MONDAY, DEC. 5TH A.D. 1836, AND ON MONDAY, MARCH 13TH, A.D. 1837, at 27 (Gale, Making of Modern Law 2011) (1837); *see Judge Thacher's Charges*, CHRISTIAN REG. & BOSTON OBSERVER, June 10, 1837, at 91.

[61] Kopel & Mocsary, *supra* note 24.
[62] N.Y. State Rifle & Pistol Ass'n v. Bruen, 142 S. Ct. 2111, 2149–50 (2022). For a historical discussion of Black abolitionists in Boston during this period and a brief allusion to the Snowden case, *see* James Oliver Horton & Lois E. Horton, *The Affirmation of Manhood: Black Garrisonians in Antebellum Boston*, *in* COURAGE AND CONSCIENCE: BLACK & WHITE ABOLITIONISTS IN BOSTON 127, 146 (Donald M. Jacobs ed., 1993).
[63] Robert Leider, *Constitutional Liquidation, Surety Laws, and the Right to Bear Arms*, *in* NEW HISTORIES OF GUN RIGHTS AND REGULATION: ESSAYS ON THE PLACE OF GUNS IN AMERICAN LAW AND SOCIETY (Joseph Blocher, Jacob D. Charles, & Darrell A.H. Miller eds., 2022). Leider omitted his discussion of Madison liquidation and repurposed his analysis for his amicus brief in *NYSRPA v. Bruen*. *See* Brief of Professors Robert Leider & Nelson Lund, & the Buckeye Firearms Association, at 19–30, N.Y. State Rifle & Pistol Ass'n, Inc. v. Bruen, 142 S. Ct. 2111 (2021) (No. 20-843) [hereinafter Leider & Lund Brief]. Leider's most recent version of his argument appears in this volume in Chapter 13.
[64] *Bruen*, 142 S. Ct. at 2177 (Breyer, J., dissenting).

were given broad new authority to hunt and return fugitive slaves. The act was seen by opponents of slavery as a repudiation of the principles of republican self-government, an unprecedented threat to individual liberty, and the latest example of the South's unrelenting campaign to bend the rule of law to further a pro-slavery agenda.[65]

Within a year of the Fugitive Slave Act's passage, Boston was convulsed by the capture of Thomas Sims, an escaped slave from Georgia. Fearing mob violence, the city took extraordinary steps to prevent abolitionists from attempting to free Sims from jail or prevent his extradition. In addition to placing the militia on alert, one hundred Boston police armed with swords and clubs (not firearms) guarded the courthouse where Sims was arraigned.[66] The 1850 Fugitive Slave Act gave federal commissioners, not local courts, the task of evaluating the claims of those seeking the return of their slaves. The commissioners ruled that Sims was a fugitive and had to be returned to Georgia to his master. Abolitionists were incensed by the news; leading opponents of slavery denounced the decision to deprive Sims of his freedom. In a series of public meetings and protests, Boston abolitionists warned that no free person was safe. To protect themselves, radical abolitionists called on the city's free Blacks to arm themselves lest they be kidnapped and enslaved by unscrupulous bounty hunters emboldened by the new Fugitive Slave Act.[67]

In the wake of the rendition of Sims, no figure in Boston was more ardent in denouncing existing law that protected slavery than the firebrand anti-slavery orator abolitionist Wendell Phillips. Among the most outspoken abolitionists in Boston, Phillips accepted the Garrisonian critique of the Constitution as a "covenant with death."[68] As was true for many Garrisonians, Phillips's views of the role of violence in abolitionism were complicated. Although he denounced the Constitution and any laws that served the interests of slavery, he stopped short of urging all abolitionists to take up arms to end slavery. An important exception to this rejection of armed violence was the situation faced by free Blacks in the North. Free Blacks were justified in arming themselves to defend against

---

[65] R.J.M. BLACKETT, THE CAPTIVE'S QUEST FOR FREEDOM: FUGITIVE SLAVES, THE 1850 FUGITIVE SLAVE LAW, AND THE POLITICS OF SLAVERY (2018); *see generally* H. Robert Baker, *The Fugitive Slave Clause and the Antebellum Constitution*, 30 LAW & HIST. REV. 1133 (2012).

[66] *See generally* Leonard W. Levy, *Sims' Case: The Fugitive Slave Law in Boston in 1851*, 35 J. NEGRO HIST. 39 (1950).

[67] Most African American abolitionists accepted a right of armed self-defense against kidnapping, but increasingly many endorsed armed insurrection as also a legitimate tool for ending slavery. *See* KELLIE CARTER JACKSON, FORCE AND FREEDOM: BLACK ABOLITIONISTS AND THE POLITICS OF VIOLENCE (2019). The best account of Phillips's thoughts, particularly in response to the Sims case and the role of violence, comes from James Brewer Stewart. JAMES BREWER STEWART, WENDELL PHILLIPS: LIBERTY'S HERO 148–58 (1986).

[68] On the politics of abolitionism during this period, *see generally* James B. Stewart, *The Aims and Impact of Garrisonian Abolitionism, 1840–1860*, 15 CIV. WAR HIST. 197 (1969); Corey M. Brooks, *Reconsidering Politics in the Study of American Abolitionists*, 8 J. CIV. WAR ERA 291 (2018).

kidnappers and anti-abolitionist violence.[69] It is important to understand the constitutional and legal argument that Phillips made to justify this stance. He did not believe that arming was legal under existing law; he argued that those choosing to act in self-defense were justified by a higher law that transcended the laws of Massachusetts or the United States.[70]

During the period of intense ferment and tumult following the rendition of Sims, two African American abolitionists were arrested in downtown Boston after attending one of the protest meetings in which Phillips urged the city's Black community to arm themselves. Isaac and Charles Snowden were the sons of a prominent Black minster allied with the radical Garrisonian wing of abolitionism, and the two were also associates of Phillips. The Snowdens were arrested late at night, not far from an armory used by one of the local militia companies that had been mobilized to deal with the unrest in the city. The two men were charged with violating the state statute prohibiting armed travel absent a good cause. Given the recent frenzied atmosphere in Boston and the fact that the two men were traveling armed, a rare occurrence in Boston, the case became a newsworthy event that drew the interest of both the local and national press.[71] To gain a full understanding of the Snowden trial and its significance as a source for understanding the enforcement of antebellum gun laws, one must situate the case in two interrelated contexts: the violent history of abolitionism in Boston and the norms governing criminal law and prosecutions in the city.

The Snowden brothers were apprehended late at night in the vicinity of one of Boston's armories at a time when city officials feared the prospect of violence between abolitionists and their opponents.[72] "Night walking" was a crime under Massachusetts law, a fact that itself would have justified members of the night watch stopping and interrogating the two men about their reason and

---

[69] Phillips's views on the role of violence in abolition were complicated. He shared the radical Garrisonian view about the Constitution's role in protecting slavery. He declared that the path forward for abolitionism "is over the Constitution, trampling it under foot; not under it, trying to evade its fair meaning." *See* WENDELL PHILLIPS, REVIEW OF LYSANDER SPOONER'S ESSAY ON THE UNCONSTITUTIONALITY OF SLAVERY 5 (Nabu Press 2010) (1847). For Phillips's relationship to abolitionist constitutionalism, *see* WILLIAM M. WIECK, THE SOURCES OF ANTISLAVERY CONSTITUTIONALISM IN AMERICA, 1760–1848, at 246 (1977). On the moral dilemma and legal quandary of being an anti-slavery judge after the passage of the Fugitive Slave Act of 1850, *see* Peter Karsten, *Revisiting the Critiques of Those Who Upheld the Fugitive Slave Acts in the 1840s and '50s*, 58 AM. J. LEGAL HIST. 291 (2018).

[70] Stewart, *supra* note 68, at 158.

[71] In his detailed study of the Boston police, historian Roger Lane concluded the public carry of guns in antebellum Boston was a rare event. *See* ROGER LANE, POLICING THE CITY: BOSTON, 1822–1885, at 103–04 (1967). If Bostonians were promiscuously traveling armed and gun-toting posed a serious threat to public safety, it seems highly unlikely that during the unrest associated with the arrest of Sims, Boston police would have deployed their force to protect the courts with nothing more than clubs and swords. *See* Levy, *supra* note 66.

[72] Anti-abolitionist papers charged the Snowden brothers with attempting to force their way into an armory, but it is difficult to verify this claim. *See The Boston Slave Case*, N.H. PATRIOT'S GAZETTE, Apr. 10, 1851, at 2; and WILMINGTON J., Apr. 11, 1851, at 2.

purpose for wandering the city's streets after dark.[73] Prior to the Snowdens' arrest, Boston had been convulsed by abolitionist and anti-abolitionist violence, so the decision to stop the Snowdens was not an overreach given contemporary police practices.[74] Members of the watch detained the two and questioned them. A search produced a loaded pistol and a large butcher's knife, a clear violation of the state law on traveling armed without a good cause.[75]

The decision of the Snowdens to arm themselves takes on a different meaning and significance when read against the unrest precipitated by the Sims case and Phillips's recent appeal to the city's Black community to arm themselves. Phillips, a lawyer by training, intervened on behalf of the two men and not only helped pay the peace bonds at their hearing but unleashed a fusillade of invective at the presiding judge in the case, Abel Cushing. Judge Cushing allowed Phillips an opportunity to vent his frustration and anger, but was resolute in defending the city's law and his commitment to the impartial administration of justice in his court. He declared that he would dispense "equal justice" and render his decision "*irrespective of color.*" The Garrisonian newspaper, *The Liberator*, denounced the judge and questioned his impartiality, but if one looks at the press coverage of the case from papers representing the full range of antebellum political views, the charge of racial bias seems unpersuasive.[76] The two men had clearly violated the state law on public carry, were apprehended at nighttime (in violation of a separate prohibition on night walking), and were in close proximity to one of the city's armories at the time of their arrest.

Because the case enraged abolitionists, it drew considerable attention from newspapers across a broad ideological spectrum. To understand the meaning of the case, one must consult the full range of extant primary sources and read those with a critical eye. One point is beyond dispute: Judge Cushing believed that armed travel without good cause violated the state law. The *Liberator*'s summary

---

[73] *See* REPORT OF THE CHIEF OF POLICE AND CAPTAIN OF THE WATCH, CITY DOCUMENT NO. 4, at 4, *in* DOCUMENTS OF THE CITY OF BOS. (1856) (listing arrests for night walking).

[74] A transcription of Phillips's speech based on an abolitionist account by a spectator was published in the ANTISLAVERY BUGLE, May 24, 1851, at 1. For other less sympathetic contemporary accounts of Phillips's call to arms to Bostonians, *see* DAILY UNION, Apr. 8, 1851, at 3, and S. PRESS, Apr. 7, 1851, at 3.

[75] The Massachusetts law allowed arming for a specified threat, but the general unrest in the city was not judged to be such a threat by the court that heard the Snowden case, for further discussion see Cornell, *supra* note 52.

[76] Abolitionist newspapers such as *The Liberator* viewed the prosecution as racist. Pro-slavery newspapers and Whig publications cast the prosecution as entirely legal. Racial harassment of African Americans in Boston was undoubtedly a problem, and many gun laws in the South were designed to disarm African Americans selectively. But the fact that gun laws sometimes were used to further an insidious agenda does not mean all gun laws and all examples of enforcement were racially motivated. *See generally* Mark A. Frassetto, *The Nonracist and Antiracist History of Firearms Public Carry Regulation*, 74 SMU L. REV. F. 169 (2021); JACKSON, *supra* note 67, at 82; WENDELL PHILLIPS, THE CONSTITUTION: A PRO-SLAVERY COMPACT, OR EXTRACTS FROM THE MADISON PAPERS, ETC. 5–10 (New York, American Anti-Slavery Society, 3d ed. 1856).

of the judge's interpretation of the state law makes this point clearly: Judge Cushing, *The Liberator* noted, "held that walking peacefully... with arms in your pocket which you neither use nor threaten to" met the statute's definition of traveling " 'armed offensively, to the terror of the people,' against the statute."[77]

Judge Abel Cushing was a respected member of the Massachusetts judiciary, who served on the Roxbury Police Court. His interpretation of the law in Massachusetts echoed the views of Senator Charles Sumner and Judge Thacher. Cushing endorsed the view that the mere act of traveling armed, even if done peaceably, without good cause, violated the statute.[78] In short, there is no evidence from any sitting judge or recognized legal authority from antebellum Massachusetts to support the modern gun rights argument about the public meaning of surety laws and their application in antebellum America.

Nor does the Snowden case support the non-enforcement thesis propounded by modern gun rights advocates that Justice Thomas accepted uncritically in *Bruen*.[79] The Snowden case proves the opposite. It forcefully demonstrated that sureties were enforced and functioned to limit public travel with guns in Massachusetts. The final resolution of Isaac Snowden's case in police court makes this point abundantly clear. Snowden having been bound to the peace and having adhered to the terms of his peace bond, the trial judge dismissed the case, correctly concluding that no further legal action was warranted by the statute.[80] The appropriate legal strategy for Snowden to avoid prosecution would have been to argue that he had a good cause to fear attack and hence armed himself in accord with the exception recognized by the statute. Indeed, Snowden had made such an argument at his hearing, but the court rejected his claim. Having failed to show a specified threat, Snowden was bound to the peace, the only mechanism for enforcement provided by the law. When Snowden later appeared in court, the judge concluded that there was no further need for prosecution because Isaac Snowden had adhered to the terms of his bond. The case does not support the

---

[77] Judge Cushing's Police Court remarks were reported in the abolitionist press. See *Arrests for Carrying Concealed Weapons*, LIBERATOR, Apr. 11, 1851, at 59.
[78] *Id.* For additional details on the case, see Complaint, Commonwealth v. Snowden, No. 1443 (Bos. Police Ct. Apr. 5, 1851) (showing the official accounts); Record Book Entry, Commonwealth v. Snowden, Bos. Police Ct. R. Book 1117 (May 1851) (same).
[79] *Bruen*, 142 S. Ct. at 2149.
[80] The Leider and Lund amicus brief erroneously argues that because Isaac Snowden was " 'caught red handed' and could not challenge the arrest using the modern exclusionary rule, he would have been prosecuted if the mere circumstances of carrying a gun had been a crime under common law." Leider & Lund Brief, *supra* note 63. In fact, the court documents and contemporary newspaper accounts make clear that crime was not charged at common law: Snowden was prosecuted for a violation of the state's prohibition on armed travel absent good cause, and the court dismissed his arguments that he had a specified need to be armed. On the norms of criminal prosecution during this period and the continuing importance of peace bonds, *see generally* Mary E. Vogel, *The Social Origins of Plea Bargaining: Conflict and the Law in the Process of State Formation, 1830–1860*, 33 LAW & SOC'Y REV. 161 (1999).

modern gun rights non-enforcement thesis; the law had been *enforced* because the peace had been kept and Snowden had adhered to the terms of his surety.[81] The claim that the Snowden case demonstrates a right to carry arms in public is mistaken and rests on a series of ahistorical claims and legal interpretive errors. The case offers dramatic evidence that confirms Judge Thacher's and Senator Charles Sumner's understanding that armed travel in public in Massachusetts was a violation of state law. This position was the orthodox legal view at the time. There is no contemporaneous account by any sitting judge in antebellum Massachusetts supporting the gun rights interpretation of surety laws, including the one pioneered by Massachusetts. The "sages of the law" who wrote about the law at the time all rejected the idea of a right to "habitual" public carry.[82]

The views of Judge Cushing confirm modern historical research on antebellum gun culture. In *Bruen*, Justice Thomas ignored this body of scholarship, preferring instead to rest his argument on gun rights historical mythology. Promiscuous public arms carry, particularly in urban areas, was relatively rare outside of the South in pre–Civil War America.[83]

Historian Roger Lane, the leading authority on crime in nineteenth-century Boston, concluded after exhaustive and meticulous research that "not many criminals in fact carried arms, even after the invention of the revolver made it possible to do so inconspicuously."[84] This conclusion is consistent with the fact that Boston police did not themselves routinely carry firearms until decades after the Civil War period: the standard weapon issued to police in the antebellum era was a club, not a firearm.[85] The absence of armed policemen in the city in the aftermath of the Sims rendition only underscores Lane's point. Not

---

[81] Both of the *Bruen* amicus briefs that discuss the Snowden case depend on the flawed scholarship of Robert Leider, *supra* note 63. Kopel and Mocsary describe Leider's work as "meticulous" but ignoring the abolitionist context of the Snowden case, confusing common law crimes with statutory offenses, and giving greater weight to radical abolitionist ideas than the views of the "sages of the law" is hardly meticulous, but rather an example of law office history at its worst. *Supra* note 63. Rather than follow orthodox legal history methods, an approach that requires consulting a wide range of sources, Leider's argument rests on cherry-picked evidence gleaned from digital keyword searches. Although keyword searches of digital sources are helpful, they are not a substitute for the accepted methods of historical research; keyword searching encourages confirmation bias because the results are shaped by the choice of terms. Tim Hitchcock, *Confronting the Digital*, 10 CULTURAL & SOC. HIST. 9, 14–17 (2013). On the dangers of historical bias and ways to minimize it, *see* C. Behan McCullagh, *Bias in Historical Description, Interpretation, and Explanation*, 39 HIST. & THEORY 39, 63 (2000). Consulting multiple sources representing diverse points of view of the same event is one of the most widely employed methods used by historians to minimize confirmation and selection bias.

[82] *Supra* note 60.

[83] SAUL CORNELL, THE POLICE POWER AND THE AUTHORITY TO REGULATE FIREARMS IN EARLY AMERICA 1–2 (2021), https://perma.cc/J6QD-4YXG.

[84] On guns in pre–Civil War Boston, *see* LANE, *supra* note 71, at 103–04.

[85] Scott W. Phillips, *A Historical Examination of Police Firearms*, 94 POLICE J.: THEORY, PRAC. & PRINCIPLES 122, 123–24 (2021).

Table 12.1. Boston Police Enforcement Data, 1864 and 1866[a]

Year	Assault and Battery	Assault with Weapons	Disturbing the Peace	Carrying Weapons Unlawfully
1864	1016	100	309	8
1866	1091	78	666	5

[a] ANNUAL REPORT OF THE CHIEF OF POLICE 1864, CITY DOCUMENT NO. 6, at 8–9 (Boston, 1865); ANNUAL REPORT OF THE CHIEF OF POLICE 1866, CITY DOCUMENT NO. 9, at 9–10 (Boston, 1867).

only did the typical Boston policeman not carry a firearm but the entire police force owned only a handful of revolvers. Property inventories of the Boston police are illuminating in this regard: the list of moveable property owned by the Boston police for the year 1862 shows a total of 270 clubs and only 7 revolvers. If Bostonians were promiscuously traveling armed and gun toting posed a serious threat to public safety, it seems highly unlikely that the entire Boston police would have owned a total of seven revolvers at the start of the Civil War era.[86]

Arrest statistics compiled by the city's chief of police further undermines the non-enforcement thesis. As the data in Table 12.1 shows, only a tiny fraction of assaults in the city involved a weapon of any kind. Moreover, the number of arrests for unlawfully carrying weapons in public were also minuscule. Contrary to the claims of modern gun rights advocates, the evidence from Boston does not support the non-enforcement thesis nor does it support the assumption that promiscuous public carry of firearms was the norm outside of the Slave South. Rather, Boston's history suggests that citizens generally obeyed their state's prohibition on armed travel, and few individuals carried weapons in public in the period leading up to the Civil War. In short, Bostonians, in contrast to their Southern brethren, did not habitually arm themselves.

The data about policing practices in Boston, the absence of pistols in the inventory of the Boston police department, and the decision to continue to arm officers with clubs, not firearms, demonstrates that the gun rights interpretation of antebellum surety laws collapses under the weight of countervailing evidence. When the disposition of the Snowden case and evidence about Boston policing are considered together, it is clear that *Bruen* rests on an egregious distortion of the historical record.

[86] *See* ANNUAL REPORT OF CHIEF OF POLICE 1864, CITY DOCUMENT NO. 3, at 13 (Boston, 1863).

V. Abolitionists, the Right to Bear Arms, and the Limits of Originalist Law Office History

Modern gun rights approaches to the history of public carry have elevated the ideas of pro-slavery judges in the South and radical abolitionists in the North to greater prominence than the views of criminal jurists charged with enforcing gun laws in antebellum America. This approach to legal history is deeply flawed, both as a matter of legal interpretation and as a matter of history.

Any competent historical account of antebellum law and gun regulation must reckon with the ideas of pro-slavery judges and radical abolitionists. Both groups adopted robust views of the right of self-defense. Yet treating two of the most radical voices in antebellum law as legally dispositive of broader views of guns and regulations violates the relevant canons of statutory construction in place in pre–Civil War America and distorts the history it invokes as binding legal authority.

If the goal of originalism is the reconstruction of the public meaning of the law, Judge Cushing's views, not those of his radical abolitionist critic Wendell Phillips, are legally dispositive. Treating the views of radical Garrisonian abolitionists, including Phillips as authoritative, distorts the past, warping it almost beyond recognition. Phillips had advised Boston's free Blacks to ignore the law, not honor it. Phillips and other Garrisonians rejected the authority of the Constitution and expressly counseled violating existing laws to achieve their laudable goals of immediate abolitionism. The modern gun rights position constitutes a type of anti-original meaning originalism. It treats the views of those who opposed the Constitution as the authoritative guide to the Constitution's meaning.[87]

In *Bruen*, Justice Breyer sounded an alarm about the continuing problem of law office history in Second Amendment jurisprudence. The majority opinion by Justice Thomas, an example of law chambers history, shows that ideologically distorted accounts of the past continue to warp Second Amendment law, distorting history almost beyond recognition.

---

[87] For a discussion of the penchant for originalists to confuse the views of those opposed to the Constitution with those supporting it, *see* Saul Cornell, *President Madison's Living Constitution: Fixation, Liquidation, and Constitutional Politics in the Jeffersonian Era*, 89 Fordham L. Rev. 1761 (2021).

13

CONSTITUTIONAL LIQUIDATION, SURETY LAWS, AND THE RIGHT TO BEAR ARMS

Robert Leider

I. INTRODUCTION

In 2008, the U.S. Supreme Court issued its landmark decision in *District of Columbia v. Heller*.[1] *Heller* held that the Second Amendment protects the right of "law-abiding, responsible citizens," including those not enrolled in state-organized militia units, to possess firearms and "to use arms in defense of hearth and home."[2] The Court qualified its holding by stating that "[l]ike most rights, the right secured by the Second Amendment is not unlimited."[3] For example, the Court seemingly accepted nineteenth-century decisions upholding prohibitions on the carrying of concealed weapons.[4]

Heller has caused litigation and academic literature to shift its focus, from the question of *which persons* are the primary holders of Second Amendment rights to the *content* and *limits* of the right.[5] Until the Supreme Court issued its opinion in *New York State Rifle & Pistol Association v. Bruen*,[6] arguably the most significant Second Amendment question was the constitutional validity of laws

---

[1] 554 U.S. 570 (2008).
[2] *Id.* at 635.
[3] *Id.* at 626.
[4] *See id.* (citing State v. Chandler, 5 La. Ann. 489, 489–90 (1850)); Nunn v. State, 1 Ga. 243, 251 (1846)).
[5] *Compare, e.g.*, Don B. Kates Jr., *Handgun Prohibition and the Original Meaning of the Second Amendment*, 82 MICH. L. REV. 204 (1983), Sanford Levinson, *The Embarrassing Second Amendment*, 99 YALE. L.J. 637 (1989), Glenn Harlan Reynolds, *A Critical Guide to the Second Amendment*, 62 TENN. L. REV. 461 (1995), Gregory Lee Shelton, *In Search of the Lost Amendment: Challenging Federal Firearms Regulation Through the "State's Right" Interpretation of the Second Amendment*, 23 FLA. ST. U. L. REV. 105 (1995), *and* Michael T. O'Donnell, *The Second Amendment: A Study of Recent Trends*, 25 U. RICH. L. REV. 501 (1991), *with* Darrell A.H. Miller, *Guns as Smut: Defending the Home-bound Second Amendment*, 109 COLUM. L. REV. 1278 (2009), Joseph Blocher, *Firearm Localism*, 123 YALE L.J. 82 (2013), *and* Eugene Volokh, *Implementing the Right to Keep and Bear Arms for Self-Defense: An Analytical Framework and a Research Agenda*, 56 UCLA L. REV. 1443 (2009).
[6] 142 S. Ct. 2111 (2022) (invalidating New York's requirement that applicants show "proper cause" for a license to carry a handgun outside the home). This chapter was primarily drafted before the Supreme Court delivered *New York State Rifle & Pistol Association v. Bruen*, 142 S. Ct. 2111 (2022). I have done my best to accommodate that decision into this chapter.

that generally prohibit individuals from carrying firearms in public. Between *Heller* and *Bruen*, scholars and judges approached this issue from at least one of two ways.

The first approach asked whether legislative restrictions are consistent with some form of means-end scrutiny.[7] The means-end approach often looks to empirical sources for answers. Do laws that generally prohibit public carry decrease crime by reducing armed confrontation?[8] Or do they increase crime by making it difficult for law-abiding citizens to defend themselves?[9] Courts, for their part, have mostly elided messy empirical questions by deferring to legislative judgments, creating a strong presumption in favor of sustaining restrictive gun control laws.[10]

The second approach—the one that this chapter will focus on (and the one ultimately adopted by the Supreme Court in *Bruen*)—looks to historical sources, especially nineteenth-century precedents.[11] For example, scholars in favor of broader gun rights note that most nineteenth-century courts struck down complete bans on public carry while sustaining prohibitions against the carrying of weapons in a concealed manner.[12] Scholars in favor of broader gun control marginalize these decisions as the product of slave states and Southern culture; they point, instead, to some laws and local ordinances that heavily restricted public carry, including in the Old West.[13] A casual reader may think that the historical debate has reached a stalemate.

---

[7] *See, e.g.*, Gould v. Morgan, 907 F.3d 659, 670 (1st Cir. 2018); Kachalsky v. Cnty. of Westchester, 701 F.3d 81, 96 (2d Cir. 2012); United States v. Marzzarella, 614 F.3d 85, 97 (3d Cir. 2010); Woollard v. Gallagher, 712 F.3d 865, 876 (4th Cir. 2013); NRA of Am., Inc. v. Bureau of Alcohol, Tobacco, Firearms, & Explosives, 700 F.3d 185, 195 (5th Cir. 2012); United States v. Reese, 627 F.3d 792, 802 (10th Cir. 2010); Allen Rostron, *The Continuing Battle over the Second Amendment*, 78 ALB. L. REV. 819 (2015).

[8] *See, e.g.*, John J. Donohue et al., *Right-to-Carry Laws and Violent Crime: A Comprehensive Assessment Using Panel Data and a State-Level Synthetic Control Analysis*, 16 J. EMPIRICAL LEGAL STUD. 198, 240 (2019) (finding that right to carry laws increase violent crime); David McDowall et al., *Easing Concealed Firearms Laws: Effects on Homicide in Three States*, 86 J. CRIM. L. & CRIMINOLOGY 193, 194 (1995) (finding that shall issue licensing regimes lead to an increase in firearm homicides).

[9] *See, e.g.*, Gary Kleck & Marc Gertz, *Armed Resistance to Crime: The Prevalence and Nature of Self-Defense with a Gun*, 86 J. CRIM. L. & CRIMINOLOGY 150, 180 (1995); JOHN R. LOTT JR., MORE GUNS LESS CRIME: UNDERSTANDING CRIME AND GUN CONTROL LAWS (3d ed. 2010); John C. Moorhouse & Brent Wanner, *Does Gun Control Reduce Crime or Does Crime Increase Gun Control?*, 26 CATO J. 103, 122 (2006).

[10] *See, e.g.*, *Gould*, 907 F.3d at 673–76; *Kachalsky*, 701 F.3d at 98–99.

[11] *See, e.g.*, Young v. Hawaii, 992 F.3d 765, 798–810 (9th Cir. 2021) (en banc); Peruta v. Cnty. of San Diego, 824 F.3d 919, 929–38 (9th Cir. 2016) (en banc); *Kachalsky*, 701 F.3d at 89–91; David B. Kopel, *The First Century of Right to Arms Litigation*, 14 GEO. J.L. & PUB. POL'Y 127 (2016); Eric M. Ruben & Saul Cornell, *Firearm Regionalism and Public Carry: Placing Southern Antebellum Case Law in Context*, 125 YALE L.J. F. 121 (2015).

[12] *See, e.g.*, David B. Kopel, *The Second Amendment in the Nineteenth Century*, 1998 BYU L. REV. 1359, 1409–33 (1998); CLAYTON E. CRAMER, CONCEALED WEAPON LAWS OF THE EARLY REPUBLIC: DUELING, SOUTHERN VIOLENCE, AND MORAL REFORM (1999).

[13] Ruben & Cornell, *supra* note 11, at 124–33; Patrick J. Charles, *The Faces of the Second Amendment Outside the Home: History Versus Ahistorical Standards of Review*, 60 CLEV. ST. L. REV. 1, 36–41 (2012).

This chapter contends otherwise. The present debate over the relevance of nineteenth-century carry laws is not about using these laws to determine the original public meaning of the right to bear arms in 1791. Instead, their relevance lies in the idea of "constitutional liquidation."

Constitutional liquidation occurs when post-enactment practices settle the meaning of "more or less obscure and equivocal" legal texts.[14] In recent years, scholars have turned some attention to how constitutional liquidation occurs. This chapter will borrow from a recent article on James Madison's theory of liquidation. Madisonian liquidation generally requires three things: (1) constitutional deliberation about the issue, (2) that results in a course of practice, and (3) that settles the constitutional issue in the public's mind.[15] Madison's is not the only theory of constitutional liquidation.[16] But to date, it is the most developed. And to the extent that other theories of liquidation become more developed in the future, many arguments and much evidence in this chapter will likely apply to them, *mutatis mutandis*.

Applying the principles of Madisonian liquidation, I argue, first, that constitutional liquidation is relevant because the full scope of the American right to bear arms was not settled in 1791. In the Anglo-American tradition, the right to have arms emerged with the English Bill of Rights in 1688 and the desire of English subjects to have some means to defend themselves against the lawless use of royal power.[17] But the English right was limited to Protestants, who could have arms "suitable to their Conditions, and as allowed by Law."[18] The American right to bear arms was broader, lacking these limitations.[19] But exactly how broad was unclear. The Framing generation said little about how they understood the full scope of the right to bear arms.[20] Constitutional liquidation is the process by which the right would develop.

Next, I turn my attention to antebellum surety laws. In 1832, Massachusetts sought to codify its statutes.[21] The result of this project was the *Revised Statutes*

---

[14] William Baude, *Constitutional Liquidation*, 71 STAN. L. REV. 1, 4 (2019) (quoting THE FEDERALIST No. 37, at 236 (James Madison) (Jacob E. Cooke ed., 1961)).

[15] *Id.* at 13–21.

[16] *Id.* at 32–35.

[17] *See, e.g.*, Aymette v. State, 21 Tenn. (2 Hum.) 154, 156–58 (1840).

[18] An Act Declaring the Rights and Liberties of the Subject, and Settling the Succession of the Crown (Bill of Rights) 1689, 1 W. & M., sess. 2, ch. 2, § 7 (Eng.), *in* 9 STATUTES AT LARGE 67, 69 (Pickering 1764).

[19] *Aymette*, 21 Tenn. at 157–58; 2 JOSEPH STORY & THOMAS MCINTYRE, COMMENTARIES ON THE CONSTITUTION OF THE UNITED STATES § 1898, at 621 (Law Book Exchange 2007) (4th ed. 1873).

[20] *See generally* THE ORIGIN OF THE SECOND AMENDMENT: A DOCUMENTARY HISTORY OF THE BILL OF RIGHTS (David E. Young ed., 2d ed. 1995) (collecting sources from the Framing on the right to bear arms).

[21] Resolve Providing for a Revision of the General Statutes of the Commonwealth, ch. 30, *in* RESOLVES OF THE GENERAL COURT OF THE COMMONWEALTH OF MASSACHUSETTS 103 (1832).

of Massachusetts, which totaled about eight hundred pages.[22] Within this large new legal code, one provision required those who went armed without reasonable cause to fear an attack to post a bond to keep the peace.[23] Nine states plus the City of Washington copied much of the *Revised Statutes*, including the surety provision. Eric Ruben, Saul Cornell, and Patrick J. Charles contend that the surety provisions serve as historical precedent that the American right to bear arms did not include a general right to carry weapons in public.[24] They call the surety law approach the "Massachusetts [M]odel."[25] They distinguish it from the so-called antebellum Southern model, which prohibited the carrying of weapons in a concealed manner, leaving individuals free to carry arms openly.[26] And they argue that the surety laws were a descendent of the common law crime of going armed to the terror of the people, which they believe generally prohibited carrying weapons in public because public carry was inherently terrifying.[27] These scholars thus conclude that historically the constitutional protection for the right to bear arms coexisted with severe limitations on public carry.

Relying on the Madisonian liquidation framework, I contend that the right to bear arms did not liquidate in favor of the Massachusetts Model. No evidence has emerged that legislatures deliberated about the meaning of the right to bear arms when they passed the surety laws. So we have no reason to think that these laws were the product of thoughtful constitutional interpretation. Second, no course of practice emerged. The surety laws were rarely invoked against those who carried weapons for lawful purposes. Finally, the lack of enforcement meant that these laws failed to settle the constitutional issue. Quite the contrary, Massachusetts Model jurisdictions switched to narrower restrictions against the carrying of weapons in a concealed manner, including in jurisdictions outside the South.

My argument in this chapter will be entirely negative. Space limitations preclude me from providing my affirmative argument, which is that the right to bear arms liquidated in favor of recognizing a general right to carry arms openly while also recognizing the government's power to prohibit the carrying of concealed weapons as a reasonable regulation of the right. Much of the evidence I cite in this chapter, however, provides the foundation for that argument.

More broadly, this chapter challenges how history intersects with constitutional interpretation. Constitutional liquidation is one attempt to reconcile

---

[22] THE REVISED STATUTES OF THE COMMONWEALTH OF MASSACHUSETTS (Boston, Dutton & Wentworth 1836).
[23] Of Proceedings to Prevent the Commission of Crimes, ch. 134, § 16, *in* THE REVISED STATUTES OF THE COMMONWEALTH OF MASSACHUSETTS 748, 750 (Boston, Dutton & Wentworth 1836).
[24] *See* Ruben & Cornell, *supra* note 11, 124–33; Charles, *supra* note 13.
[25] Ruben & Cornell, *supra* note 11, at 133.
[26] *Id.* at 124–25.
[27] Ruben & Cornell, *supra* note 11, at 129–30; Charles, *supra* note 13, at 36–41.

historical practice with constitutional law. There are other approaches. But those who argue that extensive restrictions on public carry do not violate the right to bear arms need to do more than identify a few isolated and likely unenforced nineteenth-century state laws that (arguably) support their view.

II. *HELLER*, ORIGINALISM, HISTORY, AND PUBLIC CARRY

In *District of Columbia v. Heller*, the Supreme Court held that the Second Amendment "guarantee[d] the individual right"—that is, one not conditioned on being enrolled in a state military unit—"to possess and carry weapons in case of confrontation."[28] Despite recognizing an individual right to bear arms, the Court reassured the public that "the right secured by the Second Amendment is not unlimited" and does not confer "a right to keep and carry any weapon whatsoever in any manner whatsoever and for whatever purpose."[29] The opinion notes, for example, that "the majority of the 19th-century courts to consider the question held that prohibitions on carrying concealed weapons were lawful under the Second Amendment or state analogues."[30]

Although *Heller* did not purport to "undertake an exhaustive historical analysis . . . of the full scope of the Second Amendment,"[31] lower courts and litigants have treated *Heller*'s dicta as a comprehensive road map for Second Amendment litigation. Post-*Heller*, the most significant Second Amendment issue was the validity of laws restricting private citizens from carrying firearms in public. When *Heller* was decided, eight states plus the District of Columbia heavily restricted the ability of private citizens to carry firearms in public.[32]

Subsequent litigation challenged these restrictive carry laws. In the lower courts, Justice Scalia's analysis in *Heller* became a key sticking point. Litigants challenging restrictive carry regimes argued that *Heller* implicitly adopted

---

[28] 554 U.S. 570, 592 (2008).
[29] *Id.* at 626.
[30] *Id.*
[31] *Id.*
[32] Illinois maintained a complete ban on carrying firearms in public. 720 ILL. COMP. STAT. ANN. 5/24-1, 5/24-1.6 (West 2008). Six states—California, Hawaii, Maryland, Massachusetts, New Jersey, and New York—provided for licenses to carry firearms only upon a showing of special need. CAL. PENAL CODE § 12050 (West 2008); HAW. REV. STAT. ANN. § 134-9 (2008); MASS. GEN. LAWS ANN. ch. 140, § 131 (West 2008); N.J. STAT. ANN. § 2C:58-4 (West 2008); N.Y. PENAL LAW § 400.00 (McKinney 2008). The District of Columbia had a technical discretionary licensing system, despite its complete ban on registering new handguns. D.C. CODE § 22-4506 (2001) (licenses to carry); § 7-2502.01(a), (a)(4) (registration requirement and prohibition on registering pistols). And Delaware required a special showing of need for a license to carry a weapon concealed, although state law did not regulate unconcealed weapons. DEL. CODE tit. 11, §§ 1441(a)(2), 1442.

the position that states must allow private citizens to carry firearms in some manner.[33] *Heller*'s examples of presumptively constitutional limitations on the right to bear arms included the prohibition of carrying firearms "in sensitive places such as schools and government buildings,"[34] and the Court seemingly accepted the nineteenth-century cases upholding prohibitions on concealed weapons.[35] For these litigants, the exceptions proved the rule—that the government cannot entirely prohibit private citizens from carrying firearms in public. Governments defending restrictive carry laws, however, contended that extensive restrictions on public carry were consistent with *Heller*'s emphasis on the "use of arms in defense of *hearth and home*"[36] and a full picture of historical practice.[37]

Because *Heller* featured history prominently in its decision, both sides of this debate rely on history to advance their understanding of the Second Amendment. The vast majority of nineteenth-century state court decisions upheld the state's power to prohibit the carrying of concealed weapons, while striking down laws that constituted a complete ban on pistol carry.[38] Many scholars and litigants rely on these cases as precedent that the government may regulate the carrying of firearms but may not generally prohibit it.

Those who favor a narrower interpretation of the Second Amendment argue that these nineteenth-century state cases provide dubious authority about the original meaning of the Second Amendment. These state cases came decades after the Second Amendment was adopted, when "[a] more liberal, individualistic, and ultimately democratic conception of arms-bearing emerged[.]"[39] Worse, these cases came only from the South, which had a distinctively permissive attitude towards gun carrying.[40] Other regions of the country, they argue, followed the "Massachusetts [M]odel," which generally prohibited individuals from carrying weapons unless they had reason to fear an attack.[41] And the common law, Massachusetts Model, proponents contend, for centuries generally prohibited individuals from riding or going armed with dangerous or unusual weapons.[42] So, they conclude, the Second Amendment is consistent with

[33] *See, e.g.*, Brief for Petitioners at 19–26, New York State Rifle & Pistol Ass'n v. City of New York, 140 S. Ct. 1525 (2020) (No. 18-280), 2019 WL 2068598; Brief of Plaintiffs-Appellants at 16–20, Gould v. Morgan, 907 F.3d 659 (1st Cir. 2018) (No. 17-2202), 2018 WL 1610774.
[34] 554 U.S. at 626.
[35] *Id.*
[36] *Id.* at 635 (emphasis added).
[37] *See, e.g.*, Brief of Defendant-Appellee William B. Evans at 22–26, Gould v. Morgan, 907 F.3d 659 (1st Cir. 2018) (No. 17-2202), 2018 WL 2759720; Reply Brief of Appellants at 2–15, Woollard v. Gallagher, 712 F.3d 865 (4th Cir. 2013) (No. 12-1437), 2012 WL 3598881.
[38] *See* Kopel, *supra* note 12, at 1419–36.
[39] Saul Cornell & Justin Florence, *The Right to Bear Arms in the Era of the Fourteenth Amendment: Gun Rights or Gun Regulation?*, 50 SANTA CLARA L. REV. 1043, 1055 (2010).
[40] Ruben & Cornell, *supra* note 11, at 124–28.
[41] *Id.* at 128–33.
[42] 4 WILLIAM BLACKSTONE, COMMENTARIES *149 (1979); *see supra* note 27.

heavily restricting public gun carry. As it applies to modern times, these laws may not be a perfect analog to today's discretionary licensing regimes, which require some showing of personal danger before a license to carry is issued. But these scholars contend they are close enough to be deemed constitutional on a historically based approach.[43]

To be sure, affording precedential weight to the nineteenth-century legal framework also has its critics among constitutional scholars examining original meaning. Nelson Lund has argued that nineteenth-century state decisions "do not provide direct evidence of the scope of the preexisting right [to bear arms]," as it was understood when the Second Amendment was adopted in 1791.[44] These cases, moreover, do not share *Heller*'s interpretive methodology or its understanding about the purpose of the right to bear arms.[45] Finally, Lund agrees with proponents of the Massachusetts Model that these decisions may be peculiar to the antebellum South, although for a different reason than they assert. Whereas Cornell and Ruben believe that the South had a uniquely permissive gun-carrying culture,[46] Lund argues that the South's emphasis on whether the weapon was concealed may have stemmed from a culture where the concealment of the weapon created "a presumption of criminal intent."[47] Today, in contrast, carrying a firearm *openly* may create a presumption of criminality by disturbing the peace.[48]

This dispute leaves two critical questions on the table. First, methodologically, why is the nineteenth-century legal framework relevant, if at all? As Lund notes, *Heller* fails to "explain why or to what extent judicial decisions under state analogues of the Second Amendment would be relevant to the original meaning of the Second Amendment."[49] Second, can a historical approach help elucidate the scope of the right to bear arms? Or is the history too muddy to draw any firm conclusions?

---

[43] Ruben & Cornell, *supra* note 11, at 132–33.
[44] Nelson Lund, *The Second Amendment, Heller, and Originalist Jurisprudence*, 56 UCLA L. REV. 1343, 1359 (2009).
[45] *See id.* at 1359–62.
[46] Ruben & Cornell, *supra* note 11, at 124–28.
[47] Lund, *supra* note 44, at 1361.
[48] *Id.*
[49] *Id.* at 1359; *see also* Adam Winkler, *Heller's Catch-22*, 56 UCLA L. REV. 1551, 1570 n.105 (2009) ("Whether [the antebellum cases cited in *Heller*] have anything worthwhile to show about the original understanding of the Second Amendment is highly doubtful. Notice the date of these two sources, a half-century after the ratification of the Bill of Rights.").

III. An Alternative Reading of *Heller*: Nineteenth-Century Precedent as Constitutional Liquidation

Heller offers nineteenth-century treatises and state-court decisions as evidence of "the public understanding" of the Second Amendment "in the period after its enactment or ratification."[50] One can read this claim as asserting that these sources provide authoritative evidence of the Second Amendment's original public understanding in 1791. But in this section, I want to offer a more charitable interpretation for *Heller*'s reliance on nineteenth-century precedents. Instead of being evidence of what the preexisting right to bear arms meant in 1791, nineteenth-century precedents are relevant for how the right to bear arms liquidated in America.

Constitutional liquidation is a method of resolving textual indeterminacy. In *Federalist No. 37*, Madison wrote, "All new laws, though penned with the greatest technical skill, and passed on the fullest and most mature deliberation, are considered as more or less obscure and equivocal, until their meaning be liquidated and ascertained by a series of particular discussions and adjudications."[51] Constitutional liquidation, thus, is the idea that, in proper circumstances, post-enactment practice will settle constitutional meaning.[52]

To "settle" a meaning, of course, implies that a law has some zone of ambiguity that needs to be resolved. As Caleb Nelson explains, ambiguity and vagueness could arise for many reasons:

> Some ambiguities could be traced to the human failings of the people who drafted the laws; they might have been careless in thinking about their project or in reducing their ideas to words, and they would certainly be unable to foresee all future developments that might raise questions about their meaning. Other obscurities would result simply from the imperfections of human language....[53]

Constitutional liquidation has no place, however, where the text of a written law is unambiguous. Were it otherwise, use and tradition would serve as a method to amend written law.[54] For the same reason, even in cases where a law has both unambiguous and ambiguous zones of meaning, liquidation is only appropriate when the meaning of the law is unclear in the circumstances.[55]

---

[50] 554 U.S. 570, 605 (2008) (emphasis omitted).
[51] The Federalist No. 37, at 236 (James Madison) (Jacob E. Cooke ed., 1961).
[52] Baude, *supra* note 14, at 4.
[53] Caleb Nelson, *Stare Decisis and Demonstrably Erroneous Precedents*, 87 Va. L. Rev. 1, 11 (2001).
[54] *See* Baude, *supra* note 14, at 13–16.
[55] *Id.* at 66.

The Second Amendment suffers from textual indeterminacy. The amendment provides, "A well regulated Militia, being necessary to the security of a free State, the right of the people to keep and bear Arms, shall not be infringed."[56] One (implausible) way to read the operative clause is to prohibit the government from encroaching on any individual's ability to possess and carry weapons. That meaning is obviously too broad. For example, it would divest the federal government of the power to disarm prisoners while they were in custody or to prohibit the possession of weapons in legislative chambers and judicial proceedings. A more plausible way to read the amendment is that it protects "*the* right" to keep and bear arms—that is, the general law right preexisting the Constitution and known to the Framers.[57]

But this latter reading solves the indeterminacy problem only if the *definiendum* "the right" has some known, fixed meaning. When it comes to the right to bear arms, we have good reason to believe that its meaning was not fully settled in 1791. Although the duty to bear arms existed for centuries, the legal *right* to have arms only emerged with the 1689 English Bill of Rights.[58] So unlike rights to due process of law or just compensation for eminent domain, which trace their roots to the Magna Carta, the right to bear arms had a relatively short history before our Bill of Rights was adopted.

Within that short history, the English right did not develop much. We know that the event motivating the creation of the right was the disarming of the Protestants by the Crown, thereby preventing the Protestants from resisting other illegal and unconstitutional royal edicts.[59] But the right to have arms was limited to Protestants, and even Protestants could have arms only "suitable to their Conditions, and as allowed by Law."[60] Parliament heavily restricted who could keep a gun,[61] which led Justice Story to comment that the English right "under various pretences . . . ha[d] been greatly narrowed" and was more "nominal than real."[62]

---

[56] U.S. CONST. amend. II.

[57] *See* United States v. Cruikshank, 92 U.S. 542, 553 (1875) ("'[B]earing arms for a lawful purpose' . . . is not a right granted by the Constitution. Neither is it in any manner dependent upon that instrument for its existence. The second amendment declares that it shall not be infringed; but this, as has been seen, means no more than that it shall not be infringed by Congress.").

[58] JOYCE LEE MALCOLM, TO KEEP AND BEAR ARMS: THE ORIGINS OF AN ANGLO-AMERICAN RIGHT 1 (1996).

[59] Aymette v. State, 21 Tenn. (2 Hum.) 154, 156–57 (1840) (explaining that "King James II., by his own arbitrary power, and contrary to law, disarmed the Protestant population"); *see* MALCOLM, *supra* note 58, at 94–112.

[60] An Act Declaring the Rights and Liberties of the Subject, and Settling the Succession of the Crown (Bill of Rights) 1689, 1 W. & M., sess. 2, ch. 2, § 7 (Eng.), *in* 9 STATUTES AT LARGE 67, 69 (Pickering 1764).

[61] 22 & 23 Car. II c. 25 (1671) (Eng.), *in* 5 STATUTES OF THE REALM 745 (restricting the right to keep arms to those meeting certain rank and property qualifications).

[62] 2 JOSEPH STORY & THOMAS MCINTYRE, COMMENTARIES ON THE CONSTITUTION OF THE UNITED STATES § 1898, at 621 (Law Book Exchange 2007) (4th ed. 1873).

The ability of English subjects to carry arms for private purposes is the matter of great contemporary scholarly dispute. In 1328, Parliament passed the Statute of Northampton. That statute provided:

> That no man great nor small, of what condition soever he be, except the king's servants in his presence, and his ministers in executing of the king's precepts, or of their office, and such as be in their company assisting them, and also [upon a cry made for arms to keep the peace, and the same in such places where such acts happen,] be so hardy to come before the King's justices, or other of the King's ministers doing their office, with force and arms, nor bring no force in affray of the peace, nor to go nor ride armed by night nor by day, in fairs, markets, nor in the presence of the justices or other ministers, nor in no part elsewhere, upon pain to forfeit their armour to the King, and their bodies to prison at the King's pleasure.[63]

The Statute of Northampton was considered "an affirmance of" the common law crime of going armed with dangerous or unusual weapons to the terror of the people.[64] Some claim that the Statute of Northampton made it generally unlawful to ride or go armed in public.[65] Others contend that, by the seventeenth century, the statute was understood only to apply to those "who go armed to terrify the King's subjects."[66] One reason this issue is so contested is that few judicial precedents exist, which raises the question whether the offense was enforced outside the rarest of circumstances.

Nor was the contemporary American legal picture entirely clear. Before the adoption of the federal Bill of Rights, four state constitutions guaranteed some form of the right to bear arms.[67] But there are no known judicial decisions about these provisions by the time the Second Amendment was adopted in 1791. And very little is known about how the people who drafted and ratified the Second Amendment understood the scope of the right. The ratification debates, both of the Constitution and the Bill of Rights, primarily concerned the administration of the militia and how to handle religious exemptions from military service. They did not discuss the specific limits of the federal police power to regulate guns, even in the limited cases where the federal government possessed a police

---

[63] Statute of Northampton, 2 Edw. 3, ch. 3 (1328).
[64] Sir John Knight's Case, 87 Eng. Rep. 75, 76 (K.B. 1686).
[65] *E.g.*, Charles, *supra* note 13, at 7–31.
[66] Sir John Knight's Case, 87 Eng. Rep. 75, 76 (K.B. 1686); *see, e.g.*, Kopel, *supra* note 11, at 133–42; John Anthony Gardner Davis, A Treatise on Criminal Law 249 (1838) ("In the exposition of the statute of Edward, it has been resolved, that no wearing of arms is within its meaning, unless it be accompanied with such circumstances as are apt to terrify the people. . . .").
[67] District of Columbia v. Heller, 554 U.S. 570, 601–02 (2008) (collecting provisions from Massachusetts, North Carolina, Pennsylvania, and Vermont).

power.[68] One point of departure from the English practice, however, was that the American right was broader than its English ancestor, lacking the restrictive language ("Protestants," "suitable to their condition and degree," and "as allowed by law") found in the English Bill of Rights.[69]

The American historical legislative picture adds a little clarity, but not much. Americans accepted some forms of weapons control.[70] Colonial and state legislatures readily deprived certain individuals outside the political community from having arms, including slaves, Indians, and British Loyalists. They also regulated inherently dangerous activities—for example, the storage of large quantities of gunpowder, which created a fire and explosion risk in urban areas. And they regulated the militia by requiring able-bodied men to have and train with arms. With at least one notable exception,[71] gun carrying went unregulated by statute until the nineteenth century. And while some legislatures passed laws modeled on the Statute of Northampton,[72] virtually nothing is known about how these laws were construed or enforced, assuming such prosecutions ever happened. Early American weapons regulations were much less comprehensive than modern gun-control regulations.[73] And this fact cuts both ways. Was this a sign that early American legislatures broadly respected the right to keep and bear arms? Or was this a mere legislative policy choice, not constitutionally mandated? Any historical approach to the Second Amendment has to cope with the fact that the precise scope of "the right" was "more or less obscure and equivocal"[74] in 1791.

Now some may argue that the fact the right to bear arms was ambiguous in 1791 is a reason why judges today—especially those who take originalism seriously—must defer to the legislature on the constitutionality of all gun control laws.[75] But this does not follow for two reasons.

First, the Second Amendment still has a core of unambiguous meaning. For example, under the original understanding of the Second Amendment,

---

[68] See supra note 20.
[69] Aymette v. State, 21 Tenn. (2 Hum.) 154, 158 (1840).
[70] The examples in this paragraph come from Winkler, *supra* note 59, at 1562, and SAUL CORNELL, A WELL-REGULATED MILITIA: THE FOUNDING FATHERS AND THE ORIGINS OF GUN CONTROL IN AMERICA 26–30 (2006).
[71] See New York State Rifle & Pistol Assoc. v. Bruen, 142 S. Ct. 2111, 2143–44 (2022) (recounting a New Jersey statute prohibiting "planter[s]" from carrying pistols). *Bruen* also discusses two seventeenth-century statutes from Massachusetts and New Hampshire, but those statutes just codified the common law offense of going armed to the terror of the people. *See id.* at 2142–43.
[72] Ruben & Cornell, *supra* note 11, at 129 & n.43 (collecting laws from Delaware, Massachusetts, Maine, North Carolina, Tennessee, and Virginia).
[73] Winkler, *supra* note 49, at 1562–63.
[74] THE FEDERALIST No. 37, at 236 (James Madison) (Jacob E. Cooke ed., 1961).
[75] *Cf.* United States v. Masciandaro, 638 F.3d 458, 475 (4th Cir. 2011) (urging deference on whether the Second Amendment applies outside the home because "[t]he whole matter strikes us as a vast *terra incognita*").

Congress could not enact a complete ban on the possession of rifles. And this is true whether one accepts the original understanding of the right to bear arms to be an individual, self-defense right or a common-defense, militia-centric right.[76] Deference to the legislature in core cases would elevate ordinary law over the Constitution.

Second, the Framers knew and understood that written constitutional provisions could not answer every difficult interpretive question. Over time, they expected that precedent would settle constitutional meaning. That is to say, constitutional liquidation was part of the "original methods" known to the Framers.[77] And beyond the Framers themselves, liquidation has been a traditional part of the American common law of judging since the beginning. Liquidation "dominated antebellum case law" as "[c]ourt after court used its framework to think about the effect of past decisions interpreting written laws."[78] Liquidation has resolved the interpretation of many uncertain constitutional provisions, and we should not think that the right to bear arms should be uniquely excepted.[79]

The next issue is to identify how liquidation of the Constitution happens. As Will Baude has explained, Madison's conception of liquidation has three parts.[80] First, a regular tradition or practice has to develop with respect to the interpretation of the provision.[81] That interpretation should span significant time period and not be restricted to a particular political faction or party.[82] On that front, liquidation is related to early theories of judicial precedent, which placed primacy on a series of judicial opinions rather than on a single opinion.[83] Second, the precedential interpretation must result from bona fide deliberation about the legal issue.[84] Third, a "settlement" of the issue must result, which means that (1) those holding dissenting interpretive views must accept the

---

[76] *Aymette*, 21 Tenn. (2 Hum.) 154 (1840); Andrews v. State, 50 Tenn. (3 Heisk.) 165 (1871); English v. State, 35 Tex. 473 (1872); State v. Kerner, 107 S.E. 222 (N.C. 1921).

[77] On original methods, *see* John O. McGinnis & Michael B. Rappaport, *Original Methods Originalism: A New Theory of Interpretation and the Case Against Construction*, 103 Nw. U. L. Rev. 751 (2009).

[78] Nelson, *supra* note 53, at 14.

[79] Indeed, both the *Heller* majority and dissenting opinions contain arguments essentially disputing how the Second Amendment liquidated. *Compare* District of Columbia v. Heller, 554 U.S. 570, 605–19 (majority op.) (tracing the nineteenth-century understanding of the right to bear arms), *with id.* at 638 & n.2 (Stevens, J., dissenting) (collecting the twentieth-century understanding of the Second Amendment in federal courts), *and id.* at 676–79 (noting the "substantial reliance" of "legislators and citizens for nearly 70 years" on the Court's earlier decision in *United States v. Miller*, 307 U.S. 174 (1939)).

[80] Baude, *supra* note 14, at 16–21.

[81] *Id.* at 16.

[82] *Id.*

[83] *Id.* at 38 (citing John O. McGinnis & Michael B. Rappaport, *Reconciling Originalism and Precedent*, 103 Nw. U. L. Rev. 803, 809 (2009)).

[84] *Id.* at 17.

countervailing interpretation, and (2) the public must accept the interpretation of the provision.[85]

As applied to the right to bear arms, liquidation is more complicated than it would be for purely structural federal issues, such as the constitutionality of the Bank of the United States.[86] The federal government largely lacked a de facto police power until the twentieth century.[87] Consequently, states, territories, and their localities were the primary regulators of weapons.[88] This meant that constitutional liquidation of the right to bear arms occurred in a decentralized fashion throughout the country. And many of the judicial precedents occurred under state analogs protecting the right to bear arms rather than under the Second Amendment directly.[89]

But this kind of decentralization is not fatal to the possibility of liquidation. Judicial decisions routinely accepted that the right to bear arms enumerated in both the state and federal constitutions referred to the same preexisting right, even where state constitutions used slightly different language in how they expressed the right.[90] Treatise writers also treated the various state and federal rights as coextensive, even when they were discussing doctrinal disagreements among the states.[91] One must be careful not to import post-*Erie* visions of states having entirely separate legal systems into nineteenth-century jurisprudence, which accepted that general law existed.

There is also the question of whether liquidation—which relies on the support of the public to settle an issue—is appropriate to determine the scope of countermajoritarian rights-claims? Or should liquidation be confined to questions of governmental structure,[92] as Chief Justice Marshall suggested in *McCulloch v. Maryland*?[93] I do not see any theoretical difficulty with liquidation

---

[85] *Id.* at 18–20.

[86] *Id.* at 21–29

[87] *See* Peter J. Henning, *Misguided Federalism*, 68 Mo. L. Rev. 389, 418–29 (2003) (tracing rise of federal criminal jurisdiction through the use of the Postal and Commerce Clauses).

[88] *See* Robert J. Spitzer, *Gun Law History in the United States and Second Amendment Rights*, 80 Law & Contemp. Probs. 55, 58–61 (2017) (collecting state firearms regulations prior to the National Firearms Act of 1934).

[89] *E.g.*, Andrews v. State, 50 Tenn. (3 Heisk.) 165, 175 (1871); State v. Reid, 1 Ala. 612, 614–15 (1840); Bliss v. Commonwealth, 12 Ky. (2 Litt.) 90, 90–91 (1822).

[90] *See, e.g.*, State v. Buzzard, 4 Ark. 18, 26–27 (1842) (opinion of Ringo, C.J.); Aymette v. State, 21 Tenn. (2 Hum.) 154, 157 (1840); *Ex parte Thomas*, 97 P. 260, 262 (Okla. 1908).

[91] *E.g.*, 2 Joel Prentiss Bishop, Commentaries on the Criminal Law §§ 122–23, at 74–76 (4th ed. 1868);

Thomas M. Cooley, A Treatise on the Constitutional Limitations Which Rest upon the Legislative Power of the States of the American Union 427 (Alexis C. Angell ed., 6th ed. 1890).

[92] Baude, *supra* note 14, at 50 (describing objection).

[93] 17 U.S. (4 Wheat.) 316, 401 (1819) ("It will not be denied, that a bold and daring usurpation might be resisted, after an acquiescence still longer and more complete than this. But it is conceived that a doubtful question, one on which human reason may pause, and the human judgment be suspended, in the decision of which the great principles of liberty are not concerned, but the respective powers of those who are equally the representatives of the people, are to be adjusted. . . .").

settling the meaning of the right to bear arms.[94] Madison theorized that liquidation would occur as the product of the competition for popular support among government officials with divergent views on constitutional questions.[95] In structural cases, different federal officials may line up on different sides of the constitutional question.[96] In individual rights cases, however, the concern is that "government officials may only be on one side of the dispute, so Madison's republican model would not squarely apply."[97] But this concern may be overstated. The Second Amendment protects the general law right to bear arms against federal interference.[98] Until *McDonald v. City of Chicago*,[99] the Second Amendment did not incorporate the right to bear arms against the states. So as the general law right to bear arms liquidated in the states, there was ample opportunity for "different groups of officials [to] compete for the popular sanction, developing the 'reason of society.'"[100] Furthermore, the concern that all government officers may be on one side in an individual rights case is less worrisome here because the right to bear arms liquidated in favor of a broader individual right to carry arms for self-defense.[101]

Baude gives two additional reasons why liquidation may be appropriate in individual rights cases, and I agree with those as well. First, he states that "the division between structure and rights may be somewhat artificial."[102] The Second Amendment illustrates this. The amendment secures an individual right to bear arms. But that right also serves important structural interests by reserving part of the military power to the citizenry, thereby decentralizing who has the power to use force.[103] Second, the countermajoritarian problem is mitigated by having liquidation only where the right itself is ambiguous.[104] The Second Amendment in 1791 may have had some zones of ambiguity subject to liquidation; but that does not belie that the amendment also had a clear, core zone readily capable of countermajoritarian enforcement. Refusing to allow post-enactment practice to override the clear core of a right prevents liquidation from being used to usurp "the great principles of liberty."[105] Thus, constitutional liquidation is not inherently "an odd fit for individual rights cases."[106]

---

[94] My thanks to Joseph Blocher for pressing me on this point.
[95] Baude, *supra* note 14, at 50.
[96] *Id.*
[97] *Id.*
[98] *See* United States v. Cruikshank, 92 U.S. 542, 553 (1875).
[99] 561 U.S. 742 (2010).
[100] Baude, *supra* note 14, at 50.
[101] My thanks to Will Baude for raising this point in private conversation.
[102] Baude, *supra* note 14, at 50.
[103] Robert Leider, *Federalism and the Military Power of the United States*, 73 VAND. L. REV. 989, 1068 (2020).
[104] Baude, *supra* note 14, at 50.
[105] *McCulloch*, 17 U.S. (4 Wheat.) at 401.
[106] Baude, *supra* note 14, at 50.

Finally, there is the question of how the right to bear arms actually liquidated, especially as it relates to public carry. I will offer my answer on the public carry question, although I cannot fully defend it here. The right liquidated in favor of (1) the right to carry constitutionally protected arms openly in some form, and (2) the power of the states to prohibit the carrying of concealed weapons. Throughout the nineteenth century, decision after decision of state courts recognized this distinction.[107] State and territorial legislatures accepted it; nearly all prohibited the carrying of concealed weapons, while leaving individuals free to carry arms openly in some manner.[108] And contrary to Ruben and Cornell's suggestion, this was not a distinction peculiar to the antebellum South. It spread throughout much of the West and North, as well, including after the Civil War.[109] Along the way, there were repeated examples of the issue being deemed settled by those holding dissenting views, from the Washington and Tombstone city councils to the halls of Congress.[110]

[107] *E.g.*, Nunn v. State, 1 Ga. 243, 251 (1846); State v. Chandler, 5 La. Ann. 489, 490 (1850); Aymette v. State, 21 Tenn. (2 Hum.) 154, 159–61 (1840); State v. Reid, 1 Ala. 612, 615 (1840); Fife v. State, 31 Ark. 455, 458–61 (1876). For early twentieth-century cases along the same line, *see, e.g.*, In re Brickey, 70 P. 609, 609 (Idaho 1902); State v. Kerner, 107 S.E. 222, 225 (N.C. 1921).

[108] *See, e.g., infra* notes 174–184 and accompanying text. In the nineteenth century, few states or territories maintained a complete ban on public carry. For a limited time, Arizona, Idaho, New Mexico, and Wyoming generally prohibited the carrying of weapons in incorporated areas. 1893 Ariz. Sess. Laws ch. 3, § 1; 1888 Idaho Sess. Laws ch. 23, § 1; 1860 N.M. Laws ch. 94, §1; 1876 Wyo. Sess. Laws ch. 352, § 1 (Dec. 2, 1875). Arizona's and Wyoming's were repealed around the time of statehood. Wyo. Sess. Laws 1890, ch. 73, § 6, at 140. For Arizona, compare Revised Statutes of Arizona Territory, Penal Code, Title XI, §§ 382, 385 (1901) (prohibiting carrying concealed weapons statewide and all carry within incorporated areas), with Arizona Revised Statutes, Penal Code, Title XII, § 426 (1913) (continuing only the prohibition against concealed weapons). Idaho's carry ban was invalidated by judicial decision. *In re* Brickey, 70 P. 609 (Idaho 1902). New Mexico repealed its general ban in 1962, N.M. Laws of 1963, ch. 303, § 7-2, at 842, and the law may have been unconstitutional all along, *see* City of Las Vegas v. Moberg, 485 P.2d 737, 738 (N.M. Ct. App. 1971) (holding that an analogous ordinance violated the right to bear arms). After the Civil War, Texas and West Virginia courts upheld broad restrictions on carrying pistols, though these states allowed individuals to carry rifles and shotguns. *See* State v. Duke, 42 Tex. 455 (1873); State v. Workman, 14 S.E. 9 (W. Va. 1891).

[109] *See, e.g., In re* Brickey, 70 P. 609, 609 (Idaho 1902); City of Las Vegas v. Moberg, 485 P.2d 737, 738 (N.M. Ct. App. 1971); Dano v. Collins, 802 P.2d 1021, 1022 (Ariz. Ct. App. 1990); State v. Wilforth, 74 Mo. 528, 531 (1881); Klein v. Leis, 795 N.E.2d 633, 638 (Ohio 2003) (reaffirming State v. Nieto, 130 N.E. 663, 664 (Ohio 1920)); Concealed Weapons, 1926–1928 MICH. ATT'Y GEN. BIENNIAL REP. 349 (Apr. 22, 1927); *Deadly Weapons*, PHILADELPHIA INQUIRER, Dec. 30, 1897, at 2 (recognizing that Pennsylvania law did not prohibit carrying arms openly and that "the right to openly bear arms is guaranteed by the federal constitution") (capitalization altered). Some of these decisions make the distinction implicitly by holding that a state may regulate the manner of bearing arms, including by prohibiting concealed weapons, because such regulations do not ban the carrying of arms entirely. *See, e.g., Nieto*, 130 N.E. at 664. These decisions are formally compatible with interpreting the right as guaranteeing some form of public carry, with the legislature choosing the manner (openly or concealed). But this compatibility may just result from imprecision in the language of the opinions. Prohibiting openly carried weapons while allowing concealed weapons would have raised serious constitutional concerns. *See Aymette*, 21 Tenn. at 161.

[110] Tombstone, Arizona, did not have a complete ban on public carry. Tombstone's original ordinance authorized permits to carry concealed weapons. Tombstone, Ariz. Ordinance No. 9 (Apr. 19, 1881). When Tombstone amended its ordinance to cancel those permits, it exempted weapons carried "openly in sight and in the hand," no doubt a concession to the Tennessee-Arkansas decisions that invalidated bans on public carry without those exceptions. John Carr, Mayor, *Enforcement of*

One may object that the states were not uniform in distinguishing concealed and unconcealed weapons. A very small minority of jurisdictions—most notably Texas—took a different path after the Civil War.[111] A full defense would have to explain how the existence of these isolated outliers remains consistent with the claim that the right to bear arms, in fact, liquidated in favor of the permissibility of public open carry. For now, I will say simply that liquidation does not require perfect uniformity,[112] and nearly all these jurisdictions still allowed broad avenues for public carry of constitutionally protected arms, which separate them from today's restrictive states.[113]

IV. Liquidation and the Massachusetts Model

In light of *Heller*, many scholars rely on history to argue that, outside the antebellum South, broad bans on public carry were the norm. As evidence, they cite statutes in nine states and the District of Columbia requiring sureties to keep the

---

Ordinance No. 9, The Tombstone Epitaph, Feb. 20, 1882, at 5 (canceling permits and quoting the amended ordinance). For the Tennessee-Arkansas doctrine, *see State v. Wilburn*, 66 Tenn. 57, 62–63 (1872); *Haile v. State*, 38 Ark. 564, 566–67 (1882). The City of Washington enacted a complete ban on public carry in 1857, only to amend it to a ban only on concealed weapons, for fear that the broader ban would not survive a circuit court challenge. *Compare* Act of Nov. 4, 1857, ch. 5, *in* General Laws of the Corporation of the City of Washington 75 (Robert A. Waters ed., 1860) (prohibiting all carry), *with* Act of Nov. 18, 1858, *in* General Laws of the Corporation of the City of Washington, *supra*, at 114 (prohibiting only the carrying of concealed weapons). For an explanation of the 1858 amendment, *see Concealed Weapons*, Evening Star, Nov. 11, 1858, at 3 ("Mr. Jones explained that the bill was the same as the old bill, with the exception that the word 'concealed' is here inserted. For want of that word in the former bill, it is now certain that the corporation will lose every case before the circuit court by appeal from the decisions of the police magistrates."). When legislating for the District of Columbia, Congress repeatedly refused to criminalize carrying weapons openly because of concerns that it would violate the Second Amendment. 21 Cong. Rec. 4448 (May 10, 1890) (explaining that Congress was not criminalizing unconcealed weapons); 21 Cong. Rec. 223–30 (Dec. 8, 1890) (constitutional debates); 23 Cong. Rec. 1050–51 (Feb. 11, 1892); 23 Cong. Rec. 5789 (July 6, 1892); 48 Cong. Rec. 4593 (Apr. 11, 1912) (amending a bill to prevent criminalizing "the bearing of arms openly") (statement of Mr. Johnson); 56 Cong. Rec. 9545, 9547–48 (Aug. 26, 1918); Mark Anthony Frassetto, *The First Congressional Debate on Public Carry and What It Tells Us about Firearm Regionalism*, 40 Campbell L. Rev. 335 (2018). When Congress adopted the Uniform Firearms Act for the District it 1932, it modified the act only to apply to concealed weapons. An act to control the possession, sale, transfer, and use of pistols and other dangerous weapons in the District of Columbia, Pub. L. No. 72-275, § 4, 47 Stat. 650 (1932). Congress finally prohibited carrying pistols openly without a license in 1943 because of concerns that criminals were evading the concealed weapons ban by placing their weapons in plain view when approached by law enforcement. An act to amend the law of the District of Columbia relating to the carrying of concealed weapons, Pub. L. No. 78-182, 57 Stat. 586 (1943).

[111] *See supra* note 108.

[112] *See, e.g., Bruen*, 142 S. Ct. 2111, 2153 (refusing to "give disproportionate to a single state statute and a pair of state-court decisions").

[113] All these states, for example, allowed travelers to carry arms. All except Texas also allowed public carry outside of incorporated areas. *See* sources cited *supra* note 108.

peace of those who went armed without reasonable cause to fear an attack. But the Massachusetts Model has no plausible claim to liquidating the right to bear arms. We have no evidence that these laws resulted from reasoned deliberation about the constitutional issue. The "model" never resulted in a tradition or practice. And perhaps most importantly, these laws never "settled" the constitutional question of whether a legislature could generally ban public carry.

A. Practice and Deliberation

Proponents of the Massachusetts Model assert that the model constituted a different tradition of regulating public carry outside the antebellum South. But these proponents offer no evidence that these laws resulted from any kind of constitutional deliberation. Nor have they demonstrated that these laws resulted in a tradition or practice against public carry.

Let's begin with deliberation. For constitutional meaning to liquidate, the practice "must . . . be one of constitutional interpretation,"[114] resulting from "solemn discussion."[115] This means that "[l]egislative precedents [are] entitled to little respect when they [are] without full examination & deliberation."[116]

Did the legislatures that passed these surety laws make a considered judgment that the laws were consistent with the right to bear arms? We have no evidence of this. The proponents of the Massachusetts Model have provided none to indicate that any legislature passing a surety law examined the constitutional issue.[117] I have found no evidence of constitutional deliberation, including in the Report of the Commissioners who first proposed the surety provision.[118]

Now, Massachusetts Model proponents may be right that those legislatures which passed surety laws intended them to be broad restrictions against public carry. The *Boston Morning Post* reported a Massachusetts legislative debate in which a legislator made reference to "the law forbidding individuals to carry arms."[119] This is post-enactment legislative history of the worst kind—a statement of a single member. But given the time period, it may be the best we have. In addition, a Pennsylvania code revision committee reported that the Pennsylvania analog was intended to prevent "the unnecessarily carrying [of]

---

[114] Baude, *supra* note 14, at 17.
[115] *Id.* (quoting Letter from James Madison to James Monroe (Dec. 27, 1817) *reprinted in* 1 THE PAPERS OF JAMES MADISON: RETIREMENT SERIES 190, 190–91 (David B. Mattern et al. eds., 2009)).
[116] *Id.* at 18 (quoting Madison) (internal quotation marks omitted).
[117] *See, e.g.*, Ruben & Cornell, *supra* note 11 and Charles, *supra* note 13.
[118] REPORT OF THE COMMISSIONERS APPOINTED TO REVISE THE GENERAL STATUTES OF THE COMMONWEALTH, pt. IV, ch. 134, § 16, at 42 (1834).
[119] *Massachusetts Legislature*, BOSTON MORNING POST, Feb. 6, 1840, at 2 (reporting a transcript of the Massachusetts Legislature debates of Feb. 5, 1840) (statement of Mr. Sumner).

deadly weapons" because of the "obvious necessity, arising from daily experience and observation."[120] But conspicuously lacking from this description is any analysis of whether these surety laws comported with the constitutional right to bear arms. Both the Massachusetts and Pennsylvania constitutions recognized the right.[121] Yet, we have no evidence that the legislatures considered whether the surety laws complied with these guarantees.

The mere fact that several other antebellum legislatures copied much of Massachusetts' *Revised Statutes*—including the surety provision—is not evidence that they seriously debated the surety law's constitutionality. The surety laws were a minor section, buried in a huge reform project to codify and revise existing law. There is no known evidence that the legislatures paid attention to the surety provisions or debated their constitutionality. We should be hesitant to infer a considered judgment about their constitutionality merely from legislative copy-and-paste.

We should be even more hesitant because these laws never resulted in any kind of settled practice against going armed. Proponents argue that the Massachusetts law constituted "a sweeping law that effectively prohibited the right to travel armed."[122] Here is the Massachusetts statute, which the other states copied nearly verbatim:

> If any person shall go armed with a dirk, dagger, sword, pistol, or other offensive and dangerous weapon, without reasonable cause to fear an assualt [*sic*] or other injury, or violence to his person, or to his family or property, he may, on complaint of any person having reasonable cause to fear an injury, or breach of the peace, be required to find sureties for keeping the peace.[123]

From this text, proponents of the Massachusetts Model conclude that surety law "forbade arming oneself except in unusual situations."[124] And as authority, they cite one jurist, Peter Oxenbridge Thacher, who said in a charge to a grand jury that "no person may go armed with a dirk, dagger, sword, pistol, or other offensive and dangerous weapon without reasonable cause to apprehend an assault or violence to his person, family, or property."[125]

---

[120] EDWARD KING ET AL., PA. COMM'RS APPOINTED TO REVISE THE PENAL CODE, REPORT OF THE COMMISSIONERS APPOINTED TO REVISE THE PENAL CODE OF THE COMMONWEALTH OF PENNSYLVANIA 39 (Harrisburg, A.B. Hamilton 1860).

[121] MASS. CONST. pt. I, art. XVII; PA. CONST. art. IX, § XXI (1838).

[122] Saul Cornell, *The Right to Carry Firearms Outside of the Home: Separating Historical Myths from Historical Realities*, 39 FORDHAM URB. L.J. 1695, 1720 (2012) [hereinafter *The Right*].

[123] Of Proceedings to Prevent the Commission of Crimes, ch. 134, § 16, *in* THE REVISED STATUTES OF THE COMMONWEALTH OF MASSACHUSETTS 748, 750 (Boston, Dutton & Wentworth 1836).

[124] *The Right*, *supra* note 122, at 1720.

[125] *Id.* at 1720–21; Charles, *supra* note 13, at 39–40.

But this conclusion results from a distorted picture of what the text actually says. The Massachusetts surety statute only provides that those who go armed may, in some circumstances, be required to find sureties to keep the peace. The Massachusetts Model left Massachusetts and the other states that adopted it with no coercive criminal statute actually forbidding individuals from going armed. This hardly constitutes a *ban* on public carry. And while Ruben and Cornell state that sureties were "a common enforcement tool in early America,"[126] this is wrong. These sureties were a means to *prevent* crimes, not to enforce violations of the criminal law.[127] In this case, the distinction matters.

The lack of a true ban on public carry is more evident when one examines the standing requirement. To file a complaint, a person must have "reasonable cause to fear an injury" or "breach of the peace." The standing requirement negated the ability to file a complaint based on the carrying of weapons for lawful purposes. And the standing requirement is consistent with Blackstone's explanation that a surety serves as a "caution . . . intended merely for prevention, without any crime actually committed by the party, but arising only from a probable suspicion that some crime is intended or likely to happen."[128]

Although the surety law remained on the books for decades, there is little in the way of evidence that Massachusetts viewed this law as a near-complete ban on public carry. To the contrary, the legislature enacted new criminal statutes when it wanted to restrict public carry. Beginning in 1850, Massachusetts made it a crime for a person to be "armed with any dangerous weapon, of the kind usually called slung shot" when committing or being arrested for committing a crime.[129] This statutory crime soon expanded to cover other dangerous weapons,[130] and it became the principal way in which Massachusetts punished some people for carrying concealed weapons.[131] Massachusetts slightly restricted public carry further in 1893, when it prohibited armed bodies of men from drilling and parading with firearms.[132] The passage of these laws is hardly consistent with an understanding that, since 1835, individuals had not been permitted to carry firearms in Massachusetts, except when they were in danger.

---

[126] Ruben & Cornell, *supra* note 11, at 131.

[127] 4 BLACKSTONE, *supra* note 42, at *249 (explaining that a surety to keep the peace serves as a "caution . . . intended merely for prevention, without any crime actually committed by the party, but arising only from a probable suspicion that some crime is intended or likely to happen; and consequently it is not meant as any degree of punishment, unless, perhaps, for a man's imprudence in giving just ground of apprehension.").

[128] *Id.*

[129] An Act in Relation to the Carrying of Slung Shot, ch. 194, § 1, 1850 Mass. Acts 401.

[130] 1860 Mass. Acts ch. 164, § 10.

[131] *See About Concealed Weapons*, BOSTON GLOBE, June 9, 1898, at 4 (explaining that, in Suffolk County (which includes Boston), "it is customary to prosecute" individuals found with concealed weapons when arrested for "disturbance of the peace or of any offense more serious than drunkenness").

[132] An Act Concerning the Volunteer Militia, ch. 367, § 124, 1893 Mass. Stat. 1017, 1049–50.

There is circumstantial evidence that the Massachusetts Supreme Judicial Court did not view the statute as a complete ban on public carry either. In 1896, the court resolved an appeal from a person who deliberately violated the prohibition against parading with firearms to test whether the law was constitutional.[133] Citing the federal Supreme Court's decision in *Presser v. Illinois*, the Massachusetts court held that "[t]he right to keep and bear arms for the common defence does not include the right to associate together as a military organization."[134] The court, moreover, noted that "[t]he protection of a similar constitutional provision has often been sought by persons charged with carrying concealed weapons, and it has been almost universally held that the legislature may regulate and limit the mode of carrying arms."[135] For support, the decision went on to cite seven Southern cases and an early Indiana case—the same cases that Massachusetts Model proponents claim had no influence outside the South.[136] And the court used the phrase "regulate and limit"; the court never said that the legislature could enact a general *ban* on carrying firearms. Finally, note that the court omits any mention of the 1835 surety statute. That is a curious omission. If the state had generally prohibited public carry in 1835 (and if that were thought constitutional), then it would have followed *a fortiori* that the state could ban public carry in a parade. Yet, in a case involving public carry, the Supreme Judicial Court did not cite Massachusetts' alleged sixty-year history of banning the practice.

Nor did the common folk in Massachusetts recognize that the legislature supposedly banned public carry in 1835. Percy A. Bridgham, a member of the Suffolk County Bar, answered readers' legal questions in the *Boston Globe*. In 1889, someone asked the *Boston Globe* whether it was unlawful to carry concealed weapons. Bridgham responded with the law prohibiting carrying weapons while being arrested, writing, "The above does not prohibit any one from carrying weapons with which to defend themselves."[137] In a book Bridgham published in 1890 with a collection of legal questions, he noted that "[t]here is no statute in this State which expressly forbids the carrying of weapons, but there is a statute that provides that a person so carrying may be required to give bonds to keep the peace."[138] The *Boston Globe* made a similar statement in

---

[133] Commonwealth v. Murphy, 44 N.E. 138 (Mass. 1896). *See The Right to Bear Arms*, NEW HAVEN MORNING J. AND COURIER, May 27, 1896, at 4 (discussing *Commonwealth v. Murphy*); *The Right to Carry Arms*, INDIANAPOLIS J., Apr. 5, 1896, at 12 (same).
[134] Murphy, 44 N.E. at 172 (citing *Presser v. Illinois*, 116 U.S. 252, 264, 265 (1886)).
[135] *Id.*
[136] *Id.* at 173.
[137] *Carrying Weapons*, BOSTON DAILY GLOBE, Jan. 18, 1889, at 4.
[138] PERCY A. BRIDGHAM, ONE THOUSAND LEGAL QUESTIONS ANSWERED BY THE PEOPLE'S LAWYER OF THE BOSTON DAILY GLOBE 129 (1890); *see also id.* at 170 ("There is no penalty in this State for carrying concealed weapons, except in cases where they are found on a person who is attempting to commit another crime.").

1898.[139] In 1895, the *Boston Daily Advertiser* reported that "there is still a widespread belief that to carry concealed weapons in this city is of itself a misdemeanor punishable under the law."[140] It then explained this assumption was wrong: "Massachusetts has no specific law against carrying concealed weapons.... The ordinary citizen who has not otherwise offended against the law is able to arm himself without fear of police interference, so long as he does not attempt to violate the law against the procession of armed organizations."[141] So we have some evidence that those who read the surety law did not understand it to be a near-complete ban on public carry.[142]

The Massachusetts Model's proponents, moreover, do not cite any evidence that the surety laws were actually invoked against individuals who carried firearms for lawful purposes. The proponents offer Judge Thacher's grand jury charge,[143] but that "charge" was nothing more than a welcome address to members of the grand jury.[144] The charge had no bearing on any specific case, and more importantly, it did not purport to analyze the constitutional validity of the law. Nor do nineteenth-century justice of the peace manuals help their cause.[145] These manuals simply restated the statutory surety provision. They contain no record of enforcement, and they contain no analysis of the constitutional question.[146]

For actual enforcement, the best evidence Massachusetts Model proponents have delivered is *Bullock*'s case, a case that involved the justice of the peace's *refusal* to require a surety.[147] But even setting aside the judgment line, *Bullock*'s case does not support that the surety statute restricted public carry for lawful purposes. The case involved a complaint that the defendant "did threaten to beat,

---

[139] *About Concealed Weapons*, BOSTON GLOBE, June 9, 1898, at 4 ("No Law Forbids a Man Carrying a Revolver, but It's Different if He Should Happen to be Arrested.").
[140] *Concealed Weapons*, BOSTON DAILY ADVERTISER, July 13, 1895, at 4.
[141] *Id.*
[142] A news article in Michigan offers a similar account of its analog of the Massachusetts law. The paper explained that "in this State there is no statute whatever against the carrying of concealed weapons." *Concealed Weapons*, DETROIT FREE PRESS, Feb. 26, 1873, at 2. The newspaper also expressed its belief that "[s]o far as it assumes to interfere with the rights of citizens to bear arms openly, it is in direct conflict with the Constitution of the United States and of the State; and as it makes no distinction between the open and secret carrying of weapons, there can be little question of its utter invalidity for any purpose whatever." *Id.*
[143] Charles, *supra* note 13, at 39–40; Ruben & Cornell, *supra* note 11, at 131–32.
[144] *Judge Thacher's Charges*, CHRISTIAN REG. AND BOSTON OBSERVER, June 10, 1837, at 91.
[145] *Cf.* Ruben & Cornell, *supra* note 11, at 129–31; Charles, *supra* note 13, at 35 & n.185, 36 & n.194 (all looking to justice of the peace manuals as evidence that American common law prohibited going armed to the terror of the people).
[146] *See, e.g.*, JOHN C.B. DAVIS, THE MASSACHUSETTS JUSTICE: A TREATISE UPON THE POWERS AND DUTIES OF THE JUSTICES OF THE PEACE 202 (1847); BYRON D. VERRILL, MAINE CIVIL OFFICER: A GUIDE AND HAND BOOK FOR ATTORNEYS, TRIAL JUSTICES, JUSTICES OF THE PEACE, NOTARIES PUBLIC, SHERIFFS AND THEIR DEPUTIES, CORONERS, CONSTABLES, AND OTHER OFFICERS 348 (5th ed. 1885).
[147] Ruben & Cornell, *supra* note 11, at 130 n.53.

wound, maim, and kill" the complainant—conduct well beyond a person carrying a weapon for lawful self-defense.[148] Massachusetts Model proponents do not offer a single example of the surety laws being used to restrain peaceful public carry. And they provide no recorded decisions analyzing the constitutional validity of using surety laws in such circumstances.

Next, Massachusetts Model proponents try to explain why this lack of evidence is not a problem. They contend that because these cases were resolved at the justice of the peace level, we should not expect "Westlaw-searchable case law."[149] This is highly problematic. Lack of evidence is not evidence on their behalf. They are the ones arguing that the Massachusetts Model created a constitutional precedent. They bear the burden to show a real tradition or practice, not an isolated set of ten statutes in desuetude.

If anything, the lack of evidence cuts strongly against their position. In the South and West, we have developed case law on the right to bear arms because defendants convicted of illegally carrying weapons repeatedly challenged the constitutional validity of their convictions.[150] For the Massachusetts Model, however, we have no Westlaw-searchable opinions because we have no appeals to courts of record. Now it is true that, because of the small stakes, defendants in justice of the peace court have low incentives to appeal.[151] But nine other states plus the District of Columbia adopted these laws. If surety laws were being enforced as broad bans on public carry, one would expect to see at least one appeal somewhere.

Until someone does archival research on this issue, we will have to settle for indirect means to determine the scope of enforcement. One method is to search nineteenth-century local news articles for arrests and proceedings before justices of the peace. Searching through several databases of local nineteenth-century news, I have found only one possible incident in Massachusetts of someone prosecuted for peacefully carrying weapons for self-defense.

On April 5, 1851, Boston police arrested two men, Isaac and Charles Snowden, who were armed with concealed weapons.[152] Both were charged with going armed to the terror of the people. The justice of the peace ordered Charles to find a surety to keep the peace, and I am not sure what otherwise came of his case.

---

[148] Grover v. Bullock, No. 185 (Worcester Cty. Aug.13, 1853) (on file with author).
[149] Ruben & Cornell, *supra* note 11, at 130 n.53.
[150] *See, e.g.*, Fife v. State, 31 Ark. 455 (1876); In re Brickey, 70 P. 609 (Idaho 1902); Aymette v. State, 21 Tenn. (2 Hum.) 154 (1840); Andrews v. State, 50 Tenn. (3 Heisk.) 165 (1871); English v. State, 35 Tex. 473 (1872).
[151] On the lack of appeals for weapons regulations involving minor penalties, *see, e.g.*, *Concealed Weapons*, THE SUN, Feb. 4, 1894, at 3 (explaining that the prohibition against carrying concealed weapons in New York City was "a city ordinance" and stating that there was "doubt whether it would stand if an appeal were taken to the higher courts").
[152] *Arrests for Carrying Concealed Weapons*, THE LIBERATOR, Apr. 11, 1851, at 59.

But Isaac's case proceeded to judgment. Isaac was alleged to have carried a concealed loaded pistol and a butcher knife. In court, "[t]he watchmen testified that the only reason for their arrest was being seen walking up and down before the chained Court House" at 1:00 a.m., and that "they neither spoke to, threatened, nor struck anyone" and that "there was nothing about them suspicious, but their presence in the street at that hour."[153] The defense testified that they carried the weapons for protection.[154] The justice of the peace convicted Isaac, fined him $1, taxed him $6 in costs, and required him to post a $500 bond to appeal.[155] A contemporaneous newspaper account was incredulous that "walking peacefully, up and down the street, with arms in your pocket, which you neither use nor threaten to use" could constitute going armed to the terror of the people; the newspaper believed the conviction resulted from the fact that the defendants were poor and African American.[156]

Isaac appealed his conviction to the Municipal Court. On appeal, the Commonwealth abandoned the prosecution. Isaac had "behaved quietly & peacefully" during the time he was required to post bond, so the Commonwealth's attorney had no further interest in prosecuting the case.[157] This dropped prosecution is hardly a ringing endorsement that the Commonwealth's prosecution of peaceful carry was proper.[158]

---

[153] *Id.*

[154] *Id.*

[155] *Id.* The newspaper incorrectly reported a $600 appeal bond. For the correct amounts, *see* Commonwealth v. Snowden, Bos. Police Ct. R. Book 1117 (May 1851) (on file with author).

[156] *Arrests for Carrying Concealed Weapons*, THE LIBERATOR, Apr. 11, 1851, at 59 ("As the Judge had discoursed long, and much to his own satisfaction, on the equal justice he was going to render, *irrespective of color*, he was warmly congratulated by the counsel on his success in this particular, having, on Friday, fixed the bail of Fletcher Webster, with a salary of $5000 a year, son of Daniel, and surrounded with wealthy friends, charged with striking and knocking a watchman down, at $200; and now fixing the bail of a colored man, without a wealthy friend, or a dollar in the world, allowed to have acted like a good and peaceful citizen, *at three times that amount*—$600!").

[157] Complaint, Commonwealth v. Snowden, No. 1443 (Bos. Police Ct. Apr. 5, 1851) (on file with author) ("And now said Snowden having behaved quietly & peaceably, & the object of the prosecution being satisfied by the preservation of the peace, I will no further prosecute said Snowden on this appeal & complaint."); *see also* Commonwealth v. Snowden, Bos. Police Ct. R. Book 1117 (May 1851) (on file with author) ("And now said Snowden having behaved quietly and peaceably and the object of the prosecution being satisfied by the preservation of the peace[,] the Attorney of the Commonwealth says he will no further prosecute said Snowden on this appeal and complaint.").

[158] In a recent article, Saul Cornell provides more background on the Snowden case. *See* Saul Cornell, *The Long Arc of Arms Regulation in Public: From Surety to Permitting, 1328–1928*, 55 U.C. DAVIS L. REV. 2545, 2582–87 (2022). He recounts that the Snowden brothers "were the sons of a prominent Black minister allied with the radical Garrisonian wing of abolitionism" and that they were arrested "late at night in the vicinity of one of Boston's armories at a time when city officials feared the prospect of violence between abolitionists and their opponents." *Id.* at 2583. Cornell faults me for omitting "any discussion of radical abolitionism in Boston." *Id.* at 2584. But this additional historical detail furthers my argument, not Cornell's. If it is true that the Snowden brothers were radical abolitionists headed to the Boston armory, then the complainants could have had reasonable grounds that the Snowden brothers were about to breach the peace. This, again, confirms that the surety laws were invoked when violence was anticipated. Cornell has yet to unearth any cases (let alone a significant quantity) applying the surety laws as a broad restriction against the carrying

More broadly, we lack any evidence of a *consistent* practice of prosecuting peaceful carry. A single incident in 1851 fails to demonstrate that justices of the peace routinely proceeded under surety statutes for the peaceful carrying of firearms. Again, Massachusetts Model proponents offer no cases to support their thesis, and this case is all I have found in Massachusetts on their behalf. Bridgham, the lawyer who wrote for the *Boston Globe*, claimed in an 1891 article that an "inquiry at the office of the clerk for Municipal Court reveals the fact that there has not been a single complaint before the court for the past year under [the surety statute or the crime of being armed while arrested]."[159] And the Boston Police reported only a handful of arrests each year for the crime of "carrying concealed weapons."[160] It is unclear what statute the "carrying of concealed weapons" fell under; but given that the report tracked criminal arrests, it was probably for the crime of being armed while arrested rather than a complaint for a surety. Thus, the "Massachusetts Model" did not serve as a model for restricting public carry in Massachusetts.

It is also unlikely that the Massachusetts Model served as a model anywhere else. In my search of newspaper archives, I have found two other possible cases of sureties required for peaceful carry. Both were in the District of Columbia, both appear isolated, and both (like the Snowden case) involved African American defendants. In one case, two men were arrested at a Washington fair "for having loaded pistols." The newspaper reported that "[t]he weapons were confiscated, and this morning the men were ordered to give security to keep the peace and pay costs."[161] In the other case, Lucas Dabney openly carried a loaded revolver for self-defense. It is not clear under what statute he was arrested, and Dabney was correct that District law only prohibited the carrying of concealed weapons.[162] But the judge told him to leave his weapons at home and took his "personal bonds."[163]

In ten "Massachusetts Model" jurisdictions, these three cases are all I have found involving sureties or bonds for the peaceful carrying of firearms. I recognize, of course, that my results are limited to the sources that are contained

---

firearms for self-defense. I, too, have found it extraordinarily difficult to find surety cases involving the carrying of weapons for self-defense or other lawful purposes.

[159] P.A. Bridgham, *Dangerous Weapons*, BOSTON DAILY GLOBE, Sept. 27, 1891, at 20.
[160] *See, e.g.*, CITY OF BOSTON, ANN. REP. OF THE CHIEF OF POLICE 9 (1868) (of 19,120 reported crimes, two for carrying concealed weapons); CITY OF BOSTON, ANN. REP. OF THE CHIEF OF POLICE FOR 1875, at 20, 21 (of 30,445 reported crimes, 10 for carrying concealed weapons); BD. OF POLICE COMM'RS, SIXTH ANN. REP., May 1, 1884, at 6, 7 (of 31,200 arrests made by the Boston police, 4 for carrying concealed weapons).
[161] *Carrying Concealed Weapons*, THE EVENING STAR, Nov. 26, 1856, at 3.
[162] *See supra* note 110.
[163] *Afraid of Night Doctors: Why Lucas Dabney Carried a Pistol in His Hand*, THE EVENING STAR, Dec. 5, 1887, at 5.

within the databases I used. Perhaps future research using these or other sources will uncover significantly more cases (though I doubt it for the reasons given in the next section). Most likely, Massachusetts-style surety laws were nothing more than an initial inchoate attempt to regulate public carry and had little relevance to those who carried weapons for lawful purposes.

Thus, the Massachusetts Model is not an example of liquidating the meaning of the right to bear arms in favor of broad bans on public carry. None of the materials cited by the model's proponents show any considered debate about whether these laws were consistent with the right to bear arms. Worse still, the passage of these laws did not result in a regular practice limiting public carry. Constitutional liquidation requires more than finding a handful of old statutes in the law books.

B. Settlement

The *sina qua non* of constitutional liquidation is that some settlement of the constitutional interpretive issue takes hold. Under the Madisonian framework, "settlement" exists when the dissenting voices have acquiesced to the interpretation and the result has public sanction.[164] On the surface, it looks like we can dispose of the settlement question quickly. If the surety laws produced no regular course of practice, then no settlement could have occurred, for there was no practice to which the dissenters could acquiesce and the public could sanction. Q.E.D.

But the settlement issue is actually much worse for the proponents of the Massachusetts Model. Remember that Massachusetts Model proponents consider surety laws to be a nineteenth-century descendent of the common law offense of going armed to the terror of the people. And they view the common law offense as essentially a ban on public carry because going armed would inherently terrorize the people. Citing old statutes and treatises, they claim that American jurisdictions widely recognized the offense, and thus, they never liberally allowed public carry, even for self-defense.[165]

As with the surety laws, there is little evidence that the common law offense was enforced in this country. Before 1900, there are few reported decisions. In 1833, the Tennessee Supreme Court explained that if the mere carriage of weapons constituted an affray, it would violate the right to bear arms.[166] A decade later the North Carolina Supreme Court held in *State v. Huntly* that the "the

---

[164] Baude, *supra* note 14, at 18–21.
[165] *See* Ruben & Cornell, *supra* note 11, 124–33; Charles, *supra* note 13.
[166] Simpson v. State, 13 Tenn. (5 Yer.) 356, 359–62 (1833); *cf.* State v. Bentley, 74 Tenn. 205, 206–07 (1880) (making clear that prosecution for statutory offense prohibiting going armed to the terror of the people required that someone be terrified).

carrying of a gun *per se* constitutes no offence. For any lawful purpose—either of business or amusement—the citizen is at perfect liberty to carry his gun. It is the wicked purpose—and the mischievous result—which essentially constitute the crime."[167] Common nineteenth-century cases and treatises often cite *Huntly* as the sole American judicial authority on the common law crime.[168] No recorded American decision has held that a person committed going armed to the terror of the people by carrying firearms for lawful self-defense.

Why is it so difficult to find American cases? One explanation might be that, like the surety cases, many were handled at the justice of the peace level. But another, more plausible explanation is that the common law offense never took root in this country.

Although it is difficult to search justice of the peace records, we can search nineteenth-century newspaper databases for evidence that individuals were arrested for going armed to the terror of the people.[169] Searches of the Library of Congress newspaper database from 1800 to 1900 of "armed to the terror of the people" or "armed offensively" produce sixty-eight and thirty-seven results, respectively. Of these, only two are clearly reports of arrest.[170] A search of *Newspapers.com* of "armed to the terror of the people" during the same time period produces twenty-eight results, and a handful of arrests. A search of that database for "armed offensively" produces twenty-three matches and two arrests. To be sure, these searches are limited by the newspapers in those databases. Undoubtedly, they are not capturing every arrest happening in the country. And several nineteenth-century newspaper articles recognize the legal power of various law enforcement officers to arrest those who go armed to the terror of the people.[171] But despite the recitation of these laws, there is little indication that such arrests were made, particularly when people carried weapons for lawful purposes including self-defense.

---

[167] 25 N.C. (3 Ired.) 418, 422–23 (1843). *Accord* State v. Roten, 86 N.C. 701, 704 (1882) (holding that the legislature has not prohibited carrying weapons openly, and the common law offense only applied to an "abuse[]" of "so wearing arms").

[168] *E.g.*, FRANCIS WHARTON, A TREATISE ON THE CRIMINAL LAW OF THE UNITED STATES 528 & n.j (Phila., James Kay, Jun. and Bro. 1846); 2 BISHOP, *supra* note 91 § 120, at 73 & n.5.

[169] All searches that follow were performed on August 6, 2020.

[170] *Letter from Ashland City*, CLARKESVILLE WEEKLY CHRONICLE, June 21, 1873, https://chroniclingamerica.loc.gov/lccn/sn88061082/1873-06-21/ed-1/seq-1/#words=armed+people+terror; *Police Affairs*, DELAWARE REPUBLICAN, Apr. 2, 1866, https://chroniclingamerica.loc.gov/lccn/sn87062253/1866-04-02/ed-1/seq-2/#words=armed+people+terror. A few other articles—no more than a handful—also ambiguously describe events and might be further examples of arrests for going armed to the terror of the people. *E.g.*, *General Local News*, SHENANDOAH HERALD, Nov. 20, 1896, https://chroniclingamerica.loc.gov/lccn/sn85026941/1896-11-20/ed-1/seq-3/.

[171] *E.g.*, *Acts and Joint Resolutions Passed by the Legislature of South Carolina*, NEWBERRY HERALD, Apr. 20, 1870, https://chroniclingamerica.loc.gov/lccn/sn84026909/1870-04-20/ed-1/seq-1; *Editorial Inklings: Concealed Weapons*, YORKVILLE ENQUIRER, Apr. 28, 1870, https://chroniclingamerica.loc.gov/lccn/sn84026925/1870-04-28/ed-1/seq-2.

Contrast these results with searches of the same databases for the phrase "carrying concealed weapons." In a search of newspapers between 1800 and 1900, the Library of Congress database returns 24,531 results, including reports of more arrests than I can count. The *Newspapers.com* database returns 104,474 matches for the phrase.

What explains this stark contrast? The rise of statutory criminal law. In the nineteenth century, states gradually shifted from having primarily common law crimes to having primarily written criminal codes.[172] As they did, states cracked down against weapon carrying by statutorily prohibiting the carrying of concealed weapons. They did not use the common law offense of going armed to the terror of the people.[173] And they did not rely on surety laws, which lacked a criminal penalty, did not actually ban public gun carry, and required the complainant to plead that he had reasonable cause to fear personal injury or a breach of the peace.

The passage of statutory restrictions against concealed weapons is precisely what plays out in the Massachusetts Model states. Maine, Michigan, Minnesota, Oregon, Pennsylvania, Virginia, West Virginia, Wisconsin, and the City of Washington all had laws premised on the Massachusetts Model.[174] In addition, Delaware passed a law in 1852 allowing justices of the peace to authorize arrests for going armed to the terror of the people.[175] Yet these laws were all supplemented (and supplanted) with statutory crimes. Proceeding chronologically, Virginia restricted the carrying of concealed weapons in 1838,[176] Pennsylvania in 1850,[177] the City of Washington in 1858,[178] Wisconsin in

---

[172] *See generally* Carissa Byrne Hessick, *The Myth of Common Law Crimes*, 105 VA. L. REV. 965, 979–91 (2019).

[173] As with any generality, one can find rare counterexamples. *See, e.g.*, State v. Bentley, 74 Tenn. 205, 206 (1880) (prosecution under a Tennessee statute prohibiting "publicly rid[ing] . . . armed to the terror of the people" and "privately carry[ing] . . . any dangerous weapon, to the fear or terror of any person.").

[174] Of Proceedings to Prevent and Detect the Commission of Crimes, ch. 141, § 16, *in* THE REVISED CODE OF THE DISTRICT OF COLUMBIA 570 (Washington, A.O.P. Nicholson 1857); Ruben & Cornell, *supra* note 11, at 132 & n.61 (collecting other statutes).

[175] 19 Del. Laws 733 (1852); *see The Right*, *supra* note 122, at 1722.

[176] An Act to Prevent the Carrying of Concealed Weapons, ch. 101, 1838 Va. Acts 76.

[177] Act of May 3, 1850, § 14, *in* A DIGEST OF THE LAWS OF PENNSYLVANIA 150, 150 (Philadelphia, Kay & Brother ed., 1857). The prohibition went statewide in 1875. Act of Mar. 18, 1875, Pub. L. No. 38, § 1. The 1850 Act was enforced. *See Matters in the Courts*, PHILADELPHIA INQUIRER, Dec. 10, 1872, at 7 (compiling arrest statistics for carrying concealed weapons in Philadelphia in 1871 and 1872). Conversely, people were acquitted and discharged when they carried weapons openly. *See* THE EVENING J., Dec. 15, 1899, at 2 ("His deadly weapon was not concealed and the law does not prohibit lunatics from carrying unconcealed weapons.").

[178] Act of Nov. 18, 1858, *in* GENERAL LAWS OF THE CORPORATION OF THE CITY OF WASHINGTON 114 (Robert A. Waters ed., 1860). The city first passed a law banning all public carry in 1857, Act of Nov. 4, 1857, *in* GENERAL LAWS OF THE CORPORATION OF THE CITY OF WASHINGTON 75 (Washington, Robert A. Waters ed., 1860), but modified it only to apply to concealed weapons in 1858, Act of Nov. 18, 1858, *in* GENERAL LAWS OF THE CORPORATION OF THE CITY OF WASHINGTON, *supra*, at 114. The modification occurred because of concerns that the 1857 ordinance was overbroad

1872,[179] Delaware in 1881,[180] Oregon in 1885,[181] Michigan in 1887,[182] Maine in 1917,[183] and Minnesota in 1917.[184] These laws only prohibited or restricted the carrying of concealed weapons. None of them prohibited carrying firearms openly for self-defense or other lawful purposes. Only West Virginia, in 1882, generally prohibited the carrying of handguns and other concealable weapons.[185]

And even in states like Minnesota, which passed concealed weapons restrictions fairly late, surety laws seemingly played no role in regulating the peaceful carrying of firearms. With no state criminal law governing public carry in the nineteenth century, Minnesota cities and towns filled the void through local criminal ordinances. St. Paul, for example, passed an ordinance in 1882 prohibiting concealed weapons modeled on the "antebellum Southern" approach.[186] Weapon carriers were prosecuted under these local ordinances.[187]

So not only did the Massachusetts Model not result in a settlement of the constitutional question, the other states adopting Massachusetts's surety law mostly shifted to the antebellum South's approach.[188] The truth is that the antebellum South's approach to public carry was not permissive at all. As Ruben and Cornell recognize, the antebellum South was mired in violence.[189] Laws

and would not stand up in court. *See Concealed Weapons*, EVENING STAR, Nov. 11, 1858, at 3. The District did not resume a general ban on public carry until 1942.

[179] An Act to Prohibit and Prevent the Carrying of Concealed Weapons, ch. 7, § 1, 1872 Wis. Sess. Law 17, 17.
[180] An Act Providing for the Punishment of Persons Carrying Concealed Deadly Weapons, Apr. 8, 1881, 16 Laws of Delaware ch. 548, at 987.
[181] An Act to Prevent Persons from Carrying Concealed Weapons, Feb. 18, 1885, Ore. 13th Legis. Assembly (General Law), *in* THE CODES AND GENERAL LAWS OF OREGON (San Francisco, Bancroft-Whitney Co. ed., 1887). In 1880, Portland was given the authority "[t]o regulate and prohibit the carrying of deadly weapons in a concealed manner." Ore. 11th Legis. Assembly (Special Laws) 96, 100, § 38, ¶ 22; Ore. 12th Legis. Assembly (Special Laws) 149, 152, at § 37, ¶ 20.
[182] An Act to Prevent the Carrying of Concealed Weapons, and to Provide Punishment Therefor, ch. 317, § 9113a, *in* 3 THE GENERAL STATUTES OF THE STATE OF MICHIGAN 3800, 3800 (Chicago, Callaghan & Co. ed., 1890).
[183] An Act to Prohibit the Carrying of Dangerous or Deadly Weapons Without a License, ch. 217, § 1, 1917 Me. Laws 216, 216 (prohibiting either the threatening display or the concealed carrying of weapons without a license).
[184] An Act to Amend Section 8770, General Statutes, 1913, Relating to the Manufacture, Sale, and Possession of Dangerous Weapons, ch. 243, 1917 Minn. Laws 354 (prohibiting carrying a weapon with unlawful intent, and made it "presumptive evidence" of unlawful intent that the weapon was carried concealed).
[185] An Act Amending and Re-Enacting Section Seven of Chapter One Hundred and Forty-Eight of the Code of West Virginia, and Adding Additional Sections thereto for the Punishment of Unlawful Combinations and Conspiracies to Injure Persons or Property, ch. 135, § 7, 1882 W. VA. ACTS 421, 421–22.
[186] Ord. No. 265 (Jan. 17, 1882, § 1) ("It shall be unlawful for any person, within the limits of the City of St. Paul, to carry or wear under his clothes, or concealed about his person, any pistol or pistols, dirk, dagger . . . or any other dangerous or deadly weapon.").
[187] *Made a Good Capture*, STAR TRIBUNE, May 12, 1898, at 10; *Lynchers Upheld*, STAR TRIBUNE, May 6, 1891, at 1.
[188] Ruben & Cornell, *supra* note 11, at 124.
[189] *Id.* at 125–26.

against the carrying of concealed weapons were designed to control this violence.[190] By prohibiting only the carrying of weapons in a concealed manner, these legislatures tried to fashion a solution that would "prevent the carrying of dangerous weapons—to stamp out a practice that has been and is fruitful of bloodshed, misery, and death—and yet so to prohibit the carrying as not to infringe the constitutional right to keep and bear arms."[191] For legislators who wanted to prohibit all public carry, leaving individuals free to carry arms openly was not a perfect solution. But it was a solution that recognized some constitutional limits imposed by the right to bear arms. And it was a solution that the country ultimately accepted, from Maine to California, from the St. Paul City Council to Congress. By the end of the nineteenth century, the surety laws were dead as a means of regulating public carry for lawful purposes, and there are serious doubts about whether they ever had life.

V. Conclusion

In Second Amendment litigation, the use of nineteenth-century legislative precedent has become the Wild West. Scholars on both sides sling their best examples without any theorizing about how legislative precedent fits with constitutional interpretation. Judges, too, have fallen into this trap. A search of Westlaw for the text of the surety statutes produces seven recorded decisions, only five of which discuss gun carrying.[192] All five involve challenges, during the past ten years, to public gun carry in which judges have sought to rely on the surety laws as precedent.[193]

When it comes to applying history, judges and scholars have two obligations. The first is to get the history right. Some judges, for example, have overread the surety statutes, contending based on them that "most states outside of the South in the mid-nineteenth century prohibited in most instances the carrying of firearms in public, whether carried concealed or openly."[194] As I have shown in

---

[190] See CRAMER, supra note 11, at 17.
[191] State v. Bias, 37 La. Ann. 259, 260 (1885).
[192] Two decisions from Pennsylvania cite the text but do not discuss it. Both cases involved a different part of the law, which allowed those who were threatened with interpersonal violence to seek sureties. Commonwealth v. Cushard, 132 A.2d 366, 367–68 (Pa. Super. Ct. 1957) (complaint resulting from a threat of "bodily harm"); Commonwealth v. Miller, 305 A.2d 346, 347–48 (Pa. 1973) (complaint resulting from a husband who threatened in his wife with a gun in their own home; the question was whether the defendant was entitled to a trial by jury in a surety case).
[193] Young v. Hawaii, 992 F.3d 765, 819–20 (9th Cir. 2021) (en banc); Norman v. State, 215 So. 3d 18, 30 n.12 (Fla. 2017); Grace v. District of Columbia, 187 F. Supp. 3d 124, 140–41 (D.D.C. 2016); Wrenn v. District of Columbia, 864 F.3d 650, 661 (D.C. Cir. 2017); State v. Christian, 274 P.3d 262, 279–80 (Or. Ct. App. 2012) (Edmonds, S.J., dissenting).
[194] Norman, 215 So. 3d at 30 n.12.

sections II–IV, this view of the surety statutes is mistaken. False premises result in unsound arguments.

The second is to place the history in its proper *legal* context. The proponents of the Massachusetts Model are correct that some states passed surety statutes in the nineteenth century. But this tells us nothing about what legal effect their existence should have on interpreting the right to bear arms. That is a question of constitutional law.

In this chapter, I have tried to apply a more robust framework for examining nineteenth-century practice. I have argued that the critical interpretive question is whether some form of liquidation has occurred. Madisonian constitutional liquidation using legislative precedent requires that legislation be the result of serious deliberation, that results in a regular practice, which has met the approval of the public and those holding dissenting views. The Massachusetts Model surety laws fail all three parts of this test, and judges should not be relying on them when they determine the scope of the right to carry arms.

14

Prohibitions on Private Armies in Seven State Constitutions

Darrell A.H. Miller

I. Introduction

In a period of just over twenty years, seven states constitutionalized their opposition to the employment or deployment of private armies by corporations. Largely responding to the violent suppression of labor organizations by privately employed armed groups like the Pinkerton National Detective Agency and its ilk, the states of Arizona, Idaho, Kentucky, Montana, Utah, Washington, and Wyoming all passed amendments aimed at curtailing the corporate practice of employing private bodies of armed men to supply security or suppress labor unrest. These constitutional enactments are more than an interesting anecdote in American labor history; they represent an important public statement on the nature of public and private armed violence, law enforcement, and maintenance of the public peace in the American republic.

II. Management and Labor Conflict, the Pinkertons, and "Pinkertonism"

The Gilded Age[1]—a period roughly from the end of Reconstruction in the 1870s to the first decade of the twentieth century—was marked by two interrelated economic forces: rapid industrialization and the rise of wage labor. Railroads, steel, mining, and associated businesses, captained by industrial magnates like Jay Gould, Cornelius Vanderbilt, Andrew Carnegie, and their peers, transformed the physical and economic landscape of the United States. Simultaneously, wage labor replaced a manufacturing sector formerly composed of artisans, craftsmen,

---

[1] The term comes from the title of an 1873 book by Mark Twain and Charles Dudley Warner, *The Gilded Age: A Tale of Today*. It has come to describe an age characterized by apparent opulence masking deep political, economic, and social strife below the surface.

Darrell A.H. Miller, *Prohibitions on Private Armies in Seven State Constitutions*
In: *New Histories of Gun Rights and Regulation*. Edited by: Joseph Blocher, Jacob D. Charles, and Darrell A.H. Miller,
Oxford University Press. © Oxford University Press 2023. DOI: 10.1093/oso/9780197748473.003.0014

and the self-employed.[2] By 1870, wage labor had become the dominant economic model in all employment areas outside of farming.[3]

The early years of labor organization in the United States shared little resemblance to the politically savvy, issue-focused, federally regulated unions of the New Deal era and afterward. Some unions, like the Knights of Labor, took on the trappings of masonic organizations (or, less wholesomely, racist secret societies).[4] Others, like the Workingmen's Benevolent Association, mimicked Gilded Age charitable groups.[5] Still others were ethno-anarchist organizations: the shadowy Molly Maguires, for example, were known for their violent disruption of mining operations in the coal country of Pennsylvania.[6] Unions of almost every stripe, what the laborers called "cooperations for mutual protection," were often viewed by free labor idealists and industrialists with suspicion or outright hostility.[7]

As capital consolidated power and leveraged its ability to coordinate action, it went about contracting for or employing its own police forces to investigate and disrupt labor organizations, break strikes, and act as armed guards for industrial interests.[8] Although there were a number of these kinds of organizations, including the Coal and Iron Police in Pennsylvania[9] and the Merchant Police in Chicago,[10] the name that eventually came to represent all industry-controlled private militias was the Pinkerton National Detective Agency.

Allan Pinkerton was a Scottish immigrant from Glasgow, the son of a constable.[11] Born in 1819, Pinkerton grew up in the slums of the Gorbals district, an area of Glasgow that had once been a leper colony.[12] In his youth, Pinkerton was deeply involved in Chartism—the reformist working-class politics of Victorian Britain. Amidst a crackdown on Chartists by the ruling class, in 1842 Pinkerton

---

[2] RICHARD WHITE, THE REPUBLIC FOR WHICH IT STANDS: THE UNITED STATES DURING RECONSTRUCTION AND THE GILDED AGE, 1865–1896, at 237 (2017).

[3] Id.

[4] Id. at 519; see also S. PAUL O'HARA, INVENTING THE PINKERTONS: OR, SPIES, SLEUTHS, MERCENARIES, AND THUGS 82 (2016). The history of the early labor movement is marred by episodes of ethnic and racial discrimination and terrorism. Some members of the Knights of Labor, for instance, were responsible for a massacre of Chinese laborers in Wyoming. See Joan Fitzpatrick & William McKay Bennett, A Lion in the Path? The Influence of International Law on the Immigration Policy of the United States, 70 WASH. L. REV. 589, 595 (1995) ("The most violent anti-Chinese agitation was carried out by working class white men, sometimes with the encouragement of certain labor leaders.").

[5] WHITE, supra note 2, at 311.

[6] Id. at 312–13.

[7] Id. at 241–42.

[8] O'HARA, supra note 4, at 72–73.

[9] Id. at 73.

[10] Jonathan Obert, The Coevolution of Public and Private Security in Nineteenth-Century Chicago, 43 LAW & SOC. INQUIRY 827, 849 (2018).

[11] David A. Sklansky, The Private Police, 46 UCLA L. REV. 1165, 1212 (1999).

[12] O'HARA, supra note 4, at 15.

fled the country with his wife, eventually settling in a Scottish enclave northwest of Chicago, Illinois, called Dundee.[13]

A twist of fate turned Pinkerton, the modest Dundee cooper, into the name of private security. While looking for wood for his cooperage on the Fox River, Pinkerton stumbled upon a camp of counterfeiters. Upon this discovery, he reported the camp to local law enforcement and returned to help arrest them. Leveraging his notoriety, Pinkerton hired himself out to local merchants to ferret out other criminals.[14] He built his part-time detective work into a profitable business: first by providing crime investigation services and then gradually expanding into "preventive patrols"—essentially private policemen.[15] After Allan Pinkerton died in 1884, his sons Robert and William took control of the company and rapidly expanded the preventative patrol service.[16]

Although the Pinkertons' first few decades were marked by success and public approbation (due in no small part to the company's own promotional acumen); a series of events in the latter part of the nineteenth century began to tarnish the Pinkerton brand and raise questions about the entire notion of private industry employing its own military apparatus.

Labor turmoil among miners in the Hocking Valley of Ohio was one such event. Tensions in the valley were already on the boil in 1883 after the mine owners consolidated their operations into the Columbus and Hocking Coal and Iron Company—what detractors called "the Syndicate"—and centralized labor relations.[17] Unilateral wage cuts sparked a coal strike beginning in 1884 that would last a year.[18] The company hired a hundred armed Pinkerton guards to protect strikebreakers and protect the mines, but it wasn't until the Syndicate began evicting striking miners from Syndicate housing in the summer of 1884 that sustained violence broke out.[19] In November, an attack by miners on a strikebreaker camp was repulsed by Pinkerton guards, injuring some of the striking miners.[20] By 1885, the miners had capitulated and the strike was over; but unease about the role of private armed men in the employ of industrialists was growing.[21]

---

[13] *Id.* at 15.
[14] *Id.* at 16.
[15] *Id.* at 72.
[16] *Id.* at 72.
[17] George B. Cotkin, *Strikebreakers, Evictions and Violence: Industrial Conflict in the Hocking Valley, 1884–1885*, 87 Ohio Hist. J. 140, 141 (1978).
[18] *Id.* at 142.
[19] *Id.* at 143, 146.
[20] John W. Lozier, The Hocking Valley Coal Miners' Strike 1884–1885, at 79 (1963) (M.A. thesis, the Ohio State University).
[21] O'Hara, *supra* note 4, at 76.

In the Pacific Northwest, rail, mining, and associated industries propelled rapid economic expansion, and with it, labor and management conflict.[22] The villages scattered through the Cascades and down around Puget Sound buzzed with rumor and threat.[23] A miners' strike near the town of Roslyn, Washington, prompted the Northern Pacific Railroad to hire a Pinkerton competitor called Thiel's Detective Service to escort strikebreakers to the mines. The Thiel's manager, himself a former Pinkerton, arrived in Roslyn with fifty mostly African American strikebreakers from Chicago and fifty armed men. Allegedly posing as U.S. deputy marshals, the guards, once on site, set up what amounted to a military redoubt complete with pistols, Winchester rifles, and barbed wire.[24]

Events were equally tense across the Cascades in a spot just a few miles outside of Seattle, called Newcastle. There, the Oregon Improvement Company (OIC) employed two hundred fifty workers in one of the largest mining concerns in the region.[25] In an atmosphere of confusion, with more than one union claiming to represent the interests of the miners and with unclear divisions between public and private authority, a detachment of private guards from Thiel's Detective Service descended upon Newcastle from Portland at the request of OIC, ostensibly to protect the U.S. mail. While government officials debated whether and by what authority these private agents had been deputized, citizens of the towns filed complaints with the territorial governor and the president of the United States that the private detectives were harassing residents.[26]

By the time the Washington territory was moving toward statehood in 1889, an unsettling pattern of labor threatening violence and capital hiring private troops had emerged.[27] But so had a conviction, voiced by territorial governor Eugene Semple that private armies were "a serious menace" and little more than "organized bodies of ruffians, offering for hire to become instruments of the rich and strong for the oppression of the poor and weak."[28] Given the general turmoil and flagging reputation of the Pinkertons throughout the latter part of the nineteenth century; it seems overdetermined that the violence surrounding

---

[22] Alan A. Hynding, *The Coal Miners of Washington Territory: Labor Troubles in 1888–89*, 12 ARIZ. & WEST 221, 221 (1970).
[23] *Id.*
[24] *Id.* at 223; Knute Berger, *Why Washington State's Constitution Bans Armed Militias*, CROSSCUT, Jan. 21, 2021, https://crosscut.com/politics/2021/01/why-washington-states-constitution-bans-armed-militias. Again, the racial history of this period is complicated, as the private guards were brought into the state under the auspices of a successful African American businessman named James Shepperson. *Id.*
[25] Hynding, *supra* note 22, at 228.
[26] *Id.* at 233.
[27] *Id.* at 234–35.
[28] *Id.* at 227 (quoting REP. OF THE GOVERNOR OF THE WASH. TERRITORY TO THE SEC'Y OF THE INTERIOR 49 (1889).

the infamous Homestead Massacre of 1892 in Homestead, Pennsylvania, would render the Pinkerton name synonymous with corporate militarism.

Andrew Carnegie was one of the richest men in the United States in 1888.[29] Like Pinkerton, he started off as a poor Scottish immigrant, working inauspicious jobs as a bobbin boy in a cotton mill[30] and later as a telegraph operator.[31] But through a combination of savvy, connections, and fortune, Carnegie slowly began to amass the steel empire in Pennsylvania that would underwrite his later transition into a Gilded Age patron of libraries and the arts.[32] By the 1890s, Carnegie was delegating much of his day-to-day management of the steel business to close associates. One of these associates was Henry Clay Frick, a dour, charmless, implacable foe of organized labor.[33]

Frick was the face of Carnegie Steel as labor conditions began to deteriorate in the Homestead steel mills, on the south bank of the Monongahela River, seven miles from Pittsburgh. A gargantuan operation, employing close to four thousand workers by 1892, the minority of skilled workers of Homestead were largely represented by the Amalgamated Association of Iron and Steel Workers. Successive efforts by Carnegie and Frick to break the union had failed, and in 1892, when negotiations for a new contract were underway, "[e]veryone knew a fight was coming."[34]

In anticipation, by late spring Frick had constructed a literal fort around the steel works, complete with twelve-foot fencing, electrified wires, a hot water cannon, and murder holes for rifles.[35] When Frick broke off talks on June 25, 3,000 of the 3,800 workers voted to strike. Frick responded on June 28 by locking out the workers and beginning clandestine negotiations with the Pinkertons to provide troops and reopen the mills with replacement workers.[36]

Over three hundred armed Pinkertons loaded onto barges and arrived at the Homestead Mill on the morning of July 6, but the townspeople and union were watching and confronted them with their own arms at the Monongahela's edge. Tense words between the two sides abruptly broke into the crack of gunfire. One worker, then another fell, commencing a battle between the crowd and the Pinkertons that lasted for fourteen hours.[37] Accounts differed as to who began firing; but when the battle was over that evening, nine members of the crowd and three Pinkertons lay dead, with many more injured.[38]

---

[29] WHITE, *supra* note 2, at 657.
[30] DAVID NASAW, ANDREW CARNEGIE 34 (2007).
[31] WHITE, *supra* note 2, at 657.
[32] *Id.* at 661.
[33] *Id.*
[34] *Id.* at 665.
[35] O'HARA, *supra* note 4, at 93; WHITE, *supra* note 2, at 665.
[36] *id.*
[37] *Id.* at 666.
[38] *Id.*

Media coverage of the Pinkertons, which had been romantic to positive during Allan Pinkerton's life, turned sour and skeptical after Homestead.[39] The spectacle of gun battles between a regiment of private troops and townspeople "reinforced the views of many Americans, including many who were more sympathetic to capital than to labor, that order should be kept by lawfully constituted authorities, not by 'private armies.'"[40] Responding to public pressure, both houses of Congress held a series of hearings on the Pinkerton National Detective Agency and the entire private detective business.[41]

Congressional reports criticized not only the Pinkertons but also the workers' resort to private arms: "[T]he employment of armed bodies of men for private purposes, either by employers or employees, is to be deprecated and should not be resorted to." The reason was that "[s]uch use of private armed men is an assumption of the State's authority by private citizens. If the State is incapable of protecting its citizens in their rights of person and property, then anarchy is the result . . ."[42] Although the Gilded Age Congress left the resolution of Pinkertonism to the states, it passed the Anti-Pinkerton Act of 1893 prohibiting the federal government and the District of Columbia from hiring any "employee of the Pinkerton Detective Agency, or similar agency."[43]

After nearly two decades of active participation in labor disputes,[44] the name Pinkerton had come to mean far more than the Scottish cooper's family business: "It had become a kind of shorthand for the general violence and tension that marked the struggle over labor and capital in the Gilded Age."[45]

III. Prohibitions on Employment or Deployment of Private Armies

In response to concerns about Pinkertons and Pinkertonism between 1889 and 1910, a number of states, mostly in the West, enacted constitutional amendments curtailing the use of private armies—either by stating that the right to keep and bear arms did not cover them or by prohibiting companies of men from entering the state without the express invitation of government authority.

---

[39] O'Hara, *supra* note 4, at 96.
[40] Sklansky, *supra* note 11, at 1215.
[41] *Id.*
[42] S. Rep. No. 52-1280, at XV (1893).
[43] Sklansky, *supra* note 11, at 1215 (quoting An Act of Mar. 3, 1893, ch. 208, 27 Stat. 572, 591).
[44] O'Hara, *supra* note 4, at 76.
[45] *Id.* at 82.

A. Washington and Arizona

Washington and Arizona had the most direct language concerning private armies and situated those statements alongside their provisions on the right to keep and bear arms. With only modest differences in punctuation, both states provided: "The right of the individual citizen to bear arms in defense of himself or the state shall not be impaired, but nothing in this section shall be construed as authorizing individuals or corporations to organize, maintain, or employ an armed body of men."[46]

The Washington provision resulted directly from concern with perceived Pinkerton excesses, especially during labor unrest in Roslyn and Newcastle in 1888 and 1889.[47] It was introduced by John Kinnear, a delegate to the convention. As a rough contemporary of the state constitutional convention noted in his history:

> Probably no original clause introduced for the constitution is of more importance and more in accord with strict democratic principles than that introduced by Mr. Kinnear, prohibiting the importation of armed bodies of men into the state for the purpose of keeping order. About the time of the meeting of the convention a business had sprung up in the country of peculiar interest to great corporations. Through the preceding period of strikes and labor agitations and incident rioting, these corporations had sought protection by the employment of armed bodies of men, which afterward became organized and known as Pinkerton detectives. These men, in large and small numbers, were hired out to the corporations to preserve order on their premises and protect their property. They operated for several years without legislative restrictions and eventually became a fruitful source of contention with organized labor, often being a direct cause of rioting and bloodshed. The great objection to these organizations was that they were acting as a body of troops with no responsible head save the person by whom they were organized, and it was generally believed that if troops must be employed, they should consist of state militia or regular soldiers with responsible leaders. These Pinkerton men were hired out to the highest bidder, and the viciousness of this system was too plain for argument. *It was shown that the state, and the state alone, should protect its citizens in life and property in the time of disturbance and riot, and that under no consideration should a person or corporation be permitted to call in an armed body of men, owing responsibility only to those who call them.* The Coeur d'Alene rioting

---

[46] WASH. CONST. art. I, § 24 (1889).
[47] *See* CARLOS ARNALDO SCHWANTES, RADICAL HERITAGE: LABOR, SOCIALISM, AND REFORM IN WASHINGTON AND BRITISH COLUMBIA, 1885–1917, at 30–32 (1979) (discussing labor unrest at these sites and the resulting constitutional provision).

was cited as an incident of their employment and consequent lawlessness that followed. Mr. Kinnear's resolution was favorably acted upon and became a part of the constitution.[48]

Washington enacted a prohibition on such armed bodies in its criminal law, which was upheld against a state constitutional challenge in 1907.[49]

Arizona's original 1891 charter language concerning the right to keep and bear arms did not include the language about corporations. However, concern about Pinkertonism was clearly on the minds of the progressive wing of the territorial government.[50] Progressive leader George W.P. Hunt, who would eventually become president of the Arizona constitution-drafting convention and the first governor of the state, was an ardent champion of labor and fierce opponent of corporatocracy. The Pullman Strike of 1894 had galvanized his attention, and his pro-labor, anti-corporation platform had given him a substantial working-class following.[51]

In 1895, while a territorial representative, Hunt had introduced a bill "declaring it unlawful to organize, maintain, or employ an armed body of men in the Territory of Arizona, and providing punishment therefor." But his initial proposal went nowhere.[52] However, after the ascension of the labor-friendly faction to Arizona's constitutional convention of 1910,[53] with Hunt at its helm, Arizona adopted the constitutional language concerning private armies from the Washington Constitution nearly verbatim.

B. Montana, Idaho, Wyoming, Kentucky, and Utah

Montana, Idaho, Wyoming, and Kentucky took a slightly different approach, although motivated by similar concerns. They articulated their prohibition as respecting the "importation" or "bringing" of armed men into the state. These four states form what Robert Natelson has called the "four fraternal quadruplets" that adopted similar provisions just a few years from one another in the late nineteenth century.[54]

---

[48] Lebbeus Knapp, *The Origin of the Constitution of the State of Washington*, 4 WASH. HIST. Q. 227, 267 (1913) (emphasis added).
[49] *See* State v. Gohl, 90 P. 259 (1907) (holding that the act barring private armies did not violate the state constitutional provision regarding the right to bear arms).
[50] *See* DAVID R. BERMAN, POLITICS, LABOR, AND THE WAR ON BIG BUSINESS: THE PATH OF REFORM IN ARIZONA, 1890–1920, at 43, 54 (2012).
[51] DAVID R. BERMAN, GEORGE HUNT: ARIZONA'S CRUSADING SEVEN-TERM GOVERNOR 26 (2015).
[52] JOURNALS OF THE EIGHTEENTH LEGISLATIVE ASSEMBLY OF THE TERRITORY OF ARIZONA 332 (1895); BERMAN, *supra* note 51, at 26.
[53] *See* John D. Leshy, *The Making of the Arizona Constitution*, 20 ARIZ. ST. L.J. 1, 47 (1988).
[54] Robert G. Natelson, *"No Armed Bodies of Men"—Montanans' Forgotten Constitutional Right (with Some Passing Notes on Recent Environmental Cases)*, 63 MONT. L. REV. 1, 8 (2002).

Montana and Idaho both adopted their first constitutions in 1889. Along with North Dakota, South Dakota, Washington, and Wyoming, they form what one author called the "class of 1889."[55] This was "the largest group of states to adopt their first constitutions in a single year since 1776."[56] Montana's provision reads: "No armed person or persons or armed body of men shall be brought into this state for the preservation of the peace, or the suppression of domestic violence, except upon the application of the legislature, or of the governor when the legislature cannot be convened."[57]

William Field introduced the section[58] and referred directly to the "troubles arising in different states by armed bodies being kept by corporations and companies for the preservation of the peace."[59] Field raised the specter of railroads, coal, and iron interests employing their own private policemen to "keep the peace, and keep the working men and others in servitude."[60] He continued, "I do not believe, nor I shall not believe, that any corporation or person has the right or power to employ armed bodies of men to shoot down people who assemble and congregate for the purposes of freedom."[61]

In Idaho, the specific section was not codified along with labor but with the militia.[62] Article XIV's first five sections were approved without much discussion on the fourteenth day of the convention.[63] Article XIV regarding Militia and Military Affairs was brought back up for discussion on July 30.[64] Henry Armstrong, a delegate from Logan County, proposed adding what became Section 6.[65] Delegate George Ainslie quickly supported this amendment, stating: "I move the adoption of that amendment, and I believe in it. We have had enough of Pinkerton's private squads of men ranging through the west. I see Montana has adopted the same thing, and I think it is a good idea."[66] Notwithstanding, it appears Pinkertons were hired from out of state to Montana to investigate cattle rustling, even after enactment of this provision.[67]

---

[55] G. Alan Tarr, *The Montana Constitution: A National Perspective*, 64 MONT. L. REV. 1, 2 (2003).
[56] *Id.*
[57] MONT. CONST. art. III, § 31 (1889), currently codified at MONT. CONST. art. II, § 33.
[58] PROCEEDINGS AND DEBATES OF THE CONSTITUTIONAL CONVENTION: HELD IN THE CITY OF HELENA, MONTANA, JULY 4TH, 1889, AUGUST 17TH, 1889, at 129 (1921).
[59] *Id.*
[60] *Id.*
[61] *Id.*
[62] IDAHO CONST. art. XIV, § 6.
[63] 1 PROCEEDINGS AND DEBATES OF THE CONSTITUTIONAL CONVENTION OF IDAHO OF 1889, at 397–400 (I.W. Hart ed., 1912); *see also* DENNIS C. COLSON, IDAHO'S CONSTITUTION: THE TIE THAT BINDS 81 (1991) (discussing the "quick" passage of the first five sections of Article XIV).
[64] 2 PROCEEDINGS AND DEBATES OF THE CONSTITUTIONAL CONVENTION OF IDAHO OF 1889, at 1410 (I.W. Hart ed., 1912).
[65] *Id.* at 1412.
[66] *Id.* at 1413.
[67] Natelson, *supra* note 54, at 11.

On October 7, 1890, Kentucky constitutional delegate Robert Rodes read out the new section.[68] He then made the following comments before it was passed:

> We have had evidence that there is a germ springing up in this country which may grow into something terrible unless obviated in advance. Some State Constitutions recently have made clauses equivalent to this, and I imagine that it is nothing but right. We have the right to protect our liberties, and no less our boundaries. If the Governor cannot, and the Legislature cannot be assembled in either case, when insurrection or rebellion shall arise, we can call upon the President for aid; but do not let these irresponsible armed organizations enter our territories, unless invited according to law. I do not mention any by name; it would be useless to call any men by name, for they will be Protean in shape and name hereafter often enough if we open the door wide enough for them. But I say close it, and let it be known that these armed bodies shall not be called upon to interfere in case of violence in our State, unless the Governor, at the head of the Executive Department, shall demand it or the Legislature ask it.[69]

Delegate W.R. Ramsey apparently had no compunction about identifying the Pinkertons by name in the following spring:

> You talk about it being a free contract; I deny it. The miners are compelled to submit, or else they know, when they look at their wives and little ones, they will expose them to starvation and misery. Just as it was in Ohio in the Hocking Valley. Was that a free contract? Those contracts, which the miners made and entered into, were signed by the light of the gunpowder of the Pinkerton detectives.[70]

Delegate William H. Miller was equally eager to call out this provision as against Pinkertons. On March 19, 1891, he referred to

> the danger which was threatening this country from the great aggregation of wealth manifested by the disposition of corporations to arm themselves, we passed a section which is one of the justest that we have incorporated in the Constitution.... It is responsive to the disposition of these great corporations to arm themselves in defiance of the law, and to say, when these employees of theirs assert their manhood and undertake to protect themselves, we will not

---

[68] 1 OFFICIAL REPORT OF THE PROCEEDINGS AND DEBATES IN THE CONVENTION ASSEMBLED AT FRANKFORT, ON THE EIGHTH DAY OF SEPTEMBER, 1890, TO ADOPT, AMEND, OR CHANGE THE CONSTITUTION OF THE STATE OF KENTUCKY 442 (1891).

[69] Id.

[70] 4 OFFICIAL REPORT OF THE PROCEEDINGS AND DEBATES IN THE CONVENTION ASSEMBLED AT FRANKFORT, ON THE EIGHTH DAY OF SEPTEMBER, 1890, TO ADOPT, AMEND, OR CHANGE THE CONSTITUTION OF THE STATE OF KENTUCKY 4809 (1891).

appeal to law, but we will appeal to such organizations of armed desperados as the Pinkerton Detective Agency and others of a like character.[71]

Wyoming's amendment specifically called out "detective agenc[ies]" in its prohibitions on importing men to deal with social disorder. When confronted as to whether the Wyoming provision prohibited someone from protecting their property until law enforcement could arrive, an advocate and delegate Elliott Morgan rose and said: "I think I understand that this is intended to prevent the bringing in of Pinkerton detectives as an armed force, one of the greatest outrages ever perpetrated upon any people."[72] He went on: "That is what this section is intended to prevent; that is that armed men shall be brought in from the slums of Chicago, and that they shall be clothed with authority of law to exercise the duties of United States deputy marshals. I should like to have this made even stronger, so that these outrages can be prevented by constitutional enactment."[73]

In Utah, the state passed an 1895 provision that "[n]o corporation or association shall bring any armed person or bodies of men into this State for the preservation of the peace, or the suppression of domestic trouble without authority of law." Concern with Pinkertonism was apparent from the remarks of William James: "It is to avoid such things as a year ago of the Pinkertons. That I guess will explain it so as to save time. Just say the Pinkertons."

Samuel Thurman expressed the idea that if the state was not capable of meeting basic obligations of the social compact to protect the lives and property of its citizens itself; it had no claim to be a state. "[T]he committee thought that no private company or individual had a right to import an armed body of men into the State to protect the State or the people of the State against domestic violence. We think we can do that ourselves. . . . We think the State is able to do that. If not, we have no business organizing as a State."[74]

IV. LEGAL AND CONSTITUTIONAL IMPLICATIONS

A number of opponents to Pinkertonism and to corporate power in general framed their opposition in a constitutional vernacular. They believed it violated basic republican commitments and amounted to a form of despotism to allow huge, private, unaccountable corporate interests to maintain and deploy such forces. As Terrence Powderly of the Knights of Labor told the press: "I am positive

---

[71] *Id.* at 4892–93.
[72] WYOMING JOURNAL AND DEBATES OF THE CONSTITUTIONAL CONVENTION OF THE STATE OF WYOMING. BEGUN AT THE CITY OF CHEYENNE ON SEPTEMBER 2, 1889, AND CONCLUDED SEPTEMBER 30, 1889, at 402 (1893).
[73] *Id.*
[74] STATE OF UTAH CONSTITUTIONAL CONVENTION, 54TH DAY (1895), https://le.utah.gov/documents/conconv/54.htm.

that the introduction of the Pinkerton detective as an agent in the settlement of disputes is entirely foreign to the letter and spirit of the Constitution of our common country."[75] Steelworkers at Homestead publicly declared that corporate power threatened to "eviscerate our national constitution and our common law."[76] Nothing less than the nature of a republican form of government was at stake.[77]

Certainly, when the question was armed collective action by labor, the legality of prohibitions on private armed groups was clear. On September 24, 1879, a thirty-one-year-old German radical named Herman Presser, mounted on horseback, led an armed parade of his fellow German socialists through the streets of Chicago. The march violated the recently enacted Illinois militia law, passed just that spring, which prohibited "any body of men whatever, other than the regular organized militia of [Illinois]" from "associat[ing] together as a military company or organization, or to drill or parade with arms in any city or town of [Illinois], without the license of the governor."[78]

Presser defended himself by asserting, among other things, both a right to assemble and a Second Amendment right to keep and bear arms. The Supreme Court of the United States rebuffed the defenses. The Second Amendment was not violated as the militia act "which only forbid bodies of men to associate together as military, organizations, or to drill or parade with arms in cities and towns unless authorized by law," even if one assumed that the states could not deprive a person of the right to keep and bear arms.[79] As far as violating a right to peaceably assemble, the Court was even more hostile to Presser. "Military organization and military drill . . . are subjects especially under the control of the government of every country. They cannot be claimed as a right independent of law."[80] State and federal law regulated martial organizations of every type; they were not matters of individual right. Regulation of armed assemblages, like Presser's, are "necessary to the public peace, safety, and good order. To deny the power would be to deny the right of the state to disperse assemblages organized for sedition and treason, and the right to suppress armed mobs bent on riot and rapine."[81]

---

[75] O'HARA, *supra* note 4, at 78.
[76] Richard Oestreicher, *Urban Working-Class Political Behavior and Theories of American Electoral Politics, 1870–1940*, 74 J. AM. HIST. 1257, 1259 (1988).
[77] *See id.*
[78] Presser v. Illinois, 116 U.S. 252, 262 (1886).
[79] *Id.* at 264–65. The Court was a bit unclear on its reasoning, concluding that the Second Amendment did not apply to the states (this is the era before incorporation); but even if some notion of a right to keep and bear arms applied in the sense of preventing states from disarming the organized militia, "it clear that the sections [of the Illinois militia act] do not have this effect." *Id.* at 265–66.
[80] *Id.* at 267.
[81] *Id.* at 268.

Of course, there were some skeptics. Wilfred M. Peck, a Los Angeles–based lawyer and defender of the railroads, wrote a piece in the *Yale Law Journal* in 1894 suggesting that it was every man's right to defend his property and that the railroads were simply countering union violence with their own defense of property.[82] Despite skeptics like Peck, however, what this history suggests is, although the concerns may have diverged slightly, private aggregations of military power were very much on the minds of policymakers and constitution drafters during the Gilded Age. Whether the threat manifested as a corporate power to form private armies itself, or a power to summon private agents from outside the jurisdiction, these state amendments share two common features: first, a profound distrust of the ability of large corporate interests and intrastate political interests to align in a way conducive to republican government; and second, a strong belief that the power to enforce the law and to keep the peace should be dependant on public authority and the needs of the community and not a matter of private interest or plutocracy.

---

[82] Wilfred M. Peck, *Importation of Armed Men from Other States to Protect Property*, 3 YALE L.J. 24 (1894).

Appendix

ARIZONA

(1912)

Article II—Declaration of Rights. Section 26. Bearing arms. The right of the individual citizen to bear arms in defense of himself or the state shall not be impaired, but nothing in this section shall be construed as authorizing individuals or corporations to organize, maintain, or employ an armed body of men.

IDAHO

(1889)

Article XIV—Militia. Section 6. No armed police force, or detective agency, or armed body of men, shall ever be brought into this state for the suppression of domestic violence except upon the application of the legislature, or the executive, when the legislature can not be convened.

KENTUCKY

(1891)

General Provisions. Section 225. No armed person or bodies of men shall be brought into this State for the preservation of the peace or the suppression of domestic violence, except upon the application of the General Assembly, or of the Governor when the General Assembly may not be in session.

MONTANA

(1889)

Article III. Declaration of Rights. Section 31. No armed person or persons or armed body of men shall be brought into this state for the preservation of the peace, or the suppression of domestic violence, except upon the application of the legislature, or of the governor when the legislature cannot be convened.

UTAH

(1895)

Article 12, Section 16. No corporation or association shall bring any armed person or bodies of men into this State for the preservation of the peace, or the suppression of domestic trouble without authority of law.

WASHINGTON

(1889)

Article I, Section 24. The right of the individual citizen to bear arms in defense of himself, or the state, shall not be impaired, but nothing in this section shall be construed as authorizing individuals or corporations to organize, maintain or employ an armed body of men.

WYOMING

(1889)

Article 19, Section 6. No armed police force, or detective agency, or armed body, or unarmed body of men, shall ever be brought into this state, for the suppression of domestic violence, except upon the application of the legislature, or executive, when the legislature cannot be convened.

Index

For the benefit of digital users, indexed terms that span two pages (e.g., 52–53) may, on occasion, appear on only one of those pages.

Tables are indicated by *t* following the page number

abolitionism
    carrying guns in public and, 215–20
    gun laws generally, 214–15
    incrementalism versus immediatism, 215
    self-defense and, 232
    Snowden case and, 227–30
Adams, John, 64n.62
Adams, John Quincy, 21n.63
African Americans. *See also* race, gun laws and
    enslaved persons (*see* enslaved persons)
    Republican Party and, 153–54
    self-defense and, 151n.11, 151n.12
Agnew, Daniel, 72–73, 73n.87
Ainslie, George, 271
Akerman, Amos T., 160–61
Alabama
    firing guns in public, regulation of, 207n.99
    licensing of guns in, 193
Alaska, carrying guns in public in, 163
Alder, Ken, 11
Amalgamated Association of Iron and Steel Workers, 267
Ames, Fisher, 51n.11
analogical reasoning, 132, 133
Antifa, 112–13
Anti-Pinkerton Act of 1893, 268
Arikara War, 16–17
Arizona
    carrying guns in public in, 163, 247n.108, 247–48n.110
    private militias, prohibition of, 263, 269, 270, 275
Arkansas
    concealed carry laws in, 156–57
    licensing of guns in, 193
    race and gun laws in, 159–60
    Reconstruction, gun laws during, 159–60
    registration of guns in, 173, 180, 180n.78, 182–83, 189
armed travel, prohibition of, 218–19, 220–25, 231

armories, 12–13
Armstrong, Henry, 271
Articles of Confederation, 50–51
Ashley, W.H., 16–18
Atkinson, Henry, 17–18

Balkin, Jack M., 145n.101
Banister, John, 85–87
Barber, Oliver, 103
Barbour, James, 51–52n.13, 55n.27, 57n.36
Barrett, Amy Coney, 131–32
battered women, 126–27
Baude, Will, 244–45, 246
Baum, Dan, 110–11
Baxter, Tara, 127
Bayard, James, 68
Bellesiles, Michael, 23n.81
Bill of Rights, 242–43
Black, James Augustus, 61–62
Blackbeard, 82
Black Codes, 150–51, 154–55, 159, 162
Black Hawk War, 17–19
Black Lives Matter, 97, 99–100, 112–13
Black Panthers, 107
Blackstone, William, 119–20, 121, 122, 135–36, 251, 251n.127
Bliss v. Commonwealth of Kentucky (1822), 11–12
Blocher, Joseph, 5, 28, 45, 107, 186n.123
"Boogaloo" movement, 100
Book of Common Prayer, 29–30, 34–35
Bragg, Thomas, 60–61
brandishing guns
    generally, 4, 97–101, 112–14
    "agency" of guns and, 113–14
    coercive nature of, 108
    "desensitization" of, 100–1
    early American law, in, 103–5
    English law, in, 102–3, 102n.26, 103n.27
    First Amendment and, 106
    historical myths regarding, 102–5

brandishing guns (*cont.*)
   homicide by persons brandishing guns, 101, 112–13
   hoplophobia and, 110–12
   intimidating nature of, 111, 112
   menacing or threatening manner, in, 103–5
   mere display distinguished, 103, 104–5
   mixed public opinion regarding, 109–10
   modern debate regarding, 106–12
   "normalization" of, 100–1
   other weapons, 105
   political protests, at, 97–98, 99–101, 106–7, 112–13
   "security dilemma" and, 108–9
   self-defense, for, 109–10
   "weapons instrumentality effect" and, 111, 111n.67
Breyer, Stephen, 232
Bridgham, Percy A., 252–53, 256
Brooks, Preston, 215–16
Brown, John, 40, 42–43
Bruen. See New York State Rifle & Pistol Association v. Bruen (2022)
Buchanan, George, 37–38, 40
Buchanan, James, 65–66n.66
Bureau of Alcohol, Tobacco, Firearms and Explosives, 168n.6
Bureau of Indian Affairs, 115
Burnet, Gilbert, 36–37

Calhoun, John C., 15–16
California
   "dangerous groups" prohibited from possessing guns in, 135
   licensing of guns in, 193
   registration of guns in, 167, 181n.86, 185, 185n.115, 189
Calvin, John, 37, 40
Calvinists, 34, 37
Campbell, Jud, 48–49n.3
Carberry, Caitlan, 5
Carnegie, Andrew, 263–64, 267
Carnegie Steel, 267
carrying guns in public
   abolitionism and, 215–20
   antebellum period, during, 156–57
   armed travel, prohibition of, 218–19, 220–25, 231
   brandishing (*see* brandishing guns)
   Bruen (see *New York State Rifle & Pistol Association v. Bruen* [2022])
   Colonial period, during, 156
   common law, at, 238–39, 257–58
   concealed carry laws (*see* concealed carry laws)
   constitutional liquidation and (*see* constitutional liquidation)
   debate regarding, 232
   Heller, impact of, 237–39
   historical tradition and, 234
   means–end scrutiny, 234
   open carry laws, 111–12, 235–36
   originalism and, 232
   post-Reconstruction period, during, 163
   race and, 156–57, 158–59, 163
   reasonable fear standard and, 224–25
   Reconstruction, during, 158–59
   self-defense and, 219–20
   statistics, 107n.49
   surety laws and, 235–36
   time and place restrictions, 105
Cass, Lewis, 55n.27, 65–66n.66
castle doctrine, 99
Catholics, disarmament of in England, 143
Cefali, Genesa C., 6
Charles, Jacob D., 6, 28–29, 45
Charles, Patrick J., 235–36
Charles I (England), 34–36, 38–39
Charles II (England), 36, 43
Chase, Salmon, 59
Churchill, Robert H., 199–200n.35
Cicero, 40
"civic" interpretation of Second Amendment, 47, 61–62
Civil War, 65–75
Clarke, D.A., 127–28
Clay, Clement Comer, 53–55
Coal and Iron Police, 264
Cobb, Charles, 151n.12
"collective rights" interpretation of Second Amendment, 48–49
Colonial South. *See also specific Colony*
   animals, protection from, 77–79
   enslaved persons and, 78–79, 92–95
   European powers, threat from, 81
   fire-hunting, 86–87, 87n.42
   gun laws generally, 3–4, 77–79, 95–96
   hunting and, 85–92 (*see also* hunting in Colonial South)
   piracy, threat from, 82
   threat from Native Americans and, 3–4, 78–79, 82–91, 95
   trade in arms with Native Americans and, 83–86, 88–89
   "trusty slaves," 93–94
Colt, Samuel, 22–23

INDEX

Columbus and Hocking Coal and Iron Company, 265
Commonwealth v. Leach (Mass. 1804), 219
Commonwealth v. Selfridge (Mass. 1806), 219–20
community-based policing, 218–19
Compromise of 1850, 225–26
concealed carry laws
    authority of state to prohibit concealed carry, 236, 238
    enslaved persons and, 217
    knives and, 105
    race and, 156–57, 158–59
    registration of guns compared, 186n.122
Congress
    constitutional authority over militia, 11–12, 50–51, 53, 54–55, 57–58, 63, 64–65, 68–71, 72–73
    petitions to, 55–56, 56n.32
Connecticut
    gunpowder regulation in, 206
    Hartford Convention, 70–71n.80
    licensing of guns in, 193
    registration of guns in, 179n.72, 183–84, 183n.99, 189
Conscription Act, 49–50, 66, 68–69, 70–74, 70–71n.80
Constitution
    Article I, Section 8, 11–12, 50–51, 53, 54–55, 57–58, 63, 64–65, 68–71, 72–73
    Article II, 70–71, 73
    Second Amendment (*see specific topic*)
constitutional liquidation
    generally, 7, 233–37, 261–62
    defined, 235
    deliberation, 235, 244–45
    Heller and, 237–39
    historical background, 240–48
    historical tradition and, 237–39
    individual rights, applicability to, 245–46
    Madisonian liquidation, 235, 236, 257
    Massachusetts Model (*see* Massachusetts Model)
    originalism and, 238–39, 243
    "original method," as, 244
    practice, 210–11, 235, 244–45
    settlement, 199, 235, 240, 241, 244–45, 247
    state constitutions and, 245
    surety laws and, 235–36, 248–49
    unambiguous text, inapplicable to, 240, 243–44
Continental Army, 12–13
Continental Congress, 135–36, 140–41

contractors, 13
Cony, Samuel, 73–74n.92
Cook, William A., 76n.97
Cooper, Jeff, 110–11
Cornell, Saul, 6–7, 47, 49n.4, 102, 103n.27, 106, 141n.72, 141n.78, 142n.83, 142n.88, 235–36, 239, 247, 251, 255–56n.158, 260–61
Cottrol, Robert, 150–51, 150–51nn.9–12
covenanting, 25–28, 32, 34–37, 38–40, 42–43, 44–45
coverture, 119–20, 121
COVID-19 pandemic, 28, 99–100, 107
Cowan, Edgar, 66
Cox, Samuel Smith, 68
Craft, Nikki, 127
Craighead, Alexander, 25
Cramer, Clayton, 150
Creek War, 53–54
criminal law, gunpowder regulation and, 206
Curtis, Benjamin, 69
Curtis, George Ticknor, 69
Cushing, Abel, 228–29, 230, 232

Dabney, Lucas, 256
"dangerous groups"
    felons, 134–35
    Fourteenth Amendment and, 144–45
    gun laws generally, 5, 131–34, 146–47
    Heller and, 134–35, 187n.131
    historical tradition, in, 134–36, 144–47
    loyalty oaths, persons refusing to take, 140–44
    mentally ill persons, 134–35
    Native Americans as, 5, 135–40, 144–45, 146
    "outsiders," 146
    persons "disaffected to cause of America" as, 135–36, 140–44, 146
    persons taking up arms against state as, 142–43
    Repository of Historical Gun Laws and, 5, 132, 135, 135n.32
    targeting of, 134–44
Davis, Jefferson, 60–61
Davis, John Anthony Gardner, 103, 242n.66
DeDino, Nathan, 49n.4, 141n.78, 142n.83, 142n.88
deer hunting, 85–88, 89–90, 91–92, 95
Delaware
    free Blacks, gun laws and, 155–56, 155n.24, 155n.25
    "going armed to the terror of the people" in, 259–60
    licensing of guns in, 193
    militia laws in, 201–2n.53

282 INDEX

Democratic Party
  Ku Klux Klan and, 153–54
  military conscription and, 65–69, 70–71, 73–74
  race and gun laws and, 161–63
  Reconstruction and, 161–62
  white supremacy and, 162–63
Diamond, Raymond, 150–51, 150–51nn.9–12
District of Columbia
  carrying guns in public in, 247, 247–48n.110, 254, 256
  concealed carry laws in, 259–60
  registration of guns in, 167–68, 208–10
  surety laws in, 256
  Uniform Firearms Act, 247–48n.110
District of Columbia v. Heller (2008)
  carrying guns in public, impact on, 237–39
  constitutional liquidation and, 237–39
  "dangerous groups" and, 134–35, 187n.131
  dissent in, 48–49
  federalism and, 3
  historical tradition and, 28–30, 135–36, 144–45
  individual right to bear arms and, 1, 28–29, 197, 233, 237
  prefatory language, militia clause as, 47
  registration of guns and, 187
  two-step inquiry, 186–87, 195–97
Dodd, Thomas, 150, 150n.6
Dorr Rebellion, 65–66n.66
Dred Scott v. Sandford (1857), 69, 133–34, 209–10n.111
Duke Center for Firearms Law, 2, 132, 195. *See also* Repository of Historical Gun Laws
Dworkin, Andrea, 126–27

Early, Jubal, 73–74
Eaton, John H., 17
economic liberalism, 11n.10
Edward III (England), 219
Eighteenth Amendment, 173
Elizabeth I (England), 33
England. *See also* Great Britain
  Bill of Rights (1689), 135–36, 143, 235, 241, 242–43
  Catholics, disarmament of, 143
  "dangerous groups" in, 143–44
  Declaration of Rights (1689), 28–29
  English Civil War, 29–30
  Glorious Revolution, 27, 29–30, 36–37
  House of Hanover, 27
  justices of the peace in, 102–3
  Magna Carta, 28–29, 241
  Protestants, disarmament of, 241
  Restoration in, 36–37, 38–39
  Statute of Northampton (1328), 103n.27, 242, 243
English Civil War, 29–30
English Declaration of Rights, 28–29
enslaved persons
  Colonial South, gun laws and, 78–79, 92–95
  concealed carry laws and, 217
  disarmament of, 150–51, 150–51n.9, 154–55, 213–14
  gun laws targeting, 150–51
  hunting and, 91, 95
  slave patrols, 95
  "trusty slaves," 93–94
Epps, Garrett, 107
equal protection, self-defense and, 119
Ezell v. City of Chicago (7th Cir. 2011), 210–11, 212

family, radical feminist perspective on, 120
federalism
  Heller and, 3
  "state power" interpretation of Second Amendment and, 47–50, 61–62, 65, 67, 70–71, 72–73, 74–76
Federalists, 47, 51n.11
federal police power, 245
felons, disarmament of, 134–35
feminism
  aversion to guns in second-wave feminism, 123–25, 127–28
  radical feminist perspective (*see* radical feminist perspective)
Field, William, 271
Firearm Owners Protection Act of 1986, 167–68, 168n.5
fire-hunting, 86–87, 87n.42
fire prevention law
  generally, 6, 195–96, 212
  case law, 210–12
  dangers from fires, 203–4
  firing guns in public, regulation of, 207–8, 207n.98, 207n.99
  gunpowder regulation, 204–6
  historical analogs to modern gun regulation, as, 210–12
  historical background, 203–8
  state police power and, 204
firing guns in public, regulation of, 207–8, 207n.98, 207n.99
First Amendment
  brandishing guns and, 106
  Sedition Act and, 144

Fletcher, Ryland, 60, 60n.47, 60n.49
Florence, Thomas, 65–66n.66
Florida
    acquisition of, 18–19
    discriminatory gun laws in, 18–19, 19n.51, 19n.52
    licensing of guns in, 193
    race and gun laws in, 159–60
    Reconstruction, gun laws during, 159–60
    right to bear arms in, 160n.47
    Seminole Wars, 15–16, 15n.27, 18–20, 22–23
Floyd, George, 97
Fourteenth Amendment
    Black Codes and, 150–51, 154–55
    "dangerous groups" and, 144–45
    gunpowder regulation and, 206
    incorporation under, 133n.17
    individual right to bear arms and, 100
    race and gun laws and, 151n.12
France
    guns and state authority in, 11
    raid on Charleston, 81
    Scotland, French power in, 32–33
    threat to Southern Colonies from, 81
Francis II (France), 32–33
Franklin, Benjamin, 32
Frassetto, Mark Anthony, 6, 102n.26
free Blacks
    gun laws and, 155–56, 213–14
    self-defense and, 226–27
Freedmen, 153–54, 159–60
Freedmen, John Joseph, 69n.74
Freedmen's Bureau, 161–62
Freedom Movement, 151n.12
free states model
    generally, 6–7, 213–15, 218
    good cause exception and, 220–21, 222–23
    reasonable fear standard and, 219–20, 222–23, 224–25
    Snowden case and, 227–30
    surety laws and, 220–25
Fremont, John C., 65–66n.66
Frick, Henry Clay, 267
Fugitive Slave Act of 1793, 225–26
Fugitive Slave Act of 1850, 226

Gadsden, James, 19
Gaines, Edmund P., 15, 62, 62n.54
Gardner, Kim, 98–99
Georgia
    brandishing laws in, 104–5
    concealed carry laws in, 162–63
    firearm tax in, 170, 170n.13
    licensing of guns in, 193
    militia laws in, 201–2n.53
    race and gun laws in, 160–61
    Reconstruction, gun laws during, 160–61
    registration of guns in, 176–77, 182–83, 182n.88, 182n.90, 189
    right to bear arms in, 160n.50
Germany, false association of gun control laws with Nazi period in, 150
Gilded Age, 263–64, 267, 268, 275
Glorious Revolution, 27, 29–30, 36–37
"going armed to the terror of the people," 157–58, 235–36, 238–39, 242, 250–51, 254, 257
Gordon, Margaret, 123
Gould, Jay, 263–64
governors' messages, 58–61
grand jury charges, 224
Great Britain. *See also* England
    Mexico, interests in, 21n.64
    Texas and, 20–21
Green, Michael Steven, 48–49n.3
Greene, John A., 75n.95
Gun Control Act of 1968, 11–12, 150
gunpowder regulation, 204–6
    criminal law and, 206
    Fourteenth Amendment and, 206
    nuisance law and, 204–6
    storage of firearms compared, 211

habeas corpus, 67
Hadden, Sally E., 3–4
Halbrook, Stephen P., 150, 167n.3
Hamilton, Alexander, 199n.33
Hamlin, Hannibal, 60, 60n.46, 67n.69
Harcourt, Bernard E., 167n.1
Hatley, Tom, 86n.40
Hawaii
    licensing of guns in, 193
    registration of guns in, 177, 182n.88, 183n.95, 184, 184n.104, 184n.105, 190
    Small Arms Act, 184n.104
Heller I. See *District of Columbia v. Heller* (2008)
Heller v. District of Columbia (D.C. Cir. 2011) *(Heller II)*, 208–10
Henderson, Alexander, 34–35
Henry VIII (England), 33
Heyman, Steven J., 48–49n.3
historical tradition
    Bruen and, 1–2, 6, 132, 144, 146, 187, 195, 196–98, 212
    carrying guns in public and, 234
    constitutional liquidation and, 237–39

historical tradition (*cont.*)
    "dangerous groups" in, 134–36, 144–47
    gaps in knowledge of, 2
    Heller and, 28–30, 135–36, 144–45
    importance of, 2, 7–8
    registration of guns and, 186–88
    restrictions on guns and, 133–34
    Supreme Court jurisprudence and, 1–2
Hoke, Donald, 10–11n.5
Holmes, Andrew, 30–31
Homestead Massacre, 266–67
Hooper, Shirley, 115–16
hoplophobia, 63–67
Hounshell, David, 10–11n.5
House of Hanover, 27
Hudson, Charles M., 87–88, 88n.48
Hunt, George W.P., 270
hunting in Colonial South, 85–92
    generally, 78–79
    deer hunting, 85–88, 89–90, 91–92, 95
    enslaved persons and, 91, 95
    fire-hunting, 86–87, 87n.42
    Native Americans and, 85–92
    wolf hunting, 85–86, 89–92, 95
Hyde, Alvan P., 70–71n.80

Idaho
    carrying guns in public in, 247n.108
    private militias, prohibition of, 263, 270–71, 275
    statehood of, 271
Illinois
    licensing of guns in, 193
    machine guns in, 178n.68
    registration of guns in, 170–71, 179, 181–82, 181n.84, 184n.112, 185, 190
incorporation, 133n.17, 245–46
Indiana
    brandishing laws in, 104–5
    registration of guns in, 190
Indian Removal Act of 1830, 17
individual right to bear arms
    Fourteenth Amendment, under, 100
    Heller and, 1, 28–29, 197, 233, 237
    militia laws and, 198–99
inspection of firearms, 201, 202, 208–10, 211
interchangeability, 10–11n.5, 22–23
intermediate scrutiny, 196–97

Jackson, Andrew, 15, 17, 19, 55n.27
Jacksonians, 47, 65, 65–66n.66
Jackson v. City & County of San Francisco (9th Cir. 2014), 211–12

Jacobitism, 44–45
James, William, 273
James VI (Scotland)/James I (England), 33–34
James V (Scotland), 32–33
Jefferson, Thomas, 55n.27, 64n.62
Jeffersonians, 47
Jenkins, Charles J., 160–61, 161n.52
Jim Crow, 5–6
Johnson, Andrew, 75n.96, 159
Johnson, Archibald, 34–35
Jones, Ann, 123
Justice Department, 160–61, 174
justices of the peace
    England, in, 102–3
    surety laws and, 218–19, 221–22
"Just war" doctrine and, 40

Kansas, disarmament of persons taking up arms against state in, 142–43
Kanter v. Barr (7th Cir. 2019), 131–32
Kates, Don B., 125–26, 128–29
Kavanaugh, Brett, 145n.104, 168, 208–10
Keim, George, 52–53, 52–53n.19, 53n.20, 54–55, 55n.27
Kemble, Gouverneur, 21–22
Kennedy, John F., 11–12
Kennedy, Robert, 11–12
Kentucky
    gunpowder regulation in, 206
    private militias, prohibition of, 263, 270, 272–73, 276
Khouri, Callie, 123–24
King, Martin Luther Jr., 11–12
Kinnear, John, 269–70
Kirby-Smith, Edmund, 158–59
Knights of Labor, 264, 264n.4, 273–74
knives, concealed carry laws and, 105
Knox, Henry, 50–51, 50n.8, 55n.27
Knox, John C. (special counsel), 73n.87
Knox, John (Scottish clerical reformer), 33, 37–38, 40
Konig, David Thomas, 30, 49n.4
Kopel, Dave, 167n.3
Ku Klux Klan, 153–54, 160–61
Kunstler, William, 116–17, 128–29

labor–management conflict, 263–68, 264n.4, 273–75
LadySmith (handgun), 124
Lane, Roger, 230–31
Lawson, John, 78
Leider, Robert, 7

licensing laws, 169. See also *New York State Rifle & Pistol Association v. Bruen* (2022)
Lincoln, Abraham, 67, 67n.69, 68–69, 73–74, 159–60, 160n.44
long guns, 176–77, 178
Lorde, Audre, 123
Louisiana
　concealed carry laws in, 156–57
　regulation of firing guns in public in, 207n.98
Lowrie, Walter, 72–73
loyalty oaths, disarmament of persons refusing to take, 135–36, 140–44
Lund, Nelson, 239

machine guns, 177–78, 177n.61, 178n.64
Macinnes, Allan, 34–35
MacKinnon, Catharine, 125–26
Madison, James, 51n.11, 54–55, 55n.27, 64n.62, 235, 240, 244–46
Madisonian liquidation, 235, 236, 257
Magna Carta, 28–29, 241
Mahoney, Dennis A., 69
Maine
　concealed carry laws in, 259–60
　"going armed to the terror of the people" in, 157–58
Malcolm, Joyce Lee, 48–49n.3, 50n.6, 50n.7
Malcolm X, 126
Manning, Robert B., 89n.53
marital rape, 121
marriage, radical feminist perspective on, 121
Marshall, Humphrey, 21–22
Marshall, John, 245–46
Marshall, Kevin, 134n.30, 142n.84, 143n.91
Maryland (Colony)
　militia laws in, 201n.49
　Native Americans, trade in arms with, 139–40
Maryland (State), licensing of guns in, 193
Mary of Guise, 32–33
Mary (Scotland), 32–34, 37
Massachusetts (Colony)
　militia laws in, 200n.37
　Native Americans, disarmament of, 137–38
Massachusetts Model, 248–61
　generally, 211, 235–36
　practice, 210–11
　settlement, 199
　Southern model versus, 235–36, 239, 249
　surety laws and, 249–57
Massachusetts (State)
　brandishing laws in, 103

carrying guns in public in, 156n.29, 163, 249–57
free Blacks, gun laws and, 156n.27
"going armed to the terror of the people" in, 157–58
gunpowder regulation in, 204, 206
licensing of guns in, 193
loyalty oaths, disarmament of persons refusing to take, 141–43
militia in, 60
persons "disaffected to cause of America," disarmament of, 135–36, 140–41
Revised Statutes of Massachusetts, 235–36
Shays' Rebellion, 142–43
Snowden case, 227–30
surety laws in, 220–25, 249–57
mass production, 23
Maxwell, John, 39–40
McClerland, John, 63, 63n.57
McCloskey, Mark T., 97–99
McCloskey, Patricia N., 97–99
McCord, Mary, 113
McCulloch v. Maryland (1819), 245–46
McCunn, John, 71n.81
McDonald v. City of Chicago (2010), 28–29, 245–46
McIntyre, Neil, 3
McKinley, William, 173
McLellan, George, 63n.58
Meade, George, 160–61, 161n.52
Mearsheimer, John J., 108–9
Melville, Andrew, 34
mentally ill persons, disarmament of, 134–35
mercantilism, 11n.10
Merchant Police, 264
"Me Too" movement, 121–22, 129
Mexican–American War, 21–23, 58n.37, 59, 60, 61–63
Mexico, British interests in, 21n.64
Michigan
　brandishing guns in, 112
　concealed carry laws in, 259–60
　licensing of guns in, 193
　registration of guns in, 174, 174n.42, 177, 181n.82, 182–84, 182n.87, 183n.100, 184n.111, 185, 190
Middlekauf, Robert, 30–31
military conscription
　case law on, 70–74
　Civil War, in, 65–75
　Democratic Party and, 65–69, 70–71, 73–74
　early proposals of, 50–51
　Republican Party and, 65–66, 70

militia. *See also specific topic*
   Congressional authority over militia, 11–12, 50–51, 53, 54–55, 57–58, 63, 64–65, 68–71, 72–73
   Mexican–American War, in, 62–63
   private militias (*see* private militias)
   standing armies versus (*see* standing armies)
   "state power" interpretation of Second Amendment (*see* "state power" interpretation of Second Amendment)
   training of, 200–2
   universal enrollment, 61–62
Militia Act of 1792, 12, 50n.8, 51n.11, 57n.36, 64, 202
Militia Act of 1795, 50n.8, 65
Militia Act of 1798, 57n.36
Militia Act of 1808, 13, 57n.36, 63
Militia Bill of 1862, 65
militia laws
   generally, 169
   case law, 208–12
   fire prevention law (*see* fire prevention law)
   historical background, 198–203
   individual right to bear arms and, 198–99
   inspection of firearms, 201, 202, 208–10, 211
   Native Americans and, 209–10
   race and, 152–54
   registration laws as analog to, 169, 208–10
Miller, Darrell A.H., 7, 28, 45, 106–7, 186n.123
Miller, William H., 272–73
Milton, John, 120
Minnesota
   concealed carry laws in, 259–60
   licensing of guns in, 193
   registration of guns in, 190–91
Minutemen, 201–2
Miranda v. Arizona (1966), 108
Mississippi
   Black Codes in, 155n.23, 159
   brandishing laws in, 103–4
   licensing of guns in, 193
   registration of guns in, 191
Missouri
   castle doctrine in, 99
   licensing of guns in, 193
   Native Americans, trade in arms with, 140
   stand-your-ground laws in, 99
Molly Maguires, 264
monotheism, 120
Monroe, James, 14n.24, 15, 65, 65n.65
Montana
   carrying guns in public in, 163
   licensing of guns in, 193

   private militias, prohibition of, 263, 270–71, 276
   registration of guns in, 171–73, 176–77, 179–80, 181–83, 191
   statehood of, 271
Morgan, Elliott, 273
Mosvick, Mitchell A., 48–49n.3
Mosvick, Nicholas M., 3, 48–49n.3
motivations for gun ownership, 100n.15, 103, 109

Nairne, Thomas, 93–94
Napoleonic Wars, 11
National Covenant of 1638, 25
national firearms industry
   generally, 2–3, 9–10, 23
   armories, 12–13
   contractors, 13
   government support for, 11–20
   interchangeability and, 10–11n.5, 22–23
   mass production in, 23
   Mexican–American War and, 21–23
   national expansion and, 20–23
   Native Americans, relation to wars against, 14–20
   rifles, development of, 20
   Seminole Wars and, 15–16, 15n.27, 18–20, 22–23
National Firearms Registration and Transfer Record (NFRTR), 168n.6
National Guard, 73–75, 75n.95
National Rifle Association
   anti-gun-carry laws, on, 105
   feminism and, 123
   Nazi Germany, false association of gun control laws with, 150
   open carry laws, on, 111–12
Native Americans
   Colonial South, in, 3–4, 78–79, 82–91, 95
   "dangerous group," as, 5, 135–40, 144–45, 146
   disarmament of, 135–40, 144–45, 146, 154–55
   forced removal of, 9, 17
   hunting and, 85–92
   militia laws and, 209–10
   national firearms industry, relation to wars against, 14–20
   reasonable person standard and, 119n.8
   Repository of Historical Gun Laws and, 137, 138–39
   trade in arms with, 83–86, 88–89, 138–40
   wars against, 14–20

INDEX 287

Nazi Germany, false association of gun control laws with, 150
Nebraska, licensing of guns in, 193–94
Nelson, Caleb, 240
Netherlands, threat to Southern Colonies from, 81, 82
New Hampshire
 brandishing guns in, 113–14
 gunpowder regulation in, 204
 licensing of guns in, 194
New Jersey (Colony), carrying guns in public in, 156
New Jersey (State)
 licensing of guns in, 194
 militia laws in, 200–1
New Mexico
 brandishing laws in, 104–5
 carrying guns in public in, 247n.108
New Netherland Colony
 brandishing laws in, 103
 Native Americans, disarmament of, 136–37
New Plymouth Colony, disarmament of Native Americans in, 136–37
New York
 Draft Riots, 73–74
 gunpowder regulation in, 204–5
 licensing of guns in, 194
 militia in, 57–58, 57n.35
 militia laws in, 201–2n.53
 registration of guns in, 191
 Sullivan Act, 171n.21, 179, 179n.73
New York State Rifle & Pistol Association v. Bruen (2022)
 analogous regulations and, 197–98
 distinctly similar historical regulations and, 197
 historical tradition and, 1–2, 6, 132, 144, 146, 187, 195, 196–98, 212
 "law chambers history" in, 232
 race and, 152n.13
 registration of guns and, 168–69, 187–88
 self-defense and, 100, 113
 surety laws and, 229–30
Nicholas, Samuel Smith, 69
night walking, 227–28
Noble, Patrick, 58–59, 59n.40
North Carolina (Colony)
 enslaved persons, gun laws and, 95
 hunting in, 91, 92
 militia in, 80–81, 81n.17
 piracy, threat from, 82
 threat from Native Americans in, 82–84

North Carolina (State)
 carrying guns in public in, 257–58
 licensing of guns in, 194
 militia in, 60–61
 militia laws in, 201–2n.53
 registration of guns in, 185, 191
North Dakota
 "dangerous groups" prohibited from possessing guns in, 135
 licensing of guns in, 194
 statehood of, 271
Northern Pacific Railroad, 266
Norwich University, 55n.29
nuisance law, gunpowder regulation and, 204–6
Nullification Crisis, 58–59

Ohio
 gunpowder regulation in, 206
 licensing of guns in, 194
 militia in, 59
 registration of guns in, 191
Öhman, Martin, 14n.23
open carry laws, 111–12, 235–36
Ordnance Department, 16, 22–23
Oregon
 concealed carry laws in, 259–60
 licensing of guns in, 194
 Native Americans, trade in arms with, 140
 registration of guns in, 176n.49, 180, 180n.76, 181–82, 181n.83, 191
Oregon Improvement Company, 266
originalism
 carrying guns in public and, 232
 constitutional liquidation and, 238–39, 243
O'Scannlain, Diarmuld F., 48–49n.3
"outsiders," disarmament of, 146

Page, John, 51n.11
Partridge, Alden, 55–56, 55n.29, 60–61
Patriot Prayer, 112–13
peaceful assembly, right of, 274
Peck, Wilfred M., 275
Peckham, Howard, 81
Pennsylvania (Colony)
 carrying guns in public in, 156
 loyalty oaths, disarmament of persons refusing to take, 141–43
 Middle Octorara, 25–27, 32, 36–37, 43, 46
 Presbyterians in, 25–27, 30–31
Pennsylvania (State)
 concealed carry laws in, 259–60
 gunpowder regulation in, 204
 licensing of guns in, 194

Pennsylvania (State) (*cont.*)
  Native Americans, trade in arms
    with, 139–40
  persons "disaffected to cause of America,"
    disarmament of, 135–36, 140–41
  surety laws in, 249–50, 261n.192
persons "disaffected to cause of America,"
  disarmament of, 135–36, 140–44, 146
persons taking up arms against state,
  disarmament of, 142–43
Phillips, Wendell, 226–27, 228, 232
Pierce, Franklin, 65–66n.66
Pinkerton, Allan, 264–65, 268
Pinkerton, Robert, 265
Pinkerton, William, 265
Pinkerton Detective Agency
  generally, 7
  rise of, 264–68
  state anti-Pinkerton laws, 268, 269–70,
    271, 272–73
piracy, 82
Pogrebin, Letty Cottin, 124–25
Poinsett, Joel Roberts, 50–58
police power
  federal police power, 245
  fire prevention law, state police power
    and, 204
Polk, James, 58n.37, 62–63
popular sovereignty interpretation of Second
  Amendment, 48–49, 54, 59, 76
Potter, Elisha Reynolds, 70–71n.80
Powderly, Terrence, 273–74
Powell, Lazarus, 66–67, 67n.68
Presbyterian tradition. *See* Scottish Presbyterian
  tradition
Presser, Herman, 274
Presser v. Illinois (1886), 252
private militias
  generally, 7, 263
  constitutional implications of
    prohibition, 273–75
  labor–management conflict and, 263–68,
    264n.4, 273–75
  legal implications of prohibition, 273–75
  Pinkerton Detective Agency (*see* Pinkerton
    Detective Agency)
  state prohibitions, 268–73
Prohibition, 173
Prynne, William, 40
Pullman Strike, 270

Quakers, 141–42, 142n.83
Queen Anne's War, 81

race, gun laws and
  generally, 5–6, 149–52, 164–65
  antebellum period, during, 154–58
  Black Codes, 150–51, 154–55, 159, 162
  Bruen and, 152n.13
  carrying guns in public, 156–57, 158–59, 163
  complexity of, 213–14
  concealed carry laws, 156–57, 158–59
  debate regarding, 213
  Democratic Party and, 161–63
  enslaved persons (*see* enslaved persons)
  Fourteenth Amendment and, 151n.12
  free Blacks, 155–56, 213–14
  Freedmen, 153–54, 159–60
  militia laws, 152–54
  Reconstruction, during, 150–51, 158–63
  Republican Party and, 159–63
  self-defense and, 151n.11, 151n.12
radical feminist perspective
  generally, 4–5, 115–17, 128–29
  armed women, self-defense and, 122–23,
    125, 127
  aversion to guns in second-wave feminism,
    123–25, 127–28
  battered women and, 126–27
  equal protection and, 119
  family, on, 120
  fundamental inequality and, 120–22
  male bias in law regarding self-defense
    and, 118
  marital rape and, 121
  marriage, on, 121
  nonviolence and, 127–28
  reasonable person standard, problems
    with, 117–20
  religion, on, 120
  self-defense, on, 116–20, 122–23, 125–27
  sexual aggression, resistance to, 121–22
  social conditioning of women and, 118
Ramsey, W.R., 272
reasonable fear standard, 219–20, 222–23,
  224–25
Reconstruction
  carrying guns in public during, 158–59
  Democratic Party and, 161–62
  race and gun laws during, 150–51, 158–63
  Republican Party and, 159–63
Reconstructions Act of 1867, 75n.96
Reformation, role of, 32–37, 41
Regele, Lindsay Schakenbach, 2–3, 49n.5
registration of guns
  generally, 6, 167–69
  administration of registries, 182–86

Bruen and, 168–69, 187–88
concealed carry laws compared, 186n.122
definition of "gun," 177n.57
early gun registries, 170–75
framework of, 175–86
Heller and, 187
historical tradition and, 186–88
information kept in registries, 179–82
licensing laws, 169
long guns, 176–77, 178
mail-in reporting, 183n.95
militia laws as analog to, 169, 208–10
modern debates, implications for, 186–88
Repository of Historical Gun Laws and, 169
silencers, 177
statutory design of registries, 175–82
types of arms applicable to, 175–78
religion, radical feminist perspective on, 120
Remington, 23
Repository of Historical Gun Laws
generally, 2, 195
"dangerous groups" and, 5, 132, 135, 135n.32
firing guns in public, regulation of, 207–8
Native Americans and, 137, 138–39
registration of guns and, 169
Republican Party
African Americans and, 153–54
Black Codes and, 159
discriminatory enforcement of gun laws and, 5–6
military conscription and, 65–66, 70
militia clause and, 47
race and gun laws and, 159–63
Reconstruction and, 159–63
resistance in Scottish Presbyterian tradition, 37–40, 42–45
Restoration, 36–37, 38–39
Rhode Island
carrying guns in public in, 163
Dorr Rebellion, 65–66n.66
gunpowder regulation in, 204
Rich, Adrienne, 125–26
Richardson, William, 63
rifles, development of, 20
right to bear arms. *See specific topic*
Rigor, Stephanie, 123
Rivas, Brennan Gardner, 5–6
Rodes, Robert, 272
Ruben, Eric, 235–36, 239, 247, 251, 260–61
Russell, William, 103
Rutherford, Samuel, 39–40

Sabbath laws, 207, 207n.95
Saulsbury, Willard Sr., 67–68, 67n.69, 67n.70
Scalia, Antonin, 3, 47, 144–45, 197, 211, 216–17, 218, 237–38
Scotland
"Beggars Summons," 33
Claim of Right (1689), 36–37
French power in, 32–33
gun laws in, 37–38
Lords of the Congregation, 33
Mauchline Rising, 38–39
National Covenant, 34–37, 38–40
Reformation in, 32–35
Reformation Parliament, 33–34
Restoration and, 36–37, 38–39
Western Association, 38–39
Scott, Robert Kingston, 75n.96
Scottish Enlightenment, 30
Scottish Presbyterian tradition
generally, 3, 25–28, 44–46
Calvinists and, 37
covenanting in, 25–28, 32, 34–37, 38–40, 42–43, 44–45
existing historical account versus, 28–32
"just war" doctrine and, 40
liberty in, 36–37
martial ethos of, 27, 43, 44–45
Reformation, role of, 32–37, 41
resistance in, 37–40, 42–45
right to bear arms arising in, 45–46
secession in, 27, 43
self-defense in, 40–42
suspicion of government in, 27
symbolism in, 26–27
violence in, 43–44
Secession Crisis, 61–65
Second Amendment. *See specific topic*
"Security dilemma," 108–9
Sedgwick, Theodore, 51n.11
Sedition Act, 144
self-defense
abolitionism and, 232
African Americans and, 151n.11, 151n.12
armed women and, 122–23, 125, 127
brandishing guns for, 109–10
Bruen and, 100, 113
carrying guns in public and, 219–20
equal protection and, 119
free Blacks and, 226–27
male bias in law regarding, 118
race and gun laws and, 151n.11, 151n.12
radical feminist perspective on, 116–20, 122–23, 125–27

self-defense (*cont.*)
  reasonable fear standard, 219–20, 222–23, 224–25
  reasonable person standard, problems with, 117–20
  Scottish Presbyterian tradition, in, 40–42
  social conditioning of women and, 118
Seminole Wars, 15–16, 15n.27, 18–20, 22–23
Semple, Eugene, 266–67
Seymour, Horatio, 70–71, 73–75, 74n.94, 75n.95
Sharp, James, 43
Shays' Rebellion, 142–43
Shields, Alexander, 27–28, 43–44
Shy, John, 81
Siegel, Reva, 47n.1
silencers, 177
Silver, Carol, 125–26
Silver, Timothy, 89–90
Simpson, Nicole Brown, 126
Sims, Thomas, 226–27, 228, 230–31
Slave Codes, 154–55
slave patrols, 95
slaves. *See* enslaved persons
Smith, John, 79–80, 83–84
Smith, Merritt Roe, 10–11n.5
Smith & Wesson, 124
Snowden, Charles, 227–28, 254, 255–56n.158
Snowden, Isaac, 227–28, 229–30, 254–55, 255–56n.158
social conditioning of women, 118
Solemn League and Covenant of 1643, 25, 35–36, 38–39
South Carolina (Colony)
  enslaved persons, gun laws and, 92–94
  French raid on Charleston, 81
  hunting in, 91, 92
  militia in, 80–81, 93–94, 93n.77
  piracy, threat from, 82
  Spanish raid on Charleston, 81
  Stono Rebellion, 93–94, 94n.82
  threat from Native Americans in, 83–84, 83n.24
  trade in arms with Native Americans in, 85, 88
  "trusty slaves," 93–94
  Yamasee War, 80–81
South Carolina (State)
  Black Codes in, 155n.23
  licensing of guns in, 194
  machine guns in, 178n.64, 178n.69
  militia laws in, 201–2n.53
  Nullification Crisis and, 58–59
  registration of guns in, 191
South Dakota
  machine guns in, 178n.70
  registration of guns in, 191
  statehood of, 271
Spain
  raid on Charleston, 81
  threat to Southern Colonies from, 81
Spitzer, Robert J., 4
Springfield Armory, 12
standing armies
  Civil War and, 67, 70
  governors' messages and, 58–60
  hostility toward, 47–52, 49n.5, 63–64, 76
  Poinsett plan and, 54–55, 57
  Secession Crisis and, 61–62
stand-your-ground laws, 99
Stange, Mary Zeiss, 4–5
"state power" interpretation of Second Amendment
  generally, 3, 47–50, 76
  Civil War and, 65–75
  Congress, petitions to, 55–56, 56n.32
  federalism and, 47–50, 61–62, 65, 67, 70–71, 72–73, 74–76
  governors' messages and, 58–61
  Poinsett plan versus, 50–58
  Secession Crisis and, 61–65
State v. Huntly (N.C. 1843), 257–58
Steuben, Friedrich von, 201, 202
Stevens, John Paul, 48–49
Stewart, James (American legal commentator), 103
Stewart, James (Scottish lawyer), 40–43
Stono Rebellion, 93–94, 94n.82
storage of firearms, 211
Story, Joseph, 64, 68
strict scrutiny, 196–97
Strong, Caleb, 58, 73n.87
Sumner, Charles, 215–16, 217, 219–20, 223–24, 229–30
Sununu, Chris, 113–14
surety laws
  armed travel, prohibition of, 218–19, 220–25, 231
  arrest statistics, 230–31, 231*t*
  Bruen and, 229–30
  carrying guns in public and, 235–36
  constitutional liquidation and, 235–36, 248–49
  enforcement of, 221–22
  free states model, 220–25 (*see also* free states model)
  good cause exception, 220–21, 222–23

justices of the peace and, 218–19, 221–22
  in Massachusetts, 220–25
  Massachusetts Model and, 249–57
  Snowden case and, 227–30
Sweden, threat to Southern Colonies from, 81

Taney, Roger, 73, 73n.91
Tartaro, Peggy, 124–25
Taylor, Zachary, 21–22, 65–66n.66
Teach, Edward, 82
Tennessee
  carrying guns in public in, 257–58
  gunpowder regulation in, 205
  race and gun laws in, 162–63, 162n.58
Ten Percent Plan, 159–60, 160n.44
Tenth Amendment, 68–69
Texas
  annexation of, 14n.24, 20–21
  carrying guns in public in, 163, 248
  concealed carry laws in, 158–59
  discriminatory enforcement of gun laws in, 5–6
  free Blacks, gun laws and, 155–56
  Great Britain and, 20–21
  licensing of guns in, 194
  machine guns in, 177n.61, 178n.67
  race and gun laws in, 161–62
  Reconstruction, gun laws during, 161–62
  registration of guns in, 185, 185n.116, 191
Texas Rangers, 22–23
Thacher, Peter Oxenbridge, 223–25, 229–30, 250, 253
Thelma & Louise (film), 123–24
Thiel's Detective Service, 266
Thomas, Clarence, 195, 225, 229–30, 232
Thompson, James, 72–73, 72n.85, 72n.86
Thurman, Samuel, 273
Tilly, Charles, 11n.7
training of militia, 200–2
Treaty of Ghent, 65
Trumbull, Lyman, 66
"trusty slaves," 93–94
Twiggs, David E., 22n.78
Tyler, John, 20–21

Utah
  licensing of guns in, 194
  private militias, prohibition of, 263, 273, 276

Vallandingham, Charles, 63–65, 63n.59, 64n.62
Van Buren, Martin, 51–52
Vanderbilt, Cornelius, 263–64
Vaseghi, Bardia, 107

Vermont, militia in, 60
Virginia (Colony)
  hunting in, 89–92, 90n.62, 95
  militia in, 79–81, 152–53
  piracy, threat from, 82
  threat from Native Americans in, 82–84
  trade in arms with Native Americans in, 83–84, 88, 138
Virginia (State)
  Black Codes in, 155n.23
  concealed carry laws in, 186n.122, 259–60
  licensing of guns in, 194
  persons "disaffected to cause of America," disarmament of, 135–36, 140–41
  registration of guns in, 185, 185n.117, 191–92
Volokh, Eugene, 106–7

Wadsworth, Decius, 16
Walker, Samuel, 22–23
Wanrow, Yvonne, 4–5, 115–17, 118–19, 128–29
War Department, 12–13, 15–16, 20, 21
War of 1812, 13–14, 50–51, 54–55, 55n.29, 58
War of Spanish Succession, 81
Washington
  licensing of guns in, 194
  private militias, prohibition of, 263, 269–70, 276
  statehood of, 271
Washington, George, 50–51, 55n.27, 61–62, 64, 64n.62, 64n.64
"weapons instrumentality effect," 111, 111n.67
Webster, Daniel (Senator), 62
Webster, Daniel W. (legal scholar), 167n.2
Weingarten, Dean, 167n.3
Wesler, William, 115–16, 117, 119
West Virginia
  carrying guns in public in, 163
  concealed carry laws in, 259–60
  licensing of guns in, 194
  registration of guns in, 180–81n.80, 192
Wharton, Francis, 103
Wharton, George, 71–72
Whigs, 47
Whiskey Rebellion, 50–51
White, Jonathan W., 67n.69
white supremacy, 162–63
Whitney, Eli, 13
William of Orange, 29–30
Williams, Charles Kilbourne, 59
Wilson, Henry, 66, 70–71n.80
Winkler, Adam, 102, 239n.49

Wisconsin
　concealed carry laws in, 259–60
　licensing of guns in, 194
　machine guns in, 178n.66
　registration of guns in, 192
Wodrow, Robert, 44–45
Wolf, Naomi, 122–23, 125
wolf hunting, 85–86, 89–92, 95
Wood, Fernando, 65–66n.66
Workingmen's Benevolent
　　Association, 264

Wyoming
　brandishing laws in, 104–5
　carrying guns in public in, 247n.108
　licensing of guns in, 194
　private militias, prohibition of, 263, 270, 273, 277
　registration of guns in, 176–77, 181–82, 181n.81, 192
　statehood of, 271

Yamasee War, 80–81, 93–94
Yukutake v. Connors (D. Haw. 2021), 211, 212